This book is due on the last date stamped below.
Failure to return books on the date due may
result in assessment of overdue fees.

THE
RIVALS

Also by Arthur Quinn

The Confidence of British Philosophers

Broken Shore

Figures of Speech

Before Abraham Was (with I. Kikawada)

Audiences and Intentions (with N. Bradbury)

The Poet's Work (with L. Nathan)

A New World

THE
RIVALS

William Gwin,
David Broderick,
and the Birth of California

Arthur Quinn

The Library of the American West
Crown Publishers, Inc.
New York

Copyright © 1994 by Arthur Quinn

All rights reserved. No part of this book may be reproduced or transmitted in any form or by any means, electronic or mechanical, including photocopying, recording, or by any information storage and retrieval system, without permission in writing from the publisher.

Published by Crown Publishers, Inc., 201 East 50th Street, New York, New York 10022. Member of the Crown Publishing Group.

Random House, Inc. New York, Toronto, London, Sydney, Auckland

CROWN is a trademark of Crown Publishers, Inc.

Manufactured in the United States of America

Design by Mercedes Everett

Library of Congress Cataloging-In-Publication Data

Quinn, Arthur.
    The rivals : William Gwin, David Broderick, and the birth of California / by Arthur Quinn.
      p.   cm. — (The library of the American West)
    Includes bibliographical references (p.   ) and index.
    1. California—Politics and government—1846–1850.   2. Gwin, William McKendree, 1805–1885.   3. Broderick, David C. (David Colbreth), 1820–1859.   4. Dueling—California—History—19th century.   I. Series.
F865.Q29 1994
979.4'04—dc20
94–20495
CIP

ISBN 0-517-59573-7

10 9 8 7 6 5 4 3 2 1

First Edition

PREFACE

Californians have always liked to think of their state as the great exception within American history, only incidentally involved in the history of the broader nation. Even those disdainful of the Golden State have characterized it as a lotus land where rootless Americans could go to escape the rigors of history, much as they could also go there to escape the rigors of harsh climate.

That people did come to California with such an escapism in mind is one of the two most important facts of California history. The other is that they were almost always disappointed. The history of California is strewn with Donner parties of the spirit.

Throughout most of its early history as a state, California was distinct and separate from the rest of the nation, an American outpost on the Pacific coast—but it was no exception. The tensions and problems that shook the nation were here in microcosm. All the other regions of the nation were in California mixed together. In that sense, far from being an exception, California was strangely the most representative of states. At no time was this truer than in the 1850s.

The mass migration of the 1849 gold rush brought a cross-section of ambitious young men to one place, as if in a grand experiment to see if they despite their golden dreams might establish a civil society there. But this experiment was being performed at exactly the time when the compromises necessary to preserve that social order in the nation as a whole were becoming more and more difficult to achieve, compromises over not just slavery but immigration, urbanization and a myriad of other difficult issues. Californians, new and old, were being forced to face these very issues within their state— and doing about as well as the national leaders.

Revisionist historians, such as David Potter, have argued that the American politicians of the 1850s were a bungling generation whose failure led to an unnecessary civil war. Such an interpretation would have us focus our attention not on Republican abolitionists and Southern secessionists, but rather on moderate Democrats. They constituted the center that failed to hold. Northern Democrats and Southern Unionists simply could not work together effectively enough to avoid the impending debacle.

In California this all came down to the relationship between two men, David Broderick and William Gwin. Broderick, from New York, led the loyal free-soil Democrats of California. Gwin, still owning a plantation back in Mississippi but deeply committed to the preservation of the Union, led the Chivalry, as the Southern Democrats were called.

These were the rivals for power in California who could control the young state if they would cooperate. In the end they would not, because they had come to hate each other too much.

The story of this rivalry, therefore, has much to tell us both about the building of California and about the origins of the American Civil War. I wish I could say I was drawn to it for this reason. My original attraction to it, however, arose from another source, a sense of narrative frustration. This requires a little explanation.

Czeslaw Milosz begins and ends *The Seizure of Power,* his novel on Warsaw in World War II, with the postwar meditations of the character Professor Gil. Gil has lost everything during the war, including his wife and only child. He now perseveres by translating Thucydides, the Athenian historian who narrated the destruction of most of what he himself valued. As Gil translates, it is not in his power to save Pericles or Athens, any more than it had been in his power to save his own family. His power is the power of historical imagination and collective memory—and so he spends himself trying to re-create the gestures of a sorrowing Athenian woman, the expression on the face of a man looking at his dead son, even the shape of fingers holding a jar of wine. If he can do this, then time would be, at least partially, overcome. "There would be only a great coexistence of a countless number of separate human beings, who had been and who were yet to be, each communicating to the other the same complaint"—the complaint against the finitude of this world. And yet this finitude is for Gil (and for Milosz) as inescapable as is our need to complain against it.

This left Gil with a clear sense of his own vocation as a historian: "He who would be equal to the human condition must collect blood in a basin without spilling a single drop—not to display knowledge, nor to transform heartbreak into indifference—but rather to preserve the gifts of anger and unbreakable faith." And while Gil translated, he sometimes felt that all who once were, were somehow now near him—and he was warmed by their breath, and communion with them brought peace.

But this exalted sense of the historical vocation, however comforting to the fictional character Gil, will bring little peace to most practicing historians. What humanizes and particularizes Gil's historical imagination is precisely what is usually absent in the surviving historical record. Thucydides himself, it must be said, openly admitted that he had invented some of the speeches he reported because the original words had been lost. If important speeches were lost, what chance is there for reliable descriptions of sorrowful gestures or mournful expressions?

An epistemologically fastidious historian will have to admit the truth of the old gibe of Descartes. He can spend his whole life studying Roman history and end up knowing a little less than Caesar's servant girl.

All of this was bitterly evident to me when I was writing my first book on California history, *Broken Shore*. There I tried to write the history of a small peninsula in California, one that I had chosen precisely because it was an unimportant place. To see the forces of history acting in such a place, I thought, would be to see them acting on a human scale. There, human faces would not be lost in the shadows of monumental inevitabilities. There, those displaced in the name of progress could still be heard before their leaving, heard more clearly than they could amid the noise of a larger place.

However, the book that resulted was more a mosaic than a true narrative, the sense of movement more an illusion than a true story. The historical record of this small place, not surprisingly in retrospect, was simply too in-complete to provide me with the basis for a continuous narrative. So I ended up using what I had to try to create the impression of a continuous narrative. Although an interesting literary challenge for a young writer, it was also frustrating. And then, at the peak of my frustration, I ran across Broderick and Gwin.

Their rivalry was such a great story that many of the participants them-selves realized it at the time. So they, at least on occasion, took care to record all those kinds of details that are usually lost to historians—sights, sounds, impressions, feelings, as well as the exact words of many crucial conversations. While *Broken Shore* felt to me like something I had imposed upon the frag-mentary materials, the rivalry of Broderick and Gwin was like a story I was watching. Rather than worrying about having enough of the right sources, I worried how I could possibly fully exploit their richness.

Now it has to be admitted that many of these sources on which the following narrative is based are impeachable. Those reporting were prej-udiced or remembering a vivid event decades later. Moreover, some ep-isodes are recorded in only one source. So the reader should be warned that my attitude toward these sources has been welcoming rather than critical. I have worried more if I could do justice to them than whether they were trying to hoodwink me. In fact, although I had decided by the time I finished *Broken Shore* that I would write the story of this ri-valry, I had also decided that I would wait until I felt I had fully matured as a writer, matured enough that I could hope to do justice to it—a wait of twelve years as it turned out.

I would like to thank those who read this book in manuscript, and offered their suggestions and encouragement: Thomas Brady, Howard Lamar, Mar-vin Nathan, and Gretchen von Duering. And special thanks to my agent,

Thomas D'Evelyn, and my editor, Peter Ginna, who consistently were ideal readers, as critical as they were sympathetically perceptive. Finally, I would be remiss if I did not mention that my understanding of this period of American history was shaped decades ago by conversations with the late Thomas Payne Govan, whose own published work—good as it is—gives but a faint indication of the subtlety and passion of his historical understanding.

So the whole age is at once comic and tragic—
tragic because it is perishing, comic because it goes on.
—Søren Kierkegaard

THE
RIVALS

1

This is the story of two men—of how they achieved great power and how through their implacable rivalry they destroyed each other.

This is also the story of a place, of California, and how it was transformed in only a decade from a remote province to a prosperous state—how a gold rush that brought men there to seek their individual fortunes then forced them, largely despite themselves, to produce that most precious of human goods, a community.

The story of two men and a place, this is also in part the story of a nation, a nation that recently had stretched itself, relentlessly and violently, across a continent but that was now being driven by an apparently merciless fate toward a catastrophic civil war.

So this is the story of two men, how their rise to power reflected the building of California, and how their mutual destruction foreshadowed the Civil War. Where does it begin? Not with David Broderick, for he emerges from the shadows in California only after William McKendree Gwin has well begun his ascent. It should begin with Gwin, Gwin on the deck of the steamship *Panama* as it crosses the strait called the Golden Gate and enters the bay of Saint Francis.

The steamship approached the treacherous entrance to the bay through the gray, dumb blankness of fog. It was a morning in early June, and fog was usual this time of year.

Then the baking heat of the great interior valley of California repelled the air mass above it heavenward, thereby drawing into the valley the coastal air. This atmospheric migration in turn routinely drew onto the northern California coast those billowing fog banks usually restrained far out at sea but which during the early summer could enshroud the new city and its bay for days, if not a week or two, at a time.

Yet this morning of June 4, 1849, was to be blest. Even on the best of days, the shroud was not burnt off until midmorning. But today the dawning sun somehow already was dispersing the fog with its first rays. Not that the passengers crowding the promenade deck of the *Panama* could see that yet. They strained their still-sleepy eyes eastward. Lulled into a kind of reverie by the waves, they could make out little within the billows, as if the fog had temporarily drained all objects within it of their solidity, of their full existence, leaving only ghostly demarcations where true things once stood.

The passengers knew the dawn was rising because of a disembodied radiance in the east. No quaint rosy fingers there, just a diffusion of light amid the indeterminate gray—and at its center, barely distinguishable, an intensity about the size and shape of a doubloon. The struggling paddle wheel, now reduced to cannibalizing its own barrels and spars to fuel its fire for steam, was helped by a brisk wind out of the west, a cold wind that whipped the blackish smoke forward and mingled it indiscriminately with the fog above the bow; so the brightness in the distance was accentuated by the unnatural darkness presently over the deck. It was as if the ship were moving through chaos toward the light.

When the first of these steamships chugged into the old California capital of Monterey earlier this year, the Californios on shore who had come out especially to see this nautical wonder shouted as one, "Tan feo!" (How ugly!) Ugly these squat, chugging vessels were, at least compared to those aristocrats of the ocean, the clean well-sparred frigates and sloops of war that had worked this coast before. But to most of those on the promenade deck this June morning the steamship *Panama* was as beautiful as the future of California itself, as beautiful as a nugget glittering in a millrace.

The passengers shivered in the wind, but none made a move to go below. Then, just as the ship was to enter the bay, the morning was transformed, a sudden miracle with which longtime residents become familiar if not altogether secure. The chill wind of the sea fog remained without the fog itself, while the sun now sparkled brightly on wrinkling water and distant yellow hills, hills that had the look of unchanging gold. The few fog billows left on the edges of the bay after this revolution either hovered like melting snow hills in the air or were fleeing like doomed half-hooded phantoms. It was the first morning of Creation, and the sons of God should sing.

Of course, not all the sons of man on the deck of the steamship *Panama* were thinking pious or even kindly thoughts. One of them later remembered thinking how partial a job the sun was doing. The fog was going, all right, but the morning remained bitterly cold; this morning was now, he thought, as cold and clear as Presbyterian charity. And the first sight he was going to get of San Francisco would be about as welcome.

That first sight was a while in coming, however. As the fog dissolved, the passengers could see evidences of the wilderness that almost all California still was—a wilderness beautiful, predatory, indifferent. This was most evident to those looking to the north as they entered the bay. Beyond the coastal shrubland, vast forests could be seen in a landscape dominated by a single gray-green mountain, with herds of deer grazing down to the water's edge, a few big bucks looking up unperturbed, the deer in places mingling with cattle. Someone on board who had read about this region—Joseph Revere's account of his naval visit, for instance—might speak of the extraordinary herds of elk and antelope that could be found only a few miles from here, great hunting, elk antlers bigger than a man—and bid his fellow passengers to search the land for grizzly bears and panthers, and the sky for eagles and condors. If this was an ordinary morning, some of these predators, particularly the bears, should not have been too hard to find. Nor should have seals and sea otters bobbing up and down in the north bay waters, although they had already been overhunted, especially when rifles began to be used in the 1830s. (The day was gone when the whole north bay was black with wet fir.) If the passengers were lucky, they could see a whale or two breaching, for there were usually a few in the bay this time of year, taking a respite from the long annual migration from Baja to Alaska along almost the identical route the paddle wheel had been following the past week. So pods of whales were no longer a novelty to those on deck.

The marshlands bordering the bay were larger than the bay itself, huge tule jungles teeming with life; and a ship like the *Panama* by suddenly blasting its whistle—if the captain knew just where and how to do it—could send hundreds of thousands of waterfowl into the air in an instant, a huge, dark cloud of living fright, a mob that could temporarily eclipse the sun. But the captain of the *Panama* was new to this route, having made the trip only once before. Even without such a demonstration, however, bird life was still so evident that after just a few minutes inside the bay you knew that tales of hunters bringing down six, eight, ten birds with a single shotgun blast could not be dismissed out of hand as "stretchers."

The passengers of the *Panama* who had sought out a northern position for the entry were likely not seeking animals with their eyes as much as a large island. The one book on California that many of them had read was Richard Henry Dana's *Two Years Before the Mast*. A number of them had made an excursion off the ship at San Diego to find the place where Dana had worked the hide and tallow trade, sadly all ruins now, the only constant with his descriptions the foxes barking in the night. Presently they could see to the north his Wood Island, where Dana, now a respectable Boston attorney and philanthropist, had spent frigid nights collecting fuel for his ship.

The bay itself was shaped like a giant charmed circle now broken at its westernmost point, a firmament violently breached by fresh water seeking a return to the ancient oblivion of the salt sea. And Wood Island could have been, at least in the imagination's eye, the land thrust aside so the water could make its way. Perhaps one of the passengers asked the captain if that large island to their north was really Wood Island, and he might have responded with a shrug that the Mexican charts called it something like Angel Island.

Wood to burn or angels to pray to, the alternatives said a bit about the difference between Mexicans and Americans. The island itself remained there, plucked of its trees, a fallen guardian angel of the place—and the Americans, now in charge, were still seeking fuel of one sort or another, wherever they could get it, and however much they could get.

The predominant interest on deck, however, was not toward the north—or directly to the east where the sunburnt hills rose above the tule marshlands—but toward the south. Most eyes searched the south-southeast horizon for signs of the promised city of San Francisco itself. What they saw initially was far from promising, a coastal desert of windblown sandhills with almost no vegetation. The wind was brisk, but to look at the sandstorms it was kicking up amid these dunes you would have thought it was blowing a perfect hurricane. The contrast with the lush north bay was striking for those with a vantage to look both ways. The south reminded a few on deck of the glimpses they had had of that miserable, wretched, dried-up peninsula, Baja California. If the city was in the south, it seemed in the wrong place. But it was in the south. They knew that when finally they could make out the dilapidated old Spanish presidio that once guarded the entry to this bay. Upon seeing it, some passengers looked toward one of the few ladies on deck. They would point to it—then smile or nod at this small, intense woman bundled up against the cold.

Everyone on board knew the story of how John C. Frémont in the name of the United States of America had spiked the antique cannon of this fort near the beginning of the rebellion that brought California into the Union. From his memories of these events Jessie Benton Frémont had helped her husband fashion a heroic account that had made him once again a national celebrity with a seemingly limitless future. Some unkind tongues said that she had in fact written all of it: romance fiction. And even the name Golden Gate for the strait they were now crossing was hers, not his—so they said. Any such slighting estimate of her husband's abilities or achievements, especially when grounded in truth, was sure to rile her into an immediate fury. On such occasions she could be as feisty as a weasel. But she was far from feisty now, now seeing almost wet-eyed for the first time the place that had made her husband famous, and should propel him—she was certain—to historic heights, perhaps the presidency, with her at his side. Perhaps more than the presidency. Naming this strait the Golden Gate just before the discovery of gold itself was like a prophecy beyond any human ken, a prophecy of limitless gold for the nation and of a gateway to limitless greatness for John Frémont and his beloved Jessie.

This was her first trip to California, the farthest outpost of the Manifest Destiny her father, Thomas Hart Benton, had preached to the U.S. Senate. Strange, coming to a place that was the fulfillment of your father's fondest dream, and a place you yourself had already partly named and partially created in the minds of your countrymen without ever having seen it yourself, except in your fancy. For them and for her, California had become a neutral territory between the real world and fairyland, where the actual and the imaginary could somehow meet, and each imbue itself with the nature of the other. The gold rush itself was a daydream become fact, and thereby seemed to offer a foothold in that elusive region of gliding beautiful thoughts. Here, if anywhere, fiction and reality overlapped. A quarter of a century later, remembering this very morning, she would write, "How maimed have been the lives compared to the bright hopes."

Throughout the trip she had been treated by most of the young men as if she were already the first lady of California, a treatment she took as her due, like Queen Elizabeth with her courtiers. When their attentions seemed to be waning or perhaps divided unbecomingly with the few other ladies on board, one of her coughing fits would remind them of their duties to her. During the worst of these fits she had been too weak even to walk outside for air, so had to be carried by one of the gentlemen—and then they found traces of blood on her handkerchief. That was when it was decided she should be moved out of her stifling stateroom, to a sleeping tent set up for her on deck. Clearly so delicate a woman was risking her life to join her husband, and this was the least that the other passengers could do to accommodate her.

First the name Golden Gate, then the discovery of real gold. California seemed a place where dreams could call things into being—and where those who did not dream boldly would be left behind. When the U.S. government decided in 1847 to provide a subsidy for a monthly mail run from Panama to the sparsely settled West Coast, there was some doubt that it would find a taker. Then William Aspinwall decided to do so and established the Pacific Mail Steamship Company, and his fellow New York capitalists thought him temporarily deranged. (Only temporarily, because so sound a man as Aspinwall would be soon brought back to his senses by a cold dousing in red ink.) As one of his colleagues put it baldly, the Pacific Mail company constituted "a certain sequestration of a large amount of capital for an indefinite time, with a faint prospect of profit." The first of Aspinwall's three new steamships, the *California,* had just left New York, largely empty, for the long voyage around the Horn to the Pacific when President Polk announced to the nation the California gold strike:

> It was known that mines of the precious metals existed to a considerable extent in California at the time of its acquisition. [This was a calculated fib by a one-term president on behalf of his policy of expansionism.] Recent discoveries render it probable that these mines are more extensive and valuable than was anticipated. The account of the abundance of gold in that ter-

ritory are of such an extraordinary character as would scarcely command belief were they not corroborated by the authentic reports of officers in public service.

When the *California* reached the port of New Orleans, it was swamped with eager argonauts. The Pacific Mail Steamship Company's prospects for profit were no longer faint, and William Aspinwall was being regarded by his New York colleagues as someone uncanny—he was either the luckiest man in the world or a seer.

Now the third of Aspinwall's steamships, the *Panama,* is approaching the rocky island of the middle bay, which the Mexicans called Alcatraz for the numerous pelicans that make it home, and the Yankees call Guano Island for the somewhat useful stuff the pelicans and gulls leave behind. The guano itself gives the barren rock the look of having been whitewashed and the smell of a latrine. On this unusual morning it sparkles in the rising sun, and the wind blows away the smell. So it sits there, almost beautiful in its barrenness, with the few swirling wisps of fog that still wreathe it. Having headed directly toward the island, the steamship now veers to the starboard.

A number of the passengers on deck are military men, and their blue uniforms and brass buttons show to advantage in the bright light, not that anyone is noticing. The Civil War will be the making of most of them, and the death of one. The doomed one will by then be wearing Confederate gray and the stars of a general. No less than seven generals will come from this deck, and an admiral. Perhaps the most famous of these, "Fighting Joe" Hooker (although he is not known as "Fighting Joe" yet) is congratulating a distinguished-looking gentleman. If one had to guess who will be the famous general, it would be the latter, even though he is not in uniform. He towers over Hooker, who himself is not short. He stands with the carriage and bearing of one accustomed to lead. At first it is not clear why he is so striking in appearance. But it is his head. It does not seem out of proportion, yet it is massive—mouth, chin, brow, all large together, and a profusion of carefully groomed gray hair. Not the soft leveling gray of the fog but something almost metallic in its strength. Only after looking at him for a while do you notice that his eyes seem to be gray too, taking what color they show from the immediate surroundings, but in themselves grayish and permanently distant. He is one of the two former congressmen on deck. His name is William McKendree Gwin. Hooker may be congratulating him for winning the ship pool on the exact arrival, for he has won. William Gwin is very good at calculating odds.

The passengers can now get their first glimpse of other ships. The port is on the far side of the southern peninsula that helps form the vast bay, there fully sheltered from the sea. So the location was not a complete mistake. First a few ships moored well out into the bay come into view, then a few more, and finally a forest of masts. An amazing sight, as if a great navy had collected in the middle of nowhere. Then between the masts and the sandhills San Francisco emerges—and an anxiety, if not outright panic, begins to spread across the deck. There may even have been a few curses unwittingly uttered in the presence of ladies, who themselves look startled, but not at what they hear.

San Francisco seems from this distance a tent city, and it appears deserted at that, as do some of the ships, which have had their masts removed. The passengers have immediately inferred that they are too late. This had been the largely unspoken fear throughout the humdrum of the long voyage, and now it seems to be confirmed by this odd panorama. These are the tents of prospectors returned from the quickly played out diggings. The gold rush is over; it was a proverbial flash in the pan, a bubble that had burst while they were on the *Panama*. This uncomfortable, arduous, potentially dangerous trip had been for nothing. They are a ship of fools.

Twenty-five years later, when California was still leading the world in gold production, some of these passengers would remember with amusement their premature laments and despairs at this moment. They remembered feeling so foolish at this moment, foolish as all the advice they had gotten against making the trip crowded in upon them, how they had cringed at the thought of returning home with nothing to show for their folly, nothing to say to the I-told-you-sos. The sight of those tents was a moment of absolute mortification, of titanic collective disappointment.

Eventually a navy launch approached the ship, and a young midshipman boarded and was momentarily stunned at the behavior of the passengers. Most seemed to lose their composure, and rushed at him, almost pushing him overboard, while asking questions at the same time, all asking the same question in a dozen different ways. Was it over? He calmed them with assurances that the gold rush was far from over. They had completely misinterpreted the tents. Argonauts were arriving in such great numbers and so rapidly that building in San Francisco could not possibly keep pace, especially since workers were fleeing as quickly as possible to the diggings. So were crews. Many of the ships they saw in San Francisco Bay were there because their crews had deserted before the captain could do his business and clear harbor. One trick sly captains tried was to moor far out in the bay, but this did no good; when the gold fever was bad, men would happily jump from ship and swim to shore. The last steamship in port before the *Panama,* the *Oregon,* had actually moored in the north bay; and then, after three crew members had successfully jumped ship the first night, the captain arrested all the others and put them under lock and key as prospective mutineers. Not that they were, of course; but the captain did continue his mail run on north with an almost full crew, albeit one that would have heartily enjoyed watching him walk the plank. Some of the ships closest in were now being used as hotels, jails, storehouses, and the like; these usually were without masts, which only got in the way and so were stored or—more likely—used as fuel. Accommodations were needed, and these ships weren't going anywhere until this gold fever passed. And there was no sign of that. So the ships sat there, being of use, but slowly decaying into little better than derelicts. Approaching the newborn mushroom city of San Francisco through these, it was hard not to think of it as a city that had been inhabited for ages and was now going to ruin. Eventually these ships could be broken up for lumber, as the *Panama* itself would be one day, on the northern shores of this very bay. (One of these passengers, then living nearby, would sentimentally have a cask made from some of this wood; in it he would keep only the finest imported brandy.)

Soon other launches were coming alongside. Those running the launches looked like men you would trust with nothing you valued, especially your life. They bore all the outward signs of the rough life of the common criminal. When they demanded—most in an Irish brogue—three dollars just to take a single passenger ashore, newcomers wondered whether this was a fare or petty extortion. The amount sounded more like extortion, and these men looked as if extortion would not be the worst of their enterprising activities. In this instance initial appearances were not deceptive.

Some launches carried passengers out to the ship but not for passage— and these did look respectable. A few of them were agents from the local merchants; before even clambering aboard, they were shouting out inquiries about the cargo—and then, having heard a response, began shouting out offers, bidding against one another in a free-for-all auction while the launches bobbed up and down as the agents tried to keep their balance with one hand and with the other thrust aloft large pouches of gold dust to show their earnest. (The *Panama* passengers would eventually learn that a certain percentage of such California pouches of earnestness were in fact filled with sand.) Others who had hired the launches were desperately seeking skilled labor, any labor. Labor was so scarce in San Francisco that employers regularly met passenger vessels as soon as they entered the bay in order to hire immediately likely prospects. The wages they were offering were stunning. It was said the cost to unload goods in San Francisco was greater than the whole freight charge from New York. So the wages were stunning—until, that is, one learned the prices in gold rush San Francisco. Four dollars a night for a room, a bad room at that? A passenger, who would one day be American ambassador to China, remembered that on learning this he instinctively fingered in his pocket his own total worldly wealth, a twenty-five-cent piece. What was he going to do? He couldn't afford to breathe in this place.

Another passenger, a young doctor, suddenly reached his own unexpected conclusion as to what he was going to do. He cornered a man who had just come on board, and pointing to the yellow hills in the east asked eagerly, "Is that the way to the mines?" The man said, "Yes, that is the way. Are you going to the mines?" Barely being able to contain his excitement, the doctor responded with what he thought was an air of diffident maturity.

"I thought of it." Looking at him up and down, the man said simply, "My advice to you is not to go, for I do not think you are a man calculated to succeed in the mines." He paused, and then added, "I just came from there." The young doctor's initial confusion was beginning to become defiant anger at being treated like a child, when the man who had just come from the mines started to go about his business on deck—and for the first time the doctor noticed that this Polonius was badly crippled. Just come from the mine crippled. The Californian was gone before the young doctor thought to ask him the story; but by that time he knew he might stay in California, but only to practice medicine and on the coast. Which he did for the rest of his long and productive life.

Nothing that the passengers could see from the ship, nothing that they had read about California before, nothing they had heard from the men on the launches could prepare them for what they were about to experience. Even as cool a customer as William McKendree Gwin would be temporarily disoriented by it, repulsed and invigorated all at once, staggered by a chaotic vitality that defied comprehension. Such reactions did not last long with him, but others on this ship would never quite get over this initial experience, babbling incoherently about it even years later.

The ferrymen, if they were in the mood, might point out the sights as the launch approached the wharfs. Everyone was laughing this June about that fine ship over there, so stately. The whole crew ran off, and so now the doleful captain has become an innkeeper, renting out berths, while trying to scrape together another crew—no chance. But the berths are full at least. No chance, but also no vacancy. The *Euphemia* over there is now a jail, the *Apollo* right here is a saloon.

Such benign attempts at anecdotal orientation were of little help. The first impressions of newcomers were always a blur. No one had ever seen anything like this new city, unprecedented incongruity everywhere one looked. And the most common response of new arrivals to San Francisco, once the initial excitement and perplexity wore off, was unqualified revulsion. This town might have been already planted, but it had yet to take root. The hard, makeshift character of the life was bad enough, worse than the worst New York slums—and even well-connected ladies like Jessie Frémont could not preserve themselves from rank discomfort, and a good bit of jostling of a kind suitable to bring on an attack of the vapors. William Gwin, in contrast, would somehow manage to get decent accommodations. Gwin always managed. But for ordinary mortals there was a standard repartee. You can't rent a room in San Francisco large enough to swing a cat in—but, then again, why would anyone want to swing a cat in a place where he was gonna sleep? Some new arrivals would be unable to find lodgings at all; come nightfall they would glumly be returning to their ship by launch—another three dollars lighter—to find a bunk.

The initial impression was dizzying. As one arrival put it, "There seemed no method in anything. People bustled and jostled against one another, bawled, railed, fought, cursed and swore, sweated and labored lustily, and somehow the work was done." The new arrivals were not yet part of the work, but they were certainly far from exempt from the rest of it. The jostling came about, in part, from perfect strangers coming up to the newcomer to see if he had anything to sell. One newly arrived entrepreneur had scarcely gotten off the launch when he was asked how much he wanted for the box of Panama pineapples he was carrying. Trying to enter into the spirit of broad frontier humor, he asked with a wink for ten dollars. But there was no wink or smile in reply. He instantaneously found himself relieved of his pineapples and with a ten-dollar gold piece in his hand. Already stunned, he then watched dumbstruck while half his pineapples were resold within a minute for fifteen dollars. As the rest of his pineapples walked away jauntily, a word began slowly to form itself in his mind. Greenhorn.

There was not much ceremony for important personages arriving. Captains, until moments before the enlightened despots of their floating kingdoms, were treated with offhand rudeness by mere shipping clerks. There was something delicious about watching a captain turn purple after being tweaked in a way that would have brought a severe lashing on board. One captain who made the mistake of declaring loudly that he did not like the way he was being treated was told by the smiling clerk, "Who the damned cares whether you like it or not? You can go to hell if you don't like it. Who the damned do you expect to scare?" Muffled laughter all around. Captains had to learn, and as soon as possible, that they were a dime a dozen here—but a good clerk was hard to find. And a woman, any woman, was harder.

There were only one or two women per hundred among the new San Franciscans, and most of these were what the men called "soiled doves." Jessie Frémont soon had calculated that in all San Francisco only sixteen women were such that she could socialize with them. A prospective plan to bring a shipload of marriageable young Eves was heartily, if not altogether genteelly, praised by the San Francisco newspaper; the *Alta California* editorialized that such "fresh spareribs" would "do well in this market."

When Jessie Frémont and the few other women on the *Panama* disembarked, they must have been appalled by how they were gawked at. (Jessie was already in a bad humor because Mr. Frémont had not been there to meet her.) It approached indecency, just the looks they got, and from all the men, not just the hard ones—but to tell the truth most seemed fairly hard fellows. Men were coming out of buildings, stopping their work, bridling their horses . . . just to stare. Perhaps Frémont blushingly thought this was her fame preceding her, the wife of the Pathfinder of the West. But, no, all that was required was for word to be passed—"Two women walking up Montgomery"—for a large crowd of gawkers to gather. Only after respectable women had been in California for a time would they realize that the looks they received were more sentimental than lascivious. They would be told that, of course, before they began to walk up the street, but they would not believe it until they got to know the place better, until they learned firsthand how dreadfully homesick most of these young men were. That was what a decent woman represented, a properly attired woman of European origin—Home.

This became particularly clear if the woman happened to be accompanied by children (which the women from the *Panama* were not). Then the men, or at least a few of them, would lose their inhibitions. They would crowd around, impeding the progress of the little family—and with a studied politeness, to which there was just a tinge of desperation, ask if they might touch the child. What could the mother say? And soon the child was being patted, squeezed, lifted in the air, kissed, passed around by these hard-looking men, at least one of whom would usually get misty and start blubbering about his own kids back in Vermont, Virginia, or wherever. Or his younger brother or sister who must be getting almost as big as this little gentleman by now. The women were invariably moved by all this, and a little flattered—but also somehow unnerved. Especially by the men who gratefully shoved nuggets or little bags of gold dust into the children's hands. This place was as unnatural as a desert island.

All this would have interested William Gwin not at all. The gold rush itself was for him just human frivolity writ large, a madcap adventure that used dreams of vast wealth as an excuse to escape routine and responsibility, an inept attempt to scratch the everlasting itch for things remote. Pathetically, most of those who survived this folly (and many would not) would end up with little more for their risks than fireside tales for when they were too old to repeat their mistakes, fanciful tales with which to bore others and amuse themselves. They would go to their undistinguished graves bragging that— as the boys of San Francisco now put it—they had "seen the elephant." Well, Gwin had already seen this elephant. He had seen it in the wilds of Mississippi, the Texas frontier, and the corridors of the Washington Capitol. He had seen it as he carved out his own plantation in Mississippi, using slaves and fending off Indians. He had seen it in the Texas of his friend Sam Houston, as a Mexican society was supplanted by an American one. (His own wife was a product of American Texas, one of its gorgeous yellow roses.) He had seen it among the shady entrepreneurs of New Orleans, and of course among the conniving, grasping politicians of the District of Columbia. Again and again, he had seen the elephant, and that elephant was always the same; it had fearsome tusks, big ears, and a little brain. It was a great beast, yes, but one made to do another's bidding.

Gwin was not interested in golden dreams and gauzy delusions, in exciting adventures or fireside tales. He had come west for one thing, and one thing only. That was power. And he meant to have it. He was determined to become, for all practical purposes, the human equivalent of almighty Providence for golden California. And he soon would.

★　★　★

Only a few months before—March 5, 1849, to be exact—William Mc-Kendree Gwin had been standing along a street in Washington, D.C., with a friend; together, outside the National Hotel, they were watching the inaugural procession of Zachary Taylor. They had seen the president-elect pass before them in an open carriage drawn by four stately grays. But the horses, carriage, and pageantry seemed lost on Old Rough and Ready; with his plastered hair, baggy eyes, and pleasantly empty expression, he seemed singularly miscast. As one unkind Washingtonian put it, "If he has any intellectual greatness, physiognomy is a cheat."

Some experienced politicians, even Democrats, did try to find in Taylor's victory a basis for hope. James Buchanan, the outgoing secretary of state and himself a future president, described Taylor as a "man of Providence" who might "for some purposes be greater than Washington or Jackson." It would turn out that the only such conceivable purpose was for Providence to reveal itself as a cruel jokester.

Gwin and his friend, however, had more important matters than physiognomy or pageantry or Providence to talk over. Both were Democrats and Taylor was a Whig—and that meant they both were soon to be cut off from federal patronage by the new administration, a raw wind of another kind. Their conversation naturally turned to what each expected for himself in the immediate future. Stephen A. Douglas, "the Little Giant" as he was now being called, thought he still had important challenges facing him as senator from Illinois, but the towering Gwin was now out of work as commissioner of the port of New Orleans. He told Douglas, quite matter-of-factly, that he was leaving for California the very next day, there to advocate statehood. He also offered a bet to Douglas; within a year he would be back in Washington to have Douglas present his credentials as the new senator from California. It is hard to believe that Douglas was even tempted to take that bet; he knew better than to bet with Gwin on any matter that concerned him. Douglas knew Gwin to be as shrewd as he was restlessly ambitious.

In his restlessness at least, Gwin was his father's son. The elder Gwin, a Welshman who immigrated to America shortly after it had gained independence, had himself been instinctively drawn away from the well-established life of Charleston, South Carolina, to the borderlands of the interior, following the trail blazed by Daniel Boone. There his neighbor and close friend had been a young man named Andrew Jackson. In middle age Gwin's father had taken to fretting over his own salvation, and would eventually become a Methodist parson; but his religious vocation did not prevent this old Indian fighter and frontiersman from joining Andy Jackson in New Orleans in 1812 to command fourteen hundred of his sharpshooters.

President Jackson did not forget his old friends. (Jackson never forgot friends or enemies—and counted as enemies were almost all those who had crossed him even once.) So he had taken up the young son of Gwin as a political protégé. In 1831 he brought young Gwin to live in the White House for six months and serve as his personal secretary. While still in his twenties, and when men like Douglas were still in school, Gwin already knew more about Washington politics than many senators.

More importantly, he knew Jackson, the master politician of the age. Jackson had shown how an outsider from the borderlands could beat the American elite at their own game, and thereby become their equal. Jackson would preach the cause of the common people, but he meant the people's championing of his own. So he declared that public office servers should be chosen anew by each administration since any man of ordinary intelligence was capable of doing the work—thereby he, while flattering men of ordinary intelligence, created the federal spoils system, and concentrated more power in the hands of the chief executive, himself. In private talks when his advisers began spouting republican or democratic principles, Jackson would exclaim, "Beware of your metaphysics. Hair splitting is a dangerous business." Jackson was interested in results, not metaphysics or altruism.

So Jackson's cultivation of the young Gwin was based upon more than Jackson's friendship with the father. Jackson had instinctively understood why Gwin was so restless. His was not the simple restlessness of the frontiersman, as was his father's. Rather it was the restlessness of limitless ambition. William Gwin had first studied law and passed the bar; but the law in Tennessee was dominated by old hands of his father's generation, and Gwin did not see any way to crack through. So he took up medicine, and received his medical degree. Dr. Gwin still found Tennessee confining, and joined the migration into Mississippi that would establish the cotton kingdom there. With so much money to make on this new frontier, Gwin could hardly be satisfied with treating planters' complaints. And Andy Jackson needed someone to build the Democratic Party in this new and prosperous state, a Democratic Party loyal to the central government—that is, to himself.

Jackson's chosen instruments for this were William Gwin and his brother Samuel. Jackson provided them with spoils up front in 1833. William's was to be the U.S. marshalship for southern Mississippi, worth about $75,000 annually; his brother was to get a federal land office. The Gwin brothers were to be Jackson's crown princes in Mississippi; and Jackson wanted to see to it that they would have a princely sum to work with.

The senior senator from Mississippi, George Poindexter, had other ideas. Although he had become a senator largely as a result of his support for Jackson, he now had begun to see the wisdom of states' rights, even supporting John C. Calhoun's contention that individual states had the right to nullify national legislation. Poindexter was particularly insistent that he himself should have a decisive say in federal appointments in Mississippi. General Jackson had consequently come to hate Poindexter. As far as Jackson was concerned, a loyal Democratic Party in Mississippi meant, before all else, the end of George Poindexter's political career. Of this Poindexter himself was not altogether unaware.

So he opposed the appointment of both Gwins steadfastly. He succeeded in blocking Samuel's, which in turn resulted in a minor constitutional crisis when Jackson insisted upon appointing him anyway, simply on his presidential authority. Then cooler heads prevailed, and Samuel was quietly given a different but similar post. William Gwin's appointment was also being blocked until he took the initiative by having a secret meeting with Senator Calhoun. Calhoun must have been impressed with this daring, since Jackson would have disowned Gwin, had he found out. When the opposition to William suddenly dissolved, Jackson must have interpreted this unexpectedly easy victory to his own steadfastness in the face of his enemies like the battle of New Orleans. Gwin knew better, an important political lesson for him to file away.

Once back in Mississippi, the Gwin brothers set about destroying Poindexter—first by undermining his own support, and then by seeking the right candidate to challenge him for reelection. Poindexter retaliated by launching a Senate investigation into the Gwins on charges of corruption. Relations between Jackson and Poindexter could scarcely have been worse. When a madman tried to assassinate Jackson, the president charged that Poindexter had hired him—and insisted that the Senate formally investigate this charge.

By 1835 the Gwins had settled on Robert Walker as the best candidate. Convincing Jackson himself of this was a delicate matter because Walker had recently criticized Jackson, something not normally tolerated. Gwin assured Jackson that Walker was eminently qualified to be senator from Mississippi, for he hated Poindexter as much as Jackson and the Gwins did. He wrote to Old Hickory, "If elected, he [Poindexter] will have to walk over the dead bodies of three persons before he takes his seat. Mr. Walker, my brother & myself he has used every effort to destroy. If we can not disgrace him by beating him, he shall atone for his attacks upon us by his blood." This assurance seemed to satisfy Jackson.

Walker did win; and Poindexter, if not disgraced, was humiliated, and his career in Mississippi politics was over. But this victory was at the price of blood. Samuel Gwin had hissed Poindexter during a speech so insistently that a law partner of Poindexter had lost his temper and challenged Samuel to a duel. When they met Samuel shot him dead, but died himself two and a half years later from his own wounds. This lingering death seemed to sober William Gwin. He had learned, at considerable personal cost, not to make politics personal. It was a rational game. Those who let their tempers flare were likely to lose, one way or another.

The young Gwin had one more lesson to learn during his political apprenticeship. He was typical of Jacksonian America: if he had a princely sum (as $75,000 a year certainly was), he immediately began to scheme to transform it into a kingly fortune. That this might require him to risk all daunted him not at all. He became the mastermind in some vast land speculations, involving literally millions of acres that had been opened by the brutal Indian policies of Jackson. (From the beginning Gwin's ambitions, like Jackson's, were expressed against the backdrop of the suppression of "inferior races.") This would eventually collapse, and leave Gwin in a terrible financial tangle, and his reputation a bit askew.

Happier were his adventures in Texas. There he was the guest of another family friend from the Tennessee frontier, Sam Houston. He met his wife in Houston's circle, and also began to speculate gleefully in Texas's almost virgin lands. Again the size of the tracts was boggling. The largest he would eventually control was more than half a million acres.

His avarice, however, had compromised him politically. He should have himself been grasping for the U.S. Senate or the governor's mansion. It was strange then that someone of his power and prominence should accept the nomination of the Mississippi Democratic Party to the relatively lowly position of U.S. congressman—until, that is, one realizes that this would give him immunity from his creditors. In fact, he seems to have used his term in Congress (1840–42) as an opportunity to repair his finances. Never a lover of Indians nor an advocate of their rights, he did at this time win them significant compensation for their tribal lands, for a contingency fee so high it was held up for a number of years as exorbitant.

Nonetheless, while he was attending to the mundane matter of avoiding bankruptcy, he was also being exposed to a vision of the future that he found irresistible. He happened to live in the same boardinghouse as John C. Calhoun, and the two eventually began to have long conversations about politics. Of course, as a Jacksonian, Gwin could not agree with Calhoun's advocacy of nullification. But another of Calhoun's cherished subjects Gwin found immediately convincing. At the boardinghouse table Calhoun sketched to Gwin his vision of a manifest destiny for the United States, a vast nation that would encompass Texas and much of Mexico—and would also stretch all the way to the Pacific Ocean. Calhoun could even point to the place where a great port city of this new America would be built, a port that would dwarf New Orleans and rival New York. It would be on a bay the Spanish had named San Francisco, a magnificent harbor where only a few hundred Mexican settlers lived today.

The next few years were a series of private successes and missed public opportunities for Gwin. When James K. Polk was unexpectedly elected president, Gwin was prominently mentioned as a possible cabinet member—but the choice fell to Senator Robert Walker. Walker then wanted Gwin as his replacement as senator, but the governor of Mississippi refused to have a senator so associated in the electorate's mind with what he called "broke speculators." Finally, Gwin reluctantly offered himself for renomination to the House of Representatives, but the fire-eaters for states' rights were now too strong in Mississippi.

He lost out to a promising young Democratic politician named Jefferson Davis. Davis was Poindexter returned, as if having been strengthened in defeat against any compromise with the national government. Davis insisted that intrinsically the federal government had absolutely no legitimate authority over the sovereign state of Mississippi: "It is the creature of the States. As such it could have no inherent power, all it possesses was delegated by the States." In this Davis went farther than Calhoun himself; Davis, unlike Calhoun, objected even to the federal government's improving navigation on the Mississippi. (The Constitution said "regulate commerce," not "create commerce.")

Given his reluctance to be a representative again, it was easy for Gwin to take his defeat with good grace, and thereby earn in Davis a lifelong friend. He apparently could see that the radical turn in Mississippi politics made someone with his politics unlikely to succeed. And he could let younger politicians, such as Henry Foote (who had served as a second to Samuel Gwin in his fatal duel), try to do for Davis what Gwin and his late brother had done for Poindexter. He had little taste left for such feuds.

The national Democratic Party did not forget Gwin and his loyalty, however dim his prospects for higher office in Mississippi now. At the end of the Mexican War he found himself commissioner of public works for the port of New Orleans, the same New Orleans that his father had helped defend beside Andy Jackson. The war had made the position extremely lucrative, and Gwin—his financial troubles perhaps finally behind him—was now fully prepared to grasp for power again. He had made his young man's mistakes, and was none the worse for them. He was ready to be a leader of the American republic.

When Zachary Taylor was elected, Gwin had traveled back to Washington to size up the situation. The news of the California gold discovery was all the talk. Gwin, thinking back upon his conversations with Calhoun, knew exactly what this meant for the country, and what it might mean for him. So it was that as Taylor's triumphant if slightly comic procession passed him, he turned to his friend Stephen Douglas and told him he would within a year be asking to present his credentials as senator from the new state of California.

Now, little more than three months later, Dr. William McKendree Gwin was in San Francisco observing a pageant quite different from Taylor's inauguration. There was much that was novel in San Francisco, but not much that was surprising to an experienced and single-minded man like William Gwin, nothing except for the sense of entering into a peculiarly human chaos. He was familiar with the frontier. But California was something more. On a single San Francisco street corner you could find a greater diversity of humanity than anywhere else on the continent, with the possible exception of a Nantucket whaling dock. Gwin was someone who almost as a matter of creed kept his own counsel. And yet, from his background and earlier activities, one can infer with some confidence that if he had expressed himself, he would have shared the revulsion of one contemporary account at San Francisco's unnatural mixture of the races:

> All races are represented. There were hordes of long pig-tailed, blear-eyed rank smelling Chinese, with their yellow faces and blue garbs; single dandy black fellows, of nearly as bad an odor, who strutted as only a negro can strut in holiday clothes and clean white shirt; a few diminutive Maylays, from the western archipelago, and some handsome Kanakas from the Sandwich Islands; jet-black straight-featured Abyssinians; hideously tatooed New Zealanders; Feejee sailors and even the secluded Japanese, short, thick, clumsy and ever bowing, jacketed fellows; people of many races of Hindoo land; Russians with furs and sables; a stray turbaned, stately Turk or two, and occasionally a half naked shivering Indian; multitudes of the Spanish race from every country of the Americas, partly pure, partly crossed with red blood—Chilians, Peruvians and Mexicans, all with different shades of the same complexion, black-eyed and well-featured, proud of their beards and moustaches, their grease, dirt, and eternal gaudy serapes or darker cloaks; Spaniards from the mother country, more dignified, polite and pompous than their old colonial brethren; "greasers" too, like them; great numbers of tall, goat-chinned, smooth-cheeked, oily-locked, lank-visaged, tobacco-chewing, large-limbed and featured, rough, care-worn, careless Americans from every State of the Union, dressed independently in every variety of garb, not caring a fig what people thought of them but determined to "do the thing handsomely" and "go ahead"; fat, conceited Englishmen, who pretended to compete in shrewdness with the subtle Yankee.... Then there were bands of gay easy-principled philosophical Germans, Italians and Frenchmen of every cut and figure, their faces covered with hair, and strange habiliments on their persons, and among whom might be particularly remarked numbers of thick-lipped, hook-nosed, ox-eyed, cunning, oily Jews. Among the vast motley crowd scarcely could two hats be found alike in material, size and shape; scarcely could two men be found otherwise dressed alike.

The description is from *The Annals of San Francisco,* an authoritative account of the early days of gold rush San Francisco, published in 1855, compiled by a number of local newspapermen, and told from a steadfastly American point of view. The *Annals* expressed well the preoccupations of

many of the aspiring American leaders of California. One of those preoccupations, perhaps the most persistent, was not just of a plurality observed
through stereotypes, but of a plurality suspected of being ungovernable—of
San Francisco less as a city than a conglomeration, a humanly induced social
pandemonium.

This was an extreme case of the problem presented by cities generally to
the American republic. What was it Thomas Jefferson had written? "The
mobs of great cities add just so much to the support of pure governement,
as sores do to the strength of the human body." Then there was his chilling
prediction: "When we get piled upon one another in large cities as in Europe,
we shall be corrupt as in Europe, and go on eating one another as they do
there."

Jefferson was, as usual, naive about human nature. He thought there was
pure virtue somewhere, on the small frontier farms, for instance. As anyone
who had lived on the true frontier such as Jackson or Gwin knew, such social
cannibalism was unavoidable everywhere. Nonetheless, a strong, if not a
pure, republican government was possible. But the right leaders were required, leaders who had no illusions about human nature and were not given
to dreamy hairsplitting or metaphysical hand-wringing.

The question that would have inevitably been raised in the mind of an
ambitious Jacksonian such as Gwin by that conglomeration of humanity
called San Francisco was a practical one. How were the careless Americans,
perhaps with the help of easy-principled Europeans, going to control this
new California? Or rather, how were the rest to be rendered powerless, if
not simply driven out? The answer was simply that this new California
needed to be led by someone careful, someone with sound Jacksonian principles or rather pragmatism, someone like William McKendree Gwin.

But that was in the future. Right now, there was only one person Gwin
would have liked to drive out of California. His name was Thomas Butler
King. Officially, the Honorable Thomas Butler King was the most important
personage on the *Panama,* for he was President Taylor's personal envoy to
California. When the San Francisco newspaper *Alta California* had announced
the arrival of the *Panama,* King and Jessie Frémont were the only two passengers mentioned by name.

King thought himself well suited for the role of most important personage. As one of King's friends would later say of him, "He was very brave
and manly—generous, liberal, with nice sensibility—courtly manners—and
so many of those becoming graces with which Nature refuses to endow the
mass of human beings." Not everyone would have readily agreed with this
fulsome assessment, but Butler King himself was one who would have. He
fully expected to return to Washington as the most important envoy from
California to the president—that is, as California's first elected senator. King
was coming to California for the gold of high political office.

Needless to say, Gwin had been carefully observing King during the voyage, for he also was coming to California for the same gold. Undeniably, King was a rival with an obvious edge, but gray-eyed Gwin was a careful and patient man, and had learned much about handling blowhards from Andy Jackson. And the more he saw of Butler King, the less he thought he had to worry, President Zachary Taylor or no President Zachary Taylor.

Butler King, who owned a large plantation in coastal Georgia, had been an outspoken defender of the peculiar institution. He had worried publicly that when the non–slave-holding states gained a majority in Congress, they would "resort to a course of legislation for their own benefit, that may involve us in ruinous intestine wars, or in submission to a government without limitation of powers." As a congressman from Georgia, King had decried what he called "this unnatural alliance of the West with the East." He could not understand why the rural states of the West did not ally themselves with the planters of the South rather than the manufacturers of the East.

To tell the truth, there was a great deal that Thomas Butler King did not understand. One realized this the more he spoke, and he spoke constantly. He expected to be listened to constantly as well—and undoubtedly he had been in the coastal regions of Georgia, because of his wealth, his position, and the easy good looks that reminded people of a young Henry Clay. Most of what King did not understand had to do with subtlety and indirection, of rowing toward an objective circuitously and with oars muffled. What King lacked was not so much intelligence as complexity. But he was amusing company, as long as he was the center of attention, or near it. He and Jessie Frémont made a wonderful pair.

Butler King's great achievement as a congressman, at least for California, was first sponsoring and then shepherding to passage the bill for the Pacific mail run. He, as much as any legislator, could take credit for the steamship they had ridden from Panama. He was like a young boy in his enthusiasm for ships and trains, and was already talking about a railroad line across Panama. He had also backed the right horse early for the presidency. When other Whigs were talking about Winfield Scott or another try for Henry Clay, Butler King had, for reasons not entirely clear, come out forthrightly for General Zachary Taylor. King's name even had been put forward for the vice presidential nomination; but King had his heart set upon being named secretary of the navy (there was that love of boats). He was more perplexed than angry or bitter when it was given to someone else, lacking as he did the cool vindictiveness of the truly successful politician. This mission to California was a consolation prize, one he relished almost as much for the sea trip involved as for the expected Senate seat.

Officially, he was coming to California to write a government report about California's potential. But his unofficial business was far more important. First he was to explain to Californians why the Whigs in Congress had failed to act on statehood, to explain this somehow in terms that would endear to Californians these very Whigs. That was no small task for him because the issue had been slavery; Southerners, like King himself, did not want California and New Mexico admitted as free states because they would upset the fine balance in Congress. Nonetheless, King was to encourage Californians, privately in the name of the Whig president himself, to organize a state government and petition for admission. He was quite open about this double charge, not being one to keep his cards close to his vest. And, of course, if California entered as a state while a Whig was in the White House, its people would certainly want to be represented by at least one Whig senator who had intimate ties to General Taylor. Who better to fill this position than the Honorable Thomas Butler King?

So Butler King had shown his whole hand before Gwin had played a single card. It was a very good hand, except for the lack of deviousness in the man who held it. He was too open in his strong proslavery views. And he was also remarkably vain, not an uncommon trait in a plantation owner who was used to his word being law but a weakness in a politician because it inclined him to underestimate opponents. King seemed to think all he had to do was show his cards, and everyone else would fold—and he would not have to dirty himself playing out the game. Gwin thought differently. In this particular game, the Honorable Thomas Butler King was going to have to get a little dirty or he was going to lose. And, more likely, he was going both to get a little dirty and to lose.

While Butler King on arrival was trying to impress everyone by accepting the expected adulation with aristocratic grace, Gwin was quietly forming a circle of potential supporters. One new acquaintance with no more money than that future ambassador to China was invited to spend his first nights in California in William Gwin's well-appointed quarters. Gwin also showed this young man, a Tennesseean, an open sack of money on the dresser. His friends should feel free, he said blandly, to help themselves to as much as they thought they would need. From that moment on, J. Ross Browne was a devoted friend, and he would remember this generosity warmly decades later.

There was hardly any time for Gwin to get oriented to the new city before he was involved in a whirlwind of political activity. The political situation had become, shortly before their arrival, extremely volatile. California was, quite simply, without any effective government or even legal system. The American military authorities had openly admitted that they ruled by right of conquest. This pleased neither the older Californians who were accustomed to Mexican law nor the new Americans who were continually agitating for representative government.

The military governor, General Bennet Riley, was in an impossible position, as he himself fully realized. He was continually having to swat down efforts at self-government by his compatriots while not knowing quite what to do with the indigenous Mexican institutions, which he scarcely understood. Moreover, his own superiors were giving him no orders, and his men were deserting to the goldfields right and left. His only good fortune was to have a bright young officer as his secretary, Henry Halleck (who one day as General Halleck would be Lincoln's chief of staff). Whenever things finally seemed to be calming down, some news would come from the East that would shake the populace up into a dangerous state of effervescence. To be military governor of California in 1849 would have sorely tested the patience of a monk—and General Riley was a professional soldier notable primarily in his capacity for intense exasperation at the messy ways of civilians. His predicament in California was such that even his inveterate opponents had occasionally to smile in sympathy.

At almost the same moment that Gwin had been watching Zachary Taylor's inaugural, poor Bennet Riley had been reading a letter in the *Alta California* to the people of California from no less a dignitary than Senator Thomas Hart Benton. It declared, "The treaty with Mexico makes you citizens of the United States. Congress has not yet passed the laws to give you the blessings of our government, and it may be some time before it does so. In the meantime, while your condition is anomalous and critical, the temporary civil and military government established over you as a right of war is at end." That was all bad enough, but Tom Benton, Old Bullion, did not have to go out of his way to call each of Riley's two predecessors an "ignoramus" for policies that Riley himself was following. And then there was the *Alta California* that, to add insult to injury, had taken to comparing Benton of Missouri to Paul of Tarsus, both inspired apostles of freedom against the barbaric tyranny of the old law.

If, as Benton claimed, Riley's authority had ceased to exist (and no one would more earnestly rejoice at this than Bennet Riley himself), he had the distinct impression that someone above him in the chain of command would have told him so. But, of course, no one talked to him; they just played to the grandstand as Benton was doing now, nowhere more shamelessly than in his conclusion: "Having no lawful government, nor lawful officers, you can have none that can have authority over you except by your consent." Finishing the letter, Riley might well have closed his eyes and conjured up the image of himself throttling the senior senator from Missouri before a joint session of Congress. With such help from his friends, was it any wonder that Riley at one time had had three different city councils claiming authority over San Francisco?

Riley did what he could to keep the situation from getting out of hand. He tried to explain repeatedly and with growing impatience that his was the de facto government of California. He would have to exercise his powers as governor until a viable alternative presented itself, presumably one given legal foundation by the president and Congress. Such attempts by Riley at being reasonable were usually met with lofty appeals to the Declaration of Independence or—loftier still—to Nature and Nature's God. Unfortunately, Nature's God, after having caused great mischief by strewing the Sierra Nevada foothills with gold, was not speaking very clearly on the particular matter of local governance of this mixed, itinerant, and volatile population of the new American territory of California.

Riley's own hope for deliverance was the arrival of new instructions from the federal government. Riley was so eager that he had sent his own ship down to Mexico to intercept the news and rush it back; it arrived back on May 28 with the worst possible news. Congress had not been able to decide about a government for California; but Congress, in its infinite wisdom, had decided that the federal tax codes applied there.

A few days later the news had leaked out, and everyone knew. Predictably, the cry in San Francisco was "Taxation without Representation." One group that styled itself the Legislative Assembly declared that for the first time in American history Congress had asserted "the right not only to tax us without representation but to tax us without giving us any government." The federal government, with General Riley as its instrument, had become more tyrannical than George III.

These hotheaded, latter-day Sons of Liberty were now declaring that they were going to settle the question of government for themselves. California, or that small portion of it excitable by political questions, seemed on the edge of a stampede. Riley had to get out in front to have some limited influence over subsequent events. What if Nature's God whispered to these hotheads that California was destined to be an independent republic? Then Riley would be in a pretty pickle; he didn't have enough troops to police the province, let alone to put down a rebellion. So on June 3, the day before the *Panama* arrived, Riley had issued a proclamation of his own, probably written by Halleck.

The tone was that of judiciousness barely covering extreme frustration. General Riley wished to "call attention" to the means he thought "best calculated to avoid the embarrassment of our present position." So Riley blushed briefly, and then made bold to insist that he himself was not the military governor of California but the "executive of the existing civil government." His precise position, he was sorry to say, had been by some "misinterpreted or at least misconceived." Of course, he really thought that the damned bastards had willfully misrepresented his position, but he could not say it. He did, however, insist that any interference with his exercise of his unquestionably legitimate authority was "not only uncalled for but strictly forbidden." Having done his best to assert his legitimate authority in theory, he then surrendered it in fact by ordering elections. Elections were to be held on August 1—and not just to the positions that existed in the old government of California. Delegates were also to be selected for a constitutional convention that would be held in the old capital of Monterey beginning on September 1. This convention could establish a territorial or state government for California.

Riley's proclamation was the great political news that met the arriving passengers from the steamship *Panama* on June 4. Riley could not have been particularly happy at the arrival of Jessie Frémont, given the grief her father's meddling had already caused him. Moreover, when Thomas Butler King grandly presented his credentials, the soured general was not impressed. He specifically remembered advice he'd received as a young officer from a superior he respected: "Riley, whenever you see a man with three names and he writes them all in full, depend upon it, he's a damn chit."

Thomas Butler King would not have taken kindly to being compared to a cigar butt, even though he had little time to consider possible personal slights. He needed to try to take control of a situation that was almost perfect for him if he could act fast. Butler King's first major act on arrival was to organize a rally for statehood. A large poster was produced with a ferocious American eagle at its top, a banner in the eagle's beak shouting "THE PEOPLE MUST RULE!"

Congress had not acted effectively on the California question. So it was up to Californians themselves to act on their own behalf. Otherwise, they would have only the burdens of government without any of its benefits. They must elect delegates to a constitutional convention, form a state government, and then send a duly elected congressional delegation to demand admission to the Union.

If we are to believe the *Alta California*, this proclamation created a sensation. The newspaper published the full text of the proclamation, and the story on the intense excitement caused by it appeared under the headline "A Revolution—Its Progress." The article concluded with a stanza from a recent poem by William Cullen Bryant:

> Truth crushed to earth shall rise again,
> The eternal years of God are hers,
> But Error wounded writhes in pain
> And dies amid her worshippers.

Riley could not have been pleased by all of this, but he bided his time, hoping that the damn chit of a Georgian would help calm the troubled waters.

The rally was held on June 12 at the true center of the aspiring new city, the old Plaza now to be called Portsmouth Square. On the far side of the square from the bay, wedged on the side of a hill, was a long single-story adobe with brown walls, a low-pitched tile roof, and a long rickety porch of posts and railings that had over the years been elaborately whittled. There was a flagpole in front from which flew the Stars and Stripes, the only indication that this was the U.S. customshouse instead of a Mexican ranch house.

Seen by itself and from a distance, the old adobe with its stately flagpole did give the illusion of order, an illusion which in turn was quickly broken by a glance about the rest of the square. Except on the side of the customshouse, almost the whole square was fronted with gambling emporiums. These were, as one resident put it, simply "the life and soul of the place."

The gold rush itself was a vast, improbable gamble, the city little more than a large pile of chips growing from an incredible run of luck. Roulette, faro, rondo, rouge et noir, vingt-et-un, and monte (the favorite)—these were not just games, or amusements for gold rush Californians. They were glimpses into the heart of historical reality. Not flags or customshouses or constitutions but the turn of a card on which twenty thousand dollars depended—this was history as California was experiencing it, a vast card game governed only by chance. A card game in which most players—if not all—comprehended fully neither the rules nor the odds.

Three speakers were featured at the outdoor rally: Peter Burnett, a recently arrived Oregonian; Thomas Butler King; and finally William Gwin, who knew better than to use his middle name amid such people. Each in turn addressed the large crowd, his back to the adobe customshouse, his vision beyond the crowd cut off by the temples to Chance. Nothing much is recorded about the first two speeches, except that Burnett's was too long and that Butler King's was well turned but too obviously self-serving in its continual references to the Whig administration. Gwin's speech, in contrast, went straight for the jugular.

This was not an occasion and not an audience for careful reasoning or judicious deliberations. Gwin simply and unqualifiedly attacked the usurpation of civil powers by the military authorities. He then insisted that the legitimate grievances of California could be met effectively only by full statehood.

Gwin's speech, not surprisingly, seems to have gone over well. In fact, it went over a little too well. When the time for resolutions came, the crowd was so worked up against Riley that they refused to have anything to do with the constitutional convention called by this militaristic tyrant. He had no authority to call the convention or exercise any other civil functions. They would hold their own constitutional convention, at a different place and different time, so that it would be entirely untainted by this usurper's foul hand. Gwin did not oppose this impractical petulance on the part of the crowd. Crowds were incapable of the moderation that was the key to good government. Neither capable of the moderation nor of the intelligence. He had allowed this particular crowd to enjoy itself by its posturing against Riley. His speech, in fact, had been intended to encourage just this posturing and thereby to ingratiate himself with them.

Once the oratory was done, however, the true work of politics had to begin. Gwin then could go to work on the committee that was empowered to set up the new convention. A week after the public meeting, its leaders, working in private, moderated the resolutions of the crowd in the name of prudence—their convention and Riley's would be the same one. This, it was emphasized, was a matter of convenience and not of principle, for Riley had not the least power to appoint a time and place for an election or convention or anything else. The compromise was reported in the chastened *Alta California* under the headline "The End of a Revolution."

By that time Riley must have had a name for Gwin, and one a little harsher than "damn chit." Nonetheless, Riley could take some satisfaction that early June had brought him equal measures of exasperation and relief. Until quite recently, he had been taking his exasperation straight.

Now the San Francisco committee needed to rally the rest of California for the convention, and to make sure that men who wanted statehood were elected as delegates. Thomas Butler King would head one speaking tour, and William Gwin the other. Basically they had only to adapt the speeches they had given at Portsmouth Square. The speaking tour, of course, could also serve another purpose. It was an opportunity to become known throughout the mining regions of California, and both men must have been eager for the opportunity. Not, of course, that mining camps presented ideal audiences for political discussion and constitutional discourse.

A couple of anecdotes from this period demonstrate what King and Gwin were up against. One early California politician had started his speech before a mining camp crowd only to be continually interrupted by good-natured hissing and obscenities. The boys were already pretty well liquored up. Finally, the speaker paused and peered out at the crowd, which was more jovial than ever, now that they'd gotten his goat. But the speaker calmly reached into his pocket, pulled out a revolver, placed it on the makeshift podium in full view, and said: "I have seen bigger crowds than this many a time. I want it to be fully understood that I came here to make a speech tonight, and I am going to do it, or else there will be a funeral or two." And the crowd loved him for it. Then there was the old geezer (he must have been at least forty) named Uncle Pete who began his campaign speech, "Fellow-citizens, I was born an orphan at a very early period of life." It didn't make any difference what else he said, he was going to be elected by acclamation. In short, these were not audiences before whom to play Daniel Webster.

Gwin understood this, and could adapt, for he did not care a fig what these people thought of him; they, like those at Portsmouth Square, just had something he temporarily needed, their assent. He would do whatever it took and would hit the mark, although he did not like public speaking and was never better than fair at it. In contrast, Thomas Butler King was given to aristocratic fits of eloquence, and adapted less easily. Or rather he would have, if he had had a chance. But his vanity did him in before.

Gwin was listening when old-time Californians—those who had been there more than a year—warned that he and King should travel light and watch the heat. (Anyone who had settled in Mississippi was attentive to warnings about heat.) Butler King, instead, insisted on blustering along in his own stately procession. Let one who accompanied him describe Butler's behavior as he began to travel the goldfields with his extensive entourage:

> King was one of those high toned Southern gentlemen, who, not having had much experience in rough life, did not know how to adapt himself to it, and insisted upon the day's march being made in the middle of the day. He would rise in the morning after the sun was well up, and after making an elaborate toilet, having his boots blacked, and dressing as if he was going into the Senate chamber, would then take breakfast and by the time he got ready to start it would be 8 or 9 o'clock, the sun would be hot, and the marches were made then, in the hottest and worst part of the day. Genl. Smith said to him, "Not only you but all the rest of the party are rendering themselves liable to fever and sickness by marching this time of the day."

When King refused to listen, this observer, Elisha Crosby, voted with his feet and left the tour entirely. The vain Georgian was not in the sweltering central valley much longer before he was prostrate and speechless. San Francisco fog and Thomas Butler King's speechifying, the joke went, did not stand up well in the central valley heat. Butler King, after returning to San Francisco, would eventually recover fully, but his political standing in gold rush California would never quite; jokes here could wound the ambitious as deeply as bullets. And the name Thomas Butler King now began to be known throughout the aspiring state chiefly as the butt of a good joke. Thomas Butler King, why that even sounded like the name for a damn chit who didn't have enough sense to get out of the sun.

So the distinguished-looking, well-connected, gray-haired Southern gentleman, William Gwin, now took center stage in the campaign for statehood, and without even having to give Butler King a nudge. As he traveled north from San Francisco, he would have passed launches filled with miserable victims of fever, ague, and scurvy from the mining region—young men, sallow, weak, emaciated, dispirited, old before their time. Gwin could see some of the aspiring prospectors who were traveling with him sensibly having to nerve themselves, as if for combat, as if they were fresh troops on the way to the front to replace the fallen. So they made their way up the Sacramento, that Hudson of western America, but with oak groves instead of the lofty Palisades. Not that lofty sights were absent on this trip. To the right was the golden dome of Mount Diablo, to the left could be barely made out the volcanic Mount Saint Helena, and behind, on the northern border of the bay, was the brooding green of Mount Tamalpais. But they were heading out from this mountainous triangle of the coast toward the north and east, until they were within distant sight of a forbidding ridge of white, the deathlike wall of the Sierra Nevada, looking like a huge wave of rock, already crested and poised to crash eastward.

Civilized expectations were continually tricking the eye as Gwin moved up the broad valley of the Sacramento. What looked to be a herd of sheep gamboled away as antelope; unconcerned cattle, as one approached, had their longhorns sprout until they were elk antlers. Perhaps he watched for a while those little senators of the marshlands, the grebes, who with their blood-red eyes and hatchet beaks and their feet seemingly attached to their rumps still today dive tirelessly after small fry in the oozy channels. He certainly would have noticed the insects. The insects, especially the mosquitoes, were horrific; the joke was that newcomers regularly mistook large California mosquitoes for small birds. But their sheer number was no joke. The story was told of a thief who had stolen a gold stash, had hidden it, and refused to tell where; he was simply stripped naked by his captors, and tied to a tree, to let the mosquitoes conduct their own interrogation. Three hours later he was begging for permission to testify against himself.

Of course, as Gwin moved through the goldfields themselves, everyone had stories about sudden wealth. Of a Frenchman and his son, who in just a few days, using only a hoe and a spade between them, had taken over $3,000 worth of gold. Of John Bidwell, who organized a party of seven settlers and some fifty Indians, and at the end of seven weeks had made $70,000. Of Pierson Reading, who took sixty-five Indians from near his ranch and in two months made $80,000 in gold. To Gwin's trained eye it would have been obvious that the most efficient way to work the California diggings was by plantation-style slave labor. But the prospectors were already forbidding operations such as Bidwell's and Reading's; they would no longer tolerate well-organized crews of Indians working beside them. The illogical quip of the prospectors was, "In a country where every white man makes a slave of himself, there is no use in keeping niggers." This was just envy in the service of mediocrity, while masquerading itself as a belief in free labor, the kind of unseemly concatenation of low motives and high rationalization that the Honorable Thomas Butler King would never understand, just as he would never understand the political genius of Andrew Jackson.

Gwin could now hear the various theories concerning the origin of the California gold, the theories that enlivened the nightly conversations of the miners, or at least of those not too exhausted to chew the fat. Some thought there was a huge vein of pure gold running almost the whole length of the Sierras, the fabled mother lode. It had become exposed in some places, and subsequent rains had washed bits down until they lodged in various stream beds as nuggets or were pulverized into the gravel. Whoever could find the source of the gold, one of the exposed portions of the mother lode, would have limitless wealth. So any news of a strike higher up in the Sierras would sends dozens, if not hundreds, of argonauts scurrying away from their established claims to find richer veins.

Not all the prospectors, however, believed in the mother lode. Some had noted that all the large nuggets looked as if they had once been molten. The gold, they reasoned, must have been strewn across the foothills of the Sierra Nevada by a tremendous volcanic eruption, a single fountainhead. The dream of a mother lode they pooh-poohed. They reasoned that the gold had originally existed in an ore, probably combined with quartz or other minerals; but in the heat of the volcano it was separated out from the surrounding substances. There was no gold mountain or mother lode; but there had been at least once, long ago, a cataclysm in which the sky had rained deadly gold.

The Indians had their own mythic version of the mother lode. All the gold came somehow from the bottom of a secret lake, where it had been hoarded by a demon who devoured any that endeavored to take it from him. Like a dragon of medieval lore, it would leave its lair to hunt those who were its enemies, the very prospectors who now were collecting the gold in order to take it farther from its true home. There was something attractive about the Indian version, especially if you identified the demon with human nature, and realized that it was right now feasting on the avaricious all around you.

That was not so implausible if one had actually seen a gold camp, such as that on the American River that Gwin visited. There in the midst of a broken country, parched and dried by the hot July sun, sparsely wooded with live oaks and struggling pines, Gwin could see the valley created by the American River, a bold mountain stream that connected the melting snow of the Sierra Nevada to the larger, sluggish Sacramento, which itself then meandered toward the vast delta marshlands at the northeast of San Francisco Bay. Although the valley could fill with water to its sides in the rainy season, afterwards the river receded to leave gravel beds exposed. On the edges of the reduced river hundreds of men were now digging and filling buckets with the finer gravel, which was then carried to a machine called a "rocker" because it resembled a baby's cradle. This was worked back and forth by another man, gradually separating the gold from the worthless minerals. There was an oddness to these camps as a result of the rockers; beneath the steady sound of the stream was a continual brittle rumble created by the rockers, eerie when you got close to the stream because the same sound was coming from all sides. Close your eyes and it was as if you had been enveloped in an avalanche of gravel, tumbling all about you but somehow never touching you, immune to all hurt because of some spell the gravel obeyed.

These prospectors, however, had scarcely any time for such imaginative fancy. They were each day being rewarded with gold worth ten to twenty-five dollars, nothing to sneeze at, although it usually ended up in the pockets of those who provided supplies and amusements for the miners. However, the work was full of hurt. The sun blazed down on the miners with a killing tropical heat. (Thomas Butler King could attest to that.) Moreover, the water—recently melted snow—was bitter cold. And even those who did not have to stand in the water all the time still had their clothes wet constantly. With a burning head, and freezing limbs, the prospector did the rough work of shoveling and hauling, dumping and rocking, enough to ruin a back just by itself.

The brittle rumble of the gold camp was really the sound of hundreds of young men having their physical constitutions gradually eaten away. These camps were filled with young men letting themselves be slowly devoured while dreaming of El Dorado. As one of the miners wrote home, "There are thousands of persons here who hardly saw a sick day in the States and are completely broken down, and many of them, if they live, will never fully recover." The doctor who established the first hospital for the miners concurred; he added, more clinically, "diarrhea was so general during the fall and winter months and degenerated so frequently into chronic and fatal malady that it has been popularly regarded as the disease of California."

Of course, the true disease of California was not diarrhea but dreamy-eyed greed. But even by the summer of 1849, reality was already starting to intrude upon these argonauts who had come to California, by and large, to escape it. The mining camps were raucous places, and generally not because of celebrations of newfound riches. One moralist of the mines observed, "Disappointment will make a single man sober, but when it falls on a multitude, it is often converted into a source of raillery and fun." As disappointment was these days falling on thousands in the Sierra foothills, merriment was the rule among the shivering, homesick young men, men whose chief consolation was to have company in their misery. As one wrote home, "I really hope that no one will be deterred from coming on account of what anybody else may say. The more fools the better, the fewer to laugh when we get back home."

The prospectors had begun to complain about the gold itself. The veins of gold were as uncertain and capricious as lightning. As one prospector put it, "It straggles where you least expect it, and leaves only a stain where its quick volume seemed directed. It threads its way in a rock without crevice or crack, and where its continuity becomes at times too subtle for the naked eye, and then suddenly bulges out like a lank snake that has swallowed a terrapin." He added that the Hebrew proverbs held there to be three things about which one can have no certainty: the way of an eagle in the air, the way of a serpent on a rock, and the way of a ship in the sea. To this list, the prospector humbly suggested, should be added "the way of a thread of gold in a vein of California quartz."

This litany of complaint also frequently contained an oddly interesting note of satisfaction that is heard again and again. Here is the *Placer Times* of 1849: "The mines of California have baffled all science, and rendered the application of philosophy entirely nugatory. . . . We have met with many geologists and practical scientific men in the mines, and have invariably seen them beaten by unskilled men, soldiers and sailors, and the like." Here is a prospector repeating this same common wisdom: "It's more luck than anything else. But, luck or no luck, no man can pick up gold, even here, without the very hardest labor, and that's a fact."

Gold, however perverse, was egalitarian because it especially liked common men, men who would throw away their books and roll up their sleeves. It was Jacksonian democracy written in rocks, a sermon in stone strangely like that with which Jackson himself had beguiled the nation.

As the prospectors belatedly recognized that they were not going to amass their splendid pile, they began to feed one another, by way of consolation, a delusory patter that soon had become conventional wisdom. They had not become rich because they had had indifferent luck. Intelligence had nothing to do with it. Only a willingness to work hard physically that was blest with unusually good luck.

This was a self-willed blindness among the argonauts because right before them were people accumulating considerable wealth without the killing work of the prospectors, people who relied on intelligence more than luck. These were the merchants who supplied the prospectors at exorbitant rates. And also the gamblers and whores who separated the prospectors from what was left over, or at least those gamblers and whores who could control in themselves the very appetites and shortsightedness they encouraged in others.

It was right there in front of the prospectors, but they refused to see it. Gwin himself did, of course. The prospectors were being used up, like so much cheap fuel, to produce a small wealthy class of entrepreneurs. And above these would be the politicians who would have the wealth of a whole region at their beck and call, at least once California was a state. That was the true mother lode of human society, the eye at the top of the pyramid.

Smug moralists like Henry David Thoreau might condemn the whole gold rush in scathing terms. "The rush to California," he had written with characteristic condescension, "reflects the greatest disgrace on mankind. That so many are ready to live by luck and so get the means of commanding the labor of others less lucky, without contributing any value to society—and that's called enterprise." Thoreau was wrong. These men were contributing to the future of society everything they had—namely, their health and their lives, things in themselves admittedly not of much value but of some, like the manure left in the field by a herd destined for the slaughterhouse. That they were doing it, by and large, unknowingly and unwillingly just made them typical of the overwhelming majority of mankind.

But with such profound matters Gwin did not need bother himself as he toured the mines. The men would not understand anyway. It was sufficient for his purposes to harangue against poor General Riley and to sketch out the advantages of statehood—and then quietly, on the side, to encourage the reliable, enterprising young Southerners he met to stand for election to the state convention that he could assure them would be a golden gate to wealth and power.

2

The experiences of William Gwin in his earlier career had made him into a strange kind of Democrat. He was a loyal member of the Democratic Party who deeply distrusted the people. For him the easy egalitarianism that Andy Jackson had preached made positive sense in the border states where men like Gwin's father were seeking to make their mark on the world. But it made no sense, or the wrong kind of sense, when he saw it operating, or trying to operate, elsewhere in the nation, particularly in the North.

The masses who were collecting like so much refuse in the great cities of the North, especially in New York, were scarcely fit to participate in the governance of a great nation. Theirs would be the role of the mob, a breeding ground for demagogues. In the mongrel society that New York in particular was becoming, respectable elements like the Livingstons barely kept control of the Democratic party.

In the United States Senate, in contrast, Gwin saw the true salvation of the nation. Here was a collection of men worthy of the senate of Rome, a chivalrous aristocracy headed by the triumvirate of Clay, Calhoun, and Webster. In them America had found its Cato, its Cicero, its Seneca—great orators and great citizens. On such an educated elite who could freely rule themselves by honor did the health of a civilized society depend. As for the common people, they were necessary as labor, but politically they were only a source of instability, and must—for their own sake as well as that of society as a whole—be kept at bay, lest chaos ensue. They must be kept at bay by law, by sleight of hand, or in the last resort by force. So Gwin saw civilization as a thin, precarious crust preserved by the honor, the courage, and the guile of the few, especially the guile.

If he needed further occasions to meditate upon these themes (which he did not), gold rush California supplied him with ample instances. Rosy-eyed democrats might think that government springs spontaneously from the good-hearted consent of the governed, their enlightened self-interest. A more realistic assessment of human nature was available to anyone who had experienced the brutal competitiveness of the frontier. Most respectable people, like that young doctor on the deck of the steamship *Panama,* were "not calculated" to succeed in places like the wilds of Mississippi, or the slums of New York, or the California gold country (where a place called Old Dry Diggings had recently changed its name to Hangtown).

Gold rush San Francisco was, if anything, worse. Here the old Mexican elite had been swamped without an American elite immediately to take its place. What had happened gradually and effectively in Texas had occurred overnight here, with predictable results. The only obvious public power he saw being exercised was by what passed for a police force, a comically garbed, quasi-military group called the Hounds who hung out at what passed for a saloon, a tent on Kearny (between Clay and Sacramento), called, significantly, Tammany Hall. They were, by and large, enlisted men from Stevenson's Regiment, which had been recruited in New York at the beginning of the Mexican War. Colonel Jonathan Drake Stevenson, after the discovery of gold, had allowed his men to be mustered out in California to try their luck. The Hounds had found the dissipations of San Francisco more attractive than the hard work of the diggings.

So the Hounds paraded the streets in their silly uniforms in an unintended parody of military order. They were humorous but no joke. Gwin could see how they got to their position, and why they must be destroyed. At first, they were just thugs employed to shanghai sailors back to their ships. Then businessmen began to pay them to intimidate the numerous Chileans in San Francisco. Intimidating the unruly Chileans, Gwin had no doubt, was a good thing. But who was now going to intimidate the intimidators? The newly elected alcalde—that is, mayor—certainly was not. Alcalde Leavenworth had himself been an officer in Stevenson's regiment, and had on occasion used the Hounds to enforce the law when the police did not seem up to it. Moreover, he was as much a drunk as most of the Hounds, and looked disingenuously surprised when people complained about his old comrades-in-arms.

The Hounds had already taken over the running of the launches. Bad things happened to those who tried to compete with them and their cronies, although the Chileans in particular were persistent. Moreover, the businessmen of San Francisco seemed now to pay the Hounds primarily for protection against the Hounds. They strutted the streets exercising their apparently inalienable right to eat and drink (mostly drink) wherever they wanted without payment, often charging it to the bill of the alcalde with much hilarity. When hazy with liquor, they would do whatever mischief came to their befuddled minds. Pay them off, though, and treat them with respect, and they would take out their irritability on somebody else, likely someone who spoke Spanish or wore a pigtail.

Shortly after Gwin returned from his speaking tour of the diggings the Hounds finally went too far. The chief actor was their illiterate leader, Samuel Roberts. Gwin may have met him before, or at least seen him—for Roberts worked his own small boat ferrying passengers and cargo from ships like the *Panama* to San Francisco proper. This might have seemed gainful employment quite different from his activities with the Hounds. Roberts, however, did not see it that way; being a boatman allowed him the opportunity to appropriate for himself, or at least to try, whatever he wanted before it reached dry land, where the likelihood of legal owners effectively asserting their rights was higher. So Roberts blithely skimmed off for himself the best of what he saw. Among the best that he skimmed off for himself was the best-looking woman, a hopeful Chilean prostitute named Felice Alvarez. Alvarez, like many other ladies of questionable reputation, had reasoned that since there were not many women in San Francisco, and there was much gold, she could strike it rich in her own way. This seemed a perfect place for her, until she had the misfortune to step daintily into Roberts's launch. Her favors were now to be exclusively his, or so he adamantly asserted, and convincingly after he threatened consequences in detail. Thoroughly frightened and nobody's fool, she assented to the arrangement, with her lips if not her heart. In fact, once she learned her way around San Francisco, she seems to have begun to take on other (paying) clients whenever Sam Roberts was safely busy elsewhere.

So it was that on July 15, 1849, Felice Alvarez was apparently entertaining two German gentlemen in her rooms when Sam Roberts burst in upon them. Roberts and the Hounds had gone on an excursion across the bay to practice marching in their uniforms and drinking their fill. They were also trying out a new drum they had appropriated, and Roberts had a speaking horn through which to shout out his orders, a wonderful novelty. Alas, the novelty wore off too soon. They had marched and drunk more quickly than Alvarez had reckoned. When Roberts entered the room to visit his beloved, Felice was attending in particular to the intimate needs of a Leopold Bleckschmidt. This pleasure would quickly cost him far more dearly than the price he had negotiated.

Roberts reacted to the scene before him with neither moderation nor good humor. By the time a certain amount of shouting in three languages had attracted a significant crowd in the street, Roberts was summarily dragging the undraped and unfortunate German there. Roberts then set about attempting to beat him to death. When the whip Roberts was using did not appear to be producing sufficient visible effects on the cowering Bleckschmidt, he began to club him with the handle. Thanks to it, the German soon looked to be unconscious—or perhaps he was just playing dead—anyway, Roberts mounted his horse to ride away, and then belatedly had another idea. Still in his grand uniform, he pulled off one of his ceremonial spurs—and, leaning down from the horse, began to carve up the German's face with it. (The other German had long since disappeared from the scene, sadly consigning his poor friend to a fate that could just as easily have been his; and Felice seems to have stayed behind in her room, and then to have dis-

creetly bolted for safety.) The crowd that had gathered to watch this enter-
tainment now began to show some faint signs of humane concern. The
German simply was not putting up enough of a fight for this to be fun to
watch. In fact, at this moment someone in the crowd shouted at Roberts,
"For shame! That is not manly!" Or so the words were later reported genteelly in court. The gibe in its original form apparently was pungently enough
expressed—something likely to do with Roberts's manly anatomy—to have
touched the hot-tempered, slow-witted Hound to the quick. Not manly to
cut up someone who has just been—the unjustness of this objection perplexed him into temporary inaction. He looked around the crowd with the
bloody spur in his hand. The person who had shouted tried to blend in,
while the prostrate Bleckschmidt moaned and Roberts stumped himself by
trying to think of something clever to say in rebuttal. Finally Roberts rode
off, or started to—but then paused and whirled around, to delay his exit long
enough to make the virile riposte he had finally thought of, something to
the effect that he would kill the next man he found in bed with Felice
Alvarez, a threat that likely more than a few in the crowd had reason to take
to heart.

Roberts then retired to the company of his cronies at his favorite saloon,
Tammany Hall, there to lick his psychic wounds. In this sour mood he began
his nightly ritual of drinking himself into a stupor. But tonight the drink
seemed to increase rather than to dull his sense of offended honor. The
knowing smiles which his parting threat had produced in some of the crowd
he now began to brood into a metaphysical difficulty that could not be
resolved except through action. He had reasoned far enough along the path
of forgiveness to see that the fault was not entirely the German's. It was
Felice's too—or rather it was her Chilean blood. This was what was wrong
with California.

All these Chileans coming in, competing against true Americans. Why,
they were even making it hard for him to earn a little extra as a boatman.
They reached the ships more quickly and offered lower fares. Soon there
would be no opportunities for any real Americans to get ahead in San Francisco. The Chileans ought to all go back where they came from, and leave
America to the Americans. And that went for Germans too.

Sometime during his slurred diatribe he had gained a slurred following.
About twenty men, mostly Hounds, were now ready to follow him anywhere. They accompanied him back to Alvarez's house to finish the job on
the German. The German, needless to say, was elsewhere, receiving much-
needed medical attention. So now Roberts shouted to no one in particular,
"If the damned son of a bitch would come back, I would shoot him." Unfortunately, an innocent bystander seems to have found this funny, and Roberts thought he was being laughed at by a Chilean. (The man was actually
Peruvian.) When Roberts pulled his gun, the purported Chilean took off.
Roberts got off two or three shots at close range before the man had escaped,

unharmed except for a ventilation hole in his jacket. Sam could not understand how he had missed the greaser completely at ten yards. He grabbed another bystander by the hair and began to berate him for ruining his aim, and then threatened him death or worse if he said so much as a word in response.

Now Roberts looked around at his followers. Clearly there was only one place for him to lead them, Chiletown, the group of tents and shanties where the growing population of Chileans clustered. So off they went, although one would like to think that at least one of the patriots had the presence of mind eventually to peel off and wander back on the chance that Felice Alvarez might return this evening to her habitation while Samuel Roberts was safely busy making San Francisco safe for Americans.

The first stop for the baying Hounds, predictably, was a Chilean tent saloon. Pistol in hand, Roberts commandeered the place, and ordered out all the Chileans, except the barkeep. The barkeep, it seems, was a wise and prudent man. Worried about the effect that the night air could have on delicate constitutions of the Hounds, he offered his distinguished guests ample drinks on the house as prophylactic. Roberts immediately recognized this Chilean as a notable exception to his race; if all Chileans were like him, there would be no trouble. So Roberts decreed that this saloon henceforth would serve as the command post for his movement. Amply refueled with Chilean liquor and having broken all the bottles they had finished off, Roberts's pack of Hounds now lurched out of the saloon, some still guzzling and all determined to do—well, they knew not quite what, but it was going to be the terror of the earth. And one Chilean barkeep had been left behind, quickly closing up and thinking of fair Valparaiso.

The Hounds then went on a rampage, attacking anyone who spoke Spanish, or what sounded to them like Spanish. Modest tent dwellings they simply destroyed; those that had any valuable goods were subjected to immediate impromptu auctions, proceeds going to the Hounds and their civic campaign for law and order. Any group of toughs that wanted could get into the act and loot at pleasure, so long as they did not get in the way of the Hounds and concentrated on purported Chileans. Between attacks they marched to fife and drum, with Roberts shouting out orders through his horn. When people asked who they were, they proclaimed that they were the San Francisco Regulators and they were "going to drive every damned Chilean out of town." The mob now had grown to fifty or sixty, and was dividing into marauding bands.

One of these seems to have run into the German, a Herr Koch, who had tainted his honor by failing to come to the aid of his friend—and honor was important to this aristocratic dandy, good with a sword and given to singing snatches from *Lucia di Lammermoor*. Now he comes across four looters arguing among themselves. They have already divided all the goods they had pilfered, but cannot agree which one of them is going to get the terrified young Chilean girl they had also snatched. Herr Koch comes to her rescue and quickly dispatches the four men into unconsciousness with well-placed blows from his gold-headed cane. (Impressive as the odds were, the looters were by this time of the evening likely so stupefied with drink as to be barely able to stand.) Then Koch leads off the rescued damsel while singing to her "Io son rico, / Tu sei bella." The girl's bewilderment can only be imagined. And the head-sore looters, once they came to, had to content themselves with firing their pistols into the darkness in the general direction of Koch's now fading tenor.

Not all episodes ended so happily. In one pair of tents owned by a prosperous Chilean, the Hounds opened fire at two brothers. The father heard one of his sons yell, "Do not kill me, I'm already wounded." The father and his daughter escaped to a boat in the bay; the Hounds made off with thousands of dollars of gold dust as well as destroying all the worldly possessions of this family; the brothers both had been shot, one slightly, the other to die a lingering death from a wound in the stomach.

The next day the respectable citizens of San Francisco began to act. The riot had given leaders like Gwin a temporary opportunity to make a decisive improvement in the life of the city. At the forefront with Gwin was a powerful stump of a man, with a foghorn voice, a quick fuse, and a gift for opportunism: Samuel Brannan.

Brannan was an extreme instance of the local characters with whom Gwin was going to have to strike bargains, a conniver as unprincipled as he was colorful. He had come to California in 1846 as a Mormon with pilgrims on their way to Utah; he had eventually decided that he was much more interested in wealth than salvation, especially when gold was discovered. Brannan, when he first heard of the supposed discovery of gold, dismissed it; it was, he said, a "superb take-in as was ever got up to guzzle the gullible." After he realized it was not a "take-in," he nonetheless realized it presented a superb opportunity to guzzle the gullible. And nobody, but nobody, was a better guzzler of gullibles than Samuel Brannan. It was said of him that he could turn a profit treading water.

He had started by preying on his fellow Mormons. He traveled the gold camps as the self-appointed emissary of Brigham Young to collect tithes from the many Mormon prospectors. When an inquiry was made to the military authorities about Brannan's right to collect this ten percent, the response was, "Brannan has a perfect right to collect the tax, if you Mormons are fools enough to pay it." When Young sent an emissary for this now considerable amount of gold dust, Brannan is supposed to have said, "You go back and tell Brigham that I'll give up the Lord's money when he sends me a receipt signed by the Lord, and no sooner." Rumor was that the indignant Young then sent a couple of his "Danite avenging angels" to speak a language to Brannan that even an apostate could understand, but Brannan had long since become fluent in that language. According to the story, Brannan had been warned by a presumably well-paid informant, and intercepted the avenging angels with a group of San Francisco toughs of the very type that had just gone on a rampage.

Now Brannan was on the other side. The Hounds were becoming bad for business, bad for Sam Brannan's systematic accumulation of great wealth by means fair or foul. Brannan was just the kind of man Gwin would find temporarily useful, especially because Brannan was as effective at demagoguery as anyone in this city. Gwin, like all respectable San Franciscans, wished to get rid of the Hounds, once and for all, and while observing the forms of legality as much as was convenient. Brannan through his impassioned stump oratory exploited the general outrage to gain support for setting up a special court to indict and try the Hounds. The Hounds must be muzzled.

An impromptu criminal justice system was called into existence on Portsmouth Square. Gwin was quickly selected as one of the judges to try the Hounds who had been rounded up. (Roberts himself had been captured trying to make his way to the goldfields.) The Chileans, by the way, had a word for those like Gwin and Brannan—and for that matter like the Hounds—involved with the unofficial enforcement of law and order; they called them "vigilantes."

The forms of a trial were carefully observed, with witnesses both for the prosecution and for the defense. The brief testimony of the dying Chilean boy —his stomach wound all too evident—was particularly moving. But, in general, the trial was uneventful.

Felice Alvarez was not particularly cooperative, except to insist that Roberts had stolen from her a large amount of gold dust that she wanted returned. Presumably she hoped he had been found with some on him. But then she was asked the awkward question, How had she earned this considerable pile? She assured the court that she had brought it with her from Chile as a stake. As for the Hounds, Alvarez was adamant that she knew absolutely nothing about them, even their existence. If Roberts was a member of such an organization, she said, "he never told me so." She added, by way of explanation, "He only came to my house to sleep; he did not talk at all." Likely at this point, the open-air court had to be gaveled by Gwin back to order. However, even Gwin at his sternest and most dignified would have been hard pressed to keep the crowd in order when the defense presented two of its witnesses, employees from Parker House who endeavored to provide Roberts with an alibi. One, a bartender, remembered that Roberts on the night in question took a room at Parker House; he remembered because Roberts had asked him for a lemonade before retiring. Another employee of Parker House and friend of Roberts corroborated this testimony about the lemonade. He also had run into Roberts at Parker House that very evening, and had advised him to stay inside "as there were a great many noisy men out"; Roberts had assured him he would not go out amid the noisy men for a thousand dollars.

Gwin and the other judges remained judiciously aloof from the proceedings, apart from turning down every defense motion. Gwin's hand, however, could be seen in the instructions to the jury. There it was briefly lamented that "we have not legislation in California congenial with American feelings"—and then it was added that the conscience we have received from Nature and Nature's God should nonetheless be sufficient to guide us in criminal cases such as this one. The defendants were quickly found guilty, and sentenced to be banished from California, on pain of death should they return.

The episode of the Hounds dramatized in microcosm Gwin's view of society. At the bottom was the unruly mob that included New York riffraff, Chilean whores, and dissipated Europeans. This was human nature at its worst, crooked wood out of which nothing straight could be made. Left to themselves, these were slaves to their animal instincts, and so a healthy society should endeavor to enslave them in other, more socially productive ways. Above them were the men of commerce like Samuel Brannan, cunning, selfish, shortsighted, professing to be respectable, but ultimately unprincipled. They were necessary to society but not worthy of a gentleman's respect. Still, all they wanted was to be paid off. With them one could do business. Finally, if a society was lucky, there was a small group of men like Gwin, making laws and administering justice for the common good, a common good that entailed the persistence of themselves and those like them at the top. The trial of the Hounds was likely for Gwin a gratifying and most hopeful sign.

Nonetheless, the trial of the Hounds was significant in another respect, but one of which Gwin could scarcely have been aware, at least until much later. There was likely on the edges of the crowd a scowling, disapproving presence, although one that Gwin at a glance would have concluded unworthy of his notice. The trial of the Hounds was likely the first time that David Broderick had ever laid his eyes upon William McKendree Gwin. And Gwin before that crowd was a sight Broderick, for his part, would have found neither gratifying nor hopeful.

David Broderick apparently had entered San Francisco Bay while Gwin was on the stump for statehood. He had arrived on the steamship *Stella* on June 13, 1849. Or so he always said. Or so his friends always said he had said. Unfortunately, like most things about Broderick, simple appearances quickly give way to irresoluble enigmas.

The testimony is plain, but so are the records. The records list no ship *Stella* arriving in San Francisco on the thirteenth or any other day in June 1849. In fact, as far as can be told, there never was a steamship *Stella* working the California run.

The name of this ship or the date for beginning a new life is scarcely the kind of thing Broderick would forget. But the records are reliable as far as can be known. So we are left suspecting that Broderick knowingly misrepresented his arrival. If so, why? What was the unseemly truth he was hiding? Whereas Gwin's arrival was a great public event, Broderick's arrival is wrapped in uncertainty suggestive of scandal. This is as it should be, for Broderick's earlier life was one largely lived in the shadows.

His father had been an Irish stonemason, a gifted craftsman who had brought his family to the New World so that he could work on the Capitol building in Washington, D.C. He was skilled not just with stone but with marble, and so good that he carved the huge marble columns for the east front of the Capitol. But when the work ran out, he had to move on. So he went to New York, apparently exhausted by his labors on behalf of his family and the young republic, for he soon died.

The father had started young David as an apprentice in the family craft, but now the adolescent was left the chief support of his mother and younger brother. He had the responsibility but not the means. So together they lived a life of Dickensian poverty (at the very time that Gwin was developing a taste for the medieval romances of Sir Walter Scott). The family was close, and Broderick's inner life, as little as we know of it, was filled with intense affection, but also likely with resentment, grief, and unacknowledged (because unjustified but unavoidable) guilt.

Broderick, his powerful build enhanced by the exercise of his trade, was drawn to the volunteer fire companies of the New York slums. These were much more than fire departments. They were clubs, gangs, and also instruments of the bare-knuckled ward politics of the New York Democratic machine that was run out of Tammany Hall. When there were not fires, the young workingmen demonstrated their bravery by having melees, one company against another. The "scrimmage," as this recreational violence was euphemistically called, might be between "Old Maid" and "Butt-enders," and everyone would know this was between Engine Company No. 15 and Engine Company No. 29. Violent as these contests were, it was a point of pride not to use weapons such as knives or guns. Even when the scrimmages got out of control, the participants would resort only to the tools of the fireman's trade—wrenches, pipes, hose butts (but no axes). Out of these volunteer fire departments, not surprisingly, emerged the best professional prizefighters of New York.

Broderick himself was by all accounts good at these fights, but not quite good enough to become professional. In the scrimmages he seems to have purposely sought out the best fighters of the other side to take them on, one-on-one; and in these encounters he frequently was overmatched. One nineteenth-century account of his early life listed the names of some who had bested him ("Eli Hazleton, Seth Douglas, Abe Bogart, John Williamson, Mose Cutter, Sam Baisely, and Johnny Baum"), as if they would be familiar to any fighting connoisseur. All we can conclude is that as a young man he took a number of beatings, and still kept coming back for more. The members of his company were certainly impressed, for they elected him as foreman of their company; he was the one they wanted to lead the Howard Engine Company, No. 24, into a fire or a fight.

Broderick also caught the eye of the gentleman friend of his mother, perhaps on an evening when he came back defiantly battered. The man began to lend him books and oversee his education. When Broderick took to this with the ferocity he had shown in fighting, his patron decided to free him from the manual labor of stonecutting. He set Broderick up in a saloon, one of those dank, sawdust-floored affairs that volunteer firemen used as club-houses, and where the politicians could find them when they needed some muscle to influence an election. It was a place where all the drinks were three cents apiece, and the swells could content themselves with three-cent Spanish cigars rather than the American varieties that went two or three to a cent. Other than that, everything was the same, and good enough for anybody who came in the door.

Broderick named his saloon The Subterranean, an allusion at once to its underground location and to a local radical newspaper. (The paper had as its motto the couplet: "Through the ages thou has slept in chains and night / Arise now MAN and vindicate thy right!") In one corner of the saloon the angry, brooding barkeep set up his study; there he sat, night after night, reading voraciously, especially the defiant words of his beloved Shelley and Byron. He was a Prometheus pinned to a rock, with vultures feeding on his liver, but one day he would be unbound—or would die like Byron fighting for freedom.

The saloon, of course, did sometimes intrude upon his poetical medi-tations; in the late evening or early morning he would once or twice have to interrupt his studies to use his stonecutter's hands to break up a barroom brawl, or bounce an unruly patron. His reputation was sufficient that things usually ended as soon as he made his presence felt—but not always. There was a long scar down one of his cheeks, where he had been knifed during such a scuffle.

The long scar as well as his imposing physique and his preferred dress— hobnailed boots and rough workingman's shirt and pants—all this told at a glance, no matter what books he happened to be reading, that he was some-one the roughest of ruffians might prefer to avoid. But even when Broderick eventually determined to look respectable (as he did when he became a candidate for the U.S. Senate from California), his appearance was still enough to give pause, and the pause the beginning of a stare, the stare the beginning of positive fright.

His eyes were a dark, uncompromised blue, not grayish blue as Gwin's sometimes looked, or greenish, or the beguiling bright baby blue. But the absolute blue of the day sky at its apex, or of one of those large mountain lakes locally reputed to be bottomless. He wore a beard to hide as much as possible of the scar, but that made it only more baleful as it disappeared into the beard. That scar Melville could have used as the model for Ahab's. Broderick was a darkly handsome man, but something besides the scar was unsettling. His features were not quite right, perhaps just the effect of all those beatings, but perhaps too the smoldering rage that showed up especially in the eyes and dark brows. And yet his mouth, which he kept clean shaven, was almost gentle, feminine, soft.

He never did learn how to wear fine clothes although he would eventually try; they did not seem to fit quite properly, and so he always looked a bit disheveled, as if he had dressed hurriedly, without a mirror. And nothing could hide his hands, which even in repose were full of menace. A lady who looked away from his strangely repulsive face and happened on his hands would be given a true start.

As keeper of The Subterranean, Dave Broderick ran with the roughest crowds of the roughest city in America (the roughest city, that is, until gold rush San Francisco challenged it for this particular championship, and some say won by a split decision). Take, for instance, two of the men who took him under wing as a political protégé: George Wilkes and Michael Walsh.

Wilkes was a workingman's intellectual like Broderick. He eventually would write a book on Shakespeare. His most revealing book, however, was *The Mysteries of the Tombs,* written during one of his stays in jail; there he described in lurid detail the New York underworld in which he and Broderick thrived. Wilkes once lost a slander case against a man who had stated that Wilkes "acted like the son of a prostitute, and lived like one brought up in a brothel, and had been supported by the wages of prostitution." The jury decided that it was true. Whatever the jury decided, Wilkes remained Broderick's closest friend throughout much of his adult life, and to Wilkes Broderick would eventually leave all his worldly possessions.

Then there was Mike Walsh, after whose paper Broderick named The Subterranean. Walsh was a great talker and a hard liver. (He was said to be the "fancy man" of Kate Ridgeley, who ran a bordello on Duane Street.) His fiery articles were all variations upon a single theme: "The great and fruitful source of crime and misery on earth is the *inequality of society—*the abject dependence of honest willing industry upon idle and dishonest capitalists." Again and again he would warn workers against being beguiled into thinking they were free; under the present system they were no better than slaves.

In his speeches he was even harsher, railing against "milk and water" politicians who professed to represent workingmen. They are not real men but "a mere connecting link between the animal and vegetable kingdom." They say they are respectable. Sure, they are not "lascivious" (as they put it), but that is only because they don't have enough stamina to keep their pricks hard. (When this particular speech was printed in a book-length collection of Walsh's words, this gibe was softened to read "to keep their back-bone straight.") Needless to say, Walsh's speeches were met with cheers from some

("Go it, Mike! Give it to them!"), and disgusted silence from others (he spoke "like a tramp who had graduated from the gutter," one later wrote).

Those who ran with him, such as Broderick and Wilkes, he called his Spartan Band. They called themselves the "b'hoys," to emphasize the Irish pronunciation of "boy." They were a small male band that standing together could resist the whole world, as Leonidas and his Spartans could have withstood all of Asia had they not been foully betrayed. For all the braggadocio and swagger, there was a brittleness to this self-assertion that at times made it seem almost desperate. These were Spartan warriors who expected to be betrayed and then overwhelmed. So they were always on the lookout for the beginning of the last act.

Walsh at one point thought it had come, at least for him personally, when a local district attorney took it as a personal crusade to close the *Subterranean* newspaper and put Mike Walsh behind bars. John Whiting—or "Little Bitters" as Mike, Dave, and the b'hoys called him—did finally get a conviction for criminal libel that carried a penitentiary term of six months. On the way to prison Walsh tried to commit suicide, and according to one account was only prevented because he was so obviously despondent that the guards had guessed his intention. According to another account, Broderick and Walsh had planned his suicide as a grand revolutionary gesture, after which Broderick would rally the band around his memory—and Broderick never forgave Walsh for failing. At the very least Broderick did forgive him. When Mike was released after serving his term, Broderick and his friends were there to meet him, with band and banners. They put Subterranean Mike in a large carriage drawn by six white horses and paraded noisily through the city, making it a particular point (one must think) to disrupt life in the respectable sections where his conviction had been applauded.

Broderick's was the world of violence, criminality, and prostitution. The existence of this world, Gwin, Butler King, and Jessie Frémont would only reluctantly and sadly have acknowledged. Moreover, they would take its existence as evidence that the lower orders were not fit to rule themselves, that they needed an elite to lead them, both politically and morally. Broderick saw things differently, and with conviction and passion. And we know his early views because they were articulated in detail by Walsh and Wilkes—and never really changed.

The respectability of men like Gwin was to him pure hypocrisy. Men like Gwin had their own cathouses to go to, just with prettier girls who were cleaner and in nicer petticoats, sisters and mothers and even daughters of Broderick's friends. These men made their money by working to death men like Broderick's father, money that their wives could then spend on frivolities while fretting about the fashionableness of their clothes and the delicacy of their constitutions. These men also controlled the government, using men like Broderick himself but keeping them outside the inner circles. At least in the South men and women were bought and sold out in the open. What was it that French writer had said? "Hypocrisy is the homage that vice pays to virtue." The hypocrites of the North had to pretend to be democrats, and that was their weakness—which Broderick meant to exploit.

The Democratic Party in New York, Broderick knew as well as Gwin, was controlled by the old "respectable" New York families, some of them so old and respectable they were Dutch. This was the silk-stocking crowd of pompous fogies, "upperendom" as the b'hoys contemptuously called them. But it was neither genealogy nor respectability that gave them power; it was just money. Money gave them power, and then power gave them more money, and then money gave still more power—it was a continuous cycle that went back to the Dutch. You could break the cycle only by getting into it. So Broderick tried.

Broderick, with the help of men like Wilkes, tried to work himself up the hierarchy of the Democratic Party. At first he had been quite useful to the party. Uncouth, of course, but intelligent and surprisingly well-read. (Far better read than most of them, in fact, but he was accustomed not to flaunt his learning.) And very useful—he did know how to speak to those people, and they seemed to respect him, and he seemed quite respectful of those above himself in station.

Of course, Broderick did not believe that social stations were any less arbitrary than the railroad variety. Still he kept his peace. And finally he got the support of Tammany Hall to run for Congress from a predominantly Democratic district. Broderick seemed to be on his way.

But then, as an up-and-comer in the New York party, he was invited to a Long Island reception for the new Democratic president, James K. Polk. This may have gone to his head, or maybe he was infuriated when the hostess made it clear that social priorities were going to be strictly observed, which meant of course that Mr. Broderick was to be seen and not heard. Which also meant, of course, that she would have preferred if he were not seen either. Perhaps she did not imply that, or mean to; perhaps Broderick was being too sensitive. They were all standing on the spacious back lawn of the estate, which was about as large as the city block on which Broderick's family had their skimpy rooms. That thought could not have been too far from his mind. Inevitably, he did feel out of place, and that made him smolder.

While the rest of the Democratic officials were arranging themselves in the proper receiving order and patiently waiting for the president to emerge from the mansion, Broderick slipped away, unnoticed like a servant. Finally the doors swung open, and the hostess must have almost fainted at the sight. And there was an audible growl from the men. President Polk was now slowly walking across the porch and down the steps deep in conversation with . . . David Broderick. (He had apparently circled around and intercepted the president, who assumed that he had been delegated to escort him.) One of the party officials, as soon as he recovered from the shock, immediately took charge. Polk gave a characteristically charming, brief, impromptu speech, not one word of which is remembered. However, as soon as he had finished, before the polite applause was even over, there was Broderick again, stepping forward, to offer the president his arm, and the others were forced to file on behind, as they walked toward the dock at the end of the lawn where a ship waited to take the president back to New York City and the real world.

New York did not need a congressman whom the respectable leaders of its Democratic Party would not deem fit to mingle with socially. If he made the New York Democrats uneasy, imagine what effect he would have on the Southern gentlemen who dominated the Democratic Party in Washington. It would be better to send a Whig to Congress than him. So the word went out, and the Democratic vote was split between Broderick and a splinter candidate to allow the Whig candidate to win. The other, "respectable" Democratic candidate was "Jack" Bloodgood, a dissipated rake but from good Knickerbocker stock who practiced law when he wasn't carousing, which wasn't often. So another blueblood, Frank A. Talmidge, would misrepresent the district in Washington, serving the Whig aristocracy and their rural estates, and doing a few favors for wealthy Democrats as well.

Broderick, of course, knew that he had been dumped, and knew too that he would now not be permitted to rise any further. There had been other blows, far worse, that hit him at about the same time. His mother died, to his inordinate grief. Then, not long after, his fourteen-year-old brother, Dick, was blown up in a freak accident. A bomb shell had been sold for scrap iron to the Charlton Street foundry where Dick worked, and he and a few other boys eager for quick money had been set to bore into it with a red hot bit.

Now without any family, Broderick was quietly inconsolable. He had never been affable. But now there was a hard aloofness about him. Throughout the rest of his life, he seems to have suffered from periodic depressions. When this happened, he would simply disappear for days or even weeks, holed up somewhere with his books and thoughts.

By this time he had given up liquor, tobacco, and cards (that trinity of saloon life). This abstinence also extended to women. Apart from his mother, he seems to have never had even an affectionate relationship with a woman. During his early manhood he moved daily among crowds of easy women, but with the uninterested attitude of a monk oblivious to their appeal, their blandishments. And surely there were many blandishments, but never—in New York or in California—never the hint of the slightest scandal, even from those enemies who earnestly wished him dead.

Yet throughout his subsequent life this strangeness consistently bound other men to him with a strength that someone like Gwin would find inexplicable and disturbing and perhaps even unhealthy. "More like lovers than friends," one enemy wrote. Gwin had friends, allies, rivals, enemies—but these relationships could be understood, talked about, adjusted to time and circumstance. In contrast, there was a passion to Broderick and his followers that defied reasoned calculation. It could not exist in this world, outside the madhouse. But perhaps that was what New York City now was, and what San Francisco might become, without the proper leadership. A madhouse with inexplicable men like Broderick in charge. Men who left prostitutes untouched and made respectable women cringe.

This was the David Broderick who set out for San Francisco in April 1849. With many connections to the New York underworld, political and otherwise. With no one left on earth that he could call family but with many who loved him like more than a brother. With a thwarted desire for power and no interest in mining. He too had bragged to a friend that he would return to the East as senator from California, but he put no date on this prophecy. There were too many rungs he had to climb to be able to estimate accurately. Anyway, he was not one to calculate odds; you pause to calculate odds in a bare-knuckled street fight, and you'll end up getting coldcocked.

Broderick on his trip to California followed the same route that Gwin had, but it was as if he were in a different world. Gwin was carrying a letter of introduction from outgoing secretary of state James Buchanan, much as Thomas Butler King was carrying his own from President Taylor, much as Jessie Frémont was carrying hers from William Aspinwall himself. These letters assured that everything that could be done to ease and quicken their voyages would be done. Broderick, in contrast, traveled letterless with a few of his New York cronies. He and his friends were just the kind to suffer the brunt of what was a difficult and dangerous voyage. For Gwin, King, and Frémont the voyage meant unaccustomed discomfort; for Broderick and his friends certain illness and possible death.

The first stop after New Orleans was the Panama town of Chagres. Let one traveler who arrived there about then describe it:

> Chagres at this time was a town of about seven hundred inhabitants, dwelling in some fifty windowless, bamboo huts, with thatched, palm-leaf roofs, and having open entrances, and the bare ground floor. The town was surrounded by heaps of filthy offal, the greasy, stagnant pools bordered with blue mud. It is situated on a small but exceedingly picturesque and almost land-locked bay, well nigh buried by the foliage that skirts its banks and rolls off in billowy emerald toward the hills beyond.

People in first class could afford to enjoy the picturesque village, to talk among themselves about how they had never seen such a billowy emerald green. Broderick's people rather had to worry that they might end up deposited as corpses in the greasy pools and stagnant offal. Those well-to-do could hire natives to canoe them immediately across the fifty-mile isthmus while regretting with a parting glance that Chagres was—as one put it—such "a confused mixture of dogs, hogs and naked children, Negroes and Creoles." Everyone was exposed to the contagions of Panama, of which the most feared were cholera and yellow, or Panama, fever. With enough money you could nonetheless protect yourself somewhat by a quick passage and by keeping your constitution up with good food.

Men like Broderick seldom had such luck. They usually had to wait overnight in Chagres, until the first-class passengers had been cared for; this meant that any life insurance they might have purchased was invalid, so notoriously unhealthy was the place. In Chagres or elsewhere they could not afford decent food and lodging, nor did they have the connections to get a quick berth on a steamer, since there were frequently ten aspirants for every one place. So they sat in Panama, usually on the west coast, eventually succumbing as much to their own despair as to one of the fevers, all the while watching from a distance the likes of Frémont and Gwin getting pampered.

Not surprisingly, Broderick, who started for California well before Gwin, arrived by his own account more than a week after, all because of delays in Panama. He and friends had had to spend almost a month in the fever-ravaged Panamanian coastal towns, just because they lacked connections—and, having had to wait only a month, they should have counted themselves lucky.

When they finally got passage from Panama to California (and one might imagine Broderick's threatening presence had something to do with that), their suffering was far from over, for they would be traveling steerage. The first-class cabins, reserved for people like Gwin, were located off the dining room; these were carpeted cubicles, the berths curtained for privacy and each one with its own porthole. These passengers had access to a promenade deck, partly covered by awnings to protect them from the tropical sun.

In contrast, the accommodations in steerage were, as one captain put it, "little better than a slaver." Steerage was in the bowels of the ship, hundreds of people herded into an amazingly small space filled completely with tiers of bunks. No light, no ventilation, no privacy. One captain, trying to make a joke of it, said that steerage was "filled to cramnation." The bunks were six feet long and eighteen inches wide, with two feet between a bunk and the one above. In other words, too narrow to lie comfortably on your back—and not enough height to lie on your side. Also, the bunks were jammed up in threes, three high and three wide. So there would be nine people sleeping in an area 4½ feet wide and perhaps 10 feet tall, separated from the nine people on each side only by a small aisle.

Steerage passengers were not permitted in the dining room. They would line up outside the galley with their own plates and cups. (Steerage passengers had to supply their own linens and eating utensils.) How they could manage to eat back in the stifling hole is hard to imagine. Sometimes steerage passengers were allowed onto the promenade deck. But when a lady like Jessie Frémont began to worry about her constitution and had to be moved onto a tent on deck, then, of course, free movement on deck by the steerage passengers was out of the question.

In general, those suffering below—perhaps even dying—were acknowledged by the first-class passengers only to complain about them. One sniffed, "I never witnessed so many disgusting exhibitions of the lowest passions of humanity, as during the voyage." Another wrote that of all the hardships he had experienced on ship, including fever and threatening storms, none compared to those occasioned by the "extremely disgusting persons whose presence one could not escape." Another wrote that the voyage had shaken his belief in the speedy perfection of the human race.

David Broderick, of course, would have found most of what disgusted him in life on the promenade deck itself. And one cannot imagine his being kept off the deck when the ship entered the Golden Gate. He was certainly capable of muscling himself onto deck, if he decided to; and he would have needed little provocation to express his willingness to assist the speedy perfection of the human race by throwing a few well-dressed passengers overboard.

At any rate, he would have witnessed while at anchor on the bay things that were spared the first-class passengers. For instance, sometimes a "soiled dove" had not had enough money for passage, or had not been able to work enough during the voyage. A captain then would auction her off to one of the entrepreneurs in the launches, after, of course, the respectable folks had left the ship. This may have been how Sam Roberts met Felice Alvarez.

Long after the first-class passengers had been deposited in San Francisco, the steerage passengers would arrive, having waited on the ship for hours just as they had waited in Panama for weeks or months. By that time a Jessie Frémont had already been whisked away to a closeted world of respectability, and a Butler King and a William Gwin were deep into important political meetings. Broderick, in contrast, would have no pressing business to distract him. Rather he would hook up with old friends from New York, probably at the very Tammany Hall saloon that the Hounds made their unofficial headquarters. Then the boys would show him around San Francisco, the real San Francisco. He would learn its streets and alleys, its brothels and gambling emporiums, its criminals and struggling poor in a way that Gwin and the others never would. He would know how it looked to the respectable from above, but he also would experience it as it really was, at gutter level.

Broderick, looking out at the San Francisco that so repulsed others, would have seen something quite different. His response, had he the eloquence of expression, would have been that of Herman Melville in this same year of 1849 as he looked at the various immigrants crowding a Liverpool dock for passage to America: "We are not a narrow tribe of men . . . whose blood has been debased in the attempt to ennoble it, maintaining an exclusive succession among ourselves. No: our blood is as the flood of the Amazon, made up of a thousand noble currents all pouring into one."

So the boys would show Dave Broderick around the makeshift city that seemed more likely to slide off into the bay than ever creep up over the windswept sandhills arising terracelike to its west. The boys would show him what passed for a main street in San Francisco, Kearny, named after the general who had taken over command of the conquest from Frémont. (He had died the previous year, and this was his monument, not one in which Jessie Frémont could take pleasure, for General Kearny had participated in the disgusting plot, motivated by envy and spite, to get her husband court-martialled, a subject on which she could expatiate at length.) To walk from the southern to the northern end of this street was to traverse the world, the boys said, and at times seemed about as difficult.

The northern end was mostly dominated by newly arrived Hispanics, Chileans, and Peruvians. Only a few paces away from Little Chile, toward the bay, began the Australian tents, Sydney town. Among the Chileans and the Aussies was not a place to walk at night; and even in daylight a man should make certain not to wander alone among the dunes between them because he might be caught where no one could hear a cry for help. The footpads used a kind of blackjack on the unwary, a cloth wrapped around a lump of lead, an easily disposable weapon that could dispatch a man with a single well-placed blow (it was said) and leave not a mark. The *Alta California* then would report, "Found dead—near Kearny Street—no marks of violence—apoplexy the supposed cause." And everyone could imagine what had really happened.

At the southern end of Kearny, on the other hand, was a collection of shacks almost exclusively of European immigrants. Here the business signs, as in certain districts of New York, would almost all be in either French or German or both; you would stay in a *gasthaus* and have your ills taken care of at the *pharmacie*. It said something about Kearny Street in particular, and California in general, that those from the Southern Hemisphere would be found in the north and those from the Northern in the south. This was a world turned upside down. And sprinkled throughout it were the Celestials, as the Chinese were commonly called. They usually flew long, yellow silk banners, and their restaurants gave you all you could eat for a dollar. Strange stuff, the boys thought, but filling once you developed a taste for it.

Getting from one end of Kearny to the other was no picnic. The streets were ankle deep in sand in the summer, but if Broderick thought it was bad now, just wait until winter. In the winter the mud got so deep that branches and boards were thrown into the street to make it passable. But that only made the street more dangerous. Horses and mules would sink deep into the mud, and their legs would get caught in branches that acted like hidden snares; in the struggle to get free, the horse or mule might tumble. On

Montgomery, one street over, could still be seen the carcasses of two horses that last winter had become hopelessly stuck in the mud and had to be left to starve to death. On the other hand, the drunks who drowned in the mud (three so far this year) were given a decent burial.*

So one did not want to ride up Kearny Street. But the only alternative was to walk, and that meant using the sidewalks. Oh, the sidewalks. They made one yearn for New York. Let someone who was in San Francisco in the earliest days describe them as he remembers them specifically in June on Kearny Street, as they might have been pointed out to Broderick himself:

> In front of one man's property, the walk was made of barrel-staves, nailed upon stretchers; the next one adjoining had thin, springing board, threatening at every step to let you through; then a mosaic, made of sides and ends of packing cases, some portions covered with tin or zinc—the jagged, saw-like edges making business for dealers in boots and shoes; now you trod upon the rusty tops of some old stoves, or heavy iron window-shutting, or an old ship's hatchway covering; then a dozen or two heads of kegs, set close together, imbedded in the mud of last year's rainy season; and so on, in great and curious variety.

Who could deny the jocular conclusion that the sidewalk of Kearny Street was "fearfully and wonderfully made"? If one dared look up from this obstacle course, there were sights to be seen. On the corner of Kearny and Washington there was Our House kept by the German Peter Sherrebeck, one of the oldest saloons in the city—but the old barkeep Broderick would look in vain for the bar, for Peter Sherrebeck dispensed liquor from a table in the middle of what to all the world looked like his living room. On a hot day—rare as they were in June—one might pop in for a refreshing and calming milk punch, not of course that Dave would be interested. You couldn't get a cold lager in all of San Francisco, but there was also on Kearny a pub run by an Englishman (who apparently had had an enforced sojourn Down Under; hence the name of the place, The Boomerang). He usually had warm ale and one evening a week served a good beef sirloin dinner that could be smelled up and down the street—but it was expensive. So was the French place where the boys when they had money to burn liked to go for breakfast, especially to tease Madame Rosalie by ordering their eggs boiled. (She just couldn't get them to try an omelet.) But there was no point in getting fancy, for these were not real eggs but from gulls, supposedly gathered from some islands just out of the Gate but tasting like they'd been dug up somewhere.

---

*A luckier case was described by an early San Franciscan as follows: "I saw a man try to cross Montgomery Street. . . . He was about half drunk or he would not have attempted it. He floundered in up to his waist, then up to his neck, and had not some person thrown him a rope, he would have drowned."

The usual breakfast here, by the way, was a cup of coffee, a hot biscuit, and some beans. Eggs or a glass or two of claret (or something stronger) was extra. As for Herr Sherrebeck, he was doing well, as almost everyone seemed to be who had established himself in San Francisco before the gold rush (or rather in Yerba Buena, for it was called that then, after one of the few useful things that grew here).

Another who was doing even better was the eccentric Dr. Jones, whose house would be pointed out from Kearny Street to any new arrival because of the strange goings-on reported there. Dr. Jones, who once owned much of Kearny Street, supposedly had more gold dust than anyone else in California, not that you would know it from his modest two-story wooden house. It was said that on some nights Jones would spread a sheet on the floor and sitting on it naked would pour gold dust all over his body and roll in it, and then perform a glittering dance to greed. His friends did not deny this story to the boys, but said this strange fit came over him only after he had been drinking quite a while. (Jones became a mythic figure to early Californians after he left California, which he did soon; they earnestly said that he had eventually died of exhaustion caused by his riches, for in the end he just could not bring himself to be out of sight of his gold, even to close his eyes to sleep.)

So the mosey around Kearny Street could continue. Looking back you could see the main landmark of the new city, Telegraph Hill. The name suggested its function. The little building on its peak was a signal house. When a ship entered the bay, a signal would be run up the pole by the house and could be seen throughout the shanty city. That was the telegraph. On the morning when the *Panama* was chugging into the bay, the signal of two black boards, one on each side of the pole, like outstretched arms, was run up, and everyone knew that a sidewheel steamer was approaching. Then a cheer went up all over at once, and everyone took a break from what he was doing. This was the tradition of the "universal drink." (Little did the passengers of the *Panama* know, but when they were peering at the tents and despairing that the gold rush was over, almost everyone in the city who could afford it was hoisting one in their honor.)

But, like the story about Dr. Jones and his gold dust, much that the New Yorkers would point out as fact to a new arrival like Broderick was as much imagination as real. Montgomery Street, the next street up from Kearny toward the bay, was in places not a street at all but a path up a hillside. It was on Montgomery Street, he might be told, that the Hudson's Bay Company had its office before the gold rush. The agent so despaired that his life had come to this dead end he committed suicide. His body was buried in the garden of his place, then a peaceful spot, now the bustling corner where Montgomery meets Long Wharf, the longest of the wharves that stretched out over the low tidal marshes into the bay.

The street to the old mission would also be pointed out, but this was only a horse path through sandhills and chaparral, and in the rainy season it boasted of a marshy lagoon deep enough to drown in, rider and horse all together without even falling over. Worth going out that way, though. Bob Ridley's place—he took over part of the dilapidated mission compound—serves the best milk punch in town, much better than Sherrebeck's. On a warm day so many people ride out there it looks like a cavalry post. But you should make sure you do not go there by yourself the first time. If you happen to get lost, there are just too many places you could get waylaid.

On the Kearny Street side of Portsmouth Square was the largest of the gambling saloons, Parker House, a proper two-story house the whole second floor of which was given over to gambling tables. There beautiful, well-dressed women acted the dealer and croupier beneath paintings of beautiful, undressed women. But perhaps the most representative of these establishments was El Dorado, a modest-sized tent next to Parker House, not more than fifteen by twenty-five feet. Its owner, rather than running the games himself, rented out the tables to professional gamblers; these rents totaled $40,000 a year. And the gamblers were not heard to complain. These emporiums, of course, ran day and night.

Kearny Street at night made the daytime seem calm. Traveling along the so-called sidewalks was a special trial without streetlights. But at dusk the rats came out and took over the streets, thousands of them, running in all directions, squealing and fighting, paying no attention to the humans who tried not to step on them and might try to kick them when they ran over a boot. But that was not wise; for an annoyed rat might show fight. Then the person who had started the trouble was expected to dispatch the aggressive rat by whatever means were available. Even the old timers never got used to the rats; they involuntarily jumped or kicked when a big rat ran smack into them, which was common enough if you chose to walk at dusk or later. But, like just about everything else, Californians tried to make jokes about this, and thereby impress the newcomers with their aplomb. When not being startled himself, the old-timer played the rat fancier, and for the uninitiated discriminated among varieties of rat. So our connoisseur of the Kearny sidewalks would at dusk turn naturalist and pride himself on being able to distinguish "the rat of Valparaiso, the rat of Canton or Singapore, the long, white pink-eyed rice-rat of Batavia, the New York, Boston or Liverpool wharf-rat." And if the newcomer became suspicious his leg was being pulled, the old-timer would point out some kangaroo rats from Australia, and bid him watch them for a while; they were famous among Californians for their acrobatics, as good as a circus in miniature, with the other fighting rats taking the place of lions.

Of course, the boys would know what Dave was thinking. Why didn't people get cats? Oh, they do. Cats who happen to be on board an incoming vessel bring a pretty penny, terriers too. But they do not last long. Initially they go on a killing frenzy, as if they had arrived at a ratter's heaven. But after a while, a month, two at most, they are overwhelmed; they succumb to the California fever of laziness amid plenty, and will snooze in a corner while rats cavort all around them.

It is not hard to imagine the enthusiasm and good humor with which the transplanted New Yorkers showed their admired newcomer around. They would assess for him the odds in the local card games not known in New York, and would also offer their opinions about the local grog and offer directions to the less expensive brothels. They knew, if could not quite believe, that he wasn't interested in any of this for himself. But still they talked, hardly able to contain themselves.

Nor is it hard to imagine his response to this enthusiasm and good humor. He was genuinely interested in the boys, and the intricacies of this new place. He loved the boys, but they also saddened him. They were so easily satisfied, so eager to be beguiled by rat circuses, milk punches, and the intricacies of three-card monte. So easily satisfied when there was so much to be angry about. Still, he would affectionately let them prattle on, as he used to let his brother back in New York. But he would occasionally ask serious questions that probed beneath the surface. Who owned the brothels? How much were the authorities paid off? Who controlled the *Alta California*?

He would quickly have figured out the Hounds, probably by talking to them himself. Of course, they had no power themselves. They had been tolerated because they served a purpose. At first, perhaps they did help retrieve—or shanghai—recalcitrant sailors. But sea captains who only wanted to clear harbor could not be significant players in San Francisco. Where was the real power? So he would continue to probe until he realized that the Hounds were a gang tacitly supported by the American merchants of San Francisco to intimidate the Hispanics, the second-largest group in the city and the only one with the potential to challenge American commercial predominance.

The Hounds would have especially interested him, for they were his people. Most of them were New Yorkers, and the kind of men you wouldn't mind having beside you when fighting a fire, or back-to-back behind you in a fight. An old friend of Broderick from Tammany Hall days, Jonathan Stevenson, had seen the Mexican War as an opportunity for himself. So he had quickly organized his regiment of volunteers, and had arrived in Monterey early in the war. He was accurately assessed there as "a fish out of water, with no military knowledge . . . come here to recommence a political existence." Happily seeing little action, he and his men were in the right place at the right time when gold was discovered. His men were quickly released, and some reorganized themselves into companies for gold diggings. Others stayed behind, and became the quasi-military Hounds.

Stevenson himself did better by staying at the coast, and attending to commerce, although his long-term objective was clearly politics. (Years later he claimed that he was the one who wrote to Broderick to convince him to come to California, a claim not implausible.) But to be a successful politician, in California as in New York, you needed money, lots of money. Stevenson already had made a good bit, and by the time Broderick arrived he had a scheme for making a lot more.

There was great need for coins in San Francisco. Stevenson recruited Broderick and Frederick Kohler, one of his traveling companions, to establish a private mint with his backing. Kohler had the knowledge of assaying, Stevenson an ample supply of California gold, and Broderick the experience with arduous physical labor. (Actually, there was some concern about Broderick's capacity for the last, so debilitated had he been by the voyage out; but he insisted that he would be his old self again soon.) Together, Kohler and Broderick began to produce five- and ten-dollar gold pieces. Or so they were labeled. Actually they contained only four and eight dollars' worth of gold, respectively. The scam was remarkably lucrative. Less than six months after arriving in San Francisco, Broderick would amass what for him was a small fortune.

Before that came the night of the Hounds. The b'hoys got out of control, and tried in a single night to finish the job they had been hired for. They were wrong in what they had done, of course. Worse still, they just could not be made to realize that they had more in common with the poor Chileans and Aussies than with the American businessmen who were paying them off on the side. And Sam Roberts, in particular, was a fool. But the fact was, as Broderick saw it, that respectable folks would have liked nothing more than to have the Hounds kill all the Chileans, and then to band together themselves to exile the Hounds. And then they would have San Francisco all to themselves.

The late-nineteenth-century historical apologist for the vigilantes, Hubert Howe Bancroft, wrote as much with respect to this episode: "Not that any special sympathy is due to the class against whom their wrath was kindled. The Chileans and Peruvians who infested the towns and rifled the Foothills of their treasures were low enough in the scale of humanity [that] . . . if the Hounds had extirpated them and had them themselves been hanged for it society would have been the gainer."

Broderick did not need to read Bancroft to know this attitude. He only needed to look around the crowd at the trial to see it on the smug faces, as the prosecution thundered about the great power of evil with its fangs already at the throat of our infant community, while the boys in the dock tried to look cocky. Broderick would also have known how to interpret the vague threat of the prosecutor when he spoke of possible "treason" that might be committed by certain "influential men in the community who lean to the side of the prisoners and throw obstacles in the way of justice." The slower witted of the "influential men" had to realize that the usefulness of the Hounds was over, and this was no time for sentimentality or loyalty.

What actually resulted from this episode was little different from what Bancroft had blithely envisioned. The Chileans were now terrified and leaving California by droves. And enough of the b'hoys were rounded up and exiled to strike fear in the rest, just to keep them in their place.

Broderick would have been at that trial, for it was a perfect chance to size things up. He would have hated Gwin at first sight. And when Gwin was immediately elected judge by acclamation, and then when he conducted himself during the trial with complete aplomb—well, Broderick had always suspected that the New York silk-stocking crowd was not the worst that America had to offer.

One had to admire Stevenson, however. He had actually testified for the defense, and so stood implicitly accused by the prosecutor of treason to his class of influential men. Broderick would have noticed without surprise that the *Alta California,* while reporting the testimony against the Hounds at length and having much fun with the inept attempts to provide an alibi for Roberts, did not have space for any of Stevenson's words. Stevenson's testimony about Roberts's hard background was dismissed in a line.*

So Broderick watched as the trial reached its foregone conclusion. Then, a little while after, came the election for the delegates to the constitutional convention. The results showed that Stevenson had sacrificed himself by speaking out for his men. One of the most prominent and popular men in San Francisco before the trial, now he got scarcely half the votes of the newcomer judge, William McKendree Gwin, who it was said still owned slaves back in Mississippi. Sadly, Stevenson was not going to be a partner in Broderick's pursuit of power; and, happily, Gwin—sooner or later—was going to be an obstacle that would have to be removed, one way or another. This was an inevitable fight that Broderick could look forward to with relish.

As the delegates went off to the convention, Broderick was temporarily absorbed in his pursuit of wealth. Although a full partner in the thriving mint, he did continue to do much of the manual labor. And he began slowly working toward political office. His path, unlike Gwin's, had to be slow and indirect. The first step was to join a volunteer fire department. These were functioning in San Francisco as they had in New York—a place for public-spirited workingmen to come together, a place too which enabled them to express their collective political will, especially if they happened to find in their midst someone who could articulate it for them.

Fires in San Francisco were common and dangerous, far more so even than in New York. By 1850 San Franciscans had become all too familiar with them. So, for instance, when on the morning of June 14 the cry of fire was heard, new arrivals could not understand the near hysteria in the pop-

---

*Not mentioned at all was Stevenson's plea to the court not to execute the men. He asked them to imagine how he could possibly explain to their mothers back in New York how the boys he had recruited to accompany him to California had died. This might have influenced the final sentence, but one would not know it from reading the lengthy account of the trial in the *Alta California.*

ulation, or what they took to be such. In their experience a fire meant that a building or two burned, or at worst a block or two. But San Franciscans were scurrying to clear out buildings a mile away from where the fire started. And those who had carts handy were rushing around as well, making a small fortune by carrying load after load to safety. But safety from what? Goods were being piled up in marshy empty lots where anyone could pilfer them, and yet the fire was still far away.

On this day a Captain Peter Hewlett, who had been in California so long—a year—that he was known as Don Pedro, advised some incredulous newcomers, "You'd better be looking for your baggage, if it's in the city." Against their better judgment, they followed his advice, and just managed to save their trunks, but not the rest of their belongings, from the burning building where they had stored them for safekeeping. The whole city, as Don Pedro knew, was kindling. Once a fire broke out, buildings, shacks, tents would start to go up in all directions. Then the fire, no matter how calm the day, would start to create its own wind, and the firestorm would then sweep destruction until it had reached the bay or the sandhills. Nothing else could stop it.

The fire of June 1850, for instance, took out a good bit of Portsmouth Square and Kearny Street, including Parker House. Looking down onto the city that evening from a western sandhill, one newcomer thought that the burned out district looked like it had been covered with molten lava—a low, dark red, although it still glowed yellowish in places, eerily lighting the sky and sending off into the bay black clouds that soon disappeared into the surrounding darkness.

When another major fire hit in September of that year, Heinrich Schliemann, the future discoverer of Troy, happened to be there. This gave him an image of a city being destroyed that he would carry with him the rest of his life. "The roaring of the storm, the crackling of the gunpowder, the thunder of falling walls, the cries of the people, and the wonderful spectacle of an immense city burning up in a dark night—all joined to make this catastrophe awful in the extreme." Troy on the Pacific.

The fires were so frequent and so furious that the boys did not need melees to prove their mettle. This was work they could throw themselves into with abandon, and feel good about afterwards. But it was one thing to fight fires; it was another to fight them when you were continually overmatched. That took true pluck. The boys would just fight until they dropped; Broderick would fight too and as hard, but afterwards he would also ask hard questions and find his own answers.

The fires were suspicious in their origins. A common opinion was being expressed by the San Francisco *Herald* when it reasoned that there must be "an organized band of incendiaries . . . whose fixed determination seems to be to desolate our city and ruin it beyond redemption." The respectable elements of San Francisco assumed that these perverse incendiaries were from the underclass, probably the Australians who were rumored to start fires whenever they wanted an occasion for looting. Australians had now replaced the depleted Chileans as the least desirable nationality of San Francisco. The fires *were* suspicious, and the Aussies *were* rowdy—but it didn't add up.

As far as Broderick could see, the only group who benefited from these fires were the merchants themselves. Major fires tended to start when these merchants (who worked on commission from East Coast suppliers) had such a surplus of goods that the prices were collapsing. A big fire, and suddenly demand exceeded supply—and prices shot up three or four times. If the merchant had insurance too, then all the better for him. In fact, a merchant could become wealthy on just two or three opportune fires. And always the Aussies were available as convenient bogeymen.

This was also the analysis of Broderick's mentor George Wilkes, who had arrived from New York after Broderick, and was nobody's fool. Wilkes would eventually write a story about the San Francisco fires in his magazine, *The National Police Gazette:* "The warehouses of San Francisco were glutted to the roofs; but the precious commission merchants of San Francisco could not make returns to their Atlantic shippers; and then came the terrible conflagrations which gave them a clear balance sheet. . . .'Thieves, thieves, incendiaries!' shouted the merchants. 'Hang them! Hang them!', echoed the ignorant and timid, 'They have set our city on fire.' "

Even those not as suspicious as Wilkes and Broderick could see the stimulating effect that fires had upon business. One discouraged argonaut wrote home in 1850, "The only thing that has saved California so far has been the many disastrous fires; at least that has saved the masses of merchants from failing for legitimate causes."

The San Francisco fires were typical of American society as Broderick had experienced it, Broderick whose experience left him neither ignorant nor timid. It was the workingmen who truly lost everything when a fire swept through. It was the workingmen who risked their lives to stop the fire. And it would be the workingmen of one sort or another who would be blamed for the fire by the very respectable folks who had made a killing.

Broderick did his part as a fireman. In one fire, in particular, he distinguished himself by his bravery, and soon was captain of his company, much as he had been years earlier in New York. It would be only a little step from that to running for public office, particularly because so few were interested except in the highest offices. Why do public service when there was so much money to be made? And Broderick had his own little gold mine, albeit of a peculiar type. Yet he cared not at all about money, except not having to worry about it. And he cared almost everything about power.

He wanted to help the ignorant and timid destroy the elites that exploited them—no, he wanted to destroy them himself, with his own hands, on behalf of the ignorant and timid. And by any weapons that came to hand. He had long since learned not to have scruples. He did not need to be respected by the likes of Gwin or Butler King or Sam Brannan, only feared. Being feared in his experience was better, feared by them and hence loved by his people.

Broderick wanted power. And he had not been in California very long before he saw concretely what he most wished to use that power against. There was a genteel clique of chivalrous Southerners emerging in California, led by William McKendree Gwin, who himself was acting as if he were the God Almighty providence of California. Well, here was one son of the people who would teach this Chivalry (as they were coming to be called) a thing or two about providence, as Shelley's Prometheus had taught the tyrant Zeus. Against this Chivalry, David Broderick, with his callused hands and scarred face, would build a workingman's democracy. Let the Chivalry oppose the Shovelry at its peril.

So at the very moment Dr. William Gwin was traveling to Monterey for the constitutional convention that would begin the most triumphant year and a half of his life, Mr. David Broderick was likely already starting to brood about the downfall of this man who personified everything he hated. Soon it would become a dominating passion of his life.

3

It had all been so easy, too easy almost. Such could not have been far from William Gwin's thoughts as he boarded the ship that was to take him and the other northern California delegates back down the coast to the old capital of Monterey for the constitutional convention that he expected to propel him into the United States Senate. He was coming prepared to lead, with a parliamentary handbook and a copy of the state constitution of Iowa—and with his own well-developed plans for the kind of government he wanted this state, his state, to have.

He had been in California only two months and already he was one of its leading citizens. His luck had been uncanny. He had arrived in San Francisco the day after Riley's proclamation; he had arrived back from his speaking tour the very day Brannan was haranguing the crowd in Portsmouth Square against the Hounds. Fortune was smiling upon him, and not just by the opportune timing of his arrivals.

There were also his rivals who, without any help from him, seemed bent upon ruining themselves. Butler King was still holed up somewhere in Sonoma, trying to recover from his trip to the mines, the fool, so weak that he could not participate in the convention. Neither would Frémont. He was staying in San Francisco to care for his ailing wife; the San Francisco fogs, it seems, had brought on an attack of rheumatism so severe that she could not walk without help. (The woman loved to be carried.)

Frémont was still the darling of many delegates; the very ship they were traveling on was called the *Frémont*. Others, however, who looked past the famous name to the man were beginning to take his measure. As one delegate would write, "Frémont was a very nice little gentleman, but I thought as many others did, that Jessie Benton Frémont was the better man of the two, far more intelligent and more comprehensive." That was encouraging. Anyway, there were two Senate seats.

Finally, Gwin must have had to smile to himself when he thought of Colonel Jonathan Stevenson, that quintessential Tammany Hall politician in military garb. What could he have been thinking when he testified on behalf of Sam Roberts? Who cared that this murderous miscreant was uneducated, or that he had been a good carpenter back in New York? Didn't the un-military colonel understand that sometimes you had to keep your own head down? Perhaps he understood it now, too late. So he could join Butler King in the spectators' gallery of California politics.

Gwin had been shrewd; he had taken full advantage of every opportunity that had presented itself. But he also knew he had been extremely lucky, and luck can always change, fickle as a woman. If he needed to be reminded of this, the trip down to Monterey was sufficient for that purpose. As they approached Monterey, they were engulfed in an impenetrable fog, and had to cast anchor amid the kelp forests that ringed the ample bay. There the aspiring almighty providence of California, together with his fellow passen-gers, sat while the provisions slowly ran out, and the captain, at least accord-ing to one account, consoled himself in the bottle. For day after day they could make out nothing except a few sea otters diving among the kelp next to the ship, coming up with abalone and sea urchins from the ocean floor, to feed off them at their leisure, each using his furry belly as a table. After four days even raw sea urchin started to look good, or for that matter an otter tail. Much longer, and they would have to risk coming into shore blind. That meant a future U.S. senator could end up drowned in the wreck of the *Frémont*. No luck in that.

Then the fog decided to wander off somewhere else, having had its fun here. Slowly the land came out of the water, finally visible—first the high mountains in the north above Santa Cruz, then the low beach around the Salinas River, and circling behind this the strongly marked ridge that ter-minated at the sea in a point of dark pine trees. The coastline of the bay was shaped somewhat like a fish hook with this southern headland, Point Pinos, being the point and the harbor the barb. As the ship approached the harbor, a line of whitewashed adobes rose up, and behind them a grove of dark oaks that at this distance could be mistaken for an orchard of old apple trees. And at last the ship safely made port.

Gwin's disembarkation in Monterey produced its own kind of shock. All he had seen of California before this had been dominated by the bustle of the gold rush. The Mexicans and Indians he had seen in Sacramento and Stockton were themselves scrambling to profit from the new turn of events—or, if they did not, they were being unwillingly swept up in them. In Mon-terey he could see the old California, the California of dons and ranchos, a California where a cluster of dirt-floor adobes huddled near a mission church constituted a proper town, indeed a veritable capital. The way of life seemed to have more in common with that of the sea otters than with the business of a progressive people.

Monterey, three-quarters of a century after its founding, could not ad-equately house the forty-eight delegates to the convention—to tell the truth, it could not handle comfortably one-quarter of that number. To tell the complete truth, it did not have the facilities to handle comfortably anyone, and that included its own residents. Or so it seemed to some of the new visitors.

Here was a society that looked to Gwin and others as if it had been hidden in a fog from the gaze of the nineteenth century—and now, suddenly being exposed, it was withering into nothingness. The owners of the old ranchos were having a hard time even understanding their own new wealth. There used to be so many more cattle than people in California that it had been the traveler's customary right to kill a steer for his dinner steak as long as he put the carcass in a prominent place (for it was only the hide and tallow that had any value). Now a rancher could get moderately rich just by driving his herd to the goldfields to supply the numerous hungry prospectors with meat. But the ranchers as a group did not know how to cut a good deal for themselves, and there were too many sharp operators like Sam Brannan at their elbows to help them cut bad ones. As a group they were unable to adapt to this new predatory world of commerce, and were gradually—or in some cases not so gradually—losing everything.

The town of Monterey told much about the older way of life. It was little more than a scattering of buildings about two miles from the point that sheltered the bay from the south. The main activity in the town seemed to be the birds and other wildlife. One who was at the convention wrote, "Flocks of ravens croak from the tiled roofs and cluster on the long adobe walls; magpies chatter in the clumps of gnarled oak on the hills, and as you pass through the forest, hares start up from their coverts under bearded pines. The quantity of blackbirds about the place is astonishing; in the mornings they wheel in squadrons about every housetop, and fill the air with their twitter." But cattle was king of the community, and at one point the delegates would be treated to the spectacle of a horn burning. The town occasionally had to collect all the cattle heads and horns that had been indiscriminately strewn throughout it and were becoming a nuisance; they were gathered into a pile during the day and then burned through the night, giving the incoming fog an eerie red glow and an awful stench. Apart from tending the cattle, the life of the human inhabitants of Monterey was dominated, it seemed to the Americans, by riding, dancing, and religious pageants (which the more puritanically minded of the Americans dismissed as trivializations of the gospel to the level of mere drama).

The only place to eat in Monterey was the Fonda de la Union, described by one of its visitors as "an old smoky place not uncomfortably clean." There for a dollar one had a choice of three entrées, beef and corn, beef and peppers, beef and potatoes. The coffee was thrown in free, but some thought that even free it was overpriced. You had to be careful, the delegates learned quickly, with anything that came with a red sauce; many an American had gulped down a mouthful before realizing that this was not made from tomato but was pureed chili coronado, liquid fire.

The few Americans who had settled in Mexican California tended to fare better than their Mexican contemporaries in the new order. And Gwin's window on the older way of life was largely based on his conversations with one of these Americans, Thomas Larkin, who was his host in Monterey. (Need it be said that Gwin had arranged the best accommodations available for himself?) Before the Mexican War, Larkin had served officially as American counsel in California—and secretly as a spy in the cause of American annexation.

Larkin was an interesting fellow, well involved now in commerce and real estate speculation. He would be a delegate from Monterey to the convention but was personally more intent on becoming rich, a principled version of Sam Brannan. He had felt constrained under the unstable Mexican administration, and had written secret messages to the then U.S. secretary of state, John C. Calhoun. Much of what Gwin had learned of California from Calhoun, Calhoun had in turn learned from Larkin. Larkin had been, in particular, recommended to Gwin by James Buchanan as a "shrewd observing and intelligent gentleman who judging from my correspondence with him knows more of the territory than any other individual." So Larkin was someone in whom Gwin could have confidence.

Nonetheless, like many of the older American residents of California, Larkin at times seemed to have more in common with the Mexicans than he did with the argonauts and Gwin. In fact, sometimes such Americans let slip from their lips remarks that were at once contemptuous of the new, and nostalgic for the old. The newcomers, one observed, looked upon themselves as the Israelites and this beautiful land as their Canaan. But they were no chosen people, even if this might be a promised land. Yet they persisted in believing that the happy if motley race they found already here in California were so many Hittites, Hivites, and Jebusites, to be driven out by force of arms. Or, if not to be driven out by force of arms, then to be driven into poverty by trickery.

Larkin knew better, of course. And he wanted an American California. But he could sympathize with the old-timers of Monterey who saw the gold rush as a vandal invasion that had destroyed their peaceable kingdom. The resentment now generally felt was early given apt expression by an old resident of Monterey who, after seeing the first gold nuggets from the diggings, had insisted that they were some Yankee invention, got up to reconcile the people to the change of flag.

No one could have predicted this extraordinary change that had supplanted Monterey as the chief settlement of California. The change was undeniable and irreversible, but the old residents of Monterey could not but hope that Monterey would once again reassert itself in an American California. Or so one wrote:

> Now all eyes are turned to San Francisco, with her mud bottoms, her sand hills, and her chill winds, which cut the stranger

like hail driven through the summer solstice. Avarice may erect
its shanty there, but contentment, and a love of the wild and
beautiful, will construct its tabernacle among the flowers, the
waving shade and fragrant airs of Monterey. And even they
who now drive the spade and drill in the mine, when their
yellow pile shall fill the measure of their purposes, will come
here to sprinkle these hills with the mansions and cottages of
ease and refinement. Among these soaring crags the step of
youth will still spring, and beauty garland her tresses with wild
flowers in the mirror of the mountain stream.

Such a transformation of his beloved Monterey might completely reconcile Larkin and those like him to the present, especially if he could fill the
measure of his own acquisitive purposes. Yet there must have been moments
when Larkin would find himself yearning, almost against his own conscious
will, that his California somehow be returned to the fog.

For such nostalgia Gwin would have had little time. As if human nature
would ever be satiated by a modest yellow pile, as if pretty words or garlands
of wildflowers could change reality. Decorate it, yes, but not change it.
Monterey had better enjoy its present little moment in history as the site of
the constitutional convention; this was likely to be its last of any consequence.
The future of California was in San Francisco, amid its sandhills of avarice
and its chill winds of ambition. The dangerous fog that had put Gwin and
his fellows at risk would at least convince the delegates they should move
the capital away from here. (The matter was virtually settled when it was
learned that the ship that had been sent for the delegates from southern
California had been lost on the way there, and the delegates had to straggle
in by land.)

That perverse fog indirectly had put more at risk than Gwin's physical
well-being. In fact, he would soon learn to his shock that the delay at sea
had almost undone him politically. As the ship waited for the clearing, the
delegates quite naturally began to talk about the convention—and eventually
Gwin, whether from overconfidence or out of boredom, began to hint at
his own intentions. He then seems to have taken the silence of the other
delegates as acquiescence, and so began to become more definite about his
plans. The silence had not been acquiescence, but rather sullen resentment.
These men had not come all the way to Monterey to be led around by the
nose. To hear Gwin tell it, he already had drawn up the constitution, leaving
only a few blank spaces to be filled in by the other delegates, such as that for
the date of final passage.

The ship had not been long docked before intelligence of what one called
Gwin's "haughty and dictatorial attitude" had spread throughout the delegates. The portrait of William Gwin as aspiring despot was a hotter topic for
conversation than the dangers of the voyage in, although he himself probably

did not yet realize it. Nonetheless, the reaction of the majority of the delegates was predictable. They bristled at the very notion that anybody thought himself better than anybody else, especially if that anybody was a damned Southern filibuster. The older residents were particularly riled up at this newcomer who intended to usurp their natural pride of place.

That pride was given due acknowledgment on the first day. The meeting had been called to order at Colton Hall, a large stone building used as a schoolhouse that the American alcalde of Monterey during the Mexican War (Walter Colton) had left to the community after he had decided to return east. The delegates had been led into the hall by a trio of old Californians, striding in with their arms locked together, each old-timer representing a distinct constituency. General Mariano Vallejo represented Hispanic California; commonly reputed to be the most talented of the native sons, he for years had from his vast estate in Sonoma ruthlessly defended the northern border of the Mexican ranch society, and now more recently had gotten over his resentment at having been treated presumptuously by Frémont and his men when in fact he had been sympathetic to the American cause. Arm-in-arm with Vallejo was Captain John Sutter, a Swiss of questionable origin, on whose own vast fiefdom in the Sacramento Valley the first gold was actually discovered. As a result, he should have been the wealthiest man in California by now; but Sutter did not worry about his own income, only his reputation for hospitality, throwing bigger and bigger parties while his immense wealth dwindled toward nothingness as men like Sam Brannan made a fortune trading through his fort. The third of the trio, Robert Semple, was a mountain man who looked the part because of his huge size and uncouth appearance. A Kentuckian taken to wearing a coonskin cap with the tail in front, he had been one of the leaders of the American revolt against Mexican authority in California, that comical farce called the Bear Flag Revolt that only turned serious when Frémont took charge. When the gold rush came, Semple declared, "I'd give more for a good coal mine than for all the gold mines in the universe"—but never explained quite what he meant by that.

So, with all the dignity they could muster (and for Semple it was not easy), the native son, the European settler, and the American interloper led the procession of delegates into the room where they all expected to make history.

Gwin thought that the best way for them to make history was first for them to make him president of the convention. But at this moment he got his comeuppance. Jacob Snyder, a Philadelphian who had served under Frémont, is suddenly on the floor challenging Gwin with the various suspicions that had become common knowledge among the delegates. Gwin tries to brush Snyder off by professing his complete innocence. He regards himself as but one delegate from among many, and certainly does not look down upon the pioneer residents of California. Fine, responds Snyder, who had been prepared for this; then certainly Dr. Gwin does not want to be president of this convention. Let the distinguished Dr. Semple be chosen instead. This was a wonderful piece of mischief, for the doctor of coonskins was about as far from Gwin in dignity, experience, and education as the convention could offer. The proposal appealed to the funny bone of the convention, especially because of the cunning with which Snyder had sprung it. So Semple was chosen over Gwin by a large margin. The California constitutional convention, only moments before full of dignity and self-importance, now voted to be led by a joke.

More than a quarter century later, Gwin would still remember this moment with bitterness. Referring to himself characteristically in the third person, he wrote, "So great was their prejudice against him that four-fifths of the members voted for Mr. Semple as president against Mr. Gwin, when the former acknowledged that he had never seen the inside of a legislative hall and knew no more about the rules of proceedings than a child does in learning the ABCs." Semple had been elected, Gwin still thought, simply out of spite, precisely because he was singularly unqualified for the position.

Having received such a rebuff, Butler King might have stormed out of the convention, or have challenged the impudent upstart Snyder to an affair of honor. Gwin, however, knew that he had to take this stupidity in good spirit. Tiresome as it was, Gwin now realized he had to become an apparent democrat. He was as much a Southern gentleman, by temperament and training, as King. Unlike King, however, he realized the difference between when he was on his plantation and when he was not, between when he was among his peers like James Buchanan and Jeff Davis and when he was among half-educated boors like "Captain" Sutter and "Doctor" Semple.

Such were the people Gwin had to deal with, people who needed to be led but who resented to high heaven a real leader. To succeed now, Gwin had to get out of the sun and work from the shadows, however galling that was—and, of course, he had to become a hearty good fellow, one of the boys, more galling still. Let one of the delegates describe the sudden change, the change which they took to mean that Gwin had learned his lesson:

> After the election of Dr. Semple to the Presidency of the Convention, Dr. Gwin subsided completely and took a back seat on the floor and from that time to the end of the Convention was exceedingly conciliatory, presenting his propositions with very much tact and skill and courage and won upon the Convention so much that I think he was in good fellowship with all the delegates. I know this change in his bearing was often remarked among all the delegates.

In general, Gwin was exceedingly conciliatory during the weeks of the convention. When a Mr. Jones in the heat of debate felt obliged to acquaint a Mr. Teft with the remark of Junius, "There are men who never aspire to hatred—who never rise above contempt," Teft responded, "If the gentleman was better acquainted with the works of Junius, he would not make that as a quotation." When Jones further responded, "I am better acquainted with the duties of a gentleman than with the language of Junius," Gwin was one of the delegates who worked hard and successfully to find a way for both gentlemen to save face without resorting to violence.

Nonetheless, Gwin did go out of his way to clash openly with Henry Halleck, Riley's secretary, who was another delegate from Monterey. Presumably, he judged that a little more Riley bashing would do him good with most of the delegates—and Halleck was probably still smarting over Gwin's attacks on his commanding officer. Moreover, Halleck was from New York and was constantly pressing for the New York constitution to be the model for California. Even then, Gwin seemed to have used a young admirer, one convert he had made on the *Frémont,* for the worst of the attacks. James Jones wrote to his mother as if he and Gwin had defeated the professional soldier in a battle. "On this bill we had a rich time. I started the bill, and we riddled it so completely that several of the committee turned. Their ranks once broken, to defeat them was easy. They never rallied afterwards, but concluded to change their course, and leave New York and the electorate labors of Capt. Halleck to their fate."

Beyond clashes with Halleck, Gwin rarely passed up an opportunity to twist Semple into knots, just to show the convention what a mistake it had made. When Semple out of innocent ignorance blithely suggested that acts of the California legislature should supersede those of the U.S. Congress, Gwin attacked this as a "monstrous doctrine" and called for a vote of repudiation, which he won overwhelmingly. Semple then retreated by claiming he had agreed with Gwin all along. Then Gwin, perhaps not even bothering to suppress his smile, graciously apologized to Semple; he had really thought Semple was opposing the proposed amendment. (An apologist for Semple has written, "If he might sometimes lose the thread of argument, he would never lose his composure.")

Through his gracious acceptance of his defeat for the presidency, Gwin was able to secure for himself what might have been in practice a more influential position in the convention, chairman of the committee to draw up the constitution. He also got his newly devoted young friend, J. Ross Browne, appointed as secretary to the convention. To young Browne would fall the task of editing a volume on the historic proceedings. (Somehow the initial exchange between Gwin and Snyder did not make it into the proceedings, although Riley's prior proclamation did.)

During the long, hard work of the convention, Gwin's political dexterity was tested by two difficult issues. The first was slavery. Here Gwin might have been expected to follow his mentor Calhoun, who viewed the West as a region where slavery could be profitably spread, the West thereby helping protect the South in Congress against Northern free labor advocates. So the delegate William Shannon, a captain under Stevenson in the New York

Regiment, introduced his proposal on slavery as if he were spoiling for a fight, a fight that would make Southerners like Gwin finally show their true colors. His provision read, "Neither slavery nor involuntary servitude, unless for the punishment of crimes, shall ever be tolerated in the State."

If Shannon or others expected Gwin to lead an attack on this measure, they very much underestimated his flexibility. However much Gwin might have sympathized with Calhoun's hope for a counterweight to the growing dominance of Northern power, he was not one to sacrifice his own ambition for political principle or sectional interest. So Gwin surprised probably everybody by supporting a ban on slavery in the new state. He forthrightly stated that geography itself had decided against slavery in California; Gwin not only voted for the ban, but also brought with him all of the Southern delegates, including a few like him who actually still owned slaves in their home states.*

The second issue was the establishment of the boundaries for the new state. Here Gwin, once again, had to accept graciously a defeat. He had wished for the convention to declare California to be the whole of the territory won by the United States in the Mexican War. To the argument that the U.S. government would never accept so huge a state, Gwin had an ingenious reply. That was exactly the reason these extended boundaries should be proposed—because Congress would reject them. Then the Congress would be obliged to divide California into a number of states; naturally they would give each a portion of the coast, much as the East Coast was divided among a number of states. Think how much better off the West Coast would be if it was comprised of, say, six states—and thereby had twelve senators looking after its interests.

This argument was too sophisticated by half for the plainspoken delegates at Monterey, a few of whom did not read without difficulty. It required a series of reasonings that wearied them—and when their minds were wearied, they became recalcitrant. They wanted simple solutions, solutions they could understand. And when they were pressed with arguments they did not understand, they became suspicious, even ornery. At times this could be amusing. At one point, for instance, a delegate objected to the proposed section that guaranteed Californians the right to trial by a jury of their peers. He explained, "I don't like that word 'peers,' it ain't republican. I'd like to know what we want with peers in this country—we're not a monarchy, and we've got no House of Parliament, I vote for no such law." At moments like those a California monarchy with a house of lords as its only legislative body might

---

*Years later the Frémonts would claim that their campaigning in Monterey had turned the tide against a Southern proslavery conspiracy; but the Frémonts were nowhere near Monterey during the convention, and Southerners like Gwin—whatever their private sentiments—conspired to allow this ban on slavery if they conspired at all. Equally self-serving was Gwin's later contention that he had come to California "for the express purpose of withdrawing himself and his posterity" from a slave society, believing "as he did then, and as subsequent events have proved, that the institution of slavery would be a curse on the white inhabitants where it prevailed." Gwin, no less than the Frémonts, liked to rewrite history when it seemed advantageous and there was small risk of being contradicted.

not have seemed to Gwin an altogether unreasonable proposition. But there were important things that had to be carefully calculated.

No slavery—that was plain enough. Also apparently unacceptable to Dr. Gwin was an American California that had roughly the boundaries of Mexican California. Why was Dr. Gwin making such a fuss? Later, helped by a little lubrication, some of the delegates would start to wonder what that well-spoken Southern gentleman had been really up to. If the Mexican territory was divided by congress into six states, did it not seem likely that two or three of them would be admitted as Southern states where slavery was legal? Or was the gentleman from Mississippi (who knew the Congress firsthand) really anticipating what a divisive issue slavery might be when the admission of California was debated? Was he concerned about the power of the West Coast in the Senate, or was he really trying to preserve maneuvering room for a compromise that assured the admission of California? A compromise that would also satisfy someone like Calhoun? Of course, they as a group did not know about Calhoun, but some had heard of the slave power conspiracy. And whatever that was exactly, they knew enough to know it should be kept off the Pacific Coast.

These were vague suspicions, which became much elaborated by hindsight. If this was Gwin's plan, he confided it to no one at the convention. (He had already confided more than he should have of his plans on the *Frémont*.) Conspiracy or no, the delegates to the convention had little patience with Gwin when his arguments became too sophisticated—but they were much obliged when he helped clarify things, as he usually did. Even so, they emphatically voted for a California that had as its eastern boundary the Sierra Nevada mountains.

Although slavery and borders were the big issues facing the convention, there were a myriad of lesser ones that taken together would determine the success or failure of the convention. One minor issue was the discussion of dueling. Here Gwin was obviously playing to the delegates by wanting death from dueling to be a homicide. He believed this not at all, but it played well with the delegates, especially with those who suspected him of being "too Southern." He could quiet everyone by telling the terrible tale of his brother's lingering death, or what it was like to live in New Orleans where dueling was a passion. "If you go through the cemetery of New Orleans, you will see the whole earth covered with the tombstones of the victims of honor. It is a wonderful and melancholy sight." But anything this body could do to prevent such a sight being replicated on California soil, Gwin insisted, it should do. The convention voted enthusiastically to have dueling—that destructive, predominantly Southern custom—constitutionally forbidden. William Gwin was already starting to run for the Senate.

With the work of the convention virtually over, a party was thrown. The music—a quartet of two guitars and two violins—was about as good as the coffee at the Fonda de la Union. But no one minded. All the fairest ladies of Monterey attended, including the much admired Dona Augusta Ximeno, who had read both Sir Walter Scott and James Fenimore Cooper and rode a horse better than any American. There were not enough women to go around, but the American frontiersmen were not self-conscious about dancing with one another, however distasteful this was to men like Gwin. Supper was not served until midnight, and it was lavish. These old Californios did know a thing or two about enjoying themselves. The women started to drift away only after two in the morning, but the men with plenty of liquor at hand stayed much later.

The next morning, when the convention was to be called to order for its final session, President Semple was absent. It was reported that he had been unexpectedly taken ill and was so indisposed that he could not make it out of his bed to this historic occasion. His place was taken by Sutter. As the delegates (a few of whom, one might imagine, not looking too good themselves) were formally signing the constitution, a prearranged signal was given, and the American colors were run up the flagstaff, and the local fort began a salute with its cannon. (This was probably Sutter's idea, for he loved to fire off guns in celebration.) And a British ship out of Sydney that happened to be in the harbor joined in the celebration by also running up the American colors. A moving moment, even for those whose heads throbbed. They could congratulate themselves that, as one put it, "a more sensible and dignified body of men never assembled in any portion of the world."

Sutter, like Vallejo and most of the old-timers, had had little to say during the convention; one delegate wrote in slight surprise that he "was a sort of ornamental appendage to the convention without much force, did not carry much weight, and had very little influence." But now he was in his element, the grand arena of the generous gesture. So, as the delegates continued to sign and the cannon continued to boom, Sutter finally could contain himself no more, and jumped up swinging his right hand about his head. "Gentlemen, this is the happiest day of my life. It makes me glad to hear those cannon; they remind me of the time when I was a soldier. Yes, I am glad to hear them. This is a great day for California!" Then, overcome, he burst into tears. The delegates spontaneously gave him three cheers. Then the cannon stopped at thirty-one, for California was to be the thirty-first state of the Union. The delegates understood, and some shouted, "That's for California." Then all cheered again, now three times three.

His work here finished, Gwin hurried back to San Francisco to start his campaign for the Senate. Others who witnessed the convention and participated in it lingered in Monterey to savor what they had seen. Two of these were J. Ross Browne and a new friend of his, Bayard Taylor. Taylor was almost as young as Browne, but already much more accomplished. He was an aspiring poet whose first volumes had contained odes to the promise of California; he had also already turned an account of his tramping around Europe into a best-seller. Leaving his beloved fiancée behind in Pennsylvania,

Taylor had set out to see the El Dorado of California, and had arrived on the *Panama,* on the trip after the one that had deposited Gwin.

Taylor was not looking for gold, or for political power. He was looking for heroes, and adventure, and inspiration. He would never quite fulfill his talent as an original poet, but he would be credited with having made the best translation of Goethe's *Faust* into English. And when he returned in 1850 to Pennsylvania, he found his fiancée within a few months of death from tuberculosis—and that left him permanently a wanderer, one of the greatest travelers of his age, always ready with his pen.

When Taylor heard of the constitutional convention, he knew this was something he had to observe. He had no delusions about the rude life of Monterey, especially after a few nights of little sleep because of the fleas. The party of celebration he thought wonderful, and stayed till three. But the process of the convention itself left him awestruck. He had been present at the creation, had seen the emergence of a new order. He knew that the convention had frequently stumbled, and occasionally blundered. But what they had achieved was astonishing, and as he sat in the visitors' gallery in his corduroy suit and purple flannel shirt he tried himself, as a writer, to rise to the occasion. He asked the question, "Where was ever such harmony evolved out of so wonderful, so dangerous, so magnificent a chaos?" In answering it, he sought to provide for the convention its peroration:

> The elements of which the Convention was composed were no less various, and in some respects antagonistic, than those combined in the mining population. The questions that they had to settle were often perplexing, from the remarkable position of the country and the absence of all precedent. Besides, many of them were men unused to legislation. Some had for years past known no other life than that of the mining camp; others had nearly forgotten all law in the wild life of the mountains; others again were familiar only with that practiced under the rule of a different race. Yet the courtesies of debate were never wantonly violated, and the result of every conflict has been the quiet acquiescence on the part of the minority. Now, at the conclusion, the only feeling is that of general joy and congratulation.

Now, too, Taylor was beginning to feel the eloquence flow, and he continued:

> Thus we have another splendid example of the ease and security with which people can be educated to govern themselves. From that chaos whence . . . would spring the most frightful excesses of anarchy and crime, a population of freemen peacefully and quietly develops the highest form of civil or-

der—the broadest extent of liberty and security. Governments, bad and corrupt as many of them are, and imperfect as they all must necessarily be, nevertheless at times exhibit scenes of true moral sublimity. What I have witnessed today has so impressed me; and were I a believer in omens, I would augur from the tranquil beauty of this evening—from the clear sky and the lovely sunset hues on the waters of the bay—more than all, from the joyous expression of every face I see—a glorious and prosperous career for the State of California!

Now that the convention was over, Browne and Taylor were going to have some fun by just tramping about Monterey. Taylor had fallen in love with the colors of the Pacific at sunset; these were skies for Titian to paint, and he felt at times so surrounded by the color that he felt he was floating in a hollow sphere of prismatic crystal. But now with Browne he could examine the more tangible earth. So they made their way through mazes of cypress and pine, through the bleak sandhills piled like snowdrifts, to reach finally a bare tongue of land sticking out into the sea. Taylor was attracted to the Indian myth that told of how the long southern portion of San Francisco bay was once connected to the sea through Monterey, until the land closed it off somehow. On this point Taylor could see that the civil war between gray rock and white-blue surf still continued:

> The extremity of the point is a mass of gray rock, worn by the surf into fantastic walls and turrets. The heavy swells of the open sea, striking their bases with tremendous force, fill the crevices with foaming spray, which pours off in a hundred cataracts as the wave draws back for another shock. In the narrow channels between the rocks the pent waters roll inland with great force, flooding point after point and flinging high into the air the purple flags and streamers of seaweed, till they reach the glassy, sheltered pools that are quietly filled and emptied with every pulsation of the great sea without.

This was a bleak little world; it was hard to imagine it ever evolving into an order. These sheltered pools pulsated with life, nature at its most profligate. Mussels, barnacles, the predatory starfish, the single-shelled abalone, and polyps of every sort and size and color, myriads of scuttling small crabs and crawling snails going about their business. The place was busier than the docks of San Francisco, and even less comprehensible, and all the more beautiful for that. Browne showed Taylor that the abalone and orange-fleshed mussels made good eating, and the inside of the abalone shell was iridescent like mother-of-pearl. Throughout the meal, the sea gulls swooped and cawed. And on the way back Browne and Taylor stumbled onto a pack of wolves devouring a large fish of some kind, perhaps even a whale, that had been beached, without benefit presumably of a trial by its peers. A pack of wolves gorging itself on a large beached fish—if Taylor had believed in omens, he could have done worse than to meditate upon this one. But it was life, not death, he was celebrating. The twisted pine trees of Monterey looked as if they had been tortured to death by the wind, and yet the puddles of fog-drip that collected beneath them were yellow-rimmed with their pollen. All throbbed with life here, striving to be part of some higher order yet unborn, as California itself seemed to be now striving to become part of that other higher order, the American Union.

When Taylor made it back to San Francisco, he was stunned by the changes of just a few weeks, and not simply the physical growth. There was partisan politics in the air. The new state constitution had to be ratified, and a state legislature selected. The latter then would elect the first senators from California. Three candidates were being mentioned prominently. Colonel Frémont, of course. He was holding court in his handsome house in a section of San Francisco called Happy Valley, half a mile from the center. California was already making Frémont quite rich, and he had bought a prefabricated Chinese house and had Cantonese carpenters put it together for him on one of his choice lots. Taylor visited him there, and happily confirmed his prejudgment that this was a great man.

Whigs, however, still favored for the Senate the president's man, Thomas Butler King. King himself had been convalescing from a recent illness, and was said to be in Sonoma, just to the north of San Francisco, either canvassing or further convalescing. (Taylor was not altogether sure which.) His Whig friends tried to hold a rally on his behalf on Portsmouth Square but to little effect—a bad sign for his candidacy.

The third candidate being mentioned was Dr. Gwin, a Southerner. He alone of the candidates had been active in the convention, although Taylor had scarcely noticed him, his attention having been distracted by the many more colorful characters there. He noticed him now by both his growing reputation and his absence. And Taylor seemed somewhat surprised to learn that rather than resting after those constitutional exertions, Gwin had immediately outfitted himself, and was off campaigning in the mining districts. His objective was ostensibly to make sure the constitution passed, but he also would incidentally have the opportunity to support appropriate candidates for the legislature, namely those who in turn would support him for senator. That was clear enough, but Taylor did not quite approve. He was annoyed at how quickly partisan politics had supplanted the universalizing spirit of the constitutional convention, or what he had interpreted as such.

Taylor now wanted to follow Gwin toward the mining districts. First, however, he delayed to make some money. Mail had not arrived for three months from the East. When it did, the post office was besieged. Taylor gave the beleaguered postmaster a hand in helping sort the mail, which took all night. Then they had to confront the crowds that had been lining up. Men were spending five or six hours in line just to announce their names at the desk to see if they had anything. As always, the enterprising found a way to profit from the situation. They would stand in line until they got close to the front, and then auction off their place to the highest bidder. Such entrepreneurs made more money than the postmasters and his assistants combined. Ah, California! Its universalizing spirit was becoming particularized in disturbing ways.

When Taylor finally did set out, he was far enough behind Gwin that he would never catch up, if that was what he intended. He would get glimpses of this election in a few of the mining camps. In one a leading candidate had almost lost because he had shown up at the meeting in a top hat; as serious as this election was for people like Gwin, the prospectors seemed to approach it with something like whimsy, much as the delegates had the election of the president at the convention. In one camp a philosophical dispute developed over whether you should vote only for candidates you knew personally. One prospector contended contrarily that you should vote only for candidates you did not know—that was what he was going to do. "When I left home, I was determined to go it blind. I went it blind in coming to California, and I am not going to stop now. I voted for the Constitution, and I've never seen the Constitution. I voted for all the candidates, and I don't know a damned one of them. I'm going it blind all through, I am."

Taylor must have wished that he had seen the elegant Gwin trying to solicit this man's vote. What he could not have realized was that this man epitomized Gwin's view of the electorate. In a democracy the electorate is always going it blind; the art of politics is to lead the blind so that they do not fall into a pit and pull you in after.

During the constitutional convention, beyond ingratiating himself with all the other delegates, Gwin had been campaigning for the Senate in a subtler way, which he would also have used on prospective members of the state legislature. He painted a not altogether inaccurate portrait of the Congress as dominated by their Southern delegations. They had to be effectively addressed if California was to be admitted into the Union as a state. And Californians, whatever their sectional loyalties, had to see that admission was paramount to every other consideration. There were corollaries to this that Gwin may or may not have expressed. The election of Frémont, outspoken abolitionist that he was, could scarcely be worse in the harm that it would do to the chances for admission, to say nothing of the antislavery plank in the constitution; since many thought this election of Frémont was inevitable, California had to use its second seat to assure admission. That meant electing a Southerner who could get the job done.

The constitutional convention had finished its work in October. The constitution itself was overwhelmingly ratified by a plebiscite in November; since that approval was a foregone conclusion, also elected were a state government and a two-man delegation to the House of Representatives. In December the newly elected state legislature met in San Jose, the new state capital; and its first order of business was to select the first two senators from the state of California. The choice of the first was obviously going to be the dashing John C. Frémont, hero of the American conquest. He was elected on the first ballot. Gwin had numerous rivals for the second seat, including the old blusterer Butler King. But, to the shock of some, Gwin was elected on the third ballot, by a single vote.

Elisha Oscar Crosby, who had been one of the delegates to the Monterey constitutional convention most offended by Gwin's haughty behavior in the early days, years later still remembered his response to someone who asked how he as a Northerner could vote for Gwin:

> I was asked why I favored Gwin. I said he was an extreme southern man, a most persevering and persistent man and was bound and determined to get into the Senate and he could do it by the admission of the State and he would doubtlessly work earnestly for the admission of the State and carry a good deal of influence in that direction, and I should therefore vote for him, believing that all the other matters before the Legislature were insignificant compared to the question of admission to the Union.

Crosby added that he voted for him and prayed that he would get the short term so that "he would be there only a few months and we could then send someone else." Crosby had not counted on Gwin's own incredible run of luck, which continued. When they drew straws, Frémont got the short for a two-year term, and Gwin the long for a full six years.

William Gwin left San Francisco on January 1, 1850, for the long voyage back to Washington. The steamship *Oregon* was also carrying approximately 3 million dollars' worth of gold as ballast. It stopped at Monterey where Senator-elect Frémont gallantly carried on board his indisposed wife, a most affecting scene. (Bayard Taylor, by the way, was also leaving San Francisco at almost exactly the same time; but he with characteristically romantic gusto decided to take a mail packet to Mazatlán so he could have the additional adventure of crossing Mexico by land, a decision that almost cost him his life.)

The trip of the two aspiring senators was comparatively uneventful—down the California coast and beyond, the crossing of Panama from west to east, and then a fast steamship to New Orleans. The difference in Gwin's station now (from the last time he was in New Orleans, in particular) might have been the occasion for smug reflection, and for pleasurable anticipation of his return to Washington itself. Nonetheless, this journey provided him with the opportunity to do, at his leisure, something extremely important. He had to take the measure of John C. Frémont.

Most Californians revered Frémont as an instrument of almighty providence. His politics, at least from Gwin's point of view, were extreme— extreme harshness in the treatment of Indians (whom he liked to hunt as sport) and of Mexican Californians (three of whom had been murdered in cold blood on Frémont's order). More troublesome for Gwin was Frémont's outspoken abolitionism. In Gwin's judgment Frémont's hypocrisy was typical of the abolitionist; kill Indians and Mexicans without a qualm, but then become sentimental about slaves who as valuable property were probably treated reasonably well, better than New York wage laborers for sure. That such a man was his fellow senator was potentially more than a little troublesome.

So Gwin drew Frémont out with polite questions during their long time together, much as he had earlier drawn out Thomas Butler King. He knew the wife already. She was a formidable presence who understood how to get her way. More important, she was already well established in Washington, for she was the favored daughter of Senator Thomas Hart Benton. There had been delicious gossip—delicious to those who cared about such things— when the teenaged Jessie eloped with the dashing Frémont against her father's wishes. But that breach had long since been healed. Gwin knew how much could be accomplished in Washington through the right kind of entertaining. Jessie Frémont was going to be a great asset to her husband.

Not that he could have felt at all worried about his own wife's measuring up. As one of his contemporaries wrote of Mary Gwin, "His wife was exactly the mate for such a man; fashionable, liberal, dashing, generous and full of Southern partialities. Their house was as hospitable as plenty of money and pleasant people could make it." What this observer did not think he needed to add was that Mary Gwin, while a remarkably charming hostess, was also dazzlingly beautiful—and would still be turning heads when she entered a room in her late sixties. Mary Gwin would more than hold her own with the younger, more temperamental woman.

How much of a challenge was the husband going to present? On the long voyage there was plenty of opportunity to get to know Frémont, without appearing to be trying. And, after all, they were going to be working together for the next two years and almost certainly longer. Gwin found, without particular surprise, that few things were less difficult than to get John C. Frémont to talk about himself. Gwin, of course, would not have been passive; with polite curiosity he would raise the questions that many others did at the time—about the inconsistencies, the implausibities, and the self-serving omissions in the official Frémont account of his adventures.

Frémont especially liked to talk about his role in the American rebellion in California at the beginning of the Mexican War. He claimed authorization for his initiative from the president himself, although as near as Gwin and others could tell he had no documentary evidence to support this claim. No one was likely to question, however, an action that had been so completely successful. On the other hand, Frémont was a bit defensive about his most recent exploratory expedition, the one he had been on just before Gwin and Jessie had arrived in San Francisco. Well he might have been, for he had lost fully one-third of his men to starvation and exposure in this ill-advised attempt to try to find a southern route across the Rocky Mountains in the dead of the worst winter in living memory. (There were even rumors that some survived only by resorting to cannibalism—Frémont's own little Donner party.) To hear Frémont tell it, however, all the troubles were the fault of the mountain man guide, "Old Bill" Williams, who was now past defending himself because he had recently been killed by Indians. To hear Frémont tell it, the results of the expedition were also, as he later would write, "entirely satisfactory" because despite having to turn back he was still convinced that he had found the best southern route for a transcontinental railroad. He just hadn't made it all the way across. Apparently, a hero like Frémont simply could not fail, every failure being a success misunderstood by lesser spirits. And he was perhaps right in that, given the way people fawned all over him, no matter what.

Yet this made a peculiarity about Frémont even odder, odd almost to the point of making him appear unstable, somewhat deranged. Here was a man whose lifetime of luck made Gwin's recent remarkable run look like small potatoes. He had come from nowhere to marry the daughter of one of the most powerful men in America. He had led exploratory expeditions that had made him a revered celebrity. John Greenleaf Whittier, for goodness' sake, had celebrated one of his returns in poetry in stanzas like:

> Still upward turned, with anxious strain
> Their leader's sleepless eye,
> Where splinters of the mountain chain
> Stood black against the sky.

When he returned to California, he did not have to bother himself with the hard work of politics, for a Senate seat already had his name carved into it. So he went to the Mexican land grant that he had bought earlier sight unseen; it turned out that it was riddled with gold deposits. Now the question was whether John C. Frémont was one of the wealthiest men in California or the United States or the whole world. The Mariposa grant, some said, could be worth a hundred million dollars. All this, like out of a fairy tale in which he is Prince Charming, St. George, and King Midas all in one. And yet what did one hear when listening to him at length? A litany of complaint and resentment that his wife only fueled by her bitterly angry interjections.

Amazingly, the man and his wife seemed to remember—no, to still brood upon—every slight or criticism, real or imagined, that he had ever received. There was that silly dispute with the military commander of California immediately after the Mexican War concluded. What was his name? Kearny, the one after whom the street in San Francisco was christened. Frémont petulantly had insisted on a full Washington court-martial in order to clear himself—and then the court-martial had convicted him for the simple reason that he was obviously guilty. And Frémont and his wife were still able to recount the events of this trial almost minute by minute, for each minute revealed to them a new betrayal, a new snub to his greatness.

Gwin must have expected Frémont, from the little he had seen him before, to be as vain as a peacock. And he could not have been surprised to discover that he was full of a deluded sense of personal destiny. It was a bit surprising that he was not very intelligent, but in public life a certain audacity and good luck can effectively serve the place of true ability. And Frémont certainly had more than his share of those. But it was a wonderment how all this came together in Frémont to produce an indisputable and apparently irremediable self-destructive streak. A true wonderment.

Frémont may have been Gwin's chief object of study during the long voyage, but he was not the only one. There was on board a young lieutenant who had been at the constitutional convention as an observer for General Riley. Gaunt with reddish hair, William Tecumseh Sherman seemed old before his time. Once drawn out, however, he was as irresistible as a good sour pickle. Sherman was a consistent source of amusingly terse assessments of his own encounters in California. He had found Frémont's fabled henchman Kit Carson almost moronic—smallish, with soft eyes and light greasy hair and a face with almost as many lines as freckles, Carson seemed incapable of anything more than monosyllabic answers to questions, and incapable as well of initiating conversation worthy of the name. As for Carson's vaunted leader, the now Senator Frémont, Sherman had his own private views. He had sought him out in 1847 when he still had hope of seeing some real action in California; he had spent an afternoon with Colonel Frémont, having tea—God help us!—with him in his tent; he had left "without being much impressed."

It was unusual for such a young man to have so perfect a contempt for all humbug, and also to have such a good nose for it. Sherman's response to the constitutional convention was refreshingly different from the sentimental gushing of men like Sutter and Semple. To Sherman's cold eye the only interesting issue had been slavery. He had been mildly surprised that the Southerners (who he could see perfectly well had controlled the convention) had not pushed at all on this. Of course, that would have caused an uproar in Washington, perhaps have led even to secession and civil war—then, at least, Lieutenant William Tecumseh Sherman might have had a further opportunity to practice his profession. As it was, the young man, when discussing his own prospects, was quite glum. He lamented his fate at having to spend the last years so remote from the war in Mexico, where his comrades had been reaping large honors while he enjoyed what he called the "absolute repose" of California. Of course, he had had his little adventures there; he had kidnapped the Sonoma alcalde at gunpoint and brought him all the way to Monterey because he had defied the American military authorities; he with only three men had also taken twenty-four deserters who were making their way to mines. (The deserters could not believe he would charge them without a much larger force in the rear.) But now his military career was coming to an end; and, apart from having chased Seminoles for a few years all over Florida, he had seen no action to speak of. (The government, by the way, should have left them alone; Florida was a perfect heaven for the red man, and worthless to the white.)

Compared to Frémont, Sherman was a delightful companion. Gwin, the older and more experienced man, could sympathize bemusedly with Sherman's premature world-weariness, so perceptive in its way. But when he learned that Sherman was returning to marry the daughter of a cabinet officer, and that he had friends who wanted him to help them set up a bank in California, he might well have decided that this young man of preternatural shrewdness and (despite what he protested) excellent prospects would well bear watching. Somewhere down the line he might be useful—if not to Gwin, then surely to someone else.

Frémont was Gwin's chief rival for political preeminence—and yet, despite all of his obvious advantages, he was not going to be a worthy adversary. Not that Gwin was inclined to complain. What happened in New Orleans was in its own way typical of how easy it was probably going to be to outmaneuver this celebrated Pathfinder. Frémont himself had gotten a good taste of fever in Panama, and a leg that had been badly frostbitten during his last expedition was acting up. Now Jesse Frémont took ill, how seriously was hard to say, but she'd been complaining throughout the trip. Perhaps her fits were real. But John Frémont's worries soon hardened into a conviction that he should stay by his wife's bedside, and she did nothing to dissuade her hero. And Gwin could only look sternly concerned, and do his little bit to encourage their caution.

So William Gwin was permitted to arrive in Washington as the undisputed head of the California delegation. Gwin would quickly establish himself as the almighty providence of California, while Frémont—once he did arrive with his recovered or recovering wife—would be its inconsequential afterthought, and never quite understand how it had fallen out this way.

Now Gwin returned to his Washington, the world he loved. This Washington was obviously a Southern city. Of the forty thousand inhabitants fully ten thousand were classed as colored. There were some attempts not to offend Northern sensibilities. For instance, no longer were there slave pens right behind the Smithsonian Institution.

It had been fashionable for Europeans during Gwin's earlier stays in Washington—as Jackson's private secretary and then as congressman—to ridicule the unrealized grandeur of the American capital. So many had called it "the city of magnificent distances," it was hard to know who coined this dismissive phrase—but one visitor felt obliged to improve on it lest the point be missed, "a city of magnificent distances with barren tracts and swampy morasses between them." The Englishman Frederick Marryat, who was right now writing a winningly sympathetic account of the California gold rush, superciliously compared Washington to "a general without an army, only surrounded and followed by a parcel of ragged little dirty boys." "A rich architectural joke," another wrote, "a boasting straggling, raw uncomfortable failure of infinite pretension in plan."

The Congress in the late 1840s finally had begun to make the necessary appropriations. Perhaps Gwin in 1849 during his conversations with Stephen Douglas had learned of congressional plans for massive building projects—two new wings and a new dome for the Capitol, for instance, and the oft-proposed but long-postponed monument to Washington on the great Mall. Returning in 1850, he would have seen no evidence of progress. The District of Columbia remained an uncomfortable place to live, with a bad water supply and not even adequate street lighting. But the plans were there, and the appropriations were starting to come.

Gwin just wanted to be one of those deciding on the appropriations. Only the admission of California as a state was required for him to become truly, fully, and undeniably a member of America's governing elite, the U.S. Senate—the long dark coats, the tall silk hats, the quill pens, and the two large snuff boxes placed near the vice president's desk and heavily used. And the elegantly dressed ladies filling the gallery whenever a great debate was anticipated. Even those senators who violated its decorum somehow still contributed to its sense of being the greatest senate since Rome. There was, for instance, the old Texas barbarian Sam Houston, sitting at his desk in his panther-skin waistcoat and whittling away on a piece of wood, with all the aplomb of someone who had been recently leading legions through Gaul or the forests of Germania.

Gwin shepherded the two California congressmen around the city, paying calls of courtesy to the major figures in Washington—the president, of course, and Vice President Millard Fillmore; the chief justice and other justices of the Supreme Court; the Speaker of the House of Representatives. Gwin could joke offhandedly to the aspiring new members of this body that the House was not highly regarded in Washington, as its nickname indicated: the Cave of the Winds. In that mammoth cave, it was said, men could speak in all parts and be understood in none. (The representatives had recently taken sixty-three ballots to elect the present Speaker, and would still be voting if by parliamentary sleight of hand they had not declared a simple plurality would this time be sufficient for election.)

But then there was the true ruling body. Gwin took the delegation to meet the titans of the Senate: Calhoun, Clay, Webster, Benton, and, of course, Gwin's dear friend Douglas. Stephen A. Douglas would be the one whom Gwin had chosen to present his credentials to the Senate; from Douglas they could hear the story of Gwin's prediction of his own return as senator from California.

Of all the dignitaries on whom they called, only one turned them away without an audience. Calhoun, they were told, was too weak to receive them. But later Calhoun asked to see Gwin alone. And Gwin would later record his memory of this encounter with care.

Perhaps Gwin expected to be congratulated by his old mentor. Calhoun, however, had graver matters on his mind. First, he mildly reproached Gwin for his role in the constitutional convention of California, and Gwin responded softly that Calhoun himself was responsible for inspiring Gwin to seek his political fortunes in California. Once there, he had just done what he had to do to achieve power. This open opportunism from someone he had respected, even groomed, seemed to rouse Calhoun, and his voice became hollow but deep toned, like a prophet's. He declared that the admission of California would destroy the equilibrium between North and South in the Senate, and that this would remove the only protection the South had against domination by the North, and that this would result in increased agitation against slavery, and that this in turn would lead to civil war, and that in this war the South would be destroyed, and that afterward no minority would have protection against the despotic majority—and so the American government, although republican in name, would with the blood of the South on its hands quickly become the most despotic of any in the civilized world.

This was the vatic vehemence of an obviously dying man. Gwin's own sights were not set so far into the future. He first had to become a member of the Senate, and that was almost in his grasp; then he wished to become a senator among senators, as the triumvirate of Webster, Clay, and Calhoun had been in their generation. Make no mistake about it, the timing seemed perfect. The debate over California would be this triumvirate's last great moment, and everyone understood this, including the men themselves. Who would succeed them in the stern effort required to keep this nation together and progressing? Stephen Douglas of Illinois, surely, as the voice of the growing Northwest—and perhaps for the Northeast an amiable radical like William Seward of New York. And on the Southern side, almost certainly Jefferson Davis. Might there not be room for a fourth? As chief spokesman for the aspiring new state of California and for the Pacific Coast more generally, Gwin would have ample opportunity to prove his worthiness, especially as a senator who could speak to both North and South.

However, first things first—and first California had to be admitted into the Union as the thirty-first star. As Gwin traveled out from California, he must have hoped this would be a simple matter. The representatives of the people of California had settled the disputed question of slavery for themselves. The South should respect that on the grounds of popular sovereignty. But Gwin's interview with Calhoun had shown him that admission was not going to be so simple.

Moreover, by the time Gwin returned to Washington, Zachary Taylor's administration, after less than a year in office, was already on the verge of collapse, at least according to the observers Gwin would have trusted. Old Rough and Ready had turned out to be old, all right, and also roughly ready to be put out to pasture. Horace Greeley was expressing the opinion of many—but in his own distinctive idiom—when he wrote to a confidante, "Old Zack is a good old soul but don't know himself from a side of sole leather in the way of statesmanship." One close to the administration wrote to a friend near the time Gwin was leaving California, "Unless General Taylor rouses himself and shows he has a will of his own and intelligence enough to carry it into effect, his Administration will soon be a heap of shapeless ruins."

No help was to be expected from Taylor's cabinet, which was so undistinguished, it was said, that it might have been chosen by a game of blindman's bluff at a party of Whig notables. Taylor had himself become the butt of jokes for his plain, often ungrammatical utterances ("be them Democrats and be them Whigs"); and when his speeches on occasion became more studied in their prose, he was then ridiculed for reading something he neither had written nor could understand. Here was a fake giant who had surrounded himself with real pygmies.

Taylor himself seemed perplexed by all the nastiness and contention. He had expected the Congress to be pleased when he eschewed the coercive use of his power of veto, and not to take it as a sign of stupidity and weakness. He thought they would then respect his wishes when he exhorted them to avoid "exciting topics of sectional character." He believed that the questions of the territories gained by the Mexican War would resolve themselves if left to themselves. California was a case in point; it had organized itself, and now petitioned for admission into the Union with a constitution that outlawed slavery. So California could be admitted without raising topics that would excite sectional passions. Taylor could not understand why he was consequently derided for a "no action plan." It was a patience plan, and he was commander in chief, wasn't he?

Taylor was strongly supported by Thomas Hart Benton of Missouri and William Seward of New York. What Taylor failed to appreciate was that sectional interests had already been aroused and that Benton and Seward supported him in part because admission of California as a free state would be a defeat pure and simple for the Southern section. Gwin was more than familiar with sectional rivalry and posturing. But in his absence of little more than a year sectionalism had begun to take on a life of its own.

The cotton market had temporarily collapsed because of oversupply; and that left Southern sectional leaders even more sensitive to the economic dominance of the North. To make matters worse, Northern agitators chose rather to focus attention on slavery. Daniel Webster himself, representing Massachusetts but usually speaking for the whole Northeast, had said that the issue of slavery "has arrested the religious feeling of the country; it has taken a strong hold on the consciences of men." To many a Southerner such a pronouncement exemplified the puritanical pharisaism of the Northeast in which conscience marched to the beat of economic interest. One popular Southern writer of the time had said that Massachusetts "by her lust . . . had engendered a disease which by her quackery she had turned into a cancer." To which the abolitionist would easily reply it was slavery that was the cancer and it had to excised at any risk. To which the Southerner would reply that he was not going to be coerced into a needless operation by a self-righteous quack.

Such violently expressed recriminations had for a long time been commonplace in the country; but what shocked Gwin was that they were now finding their way onto the floor of the Senate—and indeed, threatening to drive reasonable discourse out. An extreme instance is what happened with Thomas Hart Benton, Jessie Frémont's father, on the very floor of the Senate. Benton had been exhorted to make peace with the proslavery faction of his own Missouri Democratic Party, but had vehemently refused. "I would sooner sit in council with the six thousand dead who have died of cholera in St. Louis than go into convention with such a gang of scamps." The gang of scamps had returned the favor by defeating him for reelection; so he was now a lame duck, sitting in his final session as senator from Missouri. On the floor the Southern senators, especially Senator Henry S. Foote from Mississippi, baited him mercilessly. Foote was as much a Jacksonian and Unionist as Benton—but that made him all the more bitter against Benton as a border state Democrat who was betraying the South over slavery. Benton had been trying largely to ignore Foote's jabs, but then the senator from Mississippi began to speak ostensibly of his own pure motives in opposing the admission of California. "Well, sir, I at least may hereafter prove perfect disinterestedness of motive in regard to this curious affair, having no father, brother, or son-in-law to be specially benefitted by the result of this effort to drag California into the Union before her wedding garment has been cast about her person." Amazingly, Foote had managed to insinuate even Jessie's scandalous elopement into the debate over California—and Benton, not surprisingly, had decided this was a low blow. He asked rhetorically, "Can I take a cudgel to him here?" Subsequently, he decided he could, and charged Foote. Foote ran away, but only to have time to pull out a concealed pistol. Whirling with the now-cocked pistol, he was ready to make his stand. By this time, however, Benton had been grabbed by his colleagues, who were pulling him away while he shouted, "Let him fire! Stand out of the way and let the assassin fire!"*

---

*Despite the unseemly aftermath, Foote, in arguing during this speech that his own opposition to admission was based on principle, not only insulted Benton and family, but also offered a handsome little

A committee subsequently appointed to investigate the incident had nothing to recommend in the end because this incident was entirely unprecedented. What can one conclude from a unique event? In fact, there had been in that very session a similar incident in the Cave of the Winds; sectional violence almost broke out between two members with shouts of "Shoot him! Shoot him!" and "Where's your bowie knife?" coming from their fellow legislators.

In such a volatile situation a "no action" policy was clearly impossible. Gwin knew that Calhoun, revered in the South as the moral and intellectual colossus of the age, would carry with him most of the Southern senators. If Benton and Seward managed to ram through the admission of California, then fire-eaters like Jefferson Davis were prepared to insist that the North and the South part peaceably like the patriarchs of old. Here Calhoun's own failing health was a concern. As someone was quoted in the New York Tribune as saying, "The wild steed of Disunion which he has been training can only be managed by himself."

President Taylor's occasional irascible pronouncements that he would treat secessionists the way he treated deserters during the late war—namely, shoot them—did not help soothe matters. Nor did his claim that he could bring the South to its knees by a simple naval blockade. Not finding subtleties of politics congenial, General Taylor was showing a distressing hankering to settle matters once and for all, with a few orders as commander in chief.

Gwin knew where he wanted to be when this situation deteriorated, as seemed inevitable: he wanted to be somewhere else. He had no official role to play in the deliberations, and it was best if he keep his options as open as possible. So he tried to wait out the contest in New York City, but the ploy did not work. He was recalled to Washington by Henry Clay.

The great Whig statesman, now in his seventies, had been returned to the Senate by Kentucky after an absence of six years. He might have been expected to support General Taylor, his fellow Whig. But Taylor, from Clay's perspective, was no true Whig; not only had he never held public office, he had—Taylor himself impolitically once admitted—never so much as voted. He was as qualified to be president of the United States as Semple had been to be president of the California constitutional convention.

In contrast, Gwin and Clay were brothers under the skin—or perhaps nephew and uncle, for Gwin was an aspiring Clay in training. He would be to Clay what Jeff Davis was to Calhoun. No better statement of Gwin's pragmatic political philosophy could be found than Clay's famous dictum: "Life itself is but compromise. . . . All legislation, all government, all society is formed upon the principle of mutual concession, politeness, comity, courtesy; upon them, everything is based. . . . Compromises have this recom-

tribute to Gwin. There was no one he welcomed more warmly as a colleague in the Senate, no one by ability or temperament more fit to serve in this august body, than William McKendree Gwin. Foote personally regretted that he had to vote against admission.

mendation, that if you concede anything, you have something conceded to you in return."

When Gwin had taken the California delegation to see Clay, the Great Pacificator had assured them that California would be quickly admitted as a state with his own unqualified support. There were other knottier problems having to do with the conquered Mexican territories (the boundaries of Texas, for instance), but the California issue Clay thought straightforward, thanks to the California constitution for which Gwin himself could take a good deal of credit.

However, the same divisiveness that had chased Gwin to New York had now led Clay to have second thoughts. He told Gwin that since they last talked he had been attended by numerous men from the South. He no longer thought that California could be admitted except in conjunction with other measures that would be concessions to the South. He had never felt the Union to be more at risk than it was right now.

Gwin knew enough not to take this at its face. Clay might really think Taylor did not have enough votes. But Clay might also have decided that possible secession was too great a price to pay for prompt admission of California. He might also have been spoiling for an opportunity to wrest control of the Whig Party from the undeserving usurper Zachary Taylor. Now almost as frail as Calhoun, he might also have been hoping for one last, crowning achievement for his career—and what could be a better climax for the Great Pacificator of the American Republic than a comprehensive measure that would settle the issue of slavery once and for all? All of these were probably true in one degree or another, even though they were not altogether consistent. Gwin knew better than to try to sort out mixed motives in Clay's complex compromises, any more than he would try to find flaws in Calhoun's relentless syllogisms.

Clay informed Gwin that he was putting together an omnibus bill in which the admission of California would be only part of the package. He likely then outlined for Gwin the seven other provisions that were going to be included in the bill. First, territorial governments were to be set up in the rest of the conquered Mexican territory without any prejudgment on the issue of slavery. This would have the probable effect, although Clay did not need to concede this, of having slavery excluded from these territories, much as it had been in California. Second, Texas was to retain its present western borders, and not be permitted to expand to the west to swallow New Mexico as some Texans hoped. In other words, there would be no extension of slavery through the Texan backdoor. Third, to mollify the Texans for this (to buy them off?), the federal government would assume the public debt of Texas. Fourth, slaves should no longer be imported into the District of Columbia for sale or trade. Fifth, to mollify those offended by the fourth measure, slavery should never be abolished in the District of Columbia without the consent of the people and without a fair compensation of slave owners.

Sixth, Congress would formally declare it had no right to interfere with the interstate slave trade (as it just had interfered with the slave trade between the states and the District of Columbia). Finally, the South, having been in effect cut off from the West, would be given something it had long wanted, a stronger fugitive slave bill, a federal weapon to fight against the underground railroad that was being supported by Northern abolitionists.

This was the pragmatic Clay at his best and worst. He was, in effect, preventing the spread of slavery in the West and weakening it in the District of Columbia, while strengthening its position in the rest of the nation. In this complex measure there was something for everyone to cheer, and something else for everyone to denounce.

The practical politics were not hard to predict. Calhoun and those who followed him would be unyielding, and reject the whole bill because of the provisions that restricted slavery, which they would declare unconstitutional. Clay and his moderates, mostly from the border states and the old Northwest, would support it because half a loaf was better than none at all. The key in the vote would be the antislavery Northeast. Radicals like Seward of New York would almost certainly oppose the measure, with moral reasonings as unyielding as Calhoun's constitutional disquisitions. If, however, Daniel Webster could be persuaded to support the measure, he could bring enough votes with him to give the bill a good chance for passage.

How much of all this Clay discussed with Gwin is unknown. He did feel obliged as a gentleman to inform Gwin privately of his general change of position. He was informing Gwin out of courtesy, but implicitly was hoping for his support. To Clay's surprise and delight, Gwin gave it immediately. While Clay played the role of the Great Pacificator in public view, Gwin was happy to play the role of a little pacificator behind the scenes.

Part of Gwin's own mixed motives was indicated by what they talked about next. Clay said he felt he now had to inform Senator Benton, and presumably through him Senator-elect Frémont. Benton had been Clay's enemy for years, never trusting the more pliant Kentuckian. (Part of the tension may have been conflicting ambitions, for each had expected to be sooner or later the presidential nominee of his party, Benton as a successor to Jackson and Clay as the leading Whig acceptable to the South.) But the California question had brought them together, and so finally Clay had been able to count at least as an ally a fellow senator he had so long admired, even when they were completely opposed on other particular issues. He worried about the irascible Benton's reaction when he told him of this adjustment in his position. Clay, of course, knew that this would make both Benton and his son-in-law Frémont his enemies; Gwin, of course, knew that this would make his own response seem more statesmanlike, more worthily senatorial.

Gwin, after this interview, quickly retreated back to New York, diplomatically to stay as much as possible out of the line of fire. This withdrawal to New York required considerable self-discipline for Gwin, for the debate over Clay's compromise was one of those last moments of an era that everyone at the time fully recognizes as such. Watching Clay, Calhoun, and Webster, no one would have been surprised to learn that they would all be dead within a year, Calhoun himself within a month.

Henry Clay, that aspiring Prince Hal who never became king and so had to content himself with being the moral dictator of the Senate, had to be helped to walk into the chamber to give the speech outlining the compromise; his voice was so weak that the whole gallery could hear distinctly only his almost incessant hacking cough. If Clay looked like a dying man, Calhoun had the appearance of a man already dead, a corpse in everything except his eyes, which were more piercing than ever now that they seemed to have taken on a life independent from the body in which they were housed. (As he had been almost carried toward the chamber, he had passed Mary Gwin and had mumblingly apologized that he was too weak to pause.) Calhoun's appearance, in fact, was like a ghoulish confirmation of the dismissive judgment of his later career. As Calhoun aged, it was said, he became increasingly a politician who could see everything and understand nothing. He became a pair of aged eyes, trapped in a dead past and peering out disapprovingly on the living present.

Then came Webster, the American Demosthenes, to announce his support of Clay's compromise. Webster spoke slowly, haltingly, as if he were creating the language itself, or hewing it in rock. Or rather as if Something were speaking through him, as if he were only Its instrument. That was the effect Webster commonly had on his listeners. His audience, even when in disagreement, listened during the uttering of the words as if—one put it—"to one inspired." One old friend said that after hearing a Webster speech he was almost afraid to approach him: "It seemed to me as if he was like the mount that might not be touched, and that burned with fire." Another said at certain moments it was as if you "could see a halo around the orator's head like what one sees in the old pictures of saints and martyrs." The phrase that is most frequently read in various accounts of Webster's eloquence is "as if." It is the qualification of the recovered listener to what he believed while under Webster's oratorical spell. What he did believe, but later could not quite believe he ever had. It was as if "my temples would burst with the gush of blood" so great was the excitement. Such was the moment when Webster turned to the pair of eyes that was the senior senator from South Carolina and thundered, "Secession! Peaceable secession! Sir, your eyes and mine are never destined to see that miracle. The dismemberment of this vast country without convulsion!" To which the pair of eyes somehow responded, immediately and with equal finality, "No sir! the Union can be broken"—and then shrank further back under its shawl.*

---

*Sherman, who, having been unable to find room in the packed gallery, had bluffed his way onto the floor of the Senate, was not much moved by Webster's speech or Calhoun's dramatic riposte. But he did come away from the debate convinced that the dissolution of the Union would never be peaceful.

If Gwin had any influence on the debate, it was upon the pivotal Webster, who had been expected by many admirers to oppose Clay's compromise because it strengthened the federal fugitive slave law. Webster's support for all of Clay's measures made him seem a fallen archangel to abolitionists. How much influence Gwin had in this unexpected decision is impossible to say. Nonetheless, Gwin himself seems to have been convinced that he was decisive in bringing Webster to Clay's side. Webster's great speech does use Gwin's argument that nature itself had already settled the question of slavery for California, and would settle the issue in the rest of the West in favor of abolition. Such de facto abolitionism in the West more than compensated the Northeast, he reasoned, for the other measures that seemed to support slavery.

Gwin was even willing to do business, privately, with radicals like the Whig Seward, whose politics had more in common with Frémont's than Gwin's. The two surprisingly found they worked together well, although they could not disagree more about slavery. Seward was in favor of the admission of California but was against Clay's compromise because of the concessions it contained for the South. Rather than simply opposing the compromise because his president did, Seward invoked a "higher law" than the Constitution itself, which displeased President Taylor almost as much as it infuriated Southern fire-eaters.

During the actual debate Gwin was once again called back to Washington, this time to see the president himself First, he met with the secretary of the treasury, who blithely assured him that the California delegation had only to insist publicly to the houses of Congress that California should be immediately admitted before the other issues were considered, and they would acquiesce. So Gwin could be taking his seat in the Senate within a week. This was ludicrous, of course, and demonstrated beyond a reasonable doubt that Taylor's administration was as politically incompetent as everyone said it was. (If it was not incompetent, then this was insulting in the extreme.)

Gwin coolly explained his commitment to Clay's omnibus approach. Then, in an instant, the tone of the interview changed markedly. It became, Gwin wryly said later, "very exciting." Then the secretary passed Gwin on to President Taylor himself. This interview, which covered the same ground, was, Gwin remembered, "very unpleasant." Taylor likely brought up what he had done to deserters during the Mexican War. Gwin remembered that Taylor was determined and Taylor's language was violent. Apparently it was during this interview that a horrified Gwin became convinced there was going to be a civil war very soon, sometime during Taylor's term.

So the California delegation did not weigh in on the president's side, not that this would have made much difference. And the debate over the compromise continued week after week, with Clay showing preternatural strength and persistence. He looked so frail that he would collapse at any moment. And yet, whenever challenged, he seemed temporarily rejuvenated.

One admirer described the impression well: "He stands so firm and proud, with his eye all agleam, while his voice rings out clear and strong, it almost seems that his apparent debility was but a sort of Richelieu ruse, and that the hot blood of youth was still coursing through his veins, and the full vigor of manhood yet strong in every limb. The wonderful old man!"

Of course, none of the participants were in the full vigor of manhood. Rather, they were occasionally giving that impression because they were in fact spending their last, full measure of vigor. This fact was brought home when Calhoun suddenly died. Then, when Taylor's own stubbornness seemed on the verge of making Clay's effort impossible, he too sickened. When the illness turned more serious, Taylor attributed it to the office of the presidency, which he had come to detest: "God knows that I have endeavored to fulfil that which I conceived to be my honest duty. . . . My motives have been misconstrued, and my feelings most grossly outraged." A day later he was dead. His last words, uttered with the disciplined distinctness of an order, were, "My only regret is for friends I leave behind me." There seemed to be an instinctive recognition that the country itself had killed this man by demanding from him what he had not; Seward remarked with astonishment, "I never saw grief, public grief, so universal and so profound." (Not, that is, until Lincoln.)

This public grief was in marked contrast to the almost gleeful response in the Senate. As Webster put it quite baldly, "If General Taylor had lived we should have had a civil war." Gwin agreed. Hardly had the president-soldier been decently put to rest than the political struggle recommenced. With the pliable Millard Fillmore in Taylor's place the opposition to the compromise outside of the South seemed to dissolve.

Gwin was not a religious man, but this resolution of what seemed an unavoidable crisis was so neat that he could not help but think he saw the hand of providence that had beckoned Old Rough and Ready to his eternal reward at just the right time for the sake of the republic. One nation under God, indeed.

Then there was one final twist in which, worrisome as it was at the time, Gwin could take satisfaction. Suddenly, unexpectedly, Clay's omnibus bill was dismantled into its separate measures by parliamentary maneuvering. Clay withdrew from the fight in disgust, or perhaps just in exhaustion. Webster was no help because he had been taken into President Fillmore's new cabinet as secretary of state. The senator who stepped to the fore was Gwin's friend, the Little Giant, Stephen Douglas. Never before had Douglas seemed more of a giant, as he masterfully put together coalitions to pass separately each of the elements in Clay's grand proposal.

There was an unsatisfying aspect to Douglas's piecemeal method, for it meant that Congress as a whole had not voted for the compromise as a package. The Congress itself had continued to divide on sectional lines rather than assenting to the overarching national interest as Clay had hoped it would. Davis, who had taken over leadership of the opposition after Calhoun's death, had, in particular, couched the issue increasingly in uncompromising sectional terms: "I see nothing short of conquest on the one side, or submission on the other." But, beyond that, essentially everything that Clay had proposed was passed, including of course the admission of California as the thirty-first state of the Union.

Spirits were high when the final measure of what came to be called the Compromise of 1850 passed. That night it was declared to be the duty of every patriot to get drunk. Many senators, including Douglas, did their patriotic duty so well that they were unable to attend the session the next day, due to sudden infirmities.

The compromise had been passed, and so had the baton of leadership between the generations. Clay had proposed the compromise, but Douglas had gotten it through the Senate. Then, a few days later, Douglas presented to the Senate the credentials of William McKendree Gwin as the new senator from California—a glorious occasion marred only by the fact that at the same time there were also presented the credentials for Colonel John C. Frémont, a man as unfit for public office as General Zachary Taylor himself. Or so Gwin thought.

The Compromise of 1850 had taken so long to pass that only a few weeks were left in the congressional session. In fact, this Congress had already been sitting continuously now for nine months, the longest in the history of the republic. September 30 was wearily set as the date for adjournment.

Gwin knew Congress well enough to realize that there was nothing for him to do this session. Legislation simply did not have enough time to get through committee to have a chance at passage by both houses; even if somehow that happened, there would still be differences between the precise bills, and a conference committee would be required to work out a compromise—then back to both houses. Under such circumstances, it would be hard to get through the Congress a resolution in favor of the American flag and motherhood. (Gwin could content himself with social events—with his wife attending a private dinner at the White House with Fillmore and trying to accept James Buchanan's invitation to visit him with the whole Gwin family in Pennsylvania.)

Of course, this did not mean that John C. Frémont should be dissuaded from making a fool out of himself. Gwin solemnly explained to Frémont that since obviously he was going to have to return to California before the next session to start campaigning for his reelection, Gwin out of senatorial courtesy would stand aside, and let Frémont take the dominant role in what remained of the session. Frémont took the bait, and in a fury that seemed to indicate he was still suffering from Panama fever he introduced no fewer than eighteen bills.

Decades later, when he came to sketch out his memoirs, Gwin could not resist listing every one of these; he wryly added that he was doing his part in history by providing this list "as a curiosity in legislation." Frémont, of course, had about as much chance to pass any of these bills as he had to find a southern passage across the Rockies in the dead of winter.

However, even in failure, Frémont managed to do himself more grief. One of his bills was for the confirmation of Mexican land grants in California. This was a difficult issue; the treaty that ended the Mexican War specified that Mexican land grants were to be confirmed by the American government, provided they met the conditions of Mexican law. Unfortunately, very few of the larger grants did. The new government could not dispossess the Mexican citizens; on the other hand, American immigrants had to have the opportunity to settle unoccupied land. And rumor had it that former governors of Mexican California were doing a brisk business in forged grants.

Frémont characteristically did not care about subtleties. He proposed a virtual rubber stamp for the older grants; the grants would be confirmed whether or not they satisfied Mexican law. This was an awkward position for him to take. Frémont himself now owned one of the largest Mexican land grants in California—and yet one that apparently satisfied almost none of the conditions for a legal grant. He had an obvious conflict of interest. Frémont was using his seat as senator to find himself a path to vast riches— or so it looked back in California. And he was doing so against the interest of the thousands of immigrants who, having failed in the diggings, were now struggling to find a grubstake, and hated like hell the easy life of the old grandees. A continent away, Gwin could still hear the howls of protest when they got wind of this back in California. "Frémont has sold us out!"

Of course, it was not Gwin's place to discourage his eminent colleague, the American Pathfinder, from committing political suicide. Gwin quietly let it be known, both in Washington and San Francisco, that he would defend the rights of the newcomers to California, those numerous Americans without wealth and land but who—as Andy Jackson taught us—are the backbone of the American republic. They, too, should have a voice in the U.S. Senate.

Frémont pushed for his bill, and with rare good sense let his father-in-law lead the fight, Old Bullion's last in the senate. Unfortunately, Tom Benton used this occasion to try to settle some old scores. His old enemies responded in kind, and at one time it looked as if Senators Benton and Foote were going to have another go at maiming each another on the floor of the Senate.

Gwin did not himself openly oppose Frémont or Benton. He rather enlisted Senator Thomas Ewing from Ohio to show how ludicrous was the proposed legislation; Ewing was a recent secretary of the interior, and an acknowledged authority on land questions. Of course, the bill was going to be defeated, or at least deferred until the next session. And, when Frémont belatedly realized this, he became himself ill-tempered.

To make matters worse, another of Frémont's bills attempted to regulate foreigners in the diggings. Frémont thought that these foreigners should not be allowed to work in the mines unless an American employed them. Benton's nemesis, Senator Foote, was quick to see the consequences of this. Wealthy Californians with rich estates, like Frémont, would be able to employ vast numbers of skilled foreigners to work for peons' wages. Foote did not fail to point out the inconsistency of this measure with Frémont's stern abolitionism. This was too much.

Passing Senator Foote between the Senate chamber and the vice president's office, Frémont erupted in such abuse that Foote struck him. The fisticuffs were quickly broken up by some passing senators who, unlike the belligerents, were large men and had a sense of decorum. If Gwin himself had staged it, he could not have done any better, the little Pathfinder being pulled away and scolded by his betters. The stung Frémont then issued a challenge to a duel. Foote steadfastly refused to apologize—but nothing ever came of the challenge, making Frémont look even more the fool.

When the next session began, Gwin started his true work. Gwin labored tirelessly and effectively to get bill after bill through the Congress for the benefit of California. Most important and difficult was the adjudication of Mexican land titles; he felt that the system as it finally passed at once respected the legitimate land grants and also provided a means to ferret out fraudulent claims. Gwin also proposed a series of bills that gave federal employees in California much higher pay because of the inflated prices in the state; he got through the Committee on Naval Affairs, for instance, a bill granting naval employees double compensation during their service in California. He introduced a successful bill to establish a U.S. mint in California, thereby helping to eliminate shady operations like Broderick and Kohler's. He successfully proposed an extension of the coastal survey to California—and when the amount of appropriations was cut in committee to a measly $40,000, he managed to have another $250,000 restored by having it tucked into another bill. Federal judgeships, of course, had to be created and filled. He also took the first steps toward establishing a customshouse in San Francisco.

This last piece of legislation showed how he would simultaneously serve California and strengthen mightily his own political standing in the state. The customshouse would eventually employ as many as two hundred, all patronage appointments. By that time Gwin had so filled it with Southern supporters that it was locally referred to as "the Virginia poorhouse." Those, like Elisha Crosby, who thought they could send someone like Gwin to the Senate for a few years and unceremoniously dispense with his services did not understand politics.

As Congress approached its date for adjournment, Gwin was pushing a bill for a complete survey of public lands in California. He knew he had a working majority in both houses, but time was short. As he pressed for a vote, the senator from South Carolina rose, and jokingly complained that

California was like a young woman who had to be the center of every dance. There came a point when the other young ladies could justifiably object that she, pretty as she was, must finally stand aside and give them a chance. California had dominated this session of Congress, day in, day out. The time had come for the Senate to adjourn, and then give the other states a chance in the next session. The amused Senate went along; and Gwin took this defeat in good grace. The complaint of the good senator from South Carolina had, after all, been high if backhanded praise for Gwin's effectiveness.

There was more praise for Gwin when he finally returned to San Francisco in the spring of 1851. He was given ovation after ovation for his legislative triumphs. This praise was in marked contrast to the glum reception Frémont was receiving in his efforts to secure reelection. (It looked as if Frémont's career in politics was ending.) Then Gwin received a resolution from the California legislature warmly praising him for "his zeal, exertions, and untiring advocacy in the Senate of the United States of the just claims and interests of California." On April 30 Gwin responded in similarly magnanimous terms, as befitted a statesman of unquestionable achievements. "I receive," he wrote, "with profound gratitude such assurance of the confidence of the people of California, thus manifested through their Legislature, and will earnestly strive to merit a continuance of that confidence by my future efforts in securing to the State her best rights as a member of the Confederacy." He could only extend to the legislature his "most heartfelt thanks for this valued testimonial of their regard, proffered me as a public servant."

The first signature on the resolution of praise, and the first addressee for Gwin's response, was the president pro tempore of the California state senate, David C. Broderick.

Between December 1849 and April 1851, David Broderick had risen from
foreman of a volunteer fire company to president pro tempore of the California state Senate. Other than Gwin's, this was the most impressive rise to
power in the state. And yet in the spring of 1851 Broderick was as dissatisfied
as Gwin was content. Despite his successes, the whole drift of state politics
seemed to be going against him. Depression, as a result, was stalking him.
By the end of the summer he would be considering giving up his Senate seat
altogether. Broderick the bare-knuckle barroom fighter was still taking beatings without knowing when to give up, but now at least he was having
second thoughts.

The year 1850 had begun for him in much rosier fashion. To his good
fortune, the Senate seat from San Francisco had unexpectedly opened up in
January 1850 when the incumbent was appointed to the state Supreme
Court. Kohler and Broderick had just distinguished themselves in fighting
the Christmas fire of 1849; using shovels and helped by the foot of mud in
the streets, they had performed heroically to prevent the fire from spreading.
So his name was on everyone's lips. When the election was held, the heroic
young Irishman won overwhelmingly, by a margin of better than fifty
to one.

The legislative body Broderick now joined was presided over by Lieutenant Governor John McDougal. Everyone liked McDougal, especially
when he had been drinking—which meant almost always. As one of his not-
quite admirers put it, "Well, when you say he was a drunkard, you pretty
much state the whole case; there is not much in him outside the whiskey."
He had been at the convention in Monterey; however, for most of that time
he was on a bender and so little was heard from him. Now, bemused at being
lieutenant governor, he had the tendency, once well lubricated, of beginning
every sentence as if intoning an official proclamation; so he was now known
as "I, John McDougal." A hearty good fellow, all in all, he had shown
considerable courage during the Mexican War, and at thirty-four still was
remarkably handsome, although his features were getting a little puffy.

Some of the committee chairs were little better fit for public office than McDougal. Thomas Jefferson Green, for instance, was chairman of the finance committee. As one of his friends put it, "because with him everything was a frolic," Green "went to the Legislature in a frolic and made nonsense of everything that was done." Whenever he got bored (and it didn't take much), he would proclaim, "Well, boys, let's go and take a thousand drinks." Needless to say, this was all the encouragement McDougal would need. Session adjourned.

"The legislature of a thousand drinks"—this was the sobriquet that the first California legislators worked hard to earn, a thousand drinks and as many payoffs. None of this would particularly bother Broderick; in fact, it would encourage him. The ambitious teetotaling former barkeep, of course, was even more in his element here than "I, John McDougal." So raucous governmental disputes were interspersed with raucous partying. Broderick could become the shrewd observer after hours, coolly taking the measure of the men he wished to dominate, seemingly joining in the fun but never letting down his guard. Not having a single drink, or a single woman, but always calculating, he must have thought he could come to lead this collection of buffoons. However, he soon learned that he would not easily, for they were not all buffoons.

He realized that he was not the only one calculating. A significant knot of Southerners had their own agenda, and they had apparently worked out an arrangement with the moneyed merchants of San Francisco, who were lubricating the legislators with more than whiskey. Governor Peter Burnett, moreover, had been elected largely because of his experience in the territorial government of Oregon. (Burnett had been the first speaker in the Portsmouth Square rally for statehood.) Of his contributions to Oregon, he, as a former slave owner, seemed to be particularly proud of his role in excluding free blacks from the state. They were given six months to leave, after which they would be arrested and flogged; this would be repeated each six months until they finally got the message and left the state.

This also seems to have been his only legislative objective in California as well. So he was early arguing to the legislature that "colored people," since they were not permitted to vote or hold public office, should be excluded from the state. Otherwise, they would be a festering source of discontent. With respect to "coloreds," the choice for Burnett was simply either as slaves or not at all. Since the constitution was against slavery, then not at all.

Broderick held his peace initially. He was clearly trying not to cause any trouble until he had gotten a city charter for San Francisco through. He also was pleased with his appointment as chairman of the committee on public education. But then the Southerners started posturing about slavery after they heard the kind of compromise Clay was attempting to fashion in Washington. Broderick was confronted with a bevy of little Calhouns. A resolution, for instance, was proposed stating that "any attempts by Congress to interfere with the institution of Slavery . . . is unnecessary, inexpedient, and in violation of good faith.''

This was not a time for judicious silence. Even so, Broderick at first tried to avoid a confrontation. He simply moved that the resolution be sent back to committee where it could die in quiet—but he lost a narrow vote. Incredibly, some of the Mexican Californians, like Vallejo, who imagined themselves as grandees, voted with the Southerners. Didn't they realize that these Calhouns regarded them privately as colored too? This test of strength showed Broderick that he did not have the votes to defeat the measure outright. So he tried to weaken it by sleight of hand. He introduced an amendment that added to the resolution "opposition to the admission of a state . . . on account of such a prohibition [of slavery] is a policy wholly unjustifiable, unstatesmanlike, and in violation of that spirit of concession and compromise by which alone the federal constitution was adopted, and by which alone it can be perpetuated.'' A few senators now switched to his side. He was able to pick up enough swing votes to add the amendment. This changed everything, for the resolution, with its pointed repudiation of Southern fire-eaters like Jefferson Davis, became unacceptable to the very Southern senators who had originally proposed it. When Broderick then raised again his motion to table the resolution, these Southerners now felt compelled to vote with him. The provocative resolution was tabled indefinitely. And the swing senators who had voted for both the amendment and the resolution were left scratching their heads.

This was a satisfying little parliamentary victory, but inconsequential compared to Broderick's major defeat over foreign miners. This issue had been festering since the constitutional convention. There, one of the delegates had bid his fellows to look at the "degraded wretches" who were immigrating to California from South America, Mexico, and Australia. He asked, "Why do you not insert a provision preventing them from polluting the soil of California? . . . Most of them are as bad as any of the free negroes of the North, or the worst slaves of the South. Do not be partial in this matter.'' Gwin had dexterously turned aside such awkward issues by persuading delegates that these were legislative and not constitutional matters.

The California legislature now showed itself eager to rush into this issue. There was, in particular, much speechifying in the Assembly on it. Representative George Tingley intoned, "Devoid of intelligence sufficient to appreciate the true principles of a free form of government; vicious, indolent and dishonest, to an extent rendering them obnoxious to our citizens; with habits of life low and degraded; an intellect but one degree above the beast of the field, and not susceptible of elevation; all these things combined render such classes of human beings a curse to any enlightened community.'' Listening to such comments, Broderick might have thought that except for the accents he could be eavesdropping on Englishmen discussing the Irish.

At any rate, the Southerners in the Senate were shrewder than the likes of Representative Tingley. They did not want to exclude foreigners; they simply wanted to reduce them to peonage, slavery by the side door. America had always been the home of the free and oppressed. Of course, these immigrants were, as one senator put it, "lost to all social equality or national advantage." They were lost, that is, unless some wise legislative action corrected the situation. And the action was directed not toward social equality but to national advantage. The legislators had the obligation to protect these unfortunates "from the probable destruction by a national wrath which is evidently growing stronger each day." This could be done by having them "pay a small bonus for the privilege of taking from our country the vast treasure to which they have no right. This the foreigners will happily do."

The wry cynicism with which the Southerners served up this foreign miners tax was quite impressive. The "small bonus" proposed, of course, was not small for any miner except one who had struck it rich. For the rest it would drive them from the mines, unless, of course, they wished to go to work for Americans. And anyone who seriously thought that the Aussies or Chileans were going to be happy about being taxed out of existence, or were going to express their displeasure only in words, did not know them. This bill was a prescription to transform the already tense relations at the diggings into murderous ones.

The proposal was popular, and not just among the Chivalry. One San Francisco merchant wrote home, "The tax upon foreigners in the mines is likely to produce some trouble (*but the tax is right*), and they will be *obliged* to submit. The universal Yankee nation is here, and their rights there are none to dispute." On the contrary, one of the particular Gaelic nation named David Broderick was very much there to dispute.

Broderick fought the measure with whatever means he could, but it was no use. He could call it unconstitutional, but then that sage philosopher Senator Thomas Jefferson Green, sounding like Seward, would respond that there were "universal laws . . . higher, greater, and stronger than the written constitution." (This was the same frolicky T. J. Green who had written jokingly that he could "maintain a better stomach killing a Mexican" than killing a louse.) Broderick could argue pragmatically that the law was unenforceable and would increase violence in the diggings; the rosy response was that on the contrary it would pacify the Americans in the diggings and bring into state coffers $200,000 a year. Broderick was dumbfounded, once again, that the Mexican Californians in the Senate actually seemed to believe this nonsense. In the end, Broderick could only insist on a roll call vote to try to shame a few senators to his side, but it was no use. He lost 11 to 2.

The foreign miners bill was symptomatic of what he could see happening to the state government as a whole. The moneyed interests were taking over, and they in turn were being led by a Southern clique. The workingman, in contrast, was having his attentions misdirected to scapegoats like foreign miners. So the workingman went on a phony crusade against degraded foreign wretches, not realizing that the leaders whom he was serving regarded him as a degraded native wretch, no more fit for government than those being excluded.

What of those like Broderick who were inclined to raise their voices against this? The first step was to try to buy them off. Frémont had been bought off with his vast Mariposa estate. So now this vaunted abolitionist was doing his best in the U.S. Senate to make sure that large landed estates like his own were confirmed whether they were legal or not—and trying too to have a federal equivalent of the foreign miners bill passed because he needed folks to work his own diggings.

Getting rich was fine. Broderick himself hadn't minded at all. He had made his bundle in his mint, and was buying up San Francisco lots as quickly as he could—and he happily used whatever inside information he could get to make the best deals. But all that was just to get the means to be free to fight. Nonetheless, the Chivalry tried to buy off Broderick too. Not with money, though.

By January 1851, Governor Burnett realized that he was not going to get his cherished bill to exclude free blacks through the legislature. Broderick's strategy was simply to prevent it from ever coming to a vote. On April 17, 1850, the vote on it, thanks to Broderick, was indefinitely postponed, effectively killing it. Burnett, his friends sadly concluded, had everything needed to be a good governor except a backbone. He simply would not fight, even for his most cherished measure. So he sulkily waited for the legislature to reconsider. When it had not by the end of 1850, he resigned ("the most popular act" of his administration, *Alta California* ungraciously observed). Rather than fight over his racial convictions, he chose to withdraw. Publicly, he said that he had pressing business and family matters to take care of; privately, he complained to friends about the Tammany-style politics that had begun to infect the California government, an obvious swipe at none other than David Broderick. That shanty Irishman was no better than a free black.

Broderick, relishing a fight as much as Burnett cringed at the prospect, was not done with the governor yet. He alone rose in the Senate to oppose accepting the resignation of Burnett. The governor must have seen nothing but malice in the gesture. So perverse was this man that he would oppose the governor even when it was not in his interest to do so. But there was Broderick insisting that Burnett had made a contract with the people of California to serve a term as governor, and the Senate ought to do its utmost to make him honor it. Salt in the wounds.

Now the drunken buffoon I, John McDougal was governor, and his friends had begun to call the new chief executive of the state of California "His Accidency." Someone also had to be elected to preside over the Senate. The leader of the Chivalry in the Senate, Senator Solomon Heydenfeldt, who had disagreed with Broderick over almost everything (including the San

Francisco charter), sought the floor. He was the closest the California Senate had to Jefferson Davis.

Heydenfeldt was an elegant little man whose tiny feet and hands added to the impression of aristocratic daintiness. A lawyer from Alabama who preferred corporate work and had no taste for public speaking, he prided himself on both his generosity to charitable causes and his disdain for the common man. Typical of his exaggerated sense of chivalry was his claim never to have charged a woman client.

Heydenfeldt now rose to place in nomination the candidate of the Chivalry for president pro tempore of the California Senate. This would be the person against whom Broderick and his few allies were going to have to fight. Then Heydenfeldt pronounced the name, to gasps. Heydenfeldt had risen to nominate his esteemed colleague, the distinguished senator from San Francisco, David C. Broderick. It was a stunning move. Most of his fellow Southerners lined up behind him, and Broderick won on the first ballot.

That obviously was how they intended to buy him off, with a ceremonial position. He would have the honor of presiding over the Senate until a new lieutenant governor could be elected in a few months, and should be so proud at "how far he has come" that he would not mind when others exercised the real power. It was costing them little to see if he could be beguiled by this, the political equivalent of a few trinkets. Also, Broderick would now be off all Senate committees by virtue of his new office.

Broderick, of course, was not one to be beguiled by the mere trappings of power. He would show them in time that they had underestimated him, but first he would show them he knew how to play this genteel game. He got up before the Senate, and in accepting his new office gave one of those charming, throwaway addresses at which President Polk had been so good. A well-turned, magnanimous little speech in which was said exactly nothing. Or rather almost nothing.

Broderick thanked the Senate for conferring this high honor upon him. He expressed his determination to perform the duties of this office with fidelity and impartiality. He confessed that he did not doubt he would make errors. Nonetheless, he was heartened by his conviction that he could rely upon the indulgence and the wisdom of the Senate to correct him. He felt assured that the Senate would never fail him, at least in that respect.

This last little bit, a dash of vinegar amid all the oil, was likely delivered while looking directly at Heydenfeldt, and must have produced a few hearty chuckles. Nonetheless, everyone in the chamber knew what it meant. He was still going to fight. This election, whatever its motivation, was not going to placate him.

Any doubt that he really meant this was removed by his conduct in the next important business before the California legislature: the election of a U.S. senator to fill the seat now occupied by John C. Frémont. Every legislator had a vote, forty-nine in all, twenty-five needed to win. Had not

Frémont performed so miserably as senator, this seat would have been a sinecure for him—but Frémont had performed miserably and selfishly, almost everyone agreed to that. So others were throwing their hats into the ring.

Thomas Butler King had decided to run again. There were a dozen or so loyal Whig votes in the legislature—and if he could pick up a few Southern Democratic votes, then he might just be able to patch together a majority. On the other hand, Solomon Heydenfeldt represented the Southern Democrats as a candidate—and if he could gain the votes of Northern Democrats or Southern Whigs, he could reasonably expect to win. (Heydenfeldt's enthusiasm for David Broderick as president of the Senate now made complete political sense; if Broderick supported Heydenfeldt out of gratitude, his election would be virtually assured.)

The first vote, taken on February 18, made clear that the Chivalry would control the election, if they could only decide between the Southern Whig and Democratic candidates. Heydenfeldt received 16 votes, King 15, Frémont a pathetic 8. Broderick retained his independence by leading a small cluster of 4 votes for the San Francisco mayor, John Geary, not a serious candidate but someone to back until the real horse trading began. There were also 4 votes for John Weller, a Democratic congressman from Ohio, and 2 for another minor candidate.

The support for Weller was interesting. Heydenfeldt was a well-known fire-eater, a Southern radical who opposed the Compromise of 1850. Weller was as strongly pro-South, as much a member of the Chivalry; nonetheless, he was a compromiser who supported a strong national government. In other words, he was a candidate Gwin would welcome as a colleague.

The first vote was simply a test of strength. Everyone expected the election to be resolved in a few votes, a dozen at most. The minor candidacies would quickly collapse. Once these votes were distributed, then the fundamental question would be put: Heydenfeldt or King? And those doing the answering on behalf of the great state of California would be the supporters of Frémont, unless the Southerners as a group crossed party lines. A quick resolution was a reasonable expectation, but by the end of the initial session of nine ballots some were beginning to have their doubts. When the session ended, Frémont and Weller had both lost one vote to King; other than that, there was simply no movement at all. Broderick, in particular, was starting to sense an intriguing possibility. If the election was completed with the present legislature, then a Southerner was certain to get elected; if it was a stalemate and had to be postponed until the next legislature, then who knew? A Northerner might have a chance, a Northerner—say—of Irish extraction from San Francisco. And not John Geary.

So the vote continued, with little change the next day, the next day, the day after that. By the twentieth ballot, a pair of Frémont supporters had drifted over to King. Perhaps as a result, Broderick could no longer hold together his Geary delegates; they bolted to Frémont. Broderick stubbornly now voted alone for Geary. King, 20; Heydenfeldt, 13; Frémont, 9; Geary, 1; Weller, 6. The Weller men had it in their power to give King the election if they wanted, but they did not. Who was holding them together?

The legislature continued to take vote after vote, dozens of them. Broderick could now see that what had been the remote possibility of postponing the election was becoming more and more likely; if it was postponed, he himself might be ready the next time to go for himself. Anyway, he could rationalize—better only one Southern senator from California than two. Heydenfeldt and King for their parts must have by now been openly wondering who was holding the Weller support together; if they did, it was not hard to guess a likely candidate. Gwin was ruining their candidacies as effortlessly as he had ruined Frémont's senatorship.

As the sixty-fifth ballot approached, it was clear that King could not get more than 20 votes, and that usually he could control only 2 or 3 more than the 15 he had received on the first; party politics made it impossible for this Whig to be elected. That was clear, but no one should have expected so vainglorious a man to be willing to acknowledge an unflattering political reality. Heydenfeldt had drifted down to 11 votes, but now his Southerners had stiffened their lines and were rallying; so he now remained close to the 16 he had received at the very beginning. Frémont's only chance was collective weariness; but there was little likelihood the Chivalry would ever get that tired. Frémont could have named his successor if he had wanted to throw his support to someone else—but, as usual, he thought only of himself. He had been in tougher spots than this, and had not turned back. He now had a solid dozen votes. Broderick alone contined to vote for Geary, and Weller regularly would get 3 or 4. And now a few legislators each time started to vote for whoever came into their heads; since everyone could see this thing wasn't going to end anytime soon, why not get a friend or two named in the proceedings as a senatorial candidate?

The futility of it all was demonstrated on the sixty-fifth ballot when Weller finally withdrew, and no appreciable change occurred, for his votes were split among the other candidates. For dozens more ballots nobody showed any sign of budging. Broderick seemed to be taking a perverse pleasure in all this; for more than eighty ballots he impudently cast the only vote for Geary. His was a vote, as everyone must have realized by now, for an indefinite postponement of this election. On the 112th ballot he apparently decided that everyone should realize a resolution was impossible; he grandly cast his ballot for Heydenfeldt so that no one could say Heydenfeldt's failure was due to Broderick's lack of party loyalty.

Still the three major candidates insisted upon trudging on. They all knew that a postponement would mean the end of their candidacies. So they acted as if they had nothing to lose, which in a sense they did not. If this had been a Frémont exploratory expedition, it would long ago have run out of provisions, have eaten the packhorses, and now be entertaining cannibalism. The balloting had entered its second week.

On the 138th ballot, on the ninth day, Broderick decided that enough was enough. He knew exactly what would scare some sense into the divided Chivalry. He switched his vote from Heydenfeldt to Frémont. The possibility that he could start a stampede for Frémont was enough to goad the Southern Democrats to disappoint their esteemed friend Solomon Heydenfeldt. They were now willing to vote with Broderick for postponement. Apparently a deal was struck.

However, before allowing Broderick to have his postponement, the Chivalry had a nasty little surprise for him. After the first ballot the next morning—the 140th—Heydenfeldt withdrew his candidacy. He was furious and intended to vote for King. Then up popped another legislator to renominate Weller. The next vote was stunning. King got his 20, thanks to the addition of Heydenfeldt; Frémont dropped from 15 to 9 (he was as dead as Heydenfeldt); Broderick went back to voting alone for Geary; and Weller, who had not received a vote since withdrawing on the 65th ballot, got 18 on the 141st.

This vote was no sooner finished than a postponement until January 1852 was proposed and passed. As they walked out of the hall, there must have been at least one bitter glance exchanged between Broderick and Heydenfeldt. They would not have blamed each other personally; in a strange way they liked each other, and this was politics. But they knew now that they had been outmaneuvered by someone whose hand was everywhere in this convention, but nowhere to be seen. Their stubbornness and ambition had unwittingly enabled Old Man Gwin to triumph. His candidate, after hiding in the bushes for almost a hundred ballots, had emerged at the last moment as the front-runner. It was hard to see how he now could be stopped; by next January there would likely be two Gwins representing California in the U.S. Senate. Broderick and Heydenfeldt agreed on little, but they could agree that this would be a bad thing.

Shortly after the postponement of the senatorial election, the joint legislature sent its letter of congratulation to Senator William Gwin for his service to the state of California. It must have been a galling exercise for Broderick as president of the Senate to sign it. It was too galling an exercise for Heydenfeldt even to vote for it; he, alone in the legislature, voted against the resolution. By that time, however, Broderick had more to resent. He had recently so overplayed his hand in the state Senate that he had lost what little strength he had as a legislator. This did not have to do with the senatorial election.

The problem came over land titles. The treaty with Mexico that had ended the Mexican War had specified that the legitimate land titles of Mexican Californians would be respected by the new American government.

There were three problems with this reasonable provision. First, the government was slow to set up a land commission; so the status of individual titles was uncertain for years and even those confirmed were routinely appealed, increasing the delay. Second, the Mexican Californians usually had not kept adequate records for their grants, and almost as frequently used this to enlarge their claims extensively. Finally, the grants themselves, even when documented, were huge and ill defined. And, to make matters worse, there was good evidence of a flourishing trade in forged documents. This set of problems opened the door to all sorts of conflicts—and nowhere more dangerously than in Sacramento.

Most of the land around Sacramento had been claimed by John Sutter. Faced with his own declining economic fortunes and still wishing to live like a baron, he sought help by selling his title for much of the land to wealthy Americans interested in speculation. (This was a common tactic of Mexican Californians.) He, in particular, had sold off his title to the land of the growing river port of Sacramento, a leading contender to be the permanent state capital. These speculators, by and large, did not develop the land—but only held it, waiting for it to multiply in value, which it soon began to do. By then, however, much of this desirable land had been independently settled by men returning from the diggings. This land, not the elusive gold, was their stake in California, the tangible proof that their emigration had not been pure folly. So Sacramento early polarized between the speculators and the squatters, neither inclined to give an inch.

A clash of some sort seemed inevitable. Bayard Taylor had thought so already when he had visited Sacramento in 1849, but then floods during the rainy season had inundated the town. No point in fighting over a muddy mess. In the late spring of 1850 the crisis had come. The speculators then used their considerable influence over local government officials to try to have the squatters run off. But even before—as early as April—a pamphlet had been circulating which claimed to show that Sutter's land grant, even if legitimate, was much smaller than he claimed, and did not include Sacramento at all. The squatters formed their own protective association, with the motto "The Public Domain Is Free to All." So a few months after Broderick first arrived in Sacramento, there had begun a series of riots by squatters that left a number of dead, including the sheriff and assessor who were trying to enforce property rights. The demagogues who had exhorted the squatters to violence were quickly indicted for murder. Rumor had it that the wealthy of Sacramento had already kicked ten thousand dollars into a fund to make sure that the rabble-rousers swung.

Broderick seized on this as an opportunity for using his position as president of the Senate to become the moral dictator of the legislature, and to use the mob of squatters as his instrument. For Broderick the squatter question was a case of the rich versus the poor—and he would always take the side of the have-nots without ever being squeamish about the means employed to help them. Their cause was his, and also his means to greater power. Broderick was simply trying to do crudely what Gwin at about the same time was doing with sophistication and success in the U.S. Senate—serving his constituency by serving himself. (Or was it serving himself by serving his constituency?)

Broderick demanded that the California Senate intervene on behalf of the unjustly accused squatters; but his fellow senators were convinced by the arguments from the Chivalry that the constitutional separation of powers not only freed them from any responsibility in the matter but in fact made any such intervention entirely improper. Broderick did not take this lesson in constitutional law kindly. He made the mistake of trying to bully the legis-lature. Broderick threatened to lead an armed force of five thousand men to free the unjustly accused, by force if necessary. The threat did not impress the Senate in the way Broderick had hoped; and the threat itself turned out to be needless, for the men were eventually freed. Broderick with charac-teristic impatience had overplayed his hand in a way that an insider like Gwin never would have. Perhaps he was just trying to show them that he would not be controlled, but rather would do the controlling. His attempt to dom-inate the Senate had resulted only in isolating himself, and in prematurely making it clear to the Chivalry that he was a permanent enemy.

He was an enemy because he was a genuine democrat who would always stand on the side of the poor in the name of equality. When proper proce-dures or the law or even the constitution were on the other side, he would persist, invoking a higher law and appealing directly to the people. He agreed entirely with the shouts heard from squatters during the recent troubles: "If the landowners act as they do, we shall have to lick 'em" and "A fig for their laws; they have no laws." He was a dangerous combination in the eyes of the respectable—part unscrupulous demagogue, part political idealist. For the cause of right he would happily gouge an eye or knee a groin. And he would never, never cry uncle.

This steadfastness made him personally more popular than his program among his senatorial colleagues; in gold rush California raw courage meant more than Knickerbocker stock in old New York. At one point, during the second session of the legislature, Broderick had clashed bitterly with another senator, a Whig from Alabama representing Tuolumne County, Benjamin Moore. Then, later, as they approached one another on the narrow planks that passed for a sidewalk outside, there were words between them, harshly uttered, but which bystanders could not quite make out. Moore, however, was deeply offended by whatever Broderick had said, for suddenly he had pulled out his pistol. Broderick then, rather than ducking for cover, became stiff with rage. Presenting his full front to Moore, he shouted, "Shoot, you goddamned assassin! I am unarmed!" Impressed, Moore put away his pistol. Broderick, on the strength of this incident, became a hero to many senators; perhaps as significantly, Broderick and Moore, although still political foes, became fast friends. For many in the Senate, even when Broderick was defeated, he still could rise in their esteem; it was just old Dave Broderick again, standing his ground, with only his bare knuckles and nerve to back him up. For Broderick the man there developed a respect, almost an affection, that had little to do with politics. Dangerous as he was to the body politic, you could not help but like the guy.

That was what must have been most frustrating for Broderick as he signed the official letter to Gwin. Broderick was gaining admirers and respect as his power eroded, what little he had ever had of it. On the other hand, here was Gwin, whom no one really liked. And yet the less they respected or trusted him, the more powerful he seemed to become. Broderick remained strong only in his home base of San Francisco; even there, his recent reelection had been closely disputed. With Gwin now returned to California, he could expect increasingly formidable challenges; the federal patronage at Gwin's disposal was going to do wonders to make the Democratic Party a place where David Broderick would not be welcome. He was in a corner, and had to fight back before it was too late. And then, suddenly, it seemed as if he and his supporters were going to be run out of San Francisco itself.

The events began with the robbery of a respectable merchant, C. J. Jansen, in his place of business. He was sandbagged from behind without getting a good look at his assailants. Of course, there had been far worse crimes committed in San Francisco during the past year. However, this seems to have been the first of its type directed against a storekeeper. What happened at saloons or whorehouses was one thing, but this crime seemed to threaten merchants in their very conduct of business. Such lawlessness at the expense of respectable property could not be left unpunished.

The newspapers did their part by raising a hue and cry against the alleged crime wave. And there was a convenient scapegoat, the Sydney ducks. Just as the Hounds had directed their wrath primarily against Chileans and other Hispanics, so now wrath could be directed against the Australians, or any other lowlifes with a British accent. The Australians were collectively a much more plausible object of suspicion than the Chileans had ever been.

The pace of immigration from Australia had quickened dramatically in the first months of 1851, over two thousand in that short period. (As dramatically, immigration from Chile had dropped to a trickle, thanks in part to the Hounds.) At times this felt to residents of San Francisco less like an immigration than an invasion. Although only a small minority of these newcomers were actually former convicts, San Franciscans were convinced otherwise. As the *Alta California* put it in early 1851, "The state of California has been made the great rendezvous for the transported felons of Great Britain, who have either managed to escape or have been assisted in their embarkation from the penal colonies."

On this particular subject of Australian crime, many Californians refused to be reasoned with. An Australian—that is, anyone with a British accent—was a criminal, and, conversely, a criminal was an Australian. It was as simple as that. One bemused prospector wrote in his journal, "All offenses are imputed to Sydney men in this country. It matters not what they may be, the offender is certainly from Sydney, although the tone of his voice smacks of Connecticut or Massachusetts, and he came here after graduating from Sing Sing."

The fact that a few hardened criminals had joined the Australian migration enabled the paranoid fantasies of the newspapers and their readers to be more grand. Against the Hispanics, the newspapers and the Hounds had nursed the conviction that they were secretly plotting an uprising that would reunite California to Mexico; but no one, upon a moment's serious reflection, could take this as a real threat, however much the Hispanics themselves might yearn for a return to a place where they would not be ridiculed and threatened as "greasers." But to the Australians were attributed diabolical plots to destroy all San Francisco just out of pure malice. The Australian was suspected of being a demonic anarchist who did evil for its own sake. Or at least was willing to burn down a whole city just to loot a single store. Every major fire or terrible accident that occurred in San Francisco could be safely attributed to Australian hands implementing dark, nefarious schemes.

Respectable San Franciscans were always looking for evidence that pointed to a secret Australian organization of thugs, or perhaps even an evil genius behind it all, an Aussie Dr. Moriarty. But if they never found their Moriarty, there were any number of San Franciscans willing to audition for the role of Sherlock Holmes by making fearful deductions and the most elementary preemptive retributions. Let that man of high principle Sam Brannan be the first to audition: "I am very much surprised to hear people talk about grand juries, or recorders, or mayors. I am tired of such talk. These men are murderers, I say, as well as thieves. I know it, and I will die or see them hung by the neck. I am opposed to any farce in this business. . . . I want no technicalities. Such things are devised to shield the guilty."

Brannan made this statement after two suspects were arrested for the daring robbery and beating of C. J. Jansen. It had been reliably reported that the robbers had been led by a notorious cutthroat, James Stuart, a.k.a. English Jim. The vigilantes had in their power two men, one of whom was said to look like English Jim although he himself insisted his name was Berdue. They needed only a positive identification, or a rough approximation of such, to be justified in ridding the earth of a pair of villains. That Jansen, still drowsy from his concussion, drifting in and out of consciousness and difficult to rouse, could not make a certain identification of the culprits was one of those technicalities Brannan regarded as a shield for the guilty. Brannan's implicit reasoning seemed to be that if these two were not guilty of this crime they were certainly guilty of others for which they deserved to swing—and ringing the necks of this particular brace of Sydney ducks would have a desirable effect upon the others.

A handbill was circulated which began by exhorting that "each man be his own executioner"—and ended with the announcement "All those who would rid our city of its robbers and murderers, will assemble on Sunday, at two o'clock, on the Plaza." At two o'clock a huge crowd gathered, and submitted happily to a series of speeches. Mayor John Geary had tried to dissuade the crowd by pleading, "Leave it to the courts." To which Brannan had predictably retorted, "To hell with your courts! We are the courts! And the hangman!"

Then a completely unexpected thing happened. The San Francisco vigilantes found their matinee idol. William Tell Coleman, son of Napoleon Bonaparte Coleman and a distant relative of George Washington himself, had come to California to seek his fortune, but also with a vague sense that his destiny was seeking him. An important work, worthy of his name and lineage, somewhere awaited him. He had come to the assembly this day only by accident, but then felt irresistibly moved to speak, which he did. The response was one he would remember vividly decades later: "Never in my life had I heard a more instantaneous and tumultuous shout of applause. It was light breaking through the dark overhanging cloud."

With his long, dark slicked-back hair reaching toward his shoulders, his baby blue eyes, light complexion, and powerful jaw, he had permanently the look of principled determination that could also, inadvertently, melt a woman's heart by its lovely look of almost boyish innocence. Soon he would be reputed one of the two most handsome men in San Francisco, the other being a theatrical entrepreneur of questionable character (a close friend of Broderick from New York). As Brannan could rile up a crowd, so Coleman had spontaneously found himself able to calm it.

In his impromptu address he sternly supported the vigilantes' right to retribution, but wished their actions to be taken in dignified fashion. As if speaking to Geary, he said, "We will not leave it to the courts. No, we will not leave it to the courts. No, we will do no such thing." Now with the crowd on his side, he implicitly repudiated Brannan. "We don't want a mob. We won't have a mob. Let us organize as become men. Here. Now. As a committee of citizens and insist on the right. All is ready. The witnesses are at hand. Let not justice be further cheated."

He made it all seem so simple and so principled and so manly. The crowd loved him for this, for he exuded a respect for them beyond Brannan's comprehension. He instinctively realized that some formalities must be observed so the crowd could feel better about themselves later. When Coleman finished speaking by asking for their assent, the mob shouted as one, "AYE!"

Brannan wanted an immediate lynching. As he put it in a handbill, "The safety of life and property, as well as the name and credit of the city demand prompt action on the part of the people." After all, the prisoners were "both deserving of immediate punishment, as there can be no question of their guiltiness of crime." (So it was irrelevant, according to Brannan's reasoning, whether they happened to be guilty of *this* crime.) Coleman rather counseled that a trial be held, albeit one without lawyers who would delay things with their eloquent evocation of law all the way back to Moses. Coleman prevailed, and the two men (who, as it eventually turned out, were completely innocent) got an extralegal trial that resulted in a barely hung jury. Needless to say, the jurymen who found for acquittal were threatened with hanging. Weren't men who let murderers off no better than murderers themselves?

Learning of the unexpected verdict, the crowd outside the building in which the impromptu trial had been held rushed it, breaking doors and windows. The jurymen drew their revolvers, and retreated back into the jury room to make a stand. Coleman was now urging the crowd to disperse, and eventually prevailed over Brannan, who was urging them to hang the prisoners anyway. (On the issue of hanging the jurymen, Brannan seemed neutral.) Once again, Coleman prevailed, but this time it was a close thing. So the two trembling accused were turned back to the legal authorities. They were now safely behind bars, but men as different as Brannan and Coleman had been given a seductive taste of what they might do if properly banded together.

The newspapers, as usual, could be counted upon, since circulation seemed tied to fanning the conspiratorial flames. One paper even eruditely quoted Cicero on the Catiline conspiracy: "Quo usque abutere, Catilina, patientia nostra?" (How long, O Catiline, will you abuse our patience?) The consensus receiving daily confirmation in the news was that, as one newspaper put it, "there is in this city an organized band of villains who are determined to destroy the city." So a band of citizens was formally, if secretly, organized to thwart them, with Sam Brannan in the lead and Coleman modestly in the ranks. On June 9, 1851, it promulgated its constitution, a declaration of independence from regular norms of law, as its preamble made clear—the regular norms of law and also of punctuation:

> Whereas it has become apparent to the Citizens of San Francisco that there is no security for life and property either under the regulations of Society as it at present exists or under the laws now administered,—therefore, the Citizens whose names are hereunto attached do unite themselves into an association for the maintenance of the peace and good order of Society and the preservation of the lives and property of the Citizens of San Francisco and do bind ourselves each unto the other to do and perform every lawful act for the maintenance of law and order and to sustain the laws when faithfully and properly administered but we are determined that no thief burglar in-

cendiary or assassin shall escape punishment, either by the quibbles of the law the insecurity of prisons the carelessness or
corruption of the Police or a laxity of those who pretend to
administer justice.

This Committee of Vigilance had many of the trappings of a secret society, including a password and motto. The motto was derived from another
Roman orator: "Let justice be done, though the heavens may fall." The
secret signal for assembling would be given by the bell of the California
Engine Company. Two taps, a long pause (perhaps a minute), two taps,
another pause, and so on, until the count reached twenty, by which time all
the vigilantes and other law-abiding citizens should have assembled, ready
for action.

Broderick was now back in the city, and shocked at how many of his
old friends were supporting the vigilantes—Colonel Stevenson, for instance,
who had suffered recently a number of financial reverses for which he blamed
criminals. Broderick, on the other hand, knew what this organization meant,
an extralegal government for San Francisco that was directed against his people. The forms of law were there to protect the poor, the weak, and the
disreputable against the worst excesses of the rich, strong, and respectable.
Broderick had one of his own operatives, Rube Meloney, sign up for the
vigilantes so that Broderick could have inside information on their plans.
This worked only for a short period; then the password was changed and
Meloney was excluded.

Nonetheless, even Meloney at times seemed to enjoy his work as a vigilante, at one point volunteering to hide a prisoner from the sheriff. Broderick's people were in fact being divided against themselves, having been
gulled by stories of Australian criminality. One of the vigilantes would later
say that politically he and many of the others were actually "friends to Broderick": "He was against us as the Vigilance Committee; he did not think
that people should take the law into their own hands. . . . I had nothing to
say against Broderick in his position, because his theory was good enough,
but there is a time when men should take the law into their own hands."

Almost immediately the committee had a perfect case on which to demonstrate its resolve to protect the respectable citizens of San Francisco. A
second robbery was committed against a merchant, but this time the culprit
was captured fleeing the crime. There was no question that John Jenkins (as
he gave his name) was guilty of theft. Nor that he was a hardened criminal
who was foulmouthed and utterly defiant of his captors, bidding them to do
their worst. Even then, the vigilantes had temporarily quailed, until one of
them—not Sam Brannan, for once—threw his hat down and exclaimed,
"Gentlemen, as I understand it, we came here to hang somebody!"

On June 11, shortly after midnight, the bell at the California Engine
House began to toll slowly. This was the sign that the vigilantes were going

to act. Brannan clambered up onto a nearby sandhill, silver in the full moon, to address the gathered crowd. He told them of the crime, then announced the decision of the committee for an immediate execution, and asked for the approval of the people, which was given in a shout. Someone in the crowd asked loudly, "Who is speaking?" After Brannan's name was repeated through the crowd, there was the further question, "Who is the committee?" Then some in the crowd realized the questioner might be foe rather than friend. (There was already a rumor spreading that Broderick was organizing this very moment to forcibly oppose the hanging.) So now the questioner was shouted down with "No Names! No Names!"

This in turn bothered William Coleman, self-appointed caretaker of the crowd's self-respect. He began to give one of his spontaneous speeches of moral earnestness, an Emerson of the mob. In this one he argued that hanging someone under cover of night was "not bold, not manly, not creditable" and would "lay at our door an undeserved imputation of cowardice." Coleman insisted rather that Jenkins be executed at dawn, as if an offering to the rising sun of justice. But the overwrought crowd was not listening to Coleman this night, and he withdrew.

So the committee, with Jenkins in tow, began the half-mile march from their headquarters to Portsmouth Square where Jenkins was to be hung on the 110-foot flagpole, an Oregon fir sent as a gift from the people of Portland out of respect for their fellow Americans in San Francisco. Jenkins was resigned to his death, and seemed determined to keep his composure to the end. He had been jauntily derisive of the minister who had been provided him—and had enjoyed a large glass of good brandy before starting his final walk. As he was walking toward the gallows, Brannan asked him if he had any other last request. He responded, "No—Yes—Sam, I'll take a cheroot, if you've got such a thing about you." Sam did, and the procession paused for Jenkins to get a light.

When they reached the square, Broderick with a few henchmen as bodyguards was there to greet them. Broderick was standing on a wagon near the edge of the square. He harangued the crowd, trying in the moonlight to catch the eyes of those whom he counted his friends, trying to bring them at least to their senses—but, if even Coleman was ignored, things were too far along for him to be listened to, as he described in unyielding terms the barbarous enormity they were about to commit. The futility of his words was clear when the rope was defiantly put about Jenkins's neck while he was still forty yards from the flagpole. As if this were a prearranged signal, there was now a desperate rush to save Jenkins. Everything was confusion in the ensuing melee, but a few of those who were trying to get to Jenkins were policemen and others were Broderick men and others Sydney ducks. The rescuers got close enough that a tug-of-war developed over Jenkins, who had been knocked from his feet in the crush. The stately procession had become a gruesome, tug-of-war slapstick of habeas corpus. While the struggle continued, with the vigilantes making consistent progress, someone had gotten the long rope over the flagpole. Now Brannan, almost hysterical with excitement in the full moon, shouted to those holding the rope, "A long pull, and a strong pull, and a pull together—let every honest citizen be a hangman at once." This exhortation decided the matter. And during the final few minutes of struggle Jenkins apparently was strangled to death by the noose before the vigilantes finally hoisted him aloft—for when they did his legs kicked not at all. Brannan's cheroot, one vigilante close to the pole noticed, was still in Jenkins's clenched mouth, but it was out.

Once Jenkins was hoisted, it was clear to all that he was already dead. So the fighting stopped. Then the crowd began to break up, now wearily to return to bed, to get some sleep. A reporter looked at his watch. Half past two. The coroner would have Jenkins cut down first thing the next morning, at first light. At about the same time a troubled young vigilante was writing his mother about the previous night: "I do not think that I was ever blood-thirsty." He left his present doubts unexpressed, except to assure her that he "did not fix the noose around his neck nor haul on the rope."

The inquest into Jenkins's death began that afternoon. The difficulty was obvious when the first witness, one of the police officers who had performed bravely in the attempt to save Jenkins, now refused to testify. There was a secret organization ruling the city, he claimed—and if he testified against it, his own life would not be worth much. (The papers of the vigilantes show that they did indeed have a spy at the closed hearing.) When Brannan was called, he was downright jolly, simultaneously feigning ignorance while by winks and nods making sure that no one had any doubts about his role. A turning point occurred when Broderick testified; he named names, including Brannan's, and tried to be as specific as possible in describing the various roles each had played in the lynching. By the end of the day the vigilantes had changed their tactics; since anonymity was now out of the question thanks to Broderick and a few others, they decided rather to seek safety in numbers. If the list of participating vigilantes was large enough, then the inquest would be loath to move against them. The vigilantes also sought to demonstrate their popular support.*

The day after the hanging, while the inquest was still being held, there had been a spontaneous rally at Portsmouth Square. This had been encouraging; so a second was called for the next day late in the afternoon at Portsmouth Square in support of the vigilantes. No prominent vigilantes were going to make an appearance, for this too was supposed to be a spontaneous

---

*Brannan, like the typical bully when challenged, was quickly scared for his own skin. He paid to publish a notice in a San Francisco newspaper steadfastly denying any involvement in the lynching. Broderick, never one to pass up a chance to club a vulnerable enemy, then wrote a letter of rebuttal to the same newspaper. Brannan was denying what everyone knew to be the case—he had been a principal participant in the lynching. Broderick added as a parting shot, "Of that gentleman it is unnecessary for me to say anything further, notorious as he is for violence and contempt of the law. He is widely known as a turbulent man, ready to trample upon all laws that oppose his public opinions or private ends."

expression of popular support. Nonetheless, the organizers had drawn up a list of radical propositions for the little-known president of the rally, a Mr. Hoag. San Francisco had returned to the "state of nature"—they intended for him to declare—good Americans could start over to build a just society from the ground up, with the members of the Committee of Vigilance as the leaders. The elected leaders of San Francisco, ineffective as they had shown themselves to be, were irrelevant to this process. So Hoag was to ask the crowd not just for approval for the lynching, but also for approval for the lynchers to take control of San Francisco's government for as long as they saw fit.

This was heady stuff, a proposed revolution almost. The vigilantes themselves had been left giddy by their achievement of ridding this earth of Jenkins. Yet they could not have been prepared for the turnout at Portsmouth Square that afternoon. The crowd was the largest yet seen in San Francisco, or California for that matter, estimated at as many as ten thousand—come to celebrate their triumphant heroes. Hoag himself was a bit awed by the mass of humanity all about him. He had not expected to be cast as the Patrick Henry of this new political dispensation. Coleman would have risen to this occasion; Brannan would have rendered it unsavory; Mr. Hoag wasn't quite sure what to do.

He went to the front porch of the old government adobe, which because of its high foundations stood above the general level of the square, and hence had the natural effect of a platform. All, of course, could look up at the flag-pole that the dead Jenkins had recently been run up. Hoag would use the railing of the front portico as an awkward podium on which to rest his hands and steady himself. He began to read the revolutionary proposals, somewhat timidly at first; but as one after another was met with enthusiastic cheers from all around, Hoag gradually seemed to be warming to his task. The collective mood was jubilation.

Suddenly there was a disturbance near the back of the crowd, not particularly noticeable at first but then unmistakable. Initially it could not be made out from the adobe exactly what was happening, although apparently a fight had broken out. But, no, it was not a fight. Rather there was a tight formation of a few dozen men, perhaps fifty, forcing its way through the crowd. This knot of men was tossing aside those in its way, and trampling those knocked down. Some in their path, oblivious to them, had time only to turn around before they were sent sprawling, knocking over six or eight other bystanders in the process. The progress of the group was slow, but inexorable. Like a Roman legion making its way through a mob of barbarians, these men were supremely confident, this confidence itself cowing many in the crowd.

The party had made its way almost halfway across the square before Hoag could recognize the man at its head, at the center of its front row. And by then the name was spreading throughout the crowd. Broderick, it was Dave

Broderick and his shoulder strikers, come to challenge the Committee of Vigilance once again, this time in broad daylight. And this time he had brought enough men to do the job—or so their cockiness seemed to say. Fifty was enough, he seemed to think, against such a cowardly ten thousand.

Hoag had stopped speaking, and there was a stunned silence in the crowd, as if everyone were temporarily mesmerized by the spectacle of such daring. All eyes were now looking away from the adobe, toward Broderick— and some in the distant crowd were scrambling to get a better perspective from which to view the coming trouble. And Broderick and his men were for their part not rushing, just methodically removing whoever was in their way and then taking a few steps forward to the next ones. By the time they approached the adobe the gaping crowd was melting in front of them without so much as being touched.

Broderick now was up beside Hoag, who himself quickly stepped away as if he had been only a temporary stand-in for this, the true president of the assembly. Some in the crowd, misunderstanding this gesture, began shouting encouragement to Broderick; they, not having been at the lynching, inter- preted his presence as an endorsement of the coming revolution. Certainly not all in the crowd were altogether clear about what had happened that night, except that Jenkins had swung and good riddance.

If there was any suspense about Broderick's own attitude toward this meeting, he immediately dispelled it. Leaning out over the railing and glar- ing at the crowd, he began to denounce vehemently the vigilantes as no bet- ter than midnight murderers, and to denounce this crowd itself as no better than a lawless mob. This effected an immediate transformation in mood. Spontaneously from all sides came a single cry, "Hang him!" At the sound of these threats his bodyguard tightened around him, with grim smiles that dared anyone to make a move. Broderick then spoke for about twenty minutes, repeating over and over in the strongest language at his command the heinousness of what the vigilantes, this bad company of men, had done, and the outrage that this meeting should even consider expressing its ap- proval. He was not eloquent; he was too angry for that. He made no effort at persuasion but only lashed the crowd again and again. And under his un- compromising words the crowd became like a beast that writhed at each stroke, snarling continually but never quite attacking, although half a dozen times during those twenty minutes it seemed a close thing.

Finally he had finished, not that he had reached a logical conclusion, just that he had temporarily been rendered speechless by his disgust. Then the chairman tiptoed back to the front of the portico—and, with at least one furtive look over his shoulder, put the resolutions to a vote. The crowd roared, "Aye." And Broderick's men yelled back, "Nay." The b'hoys had yelled at the top of their lungs, but that only made the disproportion more impressive. It was a small band of humanity against a raging ocean; they were defiant but dwarfed. The moment Broderick's men began their "Naaaaay!"

Broderick himself shouldered aside the president to declare, "The nays have it!" The roar of the crowd now crashes again over the adobe—and Hoag, completely unnerved, timidly suggests to Broderick that the vote be repeated. Broderick, although only a few feet away, has to yell back to make himself heard, "It is no use, we'll vote it down again." For the first time he cannot keep back the flicker of a smile, and the boys are beaming impudently, as if they have never been more fully alive than at this very moment.

This is all finally too much for those at the front of the crowd. They now surge forward, perhaps a hundred of them, to seize Broderick. He's fighting them off, giving as good as he gets—and his men are protecting his flanks. But finally a few of the crowd get a good grip on him and begin to pull him kicking and fighting over the railing, which somehow does not give way. No sooner does one of those pulling him get knocked away by a blow from one of the boys than another gets a grip and continues the job. Broderick now has completely lost his feet, and is lying stretched out across the railing; it is obvious to everyone he is about to be lost into the crowd, engulfed. But the boys are equal to the threat. They jump up onto the railing, and dive out into the crowd, flattening large portions of it; one may have even used Broderick's own body as a springboard. It is pandemonium, and the fighting briefly becomes savage, with hobnail boots, brass knuckles, and sandbags doing their work. And then, as suddenly as it started, it is over. There are men sprawled all over the area in front of the adobe, some bleeding, some moaning, a few apparently unconscious. As the sand and dust start to settle, those at the back of the crowd can see, incredibly, that Broderick is back on the portico taking charge of the meeting, with his boys at his side looking little worse for the wear.

There was now an eerie calm in the crowd, a timidity perhaps from a sense that anything, just about anything, might happen next. Broderick himself, as was common of him in such extraordinary situations, looked preternaturally cool. Not moral courage so much as something that seemed physiological—as if all this excitement had the effect of chilling his blood. The boys loved Broderick for that, in a pinch as cool as a cucumber.

Looking out at the crowd now like a teacher confronting a slow class, he asked them if they really meant to overthrow the constitution by force. Once again, he had hit a nerve. Shouts came from all sides, and could be heard distinctly because the crowd in general had quieted, at least temporarily. Some simply yelled back, "Yes! Yes!" Others reverted to, "Hang him! Hang him!" One group began to chant, "We are the People! We are Supreme!" Another group, still outraged by the recent melee, repeated over and over again, "Down with the shoulder strikers." From the crowd came not one voice in support of Broderick.

He let them yell at him for a while, waited for an opening, and then shouted quickly, "All in favor of adjourning the meeting." As quickly, the boys screamed back as one, "Aye!" Then Broderick, without giving the nays a chance to drown them out, peremptorily declared the meeting adjourned—and said to his cohorts triumphantly, "Come, boys, this meeting is adjourned." Then the group of them, with a wild cheer, waving their hats in the air, marched out, down the steps of the adobe, and through the throng. They had to push aside the first few persons they confronted, but then the crowd spontaneously parted to give them a little path, not so much out of fear—it seemed—as from grudging admiration for their pluck. But that pluck was almost immediately tested again.

They had no sooner reached the far edge of the crowd than Hoag resumed the meeting. Broderick's bluff had not worked; the crowd at Hoag's timid prompting was going to start to vote on the resolutions again, this time formally to confirm them. Hearing the meeting resume, Broderick shouted, "Come on, boys, we must try it again." And try it again they did. The Spartan band wheeled around, and behind their Leonidas they once again fought their way through the crowd, back to the podium. The sheer audacity of the maneuver made the resistance perfunctory. So, once again, Broderick was on the portico, surrounded by his henchmen. But this time he did not address the meeting—he simply seized the list of resolutions from Hoag's hands, and tore it to shreds in full view of the crowd, which responded to this outrage with a deafening, wordless roar. Now hundreds from the crowd were struggling to get at Broderick. But the boys were ready for them this time. They systematically, with professional precision, beat away those who got their hands on Broderick—and, of course, Broderick did his part as well. The attack of the crowd was beaten back. The fighting, however, was beginning to take its toll on the small band. Broderick himself was panting and pale, his clothes torn, his face and knuckles bloody. The meeting, if such it could still be called, was now in its third hour—but the continual din had become so loud that one could make out only with effort what was being said by those a foot or two away. With his men regrouped, Broderick decided that the time had come for the coup de grâce: "Now, boys, adjourn them, this time sure. Spread yourselves." Then Broderick and the boys as a group charged the crowd in one direction, then wheeled around and charged it in another, and then another, always attacking the crowd at its thickest, until finally, amazingly, they had cleared virtually the whole square by their bull-like charges. With dusk having come and beginning to darken into night, the meeting was over, this time for sure. Broderick had prevailed, and the boys would have much to cheer about as they hoisted a few that night at Tammany Hall. And Broderick could sit aside, enjoying their fun and their boyish bragging, but himself beneath the surface full of worry.

One who had witnessed this whole affair from a safe distance (and who alone recorded it in detail years later) could scarcely believe what he had seen. A crowd of perhaps ten thousand had been thwarted by the nerve of one man with a few devoted friends. Yet, if the crowd had managed to seize Broderick (as it almost did on at least two occasions), it would not have strung him up as it had Jenkins. It was too maddened even for that. Undoubtedly, the crowd would have torn him limb from limb, literally. Broderick and the crowd—it was hard to say which was more frightening.

Breaking up the rally was an impressive feat, a remarkable display of determination and courage. But such a feat could scarcely be expected to intimidate the Committee of Vigilance, especially when it was being strongly supported by newspapers like *Alta California*. The editorial of the *Alta*, in particular, was all that the vigilantes could have hoped for:

> The trial and conviction of Jenkins was not the act of an inflamed and excited mob—his case was adjudged with calmness and deliberation, his guilt fully established, and penalty of death imposed by a set of men respected and esteemed by their fellows, assuming responsibility imposed on them by stern necessity, with a full perception of their accountability to their fellow men and their Maker. Who but He shall adjudge or condemn them? We dare not.

The Committee of Vigilance now largely took over the duties of the police for San Francisco. They organized night patrols for the whole of the city as well as the waterfront. Their supporters claimed that as a result they were sleeping calmly for the first time since their arrival. The committee itself was growing constantly, the number of official members approaching five hundred. Folks, reputed disreputable, would have delivered to them a simple note:

> You are hereby warned to leave this city within five days.
> By order of the Committee of Vigilance

Few declined the invitation.

Broderick supporters tried to turn this practice to their advantage. They began to send their own forged versions of the committee's notice, these to respectable citizens. For instance:

> The most eminent physicians of this place have decided that the climate of San Francisco is very injurious to your constitution. It is due to you that we should inform you of the fact and request that you will seek a place more congenial to your health, feelings and disposition, before Wednesday next.
> By order of
> The Committee

The boys had a little too much fun concocting these. The seal they added was particularly impressive, until it was realized that they had simply imprinted a Mexican silver dollar on the missive.

By this time Broderick had settled on a name for his antivigilante party, Law and Order. He put out a handbill to announce his own mass meeting, to be held at the Plaza on June 22. San Francisco's citizens must rise up against the "secret inquisition" composed of "midnight murders." It asked rhetorically, "Shall we tolerate in this enlightened age a Danton, a Robespierre or a Fource, and the paraphernalia of a secret inquisition for the suppression of our laws and courts?" Had he been able to hold that meeting, he might have broken the support for the vigilantes once and for all. However, the morning the meeting was scheduled a massive fire broke out, one that quickly spread over sixteen blocks.

Everyone conceded that this fire was obviously arson. Broderick might have had his own conspiratorial theories, but the popular view was that long proposed by the vigilantes, an anti-American crime network of Sydney ducks. The committee patrols did their work by capturing looters, one of whom, a Mexican, was publicly flogged. (A newspaper account identified him only as someone with a "long unpronounceable last name.") During the fire, however, the quibbles of law were entirely dispensed with by some irate citizens. Two men, in separate incidents, were literally stomped to death by a crowd for behaving suspiciously—one apparently had stooped to pick up a cinder to light his pipe, and then was discovered to speak with a foreign accent (the deceased was French). In another incident, an Australian ship captain, when giving advice on how to extinguish a burning tar barrel, was judged to have betrayed himself by his accent—and saved himself from an immediate hanging only by shouting the names of his employers, who happened to be prominent members of the committee.

The committee now controlled the city. Their patrols met ships, and exercised the right of turning back any undesirable immigrants, especially from Australia. Their street patrols exercised the right of search wherever and whenever they pleased. And individuals were arrested simply for looking suspicious. So sanguine had they become, they began to look beyond the confines of San Francisco itself. They issued a proclamation that could have laid the basis for the committee's taking over all of California:

> Should the order-loving portion of the citizens of Sacramento City, Stockton, Pueblo de San Jose, Monterey, Marysville, and all other towns and cities of the State find it necessary, they are invited to form themselves into Committees of Vigilance, for purposes set forth in the Constitution of the Committee of Vigilance of San Francisco.
>
> The object of formation of these committees is moreover for the purpose of corresponding with each other, so as to be able to mark and notice the movements of all disorderly and suspicious characters. By vigilance we may succeed in driving

from our midst those who have become so baneful and obnoxious to our committees.

By order of
The Committee

Everything seemed to be going the committee's way. And then they had
an incredible piece of luck. A patrol picked up a man for acting suspiciously.
He said that he had come from the diggings, but his clothes were too well
pressed. They found a pistol and a fourteen-inch bowie knife on him, but
that was not so unusual. He seemed an affable, articulate fellow, so cooperative that they almost released him but then perhaps as an oversight kept him
the night in their jail. The guard who arrived the next morning could not
believe his eyes. This was English Jim, the real James Stuart whose robbery
of Jansen had precipitated the whole vigilante movement. Moreover, he was
also wanted in at least one murder upstate. Stuart tried to bluff his way out,
but the guard was certain; he had once worked for Stuart for six months (in
what capacity exactly was left undetermined).

This discovery was awkward in a way because it meant that the vigilantes
had almost executed an entirely innocent man a few months before. Some
of the vigilantes, by way of excuse, insisted that this man and the one almost
hung earlier bore an uncanny resemblance to one another—and later a myth
would arise that the two both had a stiff middle finger on the right hand, a
scar on the right cheek, and very similar tattoos. Other vigilantes who had
seen both admitted forthrightly that there was, as one put it, "really no strong
resemblance between the two men."*

Stuart, having tried to get away first by being cooperative and then by
bluffing, now judged that his only chance of getting off was by providing
the committee what they obviously most wanted, evidence of a grand criminal conspiracy. They had promised him that if he implicated enough others
he would be spared to stand trial elsewhere for murder. Stuart clearly realized
that he had almost certainly a losing hand, but he was determined to play it
out as best he could. He kept the executive committee up all night, describing
for them his many and varied depredations.

Particularly unnerving was that the bearded, long-haired Stuart bore an
uncanny resemblance to traditional portraits of Christ, as if this amoral,
charming criminal were himself the anti-Christ. William Tell Coleman was
one of those who sat there through the night, saucer eyed. This was a night
he would never forget:

---

*This vigilante continued, "Berdue [the first man arrested] . . . was a man of about five feet and 7½ inches
in height, with full oval face, dark brown or auburn hair, a well built and good proportioned man, with
rather fair complexion, and I think grey or blue eyes. Stuart was a man full five feet 9 or 9½ inches high
with sharp features, narrow chin, darker complexion than Berdue, and very dark brown or black hair,
much darker than Berdue's, with longer arms, a slighter built man."

He went through the whole range of his many rascalities, gave vivid descriptions of his adventures, entering with great zest the details, and it was curious to see his eyes brighten and twinkle, and a smile play around his facile countenance, when describing his best successes, and recounting his best jobs. He threw off all restraint or reservation, and felt that he was bringing to light a brilliant record that had heretofore been necessarily hidden.

He named about twenty-five who had helped him at one time or another. He admitted that he had led the trio who had assaulted Jansen—and added, with respect to those who had been arrested in their stead, "We did not wish to see them hung, as they had nothing to do with it—we all agreed on Sunday night that if they hung them to burn the town down."

Throughout it all, he was utterly charming, and ended his lengthy confession, as the sun was starting to stream into his room, with the bemused observation that he had finally been arrested by the vigilantes when he had been "doing nothing." Such was life, his bemused tone seemed to suggest. Gradually it had become clear that he was telling all this not because he really expected to be spared. Nor was he confessing to unburden his soul. Rather he had been a purposeful and skillful fellow, and he thought it only fitting to leave a memorial of a life that had been lived with remarkable consistency and considerable achievement, a work of art in its own peculiar way, a fit object for human admiration.

Stuart, all agreed afterward, did act out the last scene of his drama impeccably. He murmured not a word of complaint when the leaders of the committee informed him that he had not really fulfilled his end of the agreement, and so would be executed rather than sent to Marysville for trial. At three in the afternoon they marched him through the city toward a pier where a derrick had been prepared for this special use. One near him said that he "marched as erect and with as firm a tread as any innocent man and no one could see in his actions any indications of agitation." He was hung with his face uncovered, and his hands calmly folded in front of him.

The committee was, in a strange way, grateful to English Jim. He had given them a dignified hanging, and had also provided a list of criminals to be hunted down. There was the awkward matter of the coroner having forced himself through after Stuart had been swinging a brief time. To keep the admirably dignified tone of the proceedings (so unlike Jenkins's hanging), they allowed him to cut Stuart down a little sooner than they would have liked. And then there was that ugly rumor that he was still breathing slightly when the coroner took him away. And the wags—Broderick men, no doubt—were now saying, "The first man hung by the San Francisco Vigilance Committee was dead before he was swung up, and the second was alive after he was cut down."

These witticisms, however, were but minor annoyances, and Broderick knew it. When he had heard of the planned execution of Stuart, he had offered city officials armed assistance to save him, but was politely refused. The mayor and sheriff wanted no confrontations, but Broderick was certain the committee could only be brought down by confrontations. Someone had to prevent them from hiding behind the genteel facade of respectability. Broderick's only hope was for state intervention, but that meant dealing with the governor—I, John McDougal.

McDougal had visited San Francisco shortly after Stuart's execution, and that visit could scarcely have been less promising, at least from Broderick's point of view. The committee knew that he would be stopping by their headquarters—and so laid in ten cheeses and five gallons of brandy. How far gone those five gallons were when McDougal began to praise the work of the committee was not recorded. What was recorded was a typical example of McDougal's broad humor: "He hoped that they would go on, and endeavor to act in concert with the authorities, and in case any judge should be guilty of mal-administration, to hang him, and he would appoint others."

Broderick knew better than to take anything McDougal said as an expression of deep convictions, for His Accidency had none such, as near as anyone could determine. No deep convictions, that is, beyond his abiding commitment to be a jolly good fellow. Broderick needed to find an opportunity to play on this to set McDougal against the committee. This opportunity was provided by Charles Duane.

Duane—or Dutch Charley as he was known—was one of Broderick's most loyal henchmen, and along with Ira Cole his toughest. He was always at Broderick's side when things were tight. Charley was out on his own, however, on the night of July 21. He had already drunk somewhat more than his fill when a little after midnight he heard music from a private party at the Cairo Saloon, and decided to crash it. No one had the nerve to object, and this turned out to be most unfortunate for Frank Ball.

Ball, a wiry little fellow and member of the committee, was considered quite the card around the more respectable saloons of San Francisco. Recently he had been entertaining folks with a hilarious song on the hanging of Jenkins. Dutch Charley, needless to say, did not think this lynching an appropriate subject for joking, especially by those who had had a hand in it. But Ball would do anything for a laugh, as was evidenced by his costume this night. He had come to the party in drag and blackface. Moreover, Ball's skirt bulged at the stomach, apparently to suggest pregnancy. Duane sat at the bar for a while, as Ball flounced about; but then he had had enough.

He went across to Ball, who was daintily dancing a quadrille: "I want to see you now, you damned son of a bitch." Ball tried to brush him off with some inanities. What Duane said in response was far from inane: "You god-damned son of a bitch, I want to kill you." Things were getting awfully serious; and Frank Ball, no longer flouncing around, turned to walk away. But first he said, "That is easily done, for I am unarmed." These words were ill chosen, for they seemed to imply that Dutch Charley required a weapon to kill a man. Duane then set about demonstrating, with a minimum of fuss, the falsity of that implication. With an open hand he decked Ball; then with one kick to the chest he rendered the unmanly little bastard unconscious. Ball was carried out of the room, and a physician declared that Ball's crushed chest would likely prove mortal. By that time Duane had already lurched out into the early-morning air.

Duane had soon surrendered to the sheriff, perhaps at the urging of Broderick. The committee also quickly went to work. Numerous reso-lutions were passed, from the predictable ("Whereas our Brother—Frank Ball—has been violently assaulted by one Chas. Duane, alias Dutch Char-ley, who is now in Custody of the Civil Authorities, we hereby pledge ourselves that justice shall be meted out to said Chas. Duane") to the threatening ("Resolved that the Executive recommend that if any Judge or Magistrate or other Administrator of the Laws can be detected in cor-ruption or mal-administration of their duties, they shall be arrested by this Committee, and hanged, as an example to those who have asked and re-ceived office at the hands of the people").

Fortunately, Ball had by this time started to recover. (The doctor may have exaggerated his injuries to protect him.) Fortunately, too, Duane came up before Judge Campbell, the only San Francisco judge that the committee respected, in large part because he was the only member of the judiciary who had stood up to them. The jury found Duane guilty but recommended le-niency. This recommendation was immediately met with a chorus of hisses from the courtroom spectators. Once Campbell had restored order, the de-fense was on its feet declaring that this outburst showed sufficient prejudice against Duane that the trial should be set aside. Campbell declared this ar-gument nonsense, and followed the recommendation of the jury by giving him the minimum sentence for this felony, one year. The defense now de-clared that it was appealing all the way to the California Supreme Court.

Broderick knew that he did not have to appeal to the Supreme Court; he just had to have a talk with Governor John McDougal. McDougal was not going to be governor for much longer; the Democratic Party had, not surprisingly, passed him over when nominating its candidate for the coming election. Broderick now could appeal to Lame Duck McDougal. McDougal had to remember who his friends were, friends he would need once out of office. On August 15 McDougal quietly pardoned Duane.

The governor was now feeling downright statesmanlike. In pardoning Duane he had put himself at odds with the committee; in fact, he seemed now to fit its description of a maladministrator of justice who should be hanged as an example to the rest. McDougal, although usually drunk and frequently a buffoon, was never said to be a coward. He had distinguished himself during the Mexican War, and perhaps his dissipation was an after-effect of the true horrors he had seen there. The pardoning of Duane seemed to sober him up sufficiently to give a glimpse of the McDougal of old.

The committee now had in custody two more men, Whittaker and McKenzie, whom Stuart had implicated in the robbing of Jansen. The date for their execution had already been set by the committee, and was an open secret throughout San Francisco. McDougal came to San Francisco late on August 19 to give personal support to Broderick and the city officials in their deter-mination to rescue the two men. He actually accompanied the sheriff and his deputy on a clandestine raid on committee headquarters that brought the two men under proper authority. The next morning, as news spread of the daring rescue, people had thrust into their hands a paper headed with these words in very large letters;

PROCLAMATION!
by
The Governor.

It began, "Whereas an armed and organized body of the citizens of San Francisco County, has in defiance of the Constitution and Laws of this State . . ." It continued, "Now therefore, I, John McDougal . . ." McDou-gal then urged citizens to oppose "the despotic control of a self-constituted association," and pledged his own support "at all hazards." This was such a truly fine moment for him one cannot help but wonder what he might have become had by some accident he been permitted to continue as governor.

Unfortunately, not even this one shining moment in his governorship went untarnished. The vigilantes had soon rushed the jail, seized Whittaker and McKenzie, and strung them up. One newspaper trumpeted that far from harming the committee the apparent setback initiated by the governor had served only to stimulate the committee to renewed exertion. This, however, was not quite true.

The committee had in fact spent itself. When Duane's pardon became public, there was some huffing and puffing from the committee, but no action. At least one of the leaders wrote to the members, "I would love to see it continue for all time." But active membership was now dropping, and dues increasingly difficult to collect. So the committee, a month after hanging Whittaker and McKenzie, declared its work over, at least for the time being. Its example should help those now in office by being "silently . . . a terror to all evil doers."

Broderick could not rejoice at this outcome. The committee had been allowed to dissolve on its own terms. All of his efforts to oppose it had failed, except perhaps the one confrontation on Portsmouth Square that in retrospect may not have been of any significance, however much the boys still liked to talk of it. And if Frank Ball had died, then Dutch Charley almost certainly would have meant civil war for San Francisco, a civil war to be fought to the last man if Broderick had had anything to say about it.

Broderick was realistic in his assessment of these hundred days that seemed so much longer. The committee had not been defeated. And so would remain there silently as a permanent threat. It would probably be back. The leaders of the vigilantes had successfully divided his people, and set them to killing one another. The Aussies, like the Chileans before them, were now leaving California in droves, partly because of the vigilantes, partly because of a gold strike in Australia itself. Without them it might be easier to unite his people the next time.

Yet as Broderick reflected on the struggle for law and order that he had lost, his mind would have turned on occasion to the greatest lawgiver for California, the Honorable William McKendree Gwin. Where was our California Moses during these troubles? He had been in California since that handsome tribute was delivered to him from the legislature, the tribute that Broderick had had to sign by virtue of his office. Gwin was willing to receive this tribute in his suite of rooms at the finest San Francisco hotel, and willing too to pen his own self-serving reply, which Broderick had had to read to the Senate.

Where was he when the people of San Francisco needed his leadership? He had become invisible. Nobody could find him. He could have brought the Committee down, had he opposed it, forthrightly and early. Of course, it might have cost him a few votes. Why should he lose a few votes to save some worthless blood? There he was, a great constitutional authority, a Clay, Webster, and Calhoun all in one. The almighty providence of California. And what did he do when the very Constitution of the United States was being set aside because one merchant had gotten knocked on the head? He judiciously disappeared. For one hundred days no one knew exactly where he was, except that he was obviously doing something very important. Though what, no one could quite say.

So the likes of Dave Broderick, Ira Cole, and Dutch Charley Duane had to lay their bodies on the line, while Dr. Gwin was making house calls somewhere else. And in the end it was John McDougal, His Accidency, who rose to the occasion while Gwin was off to a mountain somewhere to consult a burning bush. And no one called the Honorable William McKendree Gwin to account. Even had he been a member of the committee, that would have been something. He could have been like Coleman, a respectable lyncher. But Gwin was too smart for that, too smart really to care about little things like law and justice, life and death. What were a few people murdered by a mob compared to important things like Gwin's career?

Still, Gwin might someday be called to account in a way that would publicly reveal him as he truly was. If not on this issue, then on some other. Broderick could hope for that. A clear day of judgment when all would see the Gwins of this world as they truly were. English Jims with better breeding and better opportunities.

5

The year 1851 that had begun so promisingly for David Broderick with his election as president of the California Senate had turned out to be a dreary disappointment. The vigilantes had effectively divided Broderick's support in San Francisco itself, while the Chivalry was in control of both the California state legislature and the the Democratic Party.

His present weakness was dramatized when the California Democratic Party had its convention to nominate delegates to the national convention for the election of 1852. Broderick fully expected to be one of those who would be selecting the next presidential nominee of the party. Instead, he found himself denied his very seat in the state convention.

Broderick's delegation from San Francisco had its credentials challenged by another delegation led by someone with a familiar last name, Eclan Heydenfeldt, brother of Solomon. The Chivalry had put up its own slate in San Francisco, with the support of some former vigilantes. When this slate lost the election, a chorus shouted fraud. So both delegations showed up at the convention, demanding to be recognized. After a certain amount of unseemly scuffling, they were both ordered from the convention floor, as the other delegates took up the issue. Justice Solomon Heydenfeldt (newly appointed to the state Supreme Court) argued eloquently for the rejection of Broderick's delegation, and carried the day. So Broderick and his men were excluded from the convention.

Broderick's delegation published their outraged objections to all this in order to appeal to the general electorate. This appeal was more than pique. The convention, like the California legislature, might well be dominated by the Southerners and their sympathizers. However, they were not all as pragmatic and shrewd as their acknowledged leader, Dr. Gwin. And, also unlike him, they did not seem to realize that often in politics it is best to row toward one's objectives with muffled oars.

At one point in the convention a speaker was challenged for not having yet brought his family to California. He responded that he had not, it was true—and he did not intend to "until we make California a nigger state." Such a statement could only have made Gwin wince, and he would wince even more at the hilarity with which this remark was met by the convention as a whole. He would also note that the few Mexican Californians, after the remark was translated to them, were not smiling.

Neither was Broderick. He began to be even more cantankerous than usual, just to show that despite his defeats he was not backing down. First, he was involved in an ugly brawl with a member of the Chivalry for insulting a friend; in the fight, they used on one another whatever weapons came to hand, and Broderick ended up slashed badly by being hit over the head with an inkstand. Then Broderick insulted a former governor of Virginia so violently that he was challenged to a duel.

As Charley Duane remembered the day of the duel, the Broderick men were boyish in their jocularity. When the small boat they took over to the site of the duel in the East Bay stuck in the mudflats, Ira Cole tricked Duane into jumping into the mud to haul the boat the last mile through the chill morning fog, to the immense enjoyment of the other passengers. (They had drawn straws, and everyone except Charley had seen that Cole had cheated.) Then, just before he was to begin the duel, Broderick, who had dressed up for the occasion, came over to the boys to hand them the fine gold watch he had been given by his fire company when he had left for California. One of the boys shouted, "Put your watch in your pocket; if you are shot, die like a gentleman." Everyone had a good laugh over that one, and Broderick smilingly did as he was told.

When the duel began, the men walked toward each other with fully loaded revolvers, and could fire at will until their revolvers were empty. Suddenly Broderick's gun jammed, and he seemed doomed as he fumbled with it while his opponent approached firing coolly. Then Broderick was hit; he lurched backward, holding his stomach. He'd been gut shot. After a few seconds (which seemed much longer), he had struggled back to his feet. Having now managed finally to clear his weapon, he had begun firing himself. When the pistols stopped, the boys rushed to Broderick, fully expecting to find him mortally wounded. (His opponent was untouched.) There was much blood about his stomach, and lacerations, but no deep wound. Then they realized what had happened. The bullet had hit the watch and shattered it. The watch fragments had cut him up badly, but the bullet had not touched him.

So, as a result of this duel, Broderick had a bloody stomach, a shattered watch, and a hole in his waistcoat. Broderick saved what was left of the watch as a memento—and, displaying it, bragged to his boys, "I have been hunted by the Chivalry, but I have taught them on all occasions that I was not to be trifled with." But no one had ever thought that he was to be trifled with, at least since the days of The Subterranean. Nonetheless, he sensed that this duel would not be his last, and now began to practice his shooting regularly; soon word got out that Dave Broderick had become a crack shot with a pistol, and a damned quick draw. The Chivalry could hunt him now at their peril.

William Gwin would not have cared, of course. To him Broderick was still a political trifle, a minor nuisance the existence of which he would scarcely acknowledge. Broderick, for his part, knew he still could not touch Gwin; the man was too remote, too cunning for him. But he could get Gwin's underlings to blurt out crude testimony that Broderick could use against them all. Let the populace be convinced that the Chivalry meant to make California a "nigger state," and the Chivalry was doomed.

Californians seemed inclined to believe in conspiracies as the source of all their ills. There had been a Chilean conspiracy, a Hounds conspiracy, and an Aussie conspiracy; Broderick had to induce indiscreet Southerners to demonstrate to Californians that there was now a slave power conspiracy, a conspiracy against the ordinary, hardworking Californians. Then Old Man Gwin would be flushed from his safe lair, out into the open where he would have to fight Broderick like a man.

When the legislature met in January 1852, the first order of business was the postponed senatorial election. None of the major contenders in the earlier contest was any longer a factor. Heydenfeldt had been appointed to the California Supreme Court as a consolation for his failed bid for the Senate. King had been given patronage from the Whig administration as head of the federal mint in San Francisco, and was still an object of fun.* More importantly, Gwin had begun to enforce party discipline. The Democrats, as a result, were going to caucus first to select the candidate whom all Democratic legislators would then be obliged to support when the legislature as a whole convened. In short, the Whigs, given the Democratic majority in the state legislature, now had no chance to elect one of their own. Frémont, on the other hand, had withdrawn finally, and he had left with Jessie for a grand tour of Europe so that he would not even be on the North American continent when this most recent outrage against him was completed, more unjust and ungrateful even than his court-martial. Europeans, at least, knew how to value greatness.

As a result of all this, Weller, the Gwin-supported dark horse who had reemerged late in the last balloting, seemed unassailable. And everyone realized this, everyone except David Broderick, who was determined to assail no matter the odds.

So Broderick put himself forward as a candidate, and lost. Nonetheless, he did manage to postpone Weller's victory for a few ballots. Observers were impressed. He had made a fight out of what most had thought was an im-

---

*After a recent fire, Butler King made a great show of moving the government funds under heavy guard, and newspapers had a good time at his expense: "General King gallantly took his stand in a most exposed position upon the top of a pile of bricks, and with a six-barrelled revolver in one hand, and a formidable looking cane in the other, issued his orders for the removal of the treasure, with admirable coolness. . . . The whole conduct of the exploit exhibited military skill of the highest order and heroic devotion worthy of all praise."

possible case. The *Alta California* wrote, "His friends clung to him with a tenacity that was amazing."

Encouraging to Broderick was the steadfast support he had received from the few Mexican Californians in the legislature. They were expected to be against him as a "squatters' candidate," while they represented the large landed interests. However, they had begun to see that the Chivalry did not regard them as "white"; and they were beginning to worry about their own future if California became a "nigger state." The Californios may have profoundly disagreed with Broderick on land titles, but they knew they could count on him to fight for their rights—and they realized, if a little late, that they were going to need someone soon to fight for those rights. So they supported him to the very end.

Broderick, however, took no satisfaction in having done much better than anyone expected. In defeat he seethed against his opponents. And he behaved as if he had been the front-runner who had been cruelly denied his due. He wrote to a friend, "It would take a ream of paper to contain the account of the prohibited treachery that was used against me during the canvass."

This election, together with his experience in opposing the vigilantes, seemed to confirm him in his conviction that he had to rely on trusted ruffians, like Charley Duane and Ira Cole, rather than respectable sympathizers. A few months earlier he had been challenged about this use of toughs by such a sympathizer who had gone over to the vigilantes. Years later the man still remembered the exact words of Broderick's vehement response: "You respectable people I can't depend on. You won't go down and face the revolvers . . . so I have to take such material as I can get hold of." This election showed that, except for the Californios, respectable people would not even face down slander and threats. Except for the Californios—and they supported him only because they finally realized that they would never be respectable in the eyes of the Chivalry.

The group Broderick had gathered around him now, in addition to Charley Duane and Ira Cole, was as colorful as it was formidable. Rube Meloney was the loud gabber of the group. "His bravery was in his mouth," a Gwin man wrote, "his mouth beyond his control." If Meloney talked too much, little Billy Mulligan acted with scarcely a word; he was the embodiment of fearlessness with the size and temperament of a bull terrier, although his pinched face reminded one of a ferret. The story was told of Mulligan coming into a saloon in formal attire ready for a big evening on the town— but then he saw Broderick being berated by a man twice Billy's size. Without saying a word, Billy walked up, took the man firmly by his hands, and butted him into unconsciousness. Then Billy turned around and walked out, complaining that he needed a clean shirt since this one was covered with blood. Yankee Sullivan, former heavyweight champion of America, now a heavyweight drinker who when sober had strange bouts with fearfulness. Martin

Gallagher and Billy Carr, who took over running launches from the deported Hounds but also were Broderick stalwarts in the predominantly Irish First Ward in San Francisco. Davy Scannel, a quiet man with something of Broderick's aloofness, but without his inner rage. Scannel had been a Hound who managed to escape deportation, probably because of his mild demeanor; he would eventually be Broderick's choice for sheriff of San Francisco. Jimmy Casey, the dapper one, always dressed impeccably, prematurely balding and looking all the more mature for it. Jimmy would once take on five armed men single-handed—and, when it was over, the police arrested him for assault and battery, but then had to release him because the others were too afraid to press charges. Wooley Kearney, whom the boys liked to tease as the ugliest man in America because of his "battered, flattened twisted nose . . . at every point of the compass and more hideous at every turn." They could not understand why when Wooley blew his nose he didn't blow the damned thing off. Snaggletoothed Billy Williamson, whose teeth went with Wooley's nose, thanks to taking too many on the chops. Then there was Bill Lewis, a disreputable hanger-on no one felt comfortable with. And quiet John Crow about whom nothing was said because he was hardly ever noticed. Finally, there were the two senior citizens of the group. George Wilkes had sold his *Police Gazette* to come to California to help Broderick in any way he could. And then Edward McGowan, Old Ned who even in as colorful a crowd as this deserves a paragraph or two just to himself.

Ned McGowan was a lawyer from Philadelphia who knew the Irish political machine there as well as Broderick and Wilkes knew New York's. He also knew the leaders of the Pennsylvania Democracy, such as James Buchanan. McGowan, however, was only a politician by accident. Unlike Broderick or the sardonic Wilkes, Ned McGowan was always having a good time. A droopy, graying moustache and too much high living had given him the look of an Irish walrus, but the man was a charmer, and fancied himself a poet, and was forever reciting his own creations or adaptations:

> A little stealing is a dangerous part
> But stealing greatly is a noble art;
> It's mean to rob a hen roost of a hen
> But stealing millions makes us gentlemen.

Having left his wife and family back in Philadelphia, he had also set about making himself irresistible to all the available ladies of San Francisco, which—to hear him tell it—he was already well on his way to doing.*

McGowan had arrived in San Francisco a few months after Broderick, and had quickly fallen in with the b'hoys, who treated him as their Falstaff.

---

*Ned liked to tell the story of one conquest, a French courtesan. Having set her up in her own house, Ned caught her old pimp, a German, in her boudoir. He promptly pulled out a derringer, and plugged the retreating German in the derriere. This story was always good for a laugh, and it got better every time Ned told it.

When Broderick was running for the state Senate, they had come around to get Ned, who begged off because he was too sick to get out of bed. The boys, deciding that he was just hung over, tore the door off his bedroom, and carried him down to the polling station on it, with mattress, covers, and Ned underneath in his nightdress. Ned had to admit that he couldn't complain because they had let him vote without getting out of his bed.

It was hard not to have fun around Old Ned; he and his blarney were infectious. But he was also a man to be counted upon. He forged the link between the New York and Philadelphia Irish in San Francisco, and was always ready to turn his pen to partisan tasks. He had dismissed Gwin's crowd as "rosewater Democrats," and yet he had the kind of social polish that Broderick and Wilkes never would. Shortly after he arrived he had been elected to a judgeship in San Francisco—but then was so notoriously soft on whores and gamblers, and so hard on the respectable, that he was quickly voted out of office.

The senior citizens, Wilkes and McGowan, although not averse to rough stuff, did provide Broderick with the brains to supplement the b'hoys' exuberant brawn. This was crucial to him in his present situation. For all of Broderick's irrational resentment at losing his bid for the U.S. Senate, he could take satisfaction in his increasingly effective framing of the issues, thanks in part to the help of Wilkes and McGowan.

Broderick's views were broadly popular in the state, and he felt confident he would win any plebiscite that was decided on the issues. The problem was that these very same views were unpopular in the state government because of its dominance by Southerners. So he had no chance of winning votes in the legislature. The Chivalry would justify to the general public their rejection of him not by a discussion of the issues but by personal vilification. And this tactic was maddeningly effective.

When he was being vilified as a corrupt machine politician supported by the worst elements of society, he could barely control the terms of the debate even in San Francisco, where he was well known. His only option, therefore, was to continue to pound away against the Chivalry, no matter what the odds, and hope that the newspapers at least would finally get the message.

The people simply had to know what was being done, and more importantly what was being planned—then they would side with him. They had to know of the petition sent to the legislature in early 1852 from 1,218 citizens of South Carolina and Florida, a petition asking permission to emigrate to California with thousands of slaves. They had to ask themselves why these Southerners thought that a state with a constitutional ban on slavery might be receptive to their petition. Did these Southerners know something ordinary Californians did not? The ordinary Californians had to ask what it meant when the new governor, John Bigler from Pennsylvania, said publicly and unabashedly that those who opposed the spread of slavery were "governed by a spirit of disaffection towards the Union"—obviously, he was a Northerner with Southern views, a copperhead. They had to notice the occasional advertisement for selling slaves in California itself. For instance, in the *Democratic State Journal* in June 1852: "Negro for Sale.—On Saturday the 26th, I will sell at public auction a Negro Man, he having ageed to said sale in preference to being sent home. I value him at $300." The legislature was in practice tolerating slavery despite the state constitution. So early in 1852 they gave anyone who had brought slaves into the state before the constitutional convention a full year to remove them. That, in effect, legalized slavery from 1849 to 1853. Citizens should watch the legislature as the 1853 deadline approached; it would extend the deadline again, and again, and again—until the people rose up against the slave power conspiracy.

If they thought enough about all this, they might understand why there were continual calls from the leaders of the Chivalry for a new constitutional convention. Of course, there were minor matters in the constitution that required tinkering. Of course, too, those from the southern, less-developed portion of the state continually complained that they were being ignored by the state government except to be overtaxed—and so they yearned for a return to territorial status, or at least freedom from an uncaring Sacramento. However, these complaints were obviously insufficient to justify the drive for a new constitutional convention—and this in turn tipped you to the real motive behind the call for one. The Chivalry wanted to divide the state into two. A state of South California, once established, would then naturally drift into becoming a Southern slavery outpost on the West Coast, and might drag the territories of New Mexico and Arizona into the Southern camp, for an unbroken transcontinental belt of slave power.

Of course, the leaders of the Chivalry, at least the clever ones, would not admit this objective openly because they knew they would lose any general vote. Nonetheless, they did speak of it privately. Senator Gwin, according to one memoirist of the period, had been overheard by the writer himself talking on this very subject to the outgoing Governor McDougal late in 1851, when they both happened to be traveling on the steamship *Panama* from San Francisco to Monterey. (After challenging the vigilantes, McDougal had gone back to his old easygoing ways, which meant in political practice living in the pocket of the Chivalry.) Gwin was quietly, plausibly trying to bring the bibulous governor around to the idea. "The country is ripe for it. The initiatory steps will be taken by the legislature as fast as they can be. The people will be ready." Against an objection by McDougal about the response of the Congress, Gwin said soothingly, "The fanatics of the North could not get a corporal's guard against it." This was the kind of eavesdropping that would find its way back to Broderick and be welcomed, even rewarded.

Broderick knew he could get more than a corporal's guard to stand with him, and he would be willing to face the whole world if he could choose the men in that guard. And he knew that the people of California were far from ready to divide the state. Of course, he would know also to whom Gwin referred when he spoke of "the people"; they were *his* people, the Chivalry, the people who counted with him. Gwin's people would be ready when the constitutional convention was held, ready to get their way by gulling the easygoing and the unwary into giving them a clear majority.

A new constitutional convention was in fact called by the legislature for the summer of 1852. The Chivalry was there in force. But Broderick was there too, as a delegate and as the leader of a delegation whose credentials could not be challenged this time. He had but a simple objective. While the convention was still organizing itself and sorting out procedures, he got the floor to propose that in the name of democracy any measure which was passed should be subsequently submitted to a general plebiscite before becoming part of the state constitution. Who could be against that, except someone who was trying to pull a fast one on the California electorate?

So the convention, at Broderick's prompting, agreed that its measures would be only proposals to the general electorate. The Chivalry now realized, as well as Broderick, that their scheme for dividing the state was dead for the time being. Suddenly the instigators of constitutional reform lost interest in their own convention.

Broderick not only won at the constitutional convention, but he was also beginning to bring some newspapers along with him. The newspapers, in particular, were beginning to agree with his twin charges of elitism and slavery. The *Alta California* on February 29, 1852, observed in an editorial, "It is evidently the design of a clique in the Legislature to divide the state at all hazards." The *Alta* continued, "Those who don't want the dark cloud of slavery spread over the sunny hills and valleys of California have little to look for from the present Legislature of California."

Still the Chivalry continued to press its advantage in the state legislature, probably far more than Gwin would have wished. For instance, there was introduced a tough fugitive slave bill, "An Act respecting fugitives from labor and slaves brought to this state prior to her admission into the Union." In general, this act was needless, for a similar bill had been passed by the U.S. Congress in 1850, as part of Clay's compromise. Nonetheless, the California legislature wanted to emphasize its support for this pro-Southern portion of the compromise. The Chivalry was flexing its muscles. The legislature had already determined that "negroes, mulattos and Indians" could not give testimony in court cases. With the proposed law on fugitives strictly enforced, a free black would have no defense against a white who was willing to perjure himself to gain a valuable piece of property. This, of course, was a law that Broderick was going to fight at all costs, but by the session of April 8 it was clear he was going to lose the coming vote. He and his few supporters contented themselves with delaying the inevitable result as long as possible. Their amendments, resolutions, points of order, provisos, points of personal privilege, motions to reconsider constituted a de facto filibuster. At one point

Broderick even voted in favor of the bill in order to have parliamentary grounds to ask for a reconsideration of the question, thereby forcing a new roll call vote; at another point Broderick provided his colleagues with a slowly delivered oral interpretation of the relevant sections from the proceedings of the constitutional convention of 1849. The man had no shame.

Occasionally, one of his opponents would rise to the bait and challenge him. Then Broderick and his antagonist would verbally abuse each other for a few minutes, or maybe more than a few. Soon evening was beginning to fall on the statehouse, and candles had to be lit. Words like "abolitionist" and "chivalry" and—worse—"northern men with southern sympathies" were being thrown back and forth more frequently. Broderick was testing the parliamentary patience of his opponents every way he could think of, and sometimes they did not quite measure up. One senator, having just led the fight to defeat an amendment, when hearing another one virtually indistinguishable being immediately proposed, picked up all the papers from his desk and hurled them across the chamber in the general direction of the speaker. As the debate—or rather the delaying—went on and on, there were practical matters to be attended to. The senator from Sacramento had two large bags snuck onto the floor, one filled with a variety of cheeses, the other with a variety of crackers. These he dispensed to his ravenous allies. Later, when the bags were empty, doughnuts were smuggled in towels to weary senators. Finally, in the wee hours of the morning, the inevitable occurred, and California had its own fugitive slave bill.

Bill after bill was proposed to the legislature that Broderick could oppose with whatever means were at hand, but usually they were insufficient. A strict law for the enforcement of labor contracts came up, and everyone understood its motivation. They called it "the Coolie bill"—Asians, free blacks, and other racial inferiors could be brought into California as de facto slaves, and the state would enforce the contracts even if they violated the state constitution. Then there was the resolution that requested the federal government to remove all Indians from the territory of the state as soon as possible; this was Peter Burnett's colored-exclusion bill applied to the red man. It was all so wearisome and depressing. No wonder that Broderick had already decided he would not stand for reelection to the state Senate. Men like Gwin were calling all the shots; he had to break into their circle to have any real influence. It was New York all over again.

Broderick was having an influence, however. He was seeming more and more like a prophet as the Chivalry revealed more and more of its plans. The fugitive slave bill had further opened the eyes of the *Alta California*. The *Alta* had begun to write of a "set of politicians" who wished to transform California into "a species of aristocracy":

> Arrogating to themselves a superiority of mental endowment
> which gives them a sacred license to lord it over their less

fortunate fellow beings, they deliberately proceed to the en-
actment of laws whose direct tendency is to degrade instead of
elevating a portion of mankind. Assuming it as an inevitable
law of nature that some men were born to be masters and others
to be slaves, they belie every noble impulse of the age by seeking to sink the low still lower and elevate the high higher.

Broderick could not have put it better himself.

Yet at the very moment that this was being written relations between
Broderick and *Alta California* could scarcely have been worse. The *Alta California* had come to regard Broderick as an autocrat in egalitarian clothing,
while Broderick was for his part convinced that the newspaper had become
a mouthpiece for those who wished to make San Francisco itself into a species
of aristocracy.

The quickest way to get rich in growing California cities, especially San
Francisco, was land speculation. Broderick himself had indulged in it with the
proceeds from his shady mint operation. Frequently the state government allowed local governments to distribute state land, which had the potential of
making the new owner instantly wealthy. The degree of corruption involved
in these distributions was large even by the standards of gold rush California. By
1852 Broderick had seen what it was doing to San Francisco. An opportunity
for distributing wealth among the populace was being perverted into the service of its further concentration in the few. Or so Broderick thought.

This matter came to a head in the California legislature over some water
lots in San Francisco. The city had been gradually growing out into the bay
as the tidelands were filled in. The state officially owned the bay, but would
permit San Francisco to sell water lots—lots under water but which could
be reclaimed—for a percentage of the profits. What had been moorings for
ships would suddenly become immensely valuable waterfront property. A
great steam shovel, the Steam Paddy, was tearing away at the sandhills in the
west of San Francisco, and loading cars that would roll down the remaining
hills and dump their contents into the bay. It was a wonderfully efficient
scheme for civic advancement, or so its proponents believed. The city itself
would be leveled and extended; the city government would fill its coffers for
future improvements (better streets and sidewalks, perhaps even gas streetlights); and the leading citizens would be rewarded for their service to San
Francisco while investing more capital in its future. Needless to say, it was
the last purported advancement to which Broderick objected.

The distribution of water lots was increasing the distance between rich
and poor in San Francisco; those who could participate in their distribution
were becoming very much like a landed aristocracy, an economic elite who
could lord it over everyone else. To become immensely wealthy in San
Francisco, you had only to have enough money to offer sufficient bribes to
the right city officials. So the rich got richer.

Since the state had legal title to the water lots, each extension of them into the bay had to be approved by the state legislature. All the leading citizens of San Francisco strongly favored water lot legislation, as did the *Alta California*. Broderick as a representative for the city was expected to take the lead in advocating the water lot legislation of 1852, the third of the water lot bills. This was simply practical politics, and Broderick needed to recoup the losses he had suffered for his opposition to the vigilantes. However distasteful, he should have taken the lead in getting the water lot legislation through.

He took the lead, all right, the lead in opposing the whole procedure as hopelessly corrupt. Broderick stated the matter rather plainly, "There was fraud about many of the grants, and I want the millionaires who are wallowing in wealth to be made to disgorge."

Other legislators tried to compromise with him, but he would not hear of it. He thundered at them: do not repeal a certain section that is for the benefit of one person and leave other sections that benefit other parties unrepealed. "Let the latter parties not go unwhipped." The water lot legislation was, he insisted, "dripping with corruption."

Yet the legislature did not want to listen to him—not surprisingly, and he announced that he knew why. Colonel Jonathan Drake Stevenson was running about the streets of San Francisco, bragging about the number of legislators whose votes he had bought on this issue. (How he had risen—fallen—since his courageous defense of the Hounds!) What Stevenson indiscreetly bragged about, dozens of other aspiring plutocrats had done on the sly.

The accusation of bribes caused a rustle through the legislature, and Broderick made it clear that he was not content to make this accusation just in the abstract. And nobody who remembered his willingness to name the vigilantes could expect him to be cowed by scowling senators. He claimed he could prove that the first water lot bill was passed as a result of bribery; as for the second, he was willing to concede that the legislature might have acted in good faith. They were knaves the first time, fools the second—let there not be a third. As forcefully as Broderick expressed his charges, only one other senator among twenty-one agreed.

The *Alta California* was scathing in its analysis of Broderick's crusade against the 1852 water lot legislation. He was guilty simply of a "failure to discharge his obligations to his constituencies." As for his allegations of corruption, the *Alta* did not care "how much he bellows about fraud and knavery." Personally, he was no one to play the conscience of the state legislature, the *Alta* continued, for "we do not think the fact that Tammany Hall as the political college in which he graduated is a sure guarantee of his infinite wisdom or his immaculate honesty."

Broderick's term was now coming to an end. So did his political career seem to be to many sympathetic observers. One who wrote to the *Alta*

California to defend him conceded that "his intemperate zeal to prove himself a very paragon of legislative virtue will seal his fate as a politician."

Broderick, in fact, had lost control of himself, as if a lifetime of frustrations became somehow focused on this one issue. He would not compromise, nor could he turn away. He simply could not accept this defeat, so clearly did right seem to be on his side, so grave the consequences for California if he lost. But he seemed to be the only person who did not know that he had already lost. He was also the only person he was harming by his bitter harangues; with every futile attack his own possible effectiveness as a politician diminished. Even those who supported him on this issue and admired him generally thought he, as one put it, "has been too rigid, too inflexible, too implacable in maintaining what he has thought was right."

Broderick could not make his fellow legislators, or more importantly his supporters back in San Francisco, see the point: an aristocracy of sorts was being set up in San Francisco. It may not have been blatant like the plantation society the Chivalry loved, but it was there in the fine hotels and elegant mansions that were starting to sprout in San Francisco, wealth building upon wealth until the workingman could be effortlessly crushed beneath its weight, until his oppression seemed in the nature of things, or his own fault.

So Broderick did begin to lose all sense of proportion. His increasing depression showed itself as a mild paranoia. He began to find conspiracy and corruption where there were none. For instance, he attacked state support for a much-needed road through Red Bluff. And when he encountered the builder in a saloon, there were the inevitable hard words and then a brawl, which Broderick lost when his opponent cracked him across his much-abused face with a tumbler. In this fight Broderick had first lost his cool and then his consciousness. Crumpled there in a bloody heap on a barroom floor, he seemed finished, a spent force.*

While Broderick was flailing away in California, William Gwin was returning to Washington quietly triumphant. He could claim to have carried the state in 1852 for Franklin Pierce, the new Democratic president—an exaggerated claim but not one that anyone of any consequence in Washington would be inclined to dispute. Moreover, he had in tow a like-minded junior senator, John Weller; he had dexterously managed to replace that embarrassment John Frémont with a former Ohio congressman fully qualified to be a senator. Weller also would strengthen the moderate center of the Democratic Party. Pierce himself was from that center. Although a New Englander, he favored the South because of its steadfast support for the Mexican War, where Pierce himself had been a hero.

---

*Likely Broderick would have eventually mended personal fences with this opponent, Colonel James Freaner, as he usually did once the anger had passed—but he never had the chance. When the fight was over, Broderick was in no condition to exchange manly pleasantries. And then the next winter, when Freaner was traveling with the rest of the Shasta delegation to the Democratic convention, they were surprised by the Pitt River Indians and massacred to the last man.

Everything was working out perfectly. He was now unquestionably a member of the senatorial elite, with a man of his party and his sympathies in the White House. People had already begun to speak of him as a possible cabinet member in the new administration, secretary of the interior perhaps. The local political squabbling in California, on which the likes of Broderick spent themselves, seemed far beneath him now. There was much to do for California, and he was just the person to do it. However, he was going to do it not as a grasping politician but as a farseeing statesman who acted for the good of the nation:

> When we consider that nearly the whole products of the industry of California consist of gold, of which so many millions of dollars have been already shipped to New York, New Orleans, and to other ports, augmenting the capital of our country, the value of property and the wages of labor; furnishing a vast and rapidly augmenting market for our own products and manufactures, as well as employment for our vessels; while at the same time in the purchase also of foreign imports, adding millions of dollars annually to our revenue from customs, and giving us a new export with which to sustain the balance of trade in favor of the Union, the importance of furnishing every facility to commerce with California can not be over rated. Such facilities would not be local, but for the benefit of the revenue of the government and of the trade, industry, commerce, shipping and manufactures of the whole country.

He made this same point almost every time he spoke in the Senate. He always spoke as someone who only happened to be from California. When he referred to "us" or "our," he was talking about what California contributed to "us" Americans, and to "our" well-being. Gwin spoke not on behalf of California but on behalf of a prosperous, growing, and grateful nation. His performance was consistently grand, and usually effective, so effective that one senator had taken to complaining that the federal government had consistently discriminated in favor of its "youngest sister." This was not discrimination, Gwin repeatedly insisted. It was rather a recognition that this sister alone faced the Pacific. (Gwin, like Californians ever since, seemed at times to forget that Oregon and Washington existed.) So the future of our nation in the greatest of seas depended upon the well-being of young California.

Of course, Gwin's effectiveness depended upon more than his eloquence. Much that could be done in Washington depended upon one's social position. He and his wife entertained lavishly, and opened their house to the whole range of politicians, from Southern fire-eaters like Jefferson Davis to Northern radicals like William Seward. Many a practical coalition could be matured, after a fine dinner, over nut brown Madeira and Havana cigars.

The hard work of legislation, however, was done in committees. Needless to say, Gwin had adroitly managed to get himself well placed. By the time Gwin returned to Washington in 1852, for instance, he was already chairman of the Senate Committee on Naval Affairs. As such, he could control the flow of legislation for naval projects—and he also had a platform from which to lecture the Senate as a whole on the maritime future of the nation, a future in which California had an unparalleled importance. On this subject, he spoke with a patriotic zeal that verged on jingoism.

Who was America's greatest naval rival—indeed, the greatest naval power in the world? Britain. Where alone did the United States have a naval advantage over the British lion? In the North Pacific. There Britain lacked fortified harbors and fully equipped naval yards. If the United States had such on the Pacific, Britain would be at its mercy. We could "in an incredibly short space of time . . . sweep the Pacific Ocean, sending our prizes into San Francisco for safety and confiscation." Yes, we could successfully challenge Britain. More than that: "With the ocean supremacy on the Pacific in our hands, it would be a question of the dismemberment of her empire." America could overcome the greatest single power in the world: "In the North, we would seize her North American possessions, and in the East, we would destroy her dominion in Asia."

It is hard to say how much of all this Gwin really believed. But the evocation of such imperial visions did make it hard to quibble with him over the dowry for America's youngest sister, especially when she would offer in return nothing less than world domination. But Gwin was also capable of switching from remote grandeur to grubby immediacies:

> Here is my own State of California, which paid $3,212,127.79 into the Treasury from customs the last fiscal year, with a sea coast of 970 miles, utterly destitute of light-house establishments, necessary and indispensable to our commercial marine in approaching her coasts. . . . It is known that, perhaps with the exception of a single ship that visits the Greenland seas, the whale fishery is confined to the Pacific and the South Seas. The proceeds for the year ending June 13, 1850, from the whale fishery alone, amounted to $2,318,024. Are no means to be provided for the protection and encouragement of this valuable traffic? And are our possessions on the Pacific Coast to be deprived of a state or nation, through the miserable, parsimonious policy, on the part of a general government, when we are advancing, with rapid strides, in all that constitutes real worth and greatness?

Gwin's advocacy was relentless. If his opponents from New England wished to argue specifics, he would be happy to discuss the particulars of the whaling industry down to the last dollar, or custom duties to the last cent. If his Southern friends wanted to speak of states' rights, he would talk more broadly of the effect of California on the economy of the South—of the port of New Orleans, say, before and after the discovery of California gold, a subject on which he was an authority. No matter how one looked at it, the Southern states owed California. And if a senator from Missouri or Illinois wanted to talk about national destiny, then Gwin was happy to explain why California, a strong California, was the key to eventual world domination by the United States of America.

If Gwin's advocacy was relentless, his effectiveness at times was stunning. He got a naval yard for California included in the Naval Appropriations Act of 1852. The amount agreed to was $100,000, woefully inadequate as Gwin well knew. However, once having gotten his colleagues to accept the proposition that California had to have a fully equipped naval yard, he then convinced them to increase the fund for Mare Island, the place in the north of San Francisco Bay the secretary of the navy had chosen for the yard. So $100,000 had soon become $845,000, and soon after that $1,355,000.

Gwin progressed similarly on lighthouses and coastal fortifications. An appropriation of $40,000 in one Congress for a maritime survey became $140,000 in the next, and $700,000 a year later. Congress had become parsimonious in the matter of coastal fortifications, and would agree only to the cost of repairs, at least on the Atlantic Coast. Gwin made his colleagues realize that California, as America's bulwark on the Pacific, should be an exception to this otherwise fiscally prudent policy. By 1853 he had managed to have $500,000 appropriated for California's coastal defenses. In 1854 he somehow managed to get a further $830,000 appropriated to fortify San Francisco Bay alone. Lighthouses, a survey of islands, a dredging of the San Diego harbor, the construction of a maritime hospital—one after another bill he shepherded through Congress, mastering the details of each case, presenting the evidence to Congress, and making the necessary backroom deals, both with his colleagues and with the administration.

Gwin did not always get his way. On the matter of land titles he tried to pass legislation that would satisfy both squatter and large landholder. He argued that any real settler, one who had occupied the land and improved it significantly, should be granted as much as 160 acres, even if those happened to be within a legitimate Mexican land grant. Those who held the old Mexican titles to this land would then be compensated for their losses with an equivalent tract from the public lands. The measure was typical of Gwin in its attempt to find a compromise that would incorporate the interests of both sides. However, on this particular issue the lines had been drawn too strongly already in California; the landed interests in California vehemently opposed Gwin's bill, and Weller went along with them, effectively killing the measure. Gwin could at least show the squatters that he had tried.

Sometimes Gwin could do no better than temporize. Indian policy was one example of this. He first had the federal government appoint Indian agents to investigate conditions and make recommendations. He then supported legislation that appropriated first $25,000, then $50,000 for the president to negotiate treaties with the various California Indian groups. When these treaties were concluded, they contained a concession that the federal government would provision the Indians for the next two years; so $766,000 had to be appropriated for that. Then Gwin felt pressure from home against the treaties, and radically changing course as a result, demanded that they be presented to the Senate for formal confirmation. When they were, he opposed them, and they were rejected. Now a superintendent of Indian affairs was to start all over again. From all this it was clear that he had no idea what to do. He cared about the Indians themselves not at all, and would have been happy to see all the "wild" Indians removed from the state. (He read the resolution of the California legislature on the subject to the Senate sympathetically.) But such a removal as Andrew Jackson had effected with the Cherokees and others was not militarily feasible. So Gwin contented himself with muddling along on this issue, trying one thing and then another, always being careful to avoid angering any significant portion of his voters but also eschewing any government action that might provoke an Indian war, the last thing the growing state of California needed.

Gwin was interested only in problems that were solvable. The difficulties with establishing a federal mint in San Francisco were slowly being worked out, although far more slowly than anyone had expected. There were complications in the organization of the federal courts in California, particularly in the relationship of southern and northern California districts. And a good deal of improvisation was required before San Francisco alone was designated the Pacific Coast center for collecting federal customs. This was just the busyness of governing that took intelligence, patience and—above all—flexibility. And he loved it. This was the life he was meant for.

Thankfully, some issues were clear and could be worked on consistently. Maritime improvements for California was one; improvement of the mail service was another. A third was the development of a transcontinental railroad. California had to be linked to the nation by land. The need was as obvious as the obstacles were formidable. Unlike the maritime improvements, which Gwin had well advanced halfway through his first term, the transcontinental railroad was clearly a measure that might take a decade or more of legislative effort to accomplish.

In 1851 Gwin had read to the Senate resolutions from the California legislature urging the construction of a federally funded transcontinental railroad. He, in turn, recommended that the national government proceed slowly in order that the proper route be selected, but he acted as if so obvious a necessity for the nation was a foregone conclusion. There was going to be a rail line to California, but where was it going to be? His colleagues were not so sure. The California resolutions were submitted to the Committee on Roads and Canals for a quiet burial.

In the first session of the 1852 Congress Gwin indicated his intention to begin to push for the railroad. He submitted a two-route plan as an amendment to an unrelated piece of legislation. The amendment was passed with little discussion. The bill itself, on land grants to the indigent insane, was going nowhere; but Gwin had at least won a vote for his railroad. By the end of 1852 he produced a detailed plan for the railroad. This time he proposed an exclusively southern route. Beginning in San Francisco (with an extension up to Oregon), the railroad would swing down the great valley of California, and skirt the Sierra Nevadas at their southern end. Once the line reached Albuquerque, it would split into different branches. One line would end in New Orleans, another in Memphis, another in Texas, another in Missouri. (Gwin could at least count on the senators of four states to appreciate the wisdom of his design.)

The scale of the proposal was breathtaking. Some 5,115 miles of railroad at an estimated cost of $121,920,000. Gwin had his first opportunity to present the plan on January 13, 1853. He tried to present systematically all the advantages of this vast project—not to the youngest sister California but to the nation as a whole. He spoke of the impetus to settlement and development the railroad would provide, and also of the improvement in military defense. He tried to appeal to Northern interests, especially by distancing himself as much as possible from the Southern sectionalism of his friends. This railroad, taken together with "its great adjunct, the electric telegraph," would transform this country into a truly unified nation: "There will be established a chain, binding together each member of this confederated Union, every link of which will be united . . . by a common interest, a unity of purpose, and a deep-seated attachment to our institutions."

Years later he would point back with pride to this argument. If only his measure had been pursued by the federal government expeditiously, the Civil War itself, he would contend, would have been impossible. Others, long suspicious of Gwin, would repeat the arguments heard at the time: The railroad might increase the connection of California and Oregon to the Union, but one only had to look at the proposed route to see that it would do so through the South. The railroad, as proposed by Gwin, would have made California an appendage to the South. In any test of strength between North and South, California either would have been with the South or would have had to go its own way altogether.

As hard as Gwin worked for the railroad, he could make little headway. He thought they had a breakthrough when the Senate was about to vote $20,000,000 in bonds for the beginning of construction, with the president himself empowered to choose the final route. But then Senator James Shields successfully offered an amendment that no part of the appropriation could be spent within a state. So the railroad could run up to the boundary of California, and stop there unless the youngest sister could come up with the tens of millions to extend the road. This amendment, as far as Gwin was concerned, effectively "destroyed" the measure. He blamed Southern senators, with their insistence that federal money should be spent only in federal lands, for having gutted it. They allowed their principle of states' rights to blind them to their own interests.

In early 1854 Gwin was starting over. The government had produced, thanks to his prodding, a multivolume railroad survey. Moreover, in the Senate there was now a select committee on the railroad, with powers like Douglas and Seward on it, and Gwin as chair. The committee labored through all the various proposals—and all the constitutional objections—and came up with a compromise that benefited enough states to have a chance to pass. There would be not one but three major routes: a Southern Pacific Railroad starting in Texas and ending in Southern California; a Central Pacific from Missouri and Iowa to San Francisco; a Northern Pacific from Wisconsin to Oregon.

This measure squeaked through the Senate by a vote of 24 to 21, with all the slave senators and many of the New Englanders voting against. Although this was not a plan that Gwin liked, its passage by the Senate was a personal testimony to him. No one expected the plan to become law, for it was too late in the session for the House to act. But the Senate, or at least a bare majority of the Senate, wished to give to Gwin a vote of confidence and encouragement for his efforts that had yet to bear any tangible fruits. He continued, as long as he was in the Senate, to work indefatigably for the transcontinental railroad. His select committee continued to meet, and he tried to broaden it to include opponents he respected such as Jefferson Davis.

In talking about the transcontinental railroad he was carried beyond himself. Here was a great work worthy of his political skill, a work that would benefit thousands, millions, and into the indefinite future. He was ideally suited, he believed, to establish it as a national objective, and thereby to earn his place in history. On this subject he could become a sincere visionary, a dreamer of dreams:

> Senators, our progress as a nation has comparatively but begun; the immeasurable future lies before you. It is for us to do our part . . . to devise this means which will overcome geographical separation, and give unity to every part of this ocean-bound Republic. By the natural law of increase, aided by a swell of immigration which the shock of European War and the reconstruction of nationalities will send to our shores, the new century that approaches, even though we are yet in the springtime of national existence, will find within our limits, now greater in territorial extent than Imperial Rome, a population equal to what she possessed in the zenith of her glory, after the growth of a thousand years. Let the measure under consideration be consummated, and an act, vital to the integrity of our

territory, and to the perpetuity of our undivided Union, will have been accomplished; and then, as a united people, "WHO CAN PREDICT OUR FUTURE DESTINY?"

Oddly, when the speech was printed, Gwin insisted that this last rhetorical question be capitalized, as if suitable for being carved into stone. The Senate was never quite moved sufficiently by his eloquence and his vision to consummate this measure under any of the myriad forms in which he submitted it. Nonetheless, he was certain he would win, in time. And in the meantime there were more than enough successes to satisfy him.

Nonetheless, for all of these legislative successes, Gwin was starting to make bad mistakes as a California politician. Of course, given his growing national prominence, he might disdain the incidental details of provincial politics; sooner or later, he would have national office in a Democratic administration, as he had almost had in this one. As for California, from what he had seen during his trip back, there was no effective opposition to his designs. If he could get Weller elected behind the scenes, he certainly was in no danger himself.

This would not be the first time that he had simply overplayed a strong political hand, and thereby hurt himself. But never again would he be so grievously off his political game as he was in 1853. And there was another explanation beyond simple overconfidence. That year his favorite daughter had died, a young victim of the notorious swamp fevers of the Potomac, also then indirectly a victim—one might be tempted to say—of her own father's fevered ambition. With such a loss Gwin was not well equipped to deal. He was a man of good cheer who enjoyed calculation but not introspection. Especially not the searching of inward abysses that seemed Broderick's daily bread. When forced to look inward by such grief, Gwin appears to have temporarily lost his balance, and his extraordinary balance was his great strength. And so for a short time he seemed to stop calculating. Or rather he calculated in an uncharacteristically shortsighted manner.

Such a sacrifice of his daughter could only be weighed against great projects like the transcontinental railroad, or coastal improvements in the millions of dollars. Not two-bit appointments and petty deals. These were beneath his consideration—but, of course, such patronage was in his power. So he distributed it offhandedly, to members of what he might consider his extended family.

As a result, he disregarded his supporters who were not of Southern origin, although some had provided the Chivalry with the swing votes for power. And this included the new governor of California, John Bigler. Bigler, for reasons not entirely clear, hankered after the ambassadorship to Chile. Gwin, with culpable indifference, made little or no effort on his behalf, the first of a series of uncharacteristic mistakes on his part. What did he care whether Bigler was pleased with him?

It was one thing to displease the governor of your state by a failure to act energetically on his behalf. It was another to threaten indirectly his future political existence. Bigler had his own supporters who needed to be taken care of, and he expected them to be considered for federal positions and contracts. Gwin was managing to get vast amounts of federal money spent in California. Bigler expected his people to get their share. But he wrote bitterly to his brother, himself a prominent Pennsylvania Democrat, about Gwin's one-sided distribution of patronage: "The office holders for this state were nearly all taken from the South, but few men from the North received favors."

Gwin refused to appreciate Bigler's complaints, and never would. Years later he still looked back upon this period with pride. He described himself as a "stern party leader" whose "severest political conflicts were with members of his own party, who were not disposed to sustain the organization, unless their personal views could be carried out." He bragged that during the 1850s he had "never failed to control" the Democratic Party of California and had always managed to "carry it successfully through every conflict . . . with the exception of the year 1855." He did not seem to realize that his coming humiliation in 1855 was a consequence of his ignoring Bigler in 1852 and 1853.

Bigler in his desperation turned to Broderick for help, since he was the only prominent Democrat not under Gwin's sway. At a personal level this was not a distasteful alliance for either man. They had worked together before; when Broderick was president of the state senate, Bigler had been speaker of the state assembly. Although Bigler was moderately pro-Southern and hence the kind of Northerner whom Gwin would happily cultivate, his style offended many of the genteel Chivalry. "Big John" was an enormous man with the voice to match, a Friar Tuck of California politics whose very presence in a room could make the elegant Heydenfeldt cringe. One contemporary sniffed that Bigler was "rather low in his tastes, unrefined in conversation, and slovenly in his dress"—but admitted that he was also smart, glib, and doggedly persistent. All this must have endeared him to Broderick, especially the bad taste. Broderick had recently supported Bigler for the Democratic nomination for governor because the choice was between Bigler and some genuine Southern fire-eaters.

On most issues Bigler and Broderick still disagreed, but this new alliance was not about issues. Bigler wanted to retain his power and Broderick wanted to regain his. Moreover, Broderick's railing against the Chivalry now had in Bigler a latter-day convert.

So Broderick showed Bigler how to use the state government as a source of patronage. Commissioner of pilots, state prison inspector, district judgeships—there were many offices that could be distributed for maximum political advantage. Broderick, for his part, negotiated these appointments on behalf of Bigler. With Bigler's support he himself became chairman of the state Democratic committee, and quickly revised the rules for representation to the state convention, to the benefit of Broderick, Bigler, and San Francisco.

As a result of this alliance, the Chivalry was out in force against Bigler when he stood for reelection in 1853, another miscalculation. They challenged him at the convention with a Texan, Richard Roman; but Bigler prevailed, thanks in part to Broderick's fiddling with the representation. Then many prominent Chivalry Democrats, such as Solomon Heydenfeldt, bolted the party to support actively the Whig nominee, a Missourian named Waldo who had a farm back home worked by slaves. Worse, prominent beneficiaries of Gwin's patronage, although they could not openly support a Whig, simply sat on their hands during the campaign.

Broderick seemed to realize that this was his last chance to revive his political career, and an unexpected one at that. He pulled out all the stops; there was not a Tammany Hall trick of electioneering that he did not use. Opponents decried "Biglerism" and a "reign of ruffians." The sheer magnitude of the bribery was beyond anything California had yet seen. One estimate was that Bigler and Broderick had spent 1.5 million dollars on the election. Even with more than a million dollars and dozens of potential ballot stuffers on Broderick's side, the alliance of Whigs and Southern Democrats held firm during the campaign, and Bigler seemed a long shot on the eve of the election. Then the results were in. Bigler had won by less than 1,000 votes, out of 75,544 cast.

The resentment against Bigler and Broderick within their own party was shown by the simple fact that the Democratic nominee for lieutenant governor ran more than 10,000 votes ahead of Bigler. Still they had won, and the narrowness of the victory made it all too obvious that the election had been stolen. And so the chorus against Broderick's unscrupulous tactics was even louder. But the alliance of Bigler and Broderick had apparently broken Gwin's control of the Democratic Party, if barely.

As the news from California came back worse and worse, Gwin was resentful and short-tempered. He was still not himself. When a California congressman, Joseph McCorkle, upbraided him for his inept handling of federal patronage, he lost his temper when he should have been mollifying the other man. He was tired of dealing with people who just did not understand—did not understand politics, did not understand the density of this great nation, did not understand Gwin's importance, did not understand their own place.

Insults were exchanged, and neither would back down, and so eventually the two men found themselves facing each other across a field of honor. Rifles at thirty paces. Only then did they come to their senses—somebody might get shot. They did have to exchange a few shots just for form, and then they quickly agreed that it all had been an unfortunate misunderstanding.

A newspaperman there had understood what was happening. He wrote that this duel had been fought by two men "full of wrath, sausages, and cole slaw." Their marksmanship, he added, did leave a little to be desired. Gwin had come close to hitting a passing crow, while his opponent in making sure he missed Gwin while aiming in his general direction almost winged one of Gwin's seconds. Honor was satisfied, however, when it was discovered that a donkey half a mile away had been shot dead.

For one of the few times in his life Gwin had completely lost his temper, and as a consequence he had permitted himself to become an object of fun. Things had been going perfectly for him; and now, little more than a year after he was being considered for Pierce's cabinet, they seemed to be unraveling. Yet he could not admit to himself that he had done anything wrong. He was just a stern party leader amid Democrats for whom politics was personal, Democrats like Bigler and that damned ruffian David Broderick. They just did not understand, and never would.

Broderick understood well enough that Gwin's weakness was only temporary. The moment he was free, Old Man Gwin would be on his way back to California to mend fences. Once he turned his full attention to that, Broderick would stand little chance. Gwin would likely come back with an ambassadorship for Bigler in his back pocket, and Bigler's successor already chosen. Broderick had to get him while he was vulnerable.

In the normal course of events Gwin would have no reason to be worried for himself; his term as senator was not up until March 1855. There was plenty of time for him to regroup. When he did, this little setback might serve only to make him stronger. Moreover, the Whigs as a party seemed on the verge of collapse in California, now that they had shown they could not win a state election even with the support of many Southern Democrats. And when that party did collapse, where were the Whigs to go but to Old Man Gwin?

With Broderick's political fortunes at least temporarily rising, there was a buoyancy about him during this time. He had been rooming in the San Francisco home of Tom McGuire and his wife. Tom, the man reputedly as handsome as Coleman, was the leading theatrical impresario of the city and the owner of the Jenny Lind Theater (which Broderick would arrange to have the city of San Francisco take off his hands when it became a white elephant). Now living with them were Broderick's most trusted advisers, George Wilkes and Ned McGowan.

Living with McGuire, Wilkes, and McGowan, Broderick was less inclined to be depressed, even when enduring political setbacks. Wilkes and McGowan were always cooking up something. Now that Gwin looked weak, their minds were working overtime. And McGowan, as usual, was having one helluva time.

They had done all right on the Bigler campaign. But what were they to do next? Then they came up with it, which one first it was hard to say.

Eureka! They would move the senatorial election up a year; the legislature would vote to fill Gwin's seat a year early. Broderick could take the seat from him while suave Old Man Gwin was safely a continent away. It was beautiful, delicious, and it might just work in light of Bigler's victory. Better to act than to wait. Gwin wouldn't know what had hit him.

Intelligence of Broderick's plan was quickly passed to the Chivalry and other Gwin supporters, but they did not take it seriously. Even if Broderick somehow succeeded in engineering his election a year early, they were certain that the U.S. Senate would itself set aside this irregular election, and allow Gwin to continue. To their blithe report, Gwin responded quickly and emphatically, at least as quickly and emphatically as he could from Washington. He had checked with the powerful Southern senators who authoritatively interpreted the rules—and, as he suspected, they were loath to intervene in the affairs of a state. Gwin urged his supporters that they had to defeat Broderick's bill within the legislature itself.

At this point he might have had a few thoughts about the electric telegraph and the transcontinental railroad. With those he would have known in time to take matters into his own hands. He had been ambushed, that was for sure—and now he could only wait in Washington, and hope his men were up to the challenge ahead.

By this time Broderick had already gained considerable support, for many had already been brought to his side with state patronage before the Gwin people appreciated the threat. One shrewd episode in his campaign had been a dinner organized by Broderick and Bigler to honor two new arrivals to California: General John Wool, the new commander of the U.S. forces on the West Coast, and Henry S. Foote, former Mississippi senator and governor. Why Broderick should be honoring, in particular, a noted Mississippi politician and friend of Gwin seems perplexing. Until, that is, one knows the reason for Foote's trip west.

Foote believed that he deserved a place in the new cabinet of President Pierce as secretary of war. Instead, he was passed over by Pierce for another Mississippian, an old comrade-in-arms, Jefferson Davis. Disgusted with Washington politics, Foote decided to travel west. Wool, on the other hand, was ordered to the west by Pierce; he had obeyed, but was openly disgruntled because he too felt he was deserving of higher office. He had, after all, been second in command at Zachary Taylor's great victory at Buena Vista.

So Broderick organized for the evening of February 15, 1854, a grand public banquet in San Francisco honoring the great soldier and the great statesman. Even the Chivalry had to attend to honor their accomplished compatriot Foote. And yet effusive praise of these two deserving men could not help but produce implicit denunciation of the corruption of Washington in general, and of the cronyism of the Pierce administration in particular. And if some at the dinner came then to think of Senator William Gwin as the local personification of that corruption and cronyism . . . well, who was

David Broderick to disabuse them of their newfound political insights? And if some were too obtuse to get that point, they had only to listen to the last speaker, who happened to be none other than that distinguished journalist, the founding editor of the *Police Gazette,* George Wilkes. Watching the Chivalry squirm throughout the banquet was better than leading Mike Walsh's parade through the respectable sections of New York.

By the time the legislature had begun to consider the question of moving up the election, Broderick had produced a position paper called "The Address to the Majority," probably written by Wilkes with revisions suggested by McGowan. There Broderick marshaled precedents for this change. He also argued that only by this early election could California be assured of two senators at the very beginning of the next session of Congress; an early election was dictated by prudence, given the length and uncertainty of the Panama voyage. Had not California already been without her senator at the 1851 session because Frémont had to return home to stand for reelection?

Broderick's opponents produced their own pamphlets that attempted to rebut Broderick's claims point by point. A new state legislature was to be elected between then and the expiration of Gwin's term. This was the legislature that should fill the Senate seat, not the outgoing one. The electorate would be selecting this legislature with an eye to the impending choice of a senator, whereas this was not even considered as a possibility during the last election. Broderick's plan was a constitutional perversion that violated the democratic commitment to allow the people a say in the choice of their highest representatives.

Broderick, of course, knew it was going to take more than arguments to convince the legislature one way or the other. He brought with him his loyal, growing group of enforcers to help persuade doubtful legislators. To his regular crowd he added William Walker (soon to gain fame as a filibuster in Nicaragua) and Parker French (who had made his reputation as a polished desperado by swindling emigrants on the way out to California).*

Not that Broderick thought force would necessarily be required—after all, he had ample amounts of that mother's milk of politics, money. To be sure, the Chivalry and others were complaining that he and Bigler had virtually bankrupted the state during the last election campaign. But Broderick was only a step away, or rather two, from the prize he had so long sought. His friends advised caution. He responded arrogantly, "Leaders never take advice; leaders give direction. If it were to get whispered abroad that I ever took advice, my friends would lose their confidence in me, and leave me

---

*In 1849, the story goes, Parker French had sold passage to California to six hundred travelers from New Orleans, and gave them a gala bon voyage party with more than ample champagne; it was only when these aspiring argonauts staggered down to their berths that they found out there were only two hundred and fifty available. But they were by then well out at sea, and Parker French had slipped back to New Orleans with a tidy profit.

and go to the fountain head!" Wilkes and McGowan, hearing that, would have only shaken their heads.

The discussion had not gotten very far along on the election bill when Senator Peck arose to speak on a matter of personal privilege. He begged to inform his colleagues that on the ferry trip to the session he had been introduced to a Mr. Palmer by A. A. Selover. When they were alone, Palmer offered him $5,000 for his vote on the election law and also on the Senate seat itself, the latter vote of course going to Mr. Broderick. Peck proudly reported that he had responded, "I will not sell my vote; I cannot be bought." He demanded that a full-scale investigation be begun forthwith. It was, but to no effect.

Nonetheless, the charge did provide a rallying point for the Gwin supporters, especially when similar charges continued to be made at regular intervals by other legislators. One senator had the offer of a bribe brought to him by his brother, a clergyman who also would be in on the take if his brother accepted, which he did not. In most instances resistance to these bribes only made the bidding go higher. Rumor had it that some state senators were bragging that they had sold their votes for as much as $30,000.

One rural senator, a poor yet principled fellow who was trying to scrape together enough money to bring his family out to California, showed up at a trusted colleague's room all atremble. The rumor was correct, he blurted; he had himself just been offered $30,000 in gold. He had a favor to ask. The other senator, himself sternly anti-Broderick, was not to let him out of his sight until he cast his vote against the election bill. $30,000! Why, that was right close to his price.

The Senator Peck, who had started the bidding at $5,000, was invited to go for a supposedly apolitical buggy ride by an old business associate known to be sympathetic to Broderick. As they were going along a stretch of road with a precipitous drop off the passenger side, the driver recklessly speeded up and jumped off, to leave Peck on the buggy as it careened back and forth, and finally tumbled over. Senator Peck was unhurt, apart from cuts and bruises; but he was terrified, especially when he realized that his host had hurried off without even seeing if he had survived. This was attempted murder. No doubt about it.

Peck did make his way back to town, and put himself under the round-the-clock care of the Gwin forces. They provided him with a well-armed guard, lest another attempt be made on his life. He and his guards occupied a hotel room that could be reached only by first going up a staircase and then walking down a long hall. So no one could reach them without being heard well before. But the fact that there was no chance for surprise only served to make them more anxious. They knew how desperate a crew Broderick had assembled, and expected a full frontal assault any minute.

When reports reached the room of a "storming party" being assembled at Broderick's headquarters, a number of the guards began to have second thoughts. Yet what would happen if as they deserted Peck they ran into the Broderick men? Certain death. The Broderick men would treat them as hors d'oeuvres to the general slaughter.

The guards felt cornered, as did Peck. This whole setup had been a mistake; they had played right into Broderick's hands. One guard, in particular, began to crack. He had the look of suffering a severe attack of Panama fever, simultaneously shivering and sweating uncontrollably; soon his shirt was drenched and his teeth had taken to chattering so badly that he could scarcely talk. The others tried to laugh him out of it, but could not—and that only served to make them shakier themselves.

Then, at two o'clock in the morning, after hours of such tension, the downstairs lookout reported that the crisis was over; there would be no attack tonight. In relief, the guard with the shivers ran into the hall, and triumphantly raised his pistol in the air, challenging Billy Mulligan and the rest of Broderick's henchmen to try their worst. His cohorts now realized that he was a greater danger to them than anything Broderick was likely to do; so they forcibly disarmed him.

He was just calming down when footsteps were heard coming up the stairs. It was another Gwin man, just checking to see how things were going. But the brave guard prematurely concluded that this was Billy Mulligan who had heard his challenge and was coming for him—and him without a weapon. Immediately his teeth were chattering again, and limbs trembling, and he began running around the hall, as the others later put it, like a chicken with his head cut off. There was no place to hide. Finally, after desperately trying a number of doors, he simply broke one down, thereby awakening a soundly sleeping guest who immediately began yelling "Thief, thief!" as he fumbled under his pillow to find his pistol to shoot the intruder. After witnessing all this, Senator Peck must have thought he would be safer back in that buggy.

The next day the election bill was finally brought to a vote in the Senate. This would be the decisive vote, for Broderick—the Gwin people conceded—had control of the Assembly. The roll call began, with Lieutenant Governor Sam Purdy, a Broderick man but respected by all, in the chair as president of the Senate. "Bryan." "Aye." "Catlin." "Nay." Broderick was there, looking tense but not worried. The usually raucous Senate now was deathly quiet; neither side was certain how the vote would turn out. One or two votes could swing it. "Cofforth." "Aye." "Colby." "Aye." "Crabb." "Nay." No surprises yet, but all it would take was one. "Crenshaw." "Nay." "Gardner." "Nay." "Grewell." "Aye." There it was, a break, entirely unexpected to the Gwin supporters, who audibly groaned.

Jacob Grewell was a Whig, from a San Jose district strongly anti-Broderick. A vain old fool, a retired preacher who always looked slightly ridiculous in his cheap wig, which he insisted upon wearing but could never get on quite right. Why was he voting for Broderick? A complete surprise to Gwin's men, but apparently not to Broderick's, who were trying to suppress smiles. The roll call by now had long since passed Peck, who had of course voted "Nay." Everyone else was voting according to form. "Wade." "Nay." It would be a tie, left up to Sam Purdy. "Walkup." "Nay." Who might just be up to an act of real political courage. "Whiting." "Aye." A tie.

All eyes were on Purdy while the secretary tallied up the totals that everyone in the room knew already. As soon as the secretary announced the tie, Purdy without hesitation voted "Aye" and pronounced the bill passed, to the tumultuous cheers of Broderick's supporters. Broderick himself looked overcome. He was beaming, shaking every hand offered, but was apparently unable to speak, for the moment. Just as well, one sour observer thought: "Had he then given them the word to 'Clean out the house!'—referring to his opponents—the frantic multitude who stood prepared to receive his hint as a command would impulsively have rushed to its execution at any peril."

The story was soon all over Sacramento about how Grewell had been turned. It was his vanity that had done the trick. Not a bribe or a threat, just his vanity. Grewell had been provided with sumptuous lodgings at the Union Hotel, Broderick's headquarters. Grewell held court, lounging in his stocking feet on an elegantly upholstered chaise lounge, worthy of the best San Francisco whorehouse. He lay there, languidly, almost coquettishly, as one Broderick man after another tried to woo him. Yet they were making no headway, although clearly the old man was having the time of his life. Finally the Broderick forces decided to play their ace. They brought in his friend and former partner, the respected former congressman George Wright. And Wright did his best—but whenever he thought he was on the verge of success, Grewell would take time out to adjust yet again his ill-fitting wig. Finally, Wright in exasperation stormed out of the room, exclaiming to Joe Palmer (the same Palmer who had offered the bribe to Peck), "Great God, Palmer, nothing can be done with that old mud turtle! Why the very moment I got him all right he lifts off his god damned wig, and lets all the electricity I have worked into him escape through his spongy bald head. It is no use; you may as well give him up as a hopeless case." But Palmer was not so sure. He kept a steady stream of Broderick men, including himself, going in to talk to the vain old man who continued to adjust his wig and to lounge languidly like a surfeited French aristocrat. Palmer realized the key to what was happening at a moment when the wooing lagged a little bit. Then immediately Grewell would say something like, "Talk on, gentlemen; keep it up; you may get me yet. There's no telling. It's mighty animating." Clearly Grewell was going to vote with whoever flattered him last. All they had to do was to keep it up. They did until the vote, and they won.

That night the Broderick people had secreted Grewell in a safe room, with a single guard, while they celebrated. But the Gwin people had their own spies, including an employee in that very hotel. He informed a daring Gwin operative, who in stocking feet and with pistol drawn snuck up to the room. But, as it turned out, the guard had been celebrating too, and was dead drunk. So the Gwin man, who was prepared for manslaughter in his cause, had only to tiptoe away with the always pliable Grewell, who continued to adjust his wig periodically while whispering about this all being mighty animating. Broderick and his people learned too late that Grewell had been lost.

The next morning the election bill was brought up for reconsideration. Grewell himself grandly announced his change of mind, some howler about "telegraphic dispatches" he had just received from his constituents. Once the move to reconsider was passed, it was clear that Broderick's scheme had been belatedly, unexpectedly defeated. The vote to table the matter indefinitely, in effect to kill it, then passed 19 to 14. The look on Broderick's face was such that even his opponents in their celebration tried to avoid his gaze.

There was nothing for Broderick to do now but to wait for the state party convention that was to meet in Sacramento in July. He was the chairman of the state central committee, and could use this convention to consolidate his control over the party apparatus. They had to nominate candidates for the U.S. House of Representatives as well as the state legislature. If he could get the right slate into the state legislature, he could still be elected to the U.S. Senate–but that would not be easy given the strength and organization of the Chivalry, who knew as well as he what was at stake, and were not going to be taken by surprise this time.

Gwin was still in Washington, but his supporters now fully appreciated the seriousness of the situation. They went to Sacramento for the convention prepared for a fight, parliamentary or otherwise. And they went bolstered by their own crew, who would like nothing better than the otherwise. Everyone, needless to say, was—as they would have put it—"well-heeled." Each side took over a hotel, and transformed it into something like a fortress. It was a matter of pride that anyone passing the hotel would see plenty of drawn weapons on the alert.

The site for the convention was the large Baptist church of Sacramento, the only building in the city that could hold them all. Few of the six hundred who would gather there had either the Sermon on the Mount or spiritual cleansing in mind. The maneuvering began even before Broderick as temporary chair had called the convention to order. As a matter of fact, this convention would never come to order in any recognizable sense.

First, Broderick delayed the opening until the late afternoon. He wanted to challenge a pro-Gwin delegation from Tuolumne, and had to wait for his alternative delegation to arrive. Moreover, Broderick had planned to let many of his toughest delegates into the church secretly by a side entrance so that they could dominate the pews at the front. Once the other delegates had crowded into the back, Broderick would immediately recognize the delegate who had been chosen to nominate his man, Judge Edward Mc-Gowan, as permanent president of the convention; Broderick would call for a voice vote, declare McGowan elected by acclamation, and then be well on his way to complete control of the California Democratic Party.

Gwin's men, however, learned of the plan through their spies. To tell the truth, Broderick's men usually had a hard time keeping their mouths shut, especially after they had hoisted a few; despite Broderick's admonitions, they were always bragging, and didn't much care who heard. All it took was a few nondescript Gwin men strategically planted at the major saloons, nursing a beer or two, apparently indifferent to their surroundings but really all ears—and the Chivalry would know exactly what Broderick was up to.

So they knew how Broderick intended to stack the front of the church with his storm troopers, and they were determined to counter this with their own. As Broderick's men were reaching the side door of the church at the prearranged time of 2:30, thirty of Gwin's delegates, mostly long-haired Southerners, showed up at the main entrance to the church. They forced the door, and were marching in a phalanx to the front just as the Broderick men entered through the side. A brief melee ensued, with more shoving than fighting, until each side had staked its claim to roughly equal portions of the front rows. This had taken only a few minutes, and for the rest of the half hour before the meeting was to commence the shock troops of both sides sat uneasily side by side, while the rest of the delegates slowly arrived, some of the earlier ones visibly perplexed that the church was already so filled.

Around three o'clock Broderick walked out onto the large platform where the pulpit was. (It was estimated this platform could hold a hundred persons, an estimate that soon would be sorely tested.) He surveyed the scene with that rigidity of expression that his friends and enemies both knew signified he was in a murderous fury. Finally he took the pulpit, and called the meeting to order.

Immediately, from the midst of Gwin's thirty, a man was on his feet placing the name of the Chivalry candidate into nomination for the presidency of the convention: the former governor of the great state of California, John McDougal. For a moment, Broderick was perplexed. He was certainly not going to allow I, John McDougal to take over the chair of this convention—but he looked in vain for the man who was supposed to put his candidate in nomination. Apparently, the nominator had prudently lost himself in the shuffle, and was cowering out of Broderick's sight somewhere. Then Broderick saw him, and declared firmly, "I recognize the gentleman from Santa Clara. The seat of the other gentleman is contested. I will not recognize him."

Everyone knew that a number of delegations on both sides were going to have their credentials challenged; that issue would be one of the first tests of strength at the convention. But it could not be legitimately raised on the initiative of the temporary president, except that this was exactly what Broderick was doing. This proved too much for a Gwin delegate standing near the man Broderick refused to recognize. He was now on his feet shrieking at Broderick from the front row: "You have no right to decide on that! Your duty is to put the first motion made, no matter who made it!" However, while he was yelling this, the distinguished gentleman from Santa Clara had been shouting something else, unintelligible to everyone but the unperturbed Broderick, who announced the nomination of Judge Edward McGowan as the permanent president. Broderick no sooner had announced the nomination than he had asked for all in favor to signify by saying aye; and he had no sooner done that than he had declared McGowan elected by acclamation. At that moment noisy disorder became complete pandemonium.

From the back of the church McDougal, along with his bodyguard, was trying to push his way to the pulpit, although at least one Broderick supporter momentarily broke through the guard in a not quite successful attempt to wrestle him to the ground. The corpulent McGowan, on the other hand, perhaps to protect him from other attempted tackles, had been uneasily hoisted on the shoulders of Broderick men who were making their own triumphant if stumbling march toward the pulpit. McDougal by now had been hoisted as well, but he looked none too happy about his precarious perch. By this time the pulpit platform was itself surrounded on all three sides by men cheering, shouting, gesturing, many with guns in their hands. A few terrified souls could be seen edging their way toward doors, windows, anything that promised a quick exit. Broderick stood his ground, however, looking as if his deepest wish was to annihilate the whole vermin-infested earth.

Suddenly a man rushed to the pulpit and pointed a cocked pistol at Broderick's head, without saying a word. Broderick coolly looked him in the face as if he were a naughty child, and bade him to be careful with loaded firearms. But few seemed to notice this dramatic and potentially deadly stand-off, since all the delegates were now swirling about the church, shouting encouragement and threats, and overturning any pew or person in their way. Then the chaotic din was broken by the sharp report of a gunshot. Three terrified delegates immediately jumped out of the building through the open windows, while others dove behind pews; and then Rube Meloney screamed that he had been shot.

Meloney was quickly carried out of the church for medical attention. The rival candidates themselves were as quickly off the shoulders of their supporters and into their midst for protection. Nobody was parading now. The two sides drew themselves up into battle lines, each side glaring at the other, as if daring it to make the first move. At this moment of great tension but relative quiet, virtually the whole leadership of the California Democratic Party seemed poised to wipe itself out in a miniature civil war. But just when the tension seemed utterly unbearable, one of those who had carried out Meloney reentered the church to announce that in fact he had not been shot.

Upon careful medical examination it had been determined that the warm fluid Rube had felt running down his leg was not blood.

The whole assembly, just moments before in a murderous frenzy, now began to roll with laughter of Homeric proportions. Men who had been poised to kill one another an instant ago were now leaning together in an effort just to remain standing, so hard were they laughing. Others, holding their stomachs and with tears on their cheeks, had given up trying to stand, and were stretched out on the pews; were it not for the sound, one would think they were suffering from some agonizing fit that was racking their body with spasms. When the laughter finally started to die down after a while, and everyone in the hall was trying to catch his breath, a sheepish Rube Meloney reentered the church, and it all started again, especially when people got a glimpse at his shit-eating grin. He was treated as a hero by everyone, even by those who hated him and sincerely wished him and his kind dead. Many men were trying to do their best not to laugh because it had started to hurt so much, but they could not help themselves, and their effort at control only made it hurt more, and that somehow made them laugh still more. In fact, the laughter could never be fully stopped the rest of that evening. All it would take was for one person to be once again struck by the humor and begin to chuckle—and within seconds the whole church would be filled with muffled mirth.

Nonetheless, the feuding continued. Each side claimed to have elected its own president who in turn conducted his own meeting, pretending that the other half did not exist. Actually they did agree at a certain point to elect the same secretary, who now was supposed to record the minutes of the two meetings simultaneously. Perhaps he was ambidextrous. Of course, nothing got done, and those in the back could make out little in the jumble of words.

There were challenges to the Chivalry for having bolted the party during Bigler's reelection campaign, and challenges against Broderick and Bigler for making the party one that an honest man could scarcely support. Occasionally a conciliatory speech would be tried, as often a simply humorous one. The latter worked better. Throughout it all McDougal and McGowan were themselves remarkably good humored, as if they were pleased as punch to be the central actors in so extraordinary an event.

At one point someone in the crowd took pity on them, and passed them each up a big cocktail, which they looked at lovingly. Yet neither would drink because they were afraid of being drugged. But Ned as usual was equal to the situation. He mixed together the two drinks, poured them out again, and announced, handing one to the appreciative McDougal, "It's been a long time between drinks, and if there has been any dousing of the liquor we are both in for it." And the church rolled with laughter again.

Nothing was getting done, of course. Yet neither side wanted to adjourn first, as if leaving the church in the hands of the others would somehow give them legitimacy. When the pastor and his deacons appealed to the double convention that they were overstaying their welcome (and had already done much damage), the two sides did come together long enough to agree that these peacemakers should be bodily removed from their own church. And there was some more good-humored laughter at the sight of the pious being pitched, as there was when the prostrate preacher pleaded that if any of them ever should come to his church again, they should come as Christians, not politicians. That was a good one.

The pastor and his deacons did refuse to allow the church to be lighted, for fear that it would be eventually burned down by the tussling Democrats, which it probably would have. So for hour after hour they conducted their double meeting by the light of two little candles that they had pilfered from the sacristy. As the night deepened, the presidents could see less and less of their delegates. If open war broke out now, you wouldn't know whom to shoot. But both McGowan and McDougal were jolly good fellows, now enjoying themselves too much to instigate any real trouble. Finally, after five hours of futility, with the candles beginning to gutter out, it was agreed that both sides should adjourn simultaneously. The competing presidents, arm in arm, then led the two factions out of the church in double file and in a mood of oddly good cheer.

Mayhem had somehow been avoided, thanks perhaps to Rube Meloney's wet leg. Nonetheless, the meeting had left the Democratic Party in as bad a shape as that Baptist church, which these aspiring Ciceros had rendered a shambles.

The two factions continued their conventions, but separately in different buildings. (They were not welcomed back to what was left of the Baptist church, at any rate.) The Chivalry was eloquent in condemning both the corruption of "Biglerism" and Broderick's use of force. Broderick's men, on the other hand, produced equally eloquent defenses of democracy and the rights of the common man. They dismissed the Gwin people as "bolters"; the Gwin people dismissed them as "bogusites."

A pro-Gwin newspaper reported simply, "The democratic party of the State is severed—severed by the act of one man." Broderick, according to this account, had displayed "an arrogance never before equaled." Another newspaper wrote with disgust, "It was a task beyond the power of reasonable intelligence to reduce to shape and method the chaotic confusion into which California democracy has been thrown by a death struggle for the spoils of office."

So each faction came up with its own slate of candidates. Broderick's group, however, lacked any plausible candidates for Congress. They tried the reasonable expedient of nominating the present congressmen for reelection. This was a gamble, because no one knew whether they wanted reelection; and no one could ask them, for this very moment they were in transit back to California. Moreover, they were scarcely admirers of Broderick. When they did arrive, Broderick's gamble became a debacle. They wanted to have nothing to do with the "bogusites"; they both withdrew their candidacies and campaigned for the Gwin nominees. So Broderick's ticket had to be reconstructed; it ended up headed by latecomers who were also nonentities.

The Whigs were ecstatic. Until recently on the verge of extinction, they now expected to sweep the election, gaining a plurality against the divided Democrats, who after a few halfhearted attempts had given up any hope for a compromise slate. However, the Whigs had underestimated how badly Broderick's campaign had unraveled. In the end his candidates for Congress gained scarcely ten percent of the vote, and the other Democratic candidates managed to edge out the Whigs. Things were, if possible, even worse in the state legislature for Broderick. Between the two houses he had perhaps a dozen votes he could count upon—and dozens of votes that would go for him only after hell froze over, and perhaps not then.

By the fall of 1854 Gwin had returned to California. Broderick had caused him serious concern, but the upstart now had nothing to show for his machinations, except his own political career in ruins. Nonetheless, Gwin had to admire the cunning if not the recklessness of the attempt.

Gwin did not want to take any further chances on his reelection, and had come to realize belatedly how volatile electoral politics still were in California. One would have thought it would have settled down by now; but the place was still uncivilized. Gwin liked to talk about the process of developing legislation as the "maturing" of a bill; California, politically and otherwise, still had much maturing to do.

So he had to return; in fact, he was bringing his family with him. His wife was to set up residence in San Francisco, to begin entertaining respectable society, or what passed for such there. The hotels and restaurants were getting better, and the theater was passable, although the pride San Franciscans took in their opera productions was laughable. This move, although just until his reelection, was a considerable imposition on his wife, who loved Washington and had become a fixture in its high society. But it had to be done. One could not be too careful, and he did not want any Northern hotheads saying that he was keeping his family away from California until he and the Chivalry had made it a slave state.

Once the composition of the state legislature was known, he may have felt that he had been too careful. The Democrats easily controlled it, and his reelection should have been a sure thing. The count was 69 Democrats, 42 Whigs, and 2 independents. Broderick could not be a serious candidate, and there was no other Democrat to challenge him. The worst that might happen was that Gwin would have to make a deal with Broderick for his 12 or 13 votes, but probably not.

Broderick, however, was putting out the word that his people would never vote for Old Man Gwin. Gwin, however, thought he understood exactly the game being played. Party discipline had been destroyed in the last election; so Gwin would have to win in the legislature. If Broderick's men remained firm and the Whigs did too, then other aspiring Democrats would naturally try to position themselves in the early balloting to become the compromise candidate, as Weller had been. Broderick was encouraging such potential candidates to start thinking of themselves.

What was in this for Broderick? This was what Gwin had to ask himself. Broderick must know that he had no chance, nor did Bigler, nor did any other of their faction. It could not be personal spite because Gwin scarcely knew the man. What was Broderick after, then? The only reasonable answer was that Broderick was preparing to make a deal with Gwin—and he was doing that very well. The Irishman was cunning, crude but cunning.

But what kind of a deal? Then Gwin became certain he understood. Broderick wanted to shed Bigler, and become governor himself. From there he could make a run at Weller in two years. That was the only thing that made sense, and it could be managed, although there would be some grumbling from fire-eaters like Heydenfeldt. When the time came, Gwin would simply offer Broderick his support for the governorship—and that would be that. Weller would have to look out for himself. Having figured it all out, Gwin went into the actual election perfectly sanguine.

The early votes went as Gwin must have expected. The Whigs with nothing to lose held firm, as did Broderick's 13. Joseph McCorkle, with whom Gwin had had that embarrassing duel, made a surprisingly strong showing as the dark horse, with more votes even than Broderick. At the appropriate moment Gwin discreetly made the planned offer of the governorship to Broderick. And was turned down flat.

Gwin was left incredulous. It could not be loyalty to Bigler. The Bigler-Broderick alliance had been one of convenience on both sides. It couldn't be that Broderick actually expected the convention to turn to him, or that the eventual election of McCorkle was any tangible advantage to him. This was mad. Gwin could not comprehend it.

Gwin could comprehend Broderick's ambition, and his ruthlessness (although the latter was not fit for a gentleman); but he could not comprehend his implacability. Like the story of one of Broderick's bodyguard who had challenged another man to a duel. It was to be fought at no paces. They would start the duel with each pressing his pistol against the temple of the other; they would both then simply pull the trigger at the sign. Simple insanity.

Gwin just could not understand someone who acted as if he had nothing to lose. Or rather who with much to gain would rather lose everything than give an inch. He could not place Broderick within the conventional world of his politics.

Gwin had done everything he could. He had gone so far as to put in writing his offer of support for the governorship, a risky thing to do but a tangible sign that he was brokering in good faith. What had Broderick done then? Broderick had written back tartly that Gwin seemed to be under a misapprehension. Broderick, not Gwin, selected governors for the state of California. This was mad, and also insufferable impudence.

Despite all his efforts, the puzzled Gwin could make no progress. After thirty-eight ballots with no appreciable movement of votes among the candidates, the legislature gave up for the time being. In March 1855, Gwin's term expired, and the senatorship from California was left empty. Gallingly, Weller was given Gwin's cherished chairmanship of the select committee on the transcontinental railroad, Weller who had voted with the Southerners that federal moneys should only be spent for the railroad across the territories.

Worst of all, Gwin could think of nothing to do to break this impasse. He did not know how to deal with this man. There were now essentially two Democratic parties. Broderick proposed that this breach be healed by allowing each faction to be equally represented on the Democratic central committee. The proposal was ludicrous. Broderick's faction had been shown in the last election to be merely a splinter, less than a fifth the size of Gwin's side. Yet this outrageous bluff—and a bluff it was—he presented to the committee take-it-or-leave-it. Against all rational calculation, Gwin's people decided to take it. He could not blame them; they had to find some basis on which to deal with this man.

To bring Broderick to compromise reasonably seemed impossible, unless a common enemy emerged, a third force that threatened them both. Such a force was just about to emerge, and it was not the Whigs.

6

The challenge surfaced in San Francisco in late 1854, before the election that year. The *Alta California* began in August to refer to a secret political society that was meeting in San Francisco, the Know-Nothings. George Wilkes could tell Broderick of its origins. This particular organization had first appeared in New York at about the time Broderick had left for California; then it was called the Order of the Star-Spangled Banner. Seemingly unimportant at first, it had multiplied quickly and spawned similar secret societies in nearby states until it had become a power in the region. "I know nothing" was just the standard response to inquiries about the society from those who did not give the proper sign, handshake, or password.

Broderick may not have previously had any direct experience of the Know-Nothings, the Order of the Star-Spangled Banner, or the Party of the Dark Lantern (as it was alternatively called). He, nonetheless, knew them well enough. They were nativists, and the New York in which Broderick had grown to maturity was the center for nativist activity in the United States. Nativism meant American politics as a system of rationalized hatreds—in particular, hatred for foreigners and hatred for Roman Catholics (foreign or otherwise). In such a system of hatreds Irish immigrants served double duty.

In Broderick's New York the weekly *Anti-Romanist* and monthly *Protestant* were popular periodicals that jointly warned New Yorkers of Catholicism—"of this anti-christian system; of its soul-corrupting influence"; and of "the danger to which our country, if indifferent to its increase in political influence, is exposed." Respectable New York publishers were quite happily turning huge profits by publishing lurid anti-Catholic fabrications, such as breathless accounts of convents as popish brothels. (Maria Monk's *Awful Disclosures of the Hotel Dieu Nunnery* was the runaway best-seller of the day.)

Unlimited immigration, nativists believed, permitted this system of ignorance, priestcraft, and superstition to present a formidable threat to the American republic. Samuel Morse, inventor of the telegraph, was more widely admired for having uncovered a foreign conspiracy to use immigrants to control the American heartland: "We must first stop this leak in the ship, through which the muddy waters from without threaten to sink us."

For such political insights Morse had been nominated for mayor of New York in 1836 by the Native American Party. Although he failed, in the next election the Native Americans swept both the mayoralty and city council, as they would again in 1844. That year anti-Catholic riots broke out in Philadelphia, leaving thirteen dead, dozens injured, and many churches and convents destroyed. (Ned McGowan knew of this riot first-hand.) The archbishop of New York responded properly, at least from the standpoint of Dave Broderick and the b'hoys. Try such a thing in New York, Bishop Hughes said, and the Irish will come out in force, and leave the city in ruins, like Moscow after the retreat of Napoleon. The b'hoys were not exactly religious, but they'd have been there—and the Protestant bullies would have met their match.

The issue, as Broderick would see it, was not religious but political. It was about power. Immigrants, especially from Ireland and Germany, were crowding into the United States, hundreds of thousands each year. When they began to vote, how could those in power stay in power? Only by excluding them from citizenship.

So the nativists argued that the immigrants were incapable of participating productively in the life of a great republic, until they had been here at least twenty-one years, if then. And Roman Catholics were permanently incapable, no matter how long they had been here, because they owed higher allegiance to a foreign power, the papacy (which, by the way, had plans to relocate the Vatican to the American Middle West). Therefore, Catholics should not be allowed to hold public office at all.

Nativist changes in the immigration and naturalization laws would see to the exclusion of the foreign-born from the electoral process, and an active native American political organization would see to the exclusion of Catholics from office. (The New York Democrat who had cost Broderick a seat in the House of Representatives split the Democratic vote by running a nativist campaign against him.) But the fear behind this political program was expressed in a joke that had made the rounds. The schoolboy, having been asked to parse "America," responded: "America is a very common noun, singular number, masculine gender, in the critical case, and governed by the Irish." This answer would not have seemed to Broderick and McGowan half-bad, at least as an ideal.

Broderick had been around long enough to realize that nativism came in intense waves. During the Mexican War it seemed to be in decline, but this was an illusion since the hatred was simply projected outward. Many of those principled Northerners who had opposed that war did so because the conquest of Mexican territory would incorporate into the American republic a preponderance of people unfit for citizenship. Now in the 1850s, with immigration still rising, nativism was organizing itself again politically, and the mobs were responding, as usual not realizing that they had more in common with the people they were attacking than with people who were inciting them—or so Broderick thought.

In Washington, D.C., in 1852, someone discovered that the pope had donated a block of fine Italian marble for the building of the Washington Memorial; this was obviously part of his plot to undermine the American republic, although no one could specify quite how. (That probably meant the subtle Jesuits had their hands in this.) A mob of patriots saw to it that the block ended up at the bottom of the Potomac.

Franklin Pierce had not helped things when he appointed a Catholic postmaster general (an old associate of Ned McGowan's from Philadelphia) and a number of foreign-born Americans to diplomatic posts. This was obviously the beginning of the end for the Protestant Republic of America. The outgoing president, Millard Fillmore, thundered that the foreign vote was "fast demoralizing the whole country, corrupting the ballot box—that great palladium of our liberty—into an unmeaning mockery where the rights of native born citizens are voted away by those who blindly follow their mercenary and selfish leaders." (This apparently was all by way of saying that President Fillmore really would have liked another term.)

So nativism was on the rise again as Know-Nothingism—and nowhere was the ground more fertile for this political bigotry than California. Resentment of foreigners had been the commonplace expression for the frustration of aspiring argonauts; and suspicion of conspiracies had consistently been a chief organizing principle of local politics.

Moreover, here was Broderick, Irish and nominally Roman Catholic, widely regarded as a mercenary and selfish leader, who was supported mostly by immigrant Irish and German voters. The general points made by nativists throughout the country could be particularized with notable pungency in California. So high-toned moralists could write, as one California newspaperman did, of the "moral leprosy" that was spreading through this body politic of California; Broderick had controlled Bigler, it was said, as Cardinal Richelieu had pulled the strings on the pathetic Louis XIII. This "jesuitical system of rascality" should be decried by all true Americans, for "a more life-crushing incubus, terrible evil, nor fouler blot ever rested upon any ill-fated land, than have dark and nefarious schemers brought upon us."

For Broderick there was a life-crushing incubus here, all right; it was social oppression disguising itself as moral self-righteousness, the use of nativism by the respectable to divide the workingmen against themselves. Of this threat Gwin and his Chivs (as members of the Chivalry were now being called colloquially) had not a word to say, for they enjoyed seeing Broderick and his kind discomfited. Broderick realized that Gwin himself would never go over to the nativists; Gwin, no less than Broderick, was a party man who knew that Democratic organization and discipline was his best hope for national influence. But Gwin would wink and look the other way when his less-sophisticated or more-excitable followers went over, much as he had when they supported the Whig candidate Waldo over Governor Bigler.

More worrisome still, the Whigs themselves were looking for a new cause, and perhaps even a new organization. Their twin failures against the divided Democrats in the last two elections seemed to kill them finally as a major political force in California. The Know-Nothings, if they could organize themselves, might provide the old Whigs and disaffected Chiv Democrats with an alternative venue, untainted by Broderick and his supporters. ("King David, his courtiers and retainers," as one newspaper had dubbed them.) This was a danger, especially with the Democrats divided as deeply as they were.

As a result, Broderick must have read with mild concern the brief newspaper stories that the Know-Nothings were organizing in San Francisco. He could not get much reliable information beyond that. Newspapermen were excluded from these meetings, or sworn to leave their profession at the door. And loyal Broderickites with names like Mulligan and Casey were not likely to be welcomed. And Jimmy Casey himself had, amazingly, already gone over to the Chivs, at least partly.

Casey had managed to get control of a district ballot box in the recent election. Apparently he had used one of his own contriving, with a secret compartment that Casey filled with ballots before the polls opened. While doing so, Casey had been struck by an inspiration. Later, when the ballots were counted, Jimmy Casey had been elected county supervisor by a clear margin. This was a remarkable result, since Casey did not live in the district. Moreover, until the ballots were counted, no one had realized that Jimmy was even a candidate for the office. And no one had ever seen so many write-ins, and all in a similar hand.

Always dapper in dress and looking older than his years because of premature balding, Supervisor James P. Casey, the people's choice, now started putting on airs, or at least was acting the part of an important man by parleying with the Chivs. Ned McGowan was trying to coax Jimmy back, and Broderick so far had not written him off, as he might have if the situation within the San Francisco Democratic Party had not been so complicated.

For the election of 1854 the Democrats of San Francisco were either more or less divided than the state organization, depending upon how one looked at it. The factions had managed somehow to agree upon a single candidate for mayor, although they were fielding independent slates otherwise. Broderick's supporters were dismissed as "bogusites" by the other Democrats. However, these other Democrats themselves had split over the nominations to some minor city offices. As a consequence, they had divided themselves into two groups: the Chivalry was stuck with the nickname McGowan had given them, the "Rose-water Democrats"; and the other faction decided on a more manly appellation, "Bone-and-Sinew Democrats."

The Whigs still fielded their own ticket, naturally—and were mercifully freed from any necessity to come up with a nickname. The Know-Nothings waded in with their Citizens Reform Ticket. (A secret organization could not run under its own name apparently.) Then a wonderfully funny thing happened, funny at least to those who would not be eligible to enter the Order of the Star-Spangled Banner. It was discovered that the true-blue American nominated for mayor of San Francisco on the Citizens Reform Ticket was himself a communicant of the church headed by the bishop of Rome. So there had to be a noisy meeting during which he was replaced by a candidate whose theology was not incompatible with the institutions of the American republic. However, the dumped candidate did not take this kindly; so he and those who voted for him then formed their own ticket, Cuidado, which had as its slogan "No proscription on account of country, religion, or politics."

If all this were not complicated enough, there already were two other tickets that had been drawn up in reaction to the Know-Nothings—the Anti-Know-Nothing and the wittier Know-Something tickets. All these slates, taken together, should have presented the discerning San Franciscan voter with ample choices, but appearances sometimes are deceptive. Some organizers wanted a pox on all parties; alas, they could not agree among themselves, except that they also wanted to be independent of one another. So there were also slates put up by the Independents, Independent Citizens, and Independent Union. There were also the Anti-Slavery Men, whose objective was clear, and the Pine Tree Club and Y.I.'s, whose objectives have been lost in the mists of time.

Perhaps Broderick and his men were behind some of these organizations. They may have decided that the more divided, the more confused the non-Democratic vote, the better the chance for the divided Democrats. Whatever their machinations or hopes, the Democrats were soundly defeated by the Know-Nothing candidates. And the occasional attempts to steal ballot boxes were beaten off by Know-Nothing guards. Once a polling place was judged potentially in trouble by Know-Nothing observers, the secret call "ki-eye, ki-eye, ki-eye" would be raised, and dozens of armed men would rush to the site—"faster and more numerous," Ned McGowan said with annoyance, "than rats from a burning slaughter house." McGowan himself had tried a slier means of electioneering; he had distributed what announced itself as the Know-Nothing ticket but was really a list of Democratic candidates. None of this had much effect, and nativists now controlled San Francisco's government, and were gloating over it:

> The Know-Nothings have done the job.
> Wide-awake boys acted accordin'.
> If you want to get a lick,

Just say you're a mick
And they'll kick you on the other side of the Jordan.

That was not all the bad news for the Democrats. The Party of the Dark Lantern was being organized by reform-minded citizens in all the major northern California cities. Or so it was said. Their opponents, hearing this, were left frustrated for lack of reliable information—which was precisely the point of operating under the dark lantern.

"Where are they? We are told that the Know-Nothings are holding their meetings in town every night and their numbers are rapidly increasing. Nobody seems to know where their head-quarters are. . . . The question is, how the devil do they increase their numbers so fast, when nobody can find the right door to knock at?" So a Stockton newspaper complained.

In Sacramento the frustration was so great that a group of naturalized citizens decided secrecy itself was a compelling weapon; so they formed their own secret society, Freedom's Phalanx, to counter the Know-Nothings. It did not do any good. When the next city election came, no leading citizens would allow themselves to be nominated for office by either the Whigs or Democrats—and the Know-Nothings swept twenty-four of twenty-five offices. A Sacramento newspaper reported that naturalized citizens had boycotted the polls for lack of suitable candidates, and that the city was now in the "possession of this secret political society." It possessed San Francisco, Marysville, Stockton, Sacramento—and was rumored to be organizing just about everywhere else.

This was starting to get more than a little serious. When Broderick blocked Gwin's reelection to the senate in early 1855, he may have felt that Gwin's support and the Democratic nomination for governor might not have been sufficient to assure his election because now the Know-Nothings were poised to take over the whole state. However, it is unlikely that either Broderick or Gwin took this as a threat yet because the Know-Nothings had not shown they could organize effectively above the local level. After all, a state election would require them to go public. Nonetheless, this may help explain the generous concessions Broderick extracted from the Democratic committee. If the Know-Nothings decided to challenge for statewide office, the Democrats needed to be unified—and Broderick's people, unlike the Chivalry, would be the most reliable votes against the nativists.

By the spring of 1855 the Know-Nothings, now calling themselves the American Party, had had their first state convention. And then they began to have public rallies around the state. The one on June 25 in Sacramento made it clear that the Democrats were in trouble for the next statewide election. There was an enthusiastic crowd estimated at 1,500. A cause for even greater concern was the collection of speakers, not so much for what they said as who they were.

One was David Terry, until then a loyal member of the Democratic

Chivalry. (He wrote years later of his objectives in the 1850s, "I desired to change the constitution of the state by striking out the clause prohibiting slavery and for several years entertained strong hopes of effecting this object or, failing in that, to divide the state and thus open a portion of California to Southerners and their property.") Although an intelligent lawyer with political views similar to Heydenfeldt's, Terry otherwise could not have been more different. Unlike Heydenfeldt, who was by temperament a corporate lawyer, Terry regarded law as dueling by other means, and dismissed the businessmen of San Francisco as "damned pork peddlers." Terry, a large man more than six feet tall and weighing two hundred pounds, had been a Texas Ranger, and he had a hair-trigger temper. Oddly flat-faced with a bulbous nose, he wore his hair long, in the Southern style, and was clean shaven except for a profusion of chin whiskers. His blunt style was one of physical confrontation and intimidation, a style assisted by the common knowledge that he always carried a bowie knife and did not hesitate to use it. Terry had been at the forefront of those who challenged Broderick's men at the Baptist church convention, ready to kill or be killed. Now, apparently, he was a leading Know-Nothing. And this meant trouble for the Democrats.

More trouble still was the presence on the platform of Henry Foote, the former Mississippi senator and governor. Foote, a shrewd, practical politician after Gwin's own heart, had been an important Southern supporter of the Compromise of 1850. Afterward, he and Jefferson Davis had struggled for control of the Democratic Party in Mississippi. Foote's appointment to Pierce's cabinet, he had anticipated, would end that struggle in his favor; instead, Davis had been appointed secretary of war, another instance of Pierce's preferences for Mexican War veterans, damn the political consequences. Foote, as a result, judged that he had no future in Mississippi—and chose to emigrate to California to try to make his fortune as a lawyer. At the dinner Broderick gave for him he had foresworn politics. Subsequently he had repeated this by publishing a notice in a San Francisco newspaper in which he announced forthrightly, "I intend to take no part in the local politics of this State, now or hereafter, under any circumstances which can possibly arise." This in part was his attempt, once he realized how he had been used, to make amends with his old friend Gwin. But also it seems to have been a sincere profession of his intentions, at least then.

Obviously Foote had changed his mind. With the leading politicians of the state committed to the Democratic Party, and with the Whigs without any leaders of stature, the opening for someone of Foote's experience in a rising Know-Nothing party was irresistible. Here was another William Gwin, without the incubus of David Broderick on his back. His speech at the Sacramento rally, needless to say, was a campaign speech. If as shrewd a political weather vane as Henry Foote was pointing in the Know-Nothing direction, the California democracy was in for some rough weather indeed.

The Democrats had to wait for the Know-Nothings to misstep, but they showed no signs of doing so. In town after town the 1855 July Fourth celebrations were put in the hands of the Party of the Dark Lantern. And the speeches praising true Americanism could not but be interpreted as endorsing their program. But what was their program?

Broderick must have felt that the moment they were forced to make it explicit the Democrats would be able to attack them effectively as themselves un-American. The reports from the Know-Nothings in the East were promising. The party there seemed on the verge of splitting, with the Southern faction emphasizing anti-Catholicism and the Northern faction opposing slavery as well. (As the Chicago *Tribune* put it, American liberty was in danger of being "crushed between the upper and nether mill-stones . . . of Catholicism and Slavery.")

Perhaps the California Know-Nothings would fall into the same trap; the Democratic newspapers were doing their best to provoke them, among other things calling them Hindoos (for reasons that were not altogether clear, but at least the intended insult was plain). They could also try to be helpful by finding a biblical basis for the movement. It was the Book of Job, chapter 8, verse 9: "For we are but of yesterday, and know nothing."

Worry about the Know-Nothings as the party of tomorrow, however, dominated the state Democratic convention. (The convention was held in a theater because no church would allow them facilities in light of what had happened to that Baptist church the last time.) Delegates and nominees had to swear on oath that they were not now nor ever had been members of the secret organization, the Know-Nothings—and that, even if they were members, they would still work for Democratic nominees. This pathetic non sequitur was a measure of Democratic desperation. Of course, they also condemned as un-American not only secret organizations but also "the proscription of a man for the accident of his birth, or for his religious opinions." They also claimed that honesty and righteousness were on their side; they steadfastly assured voters that the Democratic Party "will respect the moral sentiment of the state, in the nominations which we are about to make"— and then went about business as usual by renominating Big John Bigler for governor.

The Chivalry did try to convince the convention that this nomination was suicide, and proposed instead Milton Latham. This was a shrewd choice. Latham had come to California in 1850 at age twenty-three, and was congressman at twenty-five while still looking, according to one friend, like a "handsome boy." The friend continued, "Few men have enjoyed more of the world's smiles and favors, and few deserved them more than this young man. . . . He was even and genial to all; had no angular points, and made money with the ease of fortune's favorite." He should have added that Latham was such a favorite of fortune that he often took her for granted and was incredulous when occasionally she glanced in other directions. And, moreover, that his "lack of angular points" was interpreted by some as a lack of any convictions at all, except that everyone should love Milton Latham and happily give him whatever he wanted. And, amazingly, it worked out that way for him with disconcerting regularity.

Latham had endeared himself to the Chivalry by refusing renomination to the U.S. House when Broderick had offered it on his ill-fated ticket after the party schism. Milton Latham, then not yet thirty, had not hesitated to turn this down because he had already concluded that he was meant for much bigger things. Having seen Washington, Latham had decided that he must someday soon be a senator, and did not doubt for a second that he would.

He had already been generously rewarded for turning Broderick down. Gwin had seen to it that President Pierce appoint him collector of customs, the single most important patronage appointment in the whole state with many lesser jobs under his complete control. So Latham had continued to make friends right and left. Now the charming, boyish Milton Latham would be willing to be governor of California. So he was making a run against John Bigler, or rather was allowing his Chivalry handlers to make one for him. There ensued a warm but politely conducted contest. Bigler was nominated on the third ballot, and many of the Chivalry then made plans to support the Know-Nothings if they came up with an acceptable candidate.

In August the Know-Nothings held their convention, and from the Democratic perspective it went with depressing smoothness. The platform, which the Democrats had hoped would forthrightly raise divisive issues, in fact danced around them with considerable skill. One could interpret its planks as one saw fit.

The Know-Nothings expressed "the firmest and most enduring opposition to agitation on all questions of a merely sectional character"—and Southerners, if they wished, could interpret this as a condemnation of abolitionists. The new party was inflexibly opposed to public officials who "acknowledge allegiance to any foreign government"—and this could be interpreted by nativists, if they wished, as the exclusion of practicing Roman Catholics from office. Their proposed restriction of eligibility for public office to those born within the present territory of the United States could appeal to nativists without necessarily offending Californios. "A judicious revision of the laws regulating naturalization" recommended in the platform might refer to the old proposal to require twenty-one years of residency before naturalization—but then again it might not. On the other hand, their "stern and unqualified opposition to all corruption and fraud in high places" was an unmistakable allusion to Broderick and Biglerism. Finally: "Utter disregard of ancient party names and worn out party issues, and a cordial confraternity with all who are willing to cooperate with us in support of the principles herein set forth." So, good-bye Democrats and Whigs; all were Americans now, all except perhaps Catholics and the foreign-born, and certainly sectional agitators and corrupt officials.

The nominations were equally dexterous. For governor they nominated

J. Neely Johnson, a bright young man in his twenties, without a record but with a decidedly pretty wife. David Terry and other Chivs who had gotten on the bandwagon early were rewarded, Terry himself with a nomination to the state Supreme Court. And more ambitious politicians like Foote hovered benignly on the fringes waiting for the ripe plum of a U.S. Senate seat to fall into their laps. The slate, in general, was skillfully designed to appeal to the Chivalry; as one observer put it, "There is not a man on it who is a candidate for an office of any importance who is not intensely Southern in all his views and feelings." As for Terry and the other nominee for the Supreme Court, the *Alta California* thought, "It would be impossible, probably, to find in all California two men who more completely embody the principles of the Chivalry than these two individuals."

The subsequent election in the fall was a melancholy tale for the Democrats. The Whig Party did not participate, except to endorse the Know-Nothing ticket privately. As a consequence, Know-Nothings swept the statewide offices. The state legislature was little better. The Assembly was more than two to one Know-Nothing. In the Senate the Democrats did hold on to a number of seats due to the popularity of their candidates; so the Know-Nothings had a majority there of only one.

Bigler wrote to his brother despondently that the state election had been lost in the diggings. "The prejudice in the mineral regions was great against foreigners. . . . [T]he opposition promised to turn them out of the mines and give claims to Americans by birth." The Know-Nothings, he added, dominated the state legislature taken as a whole; and by meeting in joint session this legislature was going to elect the senator to fill Gwin's seat, almost certainly now to be a Know-Nothing. They were so confident that they were talking about moving up the election for Weller's senatorship, just as Broderick had tried with Gwin's. And who was to stop them? No one. That was Bigler's despairing conclusion. The Know-Nothings "have carried everything . . . and will most assuredly elect two U.S. Senators."

Broderick was not so sure. Politics was politics, and a lot could still happen, especially with so many Know-Nothings about to get their first exposure to the rough and tumble of politics, the give and take of governing. Some earnest Know-Nothing supporters had already been shocked to find that after the election individuals were actually campaigning to be considered for the first Senate seat. Know-Nothings like Foote were acting just like politicians, and trying to make deals! But true Americans, bred on this immaculate republican soil, were supposed to be above such things. The Sacramento *Union,* the nativist paper there, was in particular outraged.

The contest for the U.S. Senate, according to the *Union,* had become one of "depravity, of low cunning, of staggering and 'hiccuping' familiarity; of profane, verdant and ridiculous pretensions and aspirations." When the paper continued by dismissing the leading candidates as so many "migratory political hacks," the irascible Henry Foote somehow took this personally. He demanded a retraction or apology. What he got was the Sacramento *Union* wondering aloud whether the man who had pulled a gun on Tom Benton on the floor of the Senate was really fit to be returned to that body. By the way, was Foote really known as "Hangman" Foote in his home state? Had he really promised to hang an abolitionist congressman personally if he so much as set foot in Mississippi?

There was something encouraging about such squabbling for both Broderick and Gwin. The new party had too many novices for its own good, and that included its governor. And too many of these wore their principles on their sleeves. Now they could not blame the Democrats for what went wrong in the state. Let these idealistic amateurs try to run things for a while.

The Know-Nothings met in caucus early in 1856. After a few votes, they had quite sensibly selected the old pro Henry Foote as their candidate for the U.S. Senate. The legislature had only to meet in joint session, and Foote was assured an overwhelming victory, even if a few Know-Nothings out of conscience refused to vote for him because he was a proslavery Southerner. The Assembly voted immediately to meet in joint session with the Senate. The measure was then brought to the Senate, and early passage was expected.

But Broderick's men had seen a possibility here for themselves to avoid disaster. If the Democrats remained firm (and Broderick and Gwin could agree that they should), then all they had to do was to turn one Know-Nothing senator in order to prevent the legislature from meeting in joint session. And they had found their man in the senator from San Francisco, Wilson Flint. Flint was originally from New Hampshire, but he had sought his fortune in Texas. There he had unexpectedly become convinced that slavery was an abomination—and, stunned by this moral revelation, he migrated farther west to escape being tainted by this depraved institution. Flint, in other words, was an uncompromising abolitionist who had joined the Know-Nothings because he was appalled not at the corruption of Broderick but at the domination of the Democratic Party by Southerners and Southern sympathizers.

Now this same group was about to dominate his new party by sending a Southern senator to Washington to join Weller, himself an out-and-out doughface. Wilson Flint was not going to be a party to this, if he could help it. His fellow Know-Nothing legislators pleaded with him. All he had to do was to abstain, and the lieutenant governor as president of the Senate would break the tie. He could then vote against Foote. His hands would be clean. To which there was a natural riposte: "You mean like Pilate's?"

Of course, the Democrats, including Chivs, were outdoing one another in their praise of Wilson as a profile in courage. Here was a man of principle, all too rare in the world of politics. The increasingly frustrated Know-

Nothings replied that here was rather another Benedict Arnold, going over to the other side at the first sign of trouble, a traitor all too common in this vale of tears.

Flint, no matter what anybody said, simply would not budge. Vote after vote was taken, and the simple measure continued to be defeated 17 to 16. And Foote, with nothing to lose, refused to withdraw his candidacy. Finally, the Know-Nothings just gave up; the U.S. Senate seat would have to remain open for another year. The legislature would try again in 1857. And the Honorable Henry Hangman Foote had been poignantly reminded why he had earlier decided to give up party politics altogether, and reminded too why the best place for an abolitionist legislator was at the end of a short rope suspended from a tall tree.

Broderick and his men themselves, however, had no opportunity to enjoy this bare victory because they were soon in a fight for their lives. The vigilantes were about to take over San Francisco again. And this time they were going to go after Broderick, Ned McGowan, and the b'hoys.

San Francisco had changed remarkably from 1851 to 1855. It now looked like a permanent city. The disastrous fires had gradually led to a replacement of wood structures with formidable brick buildings—and, as a consequence, such fires were no longer a threat, at least to burn down whole sections of the city. One of these new structures was the three-story Lucas Turner Building on Montgomery Street, which had been constructed by William Tecumseh Sherman for the bank he now managed.

Sherman, when he returned to California after finishing out his army military career (or so he thought) with a brief assignment in New Orleans, had been impressed by all this growth in San Francisco. The streets were usable now in winter, the sidewalks were recognizable as such, a sewer system was well advanced, and the roads out of town were tolerable; there were even gas streetlights in a portion of the city—and new areas, like North Beach, were being developed. Portsmouth Square had been graded and fenced, and the talk was of covering it with iron and glass, to make it a great crystal palace.

There were now ample churches of many denominations, and even two synagogues; since Mrs. Sherman was a devout Roman Catholic, Sherman had made the acquaintance of Archbishop Alemany, an ascetic Spaniard, as well as the Gallagher brothers, the priests who ran the cathedral for him. There was even an order of nuns ministering to the poor, the Sisters of Charity, and the Jesuits were setting up a college. (One of Sherman's sons would eventually join the Society of Jesus.) All this pleased his wife mightily, although she still did not give a fig for California.

At the other end of the moral spectrum, Sherman noted that the brothels were now more discreet. "The more fashionable places on Washington Street are as silent as the grave and you do not now see troops of girls displaying themselves on horseback and carriage." The gambling was not as desperate or ostentatious. The city even had a decent cemetery now, to supplement the overgrown one at the old mission. Little more than two miles from the center of the city, a large hill called Lone Mountain had been set aside for that purpose, a wonderful spot because unlike many of the large sandhills this one was covered with evergreen vegetation—live oaks, mostly—a peaceful spot with a full view of the city in one direction and the Golden Gate in another.

Sherman brooded about that cemetery a bit because his asthma was keeping him up most nights; and if it got much worse, he'd end up depositing his bones on Lone Mountain one of these winters—but there were worse ways to die. Sherman hadn't changed much, apart from his apparently deteriorating health and worries about providing for his growing family. He was not back in California long before he was taking the measure of just about everybody and everything, and leaving a record of his judgments in his frequent letters back to his home office in St. Louis.

He quickly realized that a rival bank—Palmer, Cook & Co.—was behind Broderick's machine, but he was not sure they would make out as well as they thought they would; he wrote back to St. Louis that Palmer, Cook & Co. "have been deep in bribing the present legislature for Broderick but the members charge high." He thought the Know-Nothings and their reform ticket in San Francisco as phony as their power would be ephemeral: "A new broom sweeps clean, but in one short year these immaculate gentlemen will be kicked out of office with as little ceremony and thanks as the present." He respected the members of the California Chivalry he knew: Heydenfeldt he thought "an honest, honorable good man" although unfortunately an "extremist 'states rights' Calhoun man." The younger, more aggressive and excitable Terry he thought "highly honorable and bade fair to make an excellent judge" if he only would overcome his "imprudence," what Sherman took to be his tendency to get involved when he should remain aloof. Also, Sherman detested the numerous San Francisco newspapers, which he regarded as a "perfect curse" on the community because their sole purpose seemed to be "inflaming the public mind."

Banker Sherman, of course, was mainly concerned about business. Strangely for someone who had returned to California eagerly, Sherman just could not bring himself to be comfortable with the business community of San Francisco: "It seems that nobody is proof against this country. The temptation of large profits is the soul of gambling and business here has partaken of that character." Again and again, he returned to this theme. "My opinion is the very nature of the country begets speculation, extravagance, failures and rascality. Everything is chance, everything is gambling." Bankers, he thought, were no better than the rest.

As a result, Sherman did not trust many of the leading business figures, such as "Honest Harry" Meiggs, a man-about-town who was developing

North Beach largely on credit and his good name. Then in October of 1854 Harry and more than a half-million dollars literally went south, to begin his new career as a Peruvian railroad magnate. Some banks had been rendered virtually insolvent by Meiggs's unexpected departure, but Sherman by that time had reduced his own bank's vulnerability from $80,000 to $10,000. The episode, not surprisingly, Sherman interpreted as a confirmation of his worst suspicions about California entrepreneurs.

Businessmen, no less than the miners, had come to California in expectation of a quick killing. They had thought that while mining itself was a hit-or-miss affair, mining the miners would be a sure thing. In the short run it was, and San Francisco prospered. One resident described San Francisco in 1853 as "a conglomeration of pagans, Mahommedans, Mormons, Jews, and Christians—all worshipping mammon." Another agreed: "Money is the god of our idolatry—our minds are sufficiently active—our hearts as barren as the sun-burned hills."

So when the miners were getting disillusioned in 1850, the merchants and other businessmen were still doing quite well. By 1854, however, the amount of gold had peaked, and there were simply too many businessmen in San Francisco trying to turn large profits. Then the average businessman was becoming as disillusioned with California as the average miner had been in 1850. Few were still getting rich quick, many were going broke, and most of the rest were just hanging on.

The letters back home from aspiring California businessmen now contained a litany of complaints similar to that of the miners a few years before: "There is a great deal of moonshine about the large fortunes made here." People who think "about making fortunes in a hurry" will be "very sorry if they set their feet on this place, or they will be different from all that come here now." "I cannot think that the good time of last summer will ever come to San Francisco or California again." Or more simply, "Mother, it is mighty hard to make money here." The plans for mercantile empires were proving as substantial as the billowing fog banks.

By 1854, in fact, the businesses of San Francisco had entered into a depression. In the headlong rush to progress, the downtown had been over-built, and by the end of 1854 as many as three hundred of the one thousand buildings stood unoccupied. The commission merchants had full warehouses, and were sending some ships back to New York with their cargoes un-touched, so oversupplied had the city become. There had been no fewer than seventy-seven bankruptcies in 1854. What San Francisco business needed at the beginning of 1855 was a nice big fire, but the city was no longer a tinderbox. What the city got instead was a further financial collapse, a crash that threatened every banking establishment in San Francisco with ruin.

Sherman, not a man to panic or exaggerate, described what began in

February 1855 as "the most terrible financial storm that has ever devastated any community." Banks were closing all around him, and those that remained open, like Sherman's, had to endure serious runs. Sherman could only compare it to war. "What terrible casualties we incur. . . . I thought in leaving the Army that wars and rumors of war could be forgotten but it is one continuous strife. . . . Indeed all are lucky that can report themselves in existence." In eight days an estimated 3 million dollars were paid out by San Francisco banks to panicking depositors.

Sherman's bank and a few others had survived, but the business community itself became increasingly desperate. The 1854 depression had become in 1855 apocalyptic in scope, as one after another firm failed, as one announced bankruptcy resulted soon in two or three others. The seventy-seven bankruptcies of 1854 were the worst series of failures that San Francisco had yet seen; but in 1855, there were two hundred more.

One of those who suffered most grievously in this double-dip depression was James King—or, as he preferred to be called, James King of William. The "of William" was an aristocratic affectation of his own whereby he tried to distinguish himself from all the other James Kings. This James King was the one sired by William. (King's dominating passion was to be distinguished from the mass of mankind.) His early success in California seemed to make the name prophetic of future eminence.

King had happened to be in Chile when the gold discovery was announced. Hearing the news, he had had the presence of mind to hire out a number of Chileans to come to California with him to work for him in the diggings. While some of these ran off once they arrived, others remained true to the agreement, and King had gotten to California when the miners still tolerated such crews. In a short time King had made a small fortune, and then with considerable shrewdness set out to become immensely wealthy. He set himself up as a banker—and the money, or rather the gold dust, just rolled in during the early 1850s. By 1851 his wealth was estimated as $125,000; by 1853 he had doubled it. At this rate he would be a millionaire by 1857.

He was scarcely thirty, and he could live like a prince, if not a king. He brought his family out to join him, a wife and four small children. His was one of those mansions that Broderick so resented. He was driven about the city in a carriage fit for his station, a station that would not exist in a democracy as Broderick conceived it. He had handled funds for the Committee of Vigilance in 1851, and served on both its executive and finance committees—but had remained discreetly in the background. He showed no interest in politics, only in making money and living well, both of which he did with distinction.

Then the depression of 1854 came, and King was one of those caught overextended. To save himself from the shame of bankruptcy, he had to turn over all his assets, including the mansion and carriage, to another bank, Adams & Co., which assumed his obligations and gave him a salaried job as a teller. Although he and his family were now living in rented rooms, he prided himself on being a loyal servant to his new firm, and actively solicited deposits from his old friends and clients, even as the financial situation worsened and rumors began to spread that Adams & Co. was in trouble. King was adamant that it was sound, and his clients knew that, poor though he was, his integrity was unquestionable. So King was taking deposits until noon on the very day Adams & Co. closed its doors for good. And there was some evidence that the proprietors had taken care of themselves financially while the bank had been sliding toward oblivion. King, who had not profited at all, found his own good name besmirched. In fact, people were blaming him for losing their life savings, and losing them at a time when there seemed little prospect in California of ever making them back.

King was outraged. Outraged at his own misfortunes, and his now ir-reparable penury. Outraged at the society in which this could happen to a good man. Outraged at the people who now questioned his integrity, the only thing he had left. Outraged at the owners of the bank, as well as those who had taken over its affairs. (They owed him $20,000.) Outraged at those who had betrayed his earlier bank, for surely that failure had been someone else's fault. Outraged at the Chileans who had deserted him after he had generously paid their way. Outraged, outraged, outraged. Dishonesty, pov-erty, corruption. What could the honest man do but rail against the sink of evil in which he found himself, rail so that all would know he was not of it?

King was on the verge of a breakdown, and yet even then his cleverness did not entirely desert him. He seems to have realized instinctively that if he did not find a way to express all that was seething within him he was going to lose his sanity. He decided to start a newspaper, and somehow found a backer, perhaps someone who out of charity was just trying to help him survive his apparent disgrace.

Needless to say, the San Francisco *Bulletin* was not a newspaper in the ordinary sense. It was written in vehemence and bile. King had assumed the role of self-appointed prophet to the wayward society of San Francisco. He did not look like a prophet, with his small face, dark hair, wide forehead, full beard, large ears. Only the deeply sunken eyes, half lost in the shadows of his brow and darkly circled, gave a sense of intensity, of a disillusionment projected defiantly out upon the world.

The face told less than the prose, which was that of a half-crazed prophet on a mission of inspired self-righteousness. In his violent denunciations there was the unmistakable sound of hysterical glee. The world may have thought it had taken his measure and found him wanting; but instead he, James King of William, was judging it. And his penitential ordeal of the past two years, his abject humiliation, had purified him for this providential vocation. And when exercising it, he preferred to refer to himself by the royal "we":

It would require a higher power than any earthly tribunal to release us from that moral obligation imposed on us by the silent monitor within. We have ever endeavored to do right, regardless of the consequences. We know we have made enemies by so doing, but that was to be expected. It has made us poor, but our health is as good, our slumbers as quiet, and we are prouder today than in our palmiest hours. It has kept us from church because we would not occupy the pew on which we could not afford to pay the rent, and has about forced us to first principles in domestic economy, but we enjoy our parlor and sitting room with patched carpets, and odds and ends of furniture, as much as we ever did the handsomer furnished rooms we once owned on Stockton Street.

The scales had dropped from his eyes. Suddenly James King of William saw corruption all about him, with nobody saying anything, nobody except the fearless editor of the San Francisco *Bulletin*. He attacked the banking firm of Palmer, Cook & Co., which had with Sherman's survived the bank run quite nicely. They were the "Uriah Heeps of America" who prospered only because they had become the bondmen of corrupt politicians. He refused to accept advertisements from doctors as "obscene" and not fit "for the columns of any respectable public journal." He attacked other newspapers—for instance, claiming that the San Francisco *Herald* was in debt "and the editor dare not open his lips except at the bidding of these moneyed tyrants." He attacked the Fathers Gallagher and the Sisters of Charity as agents of a foreign power, to the intense annoyance of Mrs. Sherman. (The Sisters, these Chilean peons, were making a huge profit from treating the poor and were not giving native Americans as much food as immigrants; the Gallaghers, on the other hand, were guilty of "low cunning and church Broderickism.") But most of all he attacked politicians:

> A man, unworthy to serve the humblest citizen in the land, has filled the highest office in the gift of the people. Judges have sat on the bench, whose more appropriate station would have been a prison house. Men, without one particle of claim to the position, have filled the posts of Mayor and Councilmen of this city for the sole purpose of filling their pockets with the ill-gotten gains of their nefarious schemes, their pilfering and dishonesty.

And of all the politicians he attacked, he most relished attacking Broderick, or "David Catiline Broderick" as King commonly called him: "Of all the names that grace the roll of political wire-working in this city, the most conspicuous of all . . . as high over all his compeers as was Satan among the fallen angels, and as unblushing and determined as the dark fiend, stands the name of David C. Broderick." Even when he could not connect Broderick with specific corruption in the city, King bid his readers to presume he was still behind all of it: "*His* mind is the Pandora's box from whence spring all these evils. *His* is the fertile genius that creates means for every emergency."

Almost overnight James King of William found himself a celebrity. Within a month the daily printing of the *Bulletin* had exceeded two thousand; in another month it was approaching thirty-five hundred. The San Francisco *Bulletin* had become the most widely read newspaper in San Francisco, with the possible exception of the *Alta California*. Here all the frustrations San Franciscans had endured for the last two years were finding expression. Here was someone who had suffered too, someone unafraid, someone willing to name names, to bring shady deals to light. He would expose those responsible for the blight on the community, the economic blight that threatened everyone.

Was what he wrote true? Was it fair? No one except those mentioned and their friends seemed to care. Reading it did people good, or so they felt—reading King of William, sharing his vehement outrage, with him denying the shame of financial failure, with him realizing the purity of penury—all this to feel that they, like King, were righteous and truly respectable and did not have to mince their words. And they enjoyed him most when others tried to coax him into behaving more responsibly, for he would tell all about it in the next edition, and then conclude in a peroration of moralizing self-congratulation:

> Gentleman, you have not gold enough in your vaults, nor is there enough in the hills and gulches in the State to buy us! We *have* been wealthy, and know the uses of money; but in our poverty we have learned practically that there can be *more* real happiness in the poorly furnished cottage than in the most magnificently furnished apartments. We would not exchange the hearty welcome of the mechanic and the laborer and the honest merchant for all you can offer.

Tecumseh Sherman, McKendree Gwin and Catiline Broderick all agreed that this was empty posturing, and all the more dangerous because King seemed to believe it. King's success rather than moderating him only made him wilder. As 1855 became 1856, they all could see that King's rantings were leading inexorably to some kind of explosion. King had taken to announcing that he carried a weapon, and urged potential assassins to try their worst, even suggesting a time and place where they could intercept him on any given day without endangering passersby. He seemed pleased to report that bets were being offered he would not be alive in twenty days: "War then is the cry, is it? War between the prostitutes and gamblers on the one side and the virtuous and respectable on the other! War to the knife, and knife to the hilt! Be it so, then!"

Sherman, who knew a little of war, was disgusted by all this loose, ir-responsible talk. When he found out that Jimmy Casey had rented an office on the third floor of his building to answer King's calumnies with his own paper, *The Sunday Herald,* Sherman told him to vacate, or he personally would throw Casey out the window, and his printing press right after him. Objectively, the business situation in San Francisco was precarious enough without having journalistic firebrands convincing everyone who lost money that they'd been cheated, when mostly they'd just been unlucky or greedy or stupid, or usually some invincible combination of the three.

Gwin, on the other hand, may not have liked the occasional swipes from King against the Chivalry and Democratic patronage. But they were harmless enough, and Gwin had taken care to cover his own tracks, even if King had had the patience to read the official record of Congress, which of course he did not. King's success was just another indication of how primitive a society California still was, how much in need of closer ties to the more advanced portions of the American republic, of better mails, a transcontinental railroad, and the electric telegraph. But people were not interested in talking about that here, not now. Seeing the storm clouds gathering, Old Man Gwin de-cided to take a vacation away from the city for a few months, to an unan-nounced location better for his political health where he could rest up for the upcoming presidential election, especially since his old friend James Buchanan just might be the Democratic nominee.

Broderick might have liked a vacation too, but he was stuck. He knew better than to attack King himself, for this incipient madman thrived on attacks as evidence of his own importance. (When the mayor called King a "malignant misanthrope," King delightedly responded that the mayor was a "stupid old ass.") And self-importance was all King really cared about. That was the oddity about him; professing himself a champion of equality, he hated the people. He knew no mechanics or workingmen; they were beneath him. He was as isolated from them now as he used to be in his elegant carriage. They were just objects on which he could express his virtue, a claque to confirm for him that he was a truly distinguished man. King now wore his poverty as he earlier had worn his wealth, as an indisputable sign of his superior worth.

It would have been best to ignore King, and wait for him to destroy himself. Sooner or later he would conclude that he was the only virtuous person left in the universe, with the possible exception of God, with whom King at times seemed to confuse himself. Then James King of William, this man who had forged the moral conscience of the race in the smithy of his soul, would be ready for the loony bin. But Broderick could not altogether ignore him, nor could he stay out of his way, since King was continually putting Broderick's friends at risk.

One such friend of Broderick, Charles Cora, a gambler by profession, had killed a United States marshal, William Richardson. Things looked bad for Cora—unless, that is, you knew the circumstances. Richardson was a well-connected and well-liked man; Gwin had arranged for his appointment by President Pierce as marshal, a position that Gwin regarded as the most important patronage appointment in the state after the collector of customs.

Cora had taken his common-law wife, Belle, a well-known madam, to the theater where other men could ogle her. One commonality that made their relationship so loving was that Cora liked to show her off, and she liked to be stared at. Unfortunately, Mrs. Richardson, not noticing Belle sitting near her, thought she was being stared at herself, inappropriately, by men in the cheap seats. When her misapprehension was corrected, she continued to complain of impropriety. Shameless harlots should not be allowed to sit near decent folks. She was even more incensed when the manager of the theater refused to move Belle against her wishes. (Charles Cora, although he dressed like an Italian count and was usually of an affable disposition, was not someone you pushed around.)

Later Cora and Richardson passed one another on the street, and Charles made an offhand joke about the contretemps. (How could Mrs. Richardson ever think a man would stare at her?) Richardson did not take kindly to such persiflage at the expense of his wife. Cora apologized and thought he had mollified him.

Or he did until Richardson showed up again two nights later, this time well liquored up. Everyone knew that Richardson, although a likable person generally, was a mean drunk, and he was plenty mean that night. So Cora shot him dead in self-defense. That was the way it looked to Broderick and the boys, at least.

Belle, probably with Broderick's advice, managed to get Charles a first-class attorney, the best available in fact. Edward Baker had first practiced in Illinois (where he had a partner and close friend named Abraham Lincoln), and he was a spellbinder in the courtroom and out of it. The Grey Eagle, he was called, because of his hair and his presence. He combed his prematurely silver hair forward over his receding hairline, to achieve a truly Napoleonic effect. His oratorical skills were so admired that he had given the address at the opening of Lone Mountain Cemetery; now he would use these same skills to try to make sure that Charles Cora did not arrive there prematurely. (Baker apparently was as bad with cards as he was good with words; and the $10,000 Belle was offering was irresistible, since Baker was said to be capable of losing that amount in a single night.)

Because of Richardson's prominence and Cora's profession, the trial was going to be closely scrutinized. Criticism of the San Francisco judiciary was common from the respectable elements of the city. However, apart from jolly Ned McGowan (who had been soon voted out of office), these complaints were largely unjustified. The weakness of the San Francisco criminal justice system, at least according to a loyal Gwin newspaperman, was the composition of the juries: "merchants and businessmen had a great aversion to serving on juries, particularly in important political criminal cases, which are usually protracted." This was not surprising when so many were on the verge of insolvency. So they routinely paid a fine rather than serve, and then complained bitterly when the subsequent juries turned out to be predisposed to lower-class defendants.

That could not be said of this jury, however. Baker himself was having second thoughts about his involvement because his San Francisco law partner was furious with him for compromising his firm's reputation by taking on the unpopular defense. (According to one account, Baker, badly as he needed the money, had tried to return the retainer to Belle, only to be intimidated by her womanly fury, which combined in roughly equal measures tears, threats, and questions about Baker's manhood.) So he allowed the jury to be composed almost exclusively of well-to-do men. But the case was too weak against Cora, given the circumstances and Richardson's reputation. The first trial, not surprisingly, resulted in a hung jury (with four members voting for outright acquittal on the first ballot). And James King of William reported the result as if the world were coming to an end:

> Twelve o'clock noon. Hung be the heavens in black! The money of the gambler and the prostitute has succeeded, and Cora has another respite. . . . Rejoice, ye gamblers and harlots! Rejoice with exceeding gladness! Assemble in your dens of infamy tonight and the costly wine flow freely, and let the welkin ring with your shouts of joy! Your triumph is great— oh, how you have triumphed! Triumphed over everything that is holy and virtuous and good; triumphed legally —yes legally!

Subsequently, for issue after issue of the *Bulletin,* King of William railed against Cora and his harlot, as well as against the legal system, prostitutes in general, gambling, lawyers, fraud. There was a disturbing theme in these jeremiads, and not just to Cora and Baker. (Baker, King charged, was actively plotting his assassination.) King kept writing that he was not in favor of reviving the Committee of Vigilance—he was not *if* it could be avoided, *unless* criminals would otherwise go unpunished, *although* he much admired its members.

In suggesting that the committee might well need to be revived, was King expressing his own views or those he heard expressed by others? He presented them as his own, of course; how widely they were shared was hard to say for sure. What could be said for sure was that King was trying to spread them as widely as he could. Then he discovered that the new sheriff, the old Hound Dave Scannel, had allowed Billy Mulligan to become the jailor in charge of Cora:

> Hang Billy Mulligan! That's the word! If Mr. Sheriff Scannel does not remove Billy Mulligan from his present post as keeper

of the county jail, and Mulligan lets Cora escape, hang Billy Mulligan, and if necessary get rid of the sheriff, hang him—hang the sheriff! Strong measures are now required to have justice done in this case of Cora. Citizens of San Francisco! what means this feeling so prevalent in our city that this dastardly assassin will escape the vengeance of law?

Jimmy Casey, despite Sherman's emphatic eviction, had persisted in his own efforts to shame James King of William in his *Sunday Herald*. Ned McGowan had helped by providing Jimmy with the goods on King's brother, Thomas King, a.k.a. Slippery Sim, a.k.a. Dead House Cove, a.k.a. the Nipper Kid, who had been a professional thief of no small repute on the East Coast before he joined his brother in San Francisco. A smug allusion to all this made its way into Casey's newspaper. Then the San Francisco *Bulletin* decided to discuss Casey's own exploits as a ballot stuffer, incidentally mentioning his recent residency in Sing Sing Penitentiary.

Here King had unwittingly touched a nerve. In New York Casey had had a liaison with a young woman whom he had set up in a nice apartment. After they broke up, he by way of expressing his displeasure had the furniture removed and sold. She prosecuted him, and he had ended with eighteen months in prison. The boys knew this was an episode from his past that one did not joke about. The mere mention of it would send him into a rage. It was a rank injustice to which Jimmy could never reconcile himself. It enraged him, in much the same way that almost everything enraged James King of William. Moreover, Casey felt that he was beginning to make his mark in California, as a county supervisor as well as a newspaper editor—and was proudly sending money home each month to his mother as evidence of his new status. What happened now but he had Sing Sing thrown in his face?

This mention of his earlier difficulties by the San Francisco *Bulletin* was offensive to him as a gentleman, he decided—and he felt it within his rights to demand satisfaction. Supervisor Casey confronted editor King of William at his place of business. The exchange of words that followed was reported in most contemporary accounts—and it has the ring of truth, for one can hear Casey trying to be dignified while King of William persists in dismissing him as a miscreant beneath his notice. Casey began the dialogue.

"What do you mean by that article?"

"What article?"

"That which says I was a former inmate of Sing Sing prison."

"Is that not true?"

"That is not the question. I don't wish my past acts raked up; on that point I am sensitive."

"Are you done? There's the door—go! Never show your face again."

Casey was obviously feeling humiliated at this point, and tried to remind King that he was a journalist too, with his own power over reputations.

"I'll say in *my* paper what I please."

"You have a perfect right to do as you please. I'll never notice your paper."

"If necessary, I'll defend myself."

"Go! Never show your face again!"

Casey retreated in complete humiliation. He might as well never show his face again, if he did not do something about how badly he had just been used. Knowing King, Casey would expect a report on their conversation to figure prominently in the next issue of the *Bulletin*.

Casey could challenge King to a duel; but, given the way he had been treated in King's office, he should expect his challenge to be refused because of an unsuitable difference in their stations. And then there'd be another story on that, and more public humiliation. Not that there was any difference in their stations now; Jimmy thought he could buy and sell King with the money he got as supervisor. But King clearly thought himself above him. And that was going to make Casey a laughingstock.

Nonetheless, Casey could completely turn tables if he had the daring. He could this very day force King into a duel by confronting him in the street. Since he knew King now always carried a weapon (he had bragged about that enough in the *Bulletin*), Casey had only to give sufficient warning before drawing and shooting. Casey, when he was worried about Slippery Sim getting violent, had already borrowed a good pistol from Ned McGowan, who always had a mini arsenal at his disposal, although he was not inclined to use it himself.

So Casey waited along the street where King would pass on his way to get a cigar after finishing at the *Bulletin*, as he usually did. Shortly after five, he saw him, and shouted, "Arm yourself!" King was still a considerable distance away, and looked up perplexed. The shout as he heard it was "Come on!" Then Casey quickly threw off his short cloak and fired. King staggered backward, saying, "Oh God. I am shot." Then King, rather than attempting to return fire, fled before Casey, and was on the verge of collapse when passersby seeing the blood on the left of his chest helped him into a nearby office. Medical attention was soon rushed to him, and the wound was pronounced serious but not life threatening. King was flat on his back, weakened by a considerable loss of blood from a flesh wound—but not so weak he could not recount what had happened that day between himself and Casey.

Casey himself could scarcely have been more satisfied. He had shot King of William in a fair fight, and had shown him to all the world for the coward that he was. Casey said later that when he saw that King made no effort to shoot back he thought him a "dunghill" and not worth trying another shot on. It was only when King collapsed as he retreated that Casey knew he must have hit him. He had only hit King in the shoulder, and perhaps he had only meant to wing him. At any rate, he calmly turned himself in to Sheriff Scannel, expecting to be placed in the county jail next to Charles

Cora—and to have the good fun of telling him and Billy Mulligan in detail of his exploit. They were going to be the perfect audience for this, what was undoubtedly the finest moment in his life.

Dave Scannel, however, was just getting him into the carriage to be transferred from the station house to the county jail when both he and Casey realized the situation had already gotten out of hand. Somehow a large, angry crowd had already assembled, and were screaming for Casey's immediate execution. Scannel had then given Casey a revolver to help defend himself. And at least one aspiring vigilante was sent sprawling from the step of the carriage as it sped off. But as they got away, they could hear above the din of the crowd the slow tolling of the bell that had called together the vigilantes in 1851.

The Committee of Vigilance was revived with breathtaking swiftness. Those who thought in terms of conspiracies could be forgiven if they suspected that a plan had already existed to be implemented at the first opportune moment. McGowan sourly noted that the first meeting of the new committee was "at the counting house of G. B. Post, who was upon the verge of bankruptcy, and was willing with others similarly situated, to ward off, for a brief period, their impending ruin." Others noted that the organizational meeting had been held at the building that was the old Know-Nothing headquarters. James O'Meara, who had put McGowan's rival, John McDougal, in nomination at the tumultuous Democratic convention, added that some of the worst criminals of San Francisco, having seen what had happened in 1851, "hastened to join the band, in order to save themselves from arrest, and the rope and bullet." So the committee quickly had considerable muscle, particularly ruffians who had scores to settle with Broderick men.

What the organizers of the new Committee of Vigilance wanted, of course, was a sense of decorum, of dignity. Sam Brannan was eager to take over as he had in 1851, and was a bit miffed to find himself quickly pushed aside. Near the end of the last committee he had defied it by getting a horse thief released just because he liked him. Brannan was now scandalizing his commercial brethren by his panting pursuit of a well-known young dancing lady (who was not the kind of woman Mrs. Richardson would want to sit near). The Know-Nothing mayor of San Francisco was saying what had been oft thought but ne'er so well expressed when he dismissed Brannan as "a thing of booty and a bore forever."

There was only one man to lead this revolution, it was agreed: William Tell Coleman. He was now held in awe for more than his role in the committee of 1851. He had somehow anticipated the financial collapse of 1854–55, and he had withdrawn from San Francisco to the East near the end of 1853. The recent return of this great leader and prescient businessman itself presaged a return of San Francisco to order and prosperity.

Coleman was at first reluctant, and that coyness only made him more attractive to the organizers. Then he agreed, but on two conditions. There would be absolute secrecy; so the members would only be known by numbers, as they had in 1851. Second, Coleman would have, as he put it, "authority supreme." So it was that William Tell Coleman, or rather Citizen No. 1, became the aspiring dictator of San Francisco.

Within twenty-four hours more than fifteen hundred men had signed up—and the number would grow until over six thousand. (In contrast, the committee of 1851 had scarcely reached seven hundred.) They took over the motto from the old committee, but now had a new symbol, a great open eye. This eye dominated a whole wall on the inside of their headquarters, an imposing brick building that they transformed into a fort, including four pieces of ordnance on the roof, requisitioned from ships in the harbor. The first floor of the building was an armory and drill room; the second, offices for the committee as well as eight cells for prisoners. For defensive positions around the fort and as placements for cannon, the vigilante recruits piled sandbags. The Broderick men henceforth called the place, in derision, Fort Gunnybags, a name the vigilantes eventually started using themselves. The bags were piled ten feet high and to a thickness of six feet, for two hundred feet along the street and extending out at the corners into the road. The membership was organized militarily, with numerous companies of infantry, two of cavalry, and four of artillery. Citizen No. 1 and his inner circle obviously had more in mind than the punishment of a few criminals.

For Coleman, always excitable, the scope and rapidity of the developments were intoxicating. Years later he would claim to have had the support of 85 percent of the population, although he conceded that the opposition was "active, persistent and plucky." With him as supreme authority, the committee within a few weeks had constituted itself as a completely independent entity, its eye overseeing all of San Francisco and beyond. "Our police and military systems were now equal, if not superior, to any on the continent," Coleman would write. If "on the continent" seemed a bit of an exaggeration since it made the committee equal to the U.S. government, Coleman coolly added that within twenty-four hours' time he could call out fifty-seven thousand disciplined men "ready for any service."

Here Coleman's memory was flattering him into gross exaggeration, but it was also the memory of a man who had once had a taste of being a dictator and who had never quite recovered from the experience. Even at the time, it seemed that this committee was more than just vigilantism; it was a political revolution that with wide enough support within the state could result in the secession of California from the Union. Then complicated questions about immigration, naturalization, and office qualification could be handled more simply than seemed possible under the present American governing system.

However disproportionate the preparations, the immediate problems were Casey and Cora. Significantly, there was another inmate of the country jail who had committed a homicide without any mitigating circumstances. Rodney Backus, at the behest of a prostitute friend, had murdered in cold blood a prominent German citizen, and had gotten off with a light sentence for manslaughter. However, he had killed an immigrant, was not himself (unlike the German) of Catholic origins, and had friends who had quickly joined the committee. So he was in no danger, although he did plead to be transferred to the state penitentiary the moment the vigilance bell started to toll. (It tolled not for the likes of him.)

Sherman could not observe these developments with his usual detachment. In a moment of weakness he had allowed himself to be appointed major general in the California militia; so he now had ample grounds to curse himself for his misplaced civic-mindedness. The mayor wanted him to do something, but Sherman refused without explicit orders from the governor. He did look over the jail, and pronounced it indefensible: "I would rather be in the open prairie than in that jail." The only possibility for defense was to occupy all the buildings nearby, but they were already occupied by vigilantes who kept an ominous watch over the jail. He commiserated with the jailors for their "most disagreeable" duty of having to defend a couple of scoundrels, but it was a question of organized law versus mob violence.

Governor Neely Johnson, to his credit as far as Sherman was concerned, realized that he had to do something. The vigilantes were primarily from his main constituency, nativists committed to political reform. And yet they were now in defiance of the very government authority that he had just sworn to defend. Johnson must have thought he could reach an accommodation with the committee, but he also obviously recognized the potential seriousness of the situation they had created. The best course, he decided, was for him to talk with them face-to-face. So he rushed to San Francisco from Sacramento, and first met with Sherman, who apprised him of the situation at the jail. Sherman also informed the young governor that he had already picked out a hill from which with a little artillery he could blow Fort Gunnybags to smithereens in no time. Together, Sherman and Johnson arranged to meet with Citizen No. 1, William Tell Coleman.

They met at the committee's headquarters, on the night of Friday the sixteenth. Sherman, to his own surprise, had taken a liking to Johnson, a bright young man—he thought—pleasing in his ways and sincerely desiring to do the right thing, although his inexperience might well express itself eventually in either timidity or rashness. Coleman, Sherman judged in a more finely measured fashion. Coleman struck Sherman as someone quite admirable—"of fine impulses, manners, character and intelligence." But there was something lacking in Coleman, as if he had not had much education and hence did not acknowledge the complexities of life. Coleman had "not the least doubt of himself, his motives or intentions." A man constitutionally unable to question his own motives or intentions was dangerous, for he was ultimately a man without a conscience.

Governor Johnson asked Citizen Coleman plainly what he wanted. The response was slippery: "Peace—and, if possible, without a struggle. But if need be we will seek it even at the cost of war." At this Sherman might have started thinking about his artillery position. Johnson patiently pressed Coleman to be more specific. What exactly did Coleman and his committee expect to achieve?

Here Johnson had raised the key question. Within the committee, there was a whole range of expectations, all the way from simple lynching to complete revolution, from the simple punishment of Casey and a few others to the taking over of the San Francisco city government and from there to the complete secession of California from the Union and the establishment of an independent Pacific Republic (perhaps on broadly nativist lines). How far they were going to go along this path was going to depend upon circumstances. Most of the executive committee probably themselves had not decided how far they were willing to go, how much they were willing to risk. In Coleman they had the perfect leader, or rather spokesman, to present whatever they did decide in the best possible light, and someone who instinctively knew what would look dignified. In the short run, they could express their objectives in the most modest terms, once it had been made clear that if pushed by the authorities there would be civil war.

Coleman assured the governor that they had no broader objectives than the committee of 1851. They wanted to see some notorious criminals punished, some others deported. In short, they wished only "to purify the moral and political atmosphere, and then disband." Coleman added that he knew the mayor and others (like Sherman, although he did not specifically mention him) were pressuring the governor to put down the movement. Coleman assured him that it simply could not be done. And if the governor tried, it would cause them both a good deal of unnecessary trouble.

Once again, Johnson quite sensibly wanted to talk specifics. He would not under any circumstances give up Casey to the committee. He would, however, guarantee that, if King died, he would be brought to trial for murder with a judge and a jury whom the committee would find acceptable. Beyond that, he promised he would not subsequently exercise his power of clemency in that particular case under any circumstances.

Coleman seemed pleased by this, and left the room to consult with others. When he returned, his demeanor had changed. He said brusquely that the offer was insufficient. Casey might still be permitted to escape by his cronies in charge of the jail. (A number of them, including Ned McGowan, were now guarding the jail.) The vigilantes had to be permitted to put their own guards in the jail to protect against a breakout.

Sherman now began to suspect the complexity of the situation within the committee itself. Coleman was being overruled by men within his own committee—either that, or he was being disingenuous in the extreme.

Such would be Coleman's enigmatic role throughout this summer. He presented himself to the world as the first citizen, the man in absolute control. How much he was in control, how much a mere spokesman or figurehead was never clear. Perhaps he was just a spokesman, but in his pride was continually deluding himself that he was not. He was an actor who could not separate himself from his role, and was all the better in it for that.

Johnson now showed weakness. Trusting the good faith of Coleman, he gave in. They could have their guards. Johnson left thinking he had struck a deal, not a good deal but the best he could get. What Sherman thought he kept to himself.

McGowan and the boys at the jail thought differently from the governor. When the vigilantes showed up to take their positions inside, McGowan and a number of others threw down their arms in disgust, and repaired to the nearest saloon, to begin a premature Irish wake for their friends. It did not take long for McGowan and the boys to be proven right in their pessimism.

The vigilante battalions were drilled for the next two days, to make sure they were ready for action. Then the governor received a note:

> To His Excellency J. Neely Johnson
> Dear Sir:
> We beg to advise you that we have withdrawn our guard
> from the county jail.
> By the order of the Committee.
> No. 33, Secretary

A few hours later the county jail was surrounded by three thousand men, with Coleman in command. They demanded Casey. Sheriff Scannel, with not thirty men left to defend the jail, expressed his regrets to Jimmy (who understood) and turned him over. As he was led out of the door, a cheer began to build among the vigilantes, until Coleman decided that this was not dignified. He removed his hat and gestured to the crowd to become silent, which it did almost immediately. One among the crowd wrote that the dignified silence with which they took Casey back to their headquarters was "something frightful, something unnatural, a silence that could be felt, like the darkness that fell upon the land of Egypt."

A little while later, almost as an afterthought, they came back for Cora. (Had Coleman been overruled again?) Sherman and Johnson had watched the whole proceedings as best they could from the roof of a nearby hotel. Others were watching too; in fact, most roofs downtown were filled with spectators, and Telegraph Hill was black with them.

Throughout these days since the shooting, notices of King's condition were being posted every half hour. Almost all the leading doctors of San Francisco were being consulted, and predictably squabbling among themselves over proper treatment. In the process they had managed gradually to transform a serious wound into a mortal one. King died a martyr on Tuesday,

May 20. That Thursday, an exceedingly beautiful spring day by all accounts, as King's large funeral procession (led by the Freemasons) was winding through the city toward Lone Mountain, a crowd at least as large had congregated around the vigilante headquarters.

From the roof of the building were extended two projecting beams. Then, directly beneath them, out of second-story windows, were placed two thick planks, sixteen inches wide. The two men were made to walk out to the end of these. From beneath it could be seen that these planks had hinges; they were like trap doors.

The man in charge, the hangman, was one of the least reputable of the committee, Sydney Hopkins. He was one of those who with a different nationality could have just as easily been a target of the committee rather than its instrument. But he was an eager instrument this day. He had had trouble with the boys the last year or two, and detested them as thoroughly as they detested him. (Ned McGowan said that Hopkins's only distinction was that he had once been pimping simultaneously for both his wife and mother.)

The ropes, suspended from the upper beams, were placed around the men's necks. Cora declined to say any last words from this perch; Casey, who did not look so dapper next to the elegant Cora, gave a brief, excited speech, to as little effect as his semiliterate editorials in the *Sunday Herald*. When Hopkins (who himself would die a few years later in the Battle of the Wilderness) placed the white hood over Casey, he could not resist whispering a gloating remark in his ear. The enraged, still-hooded Casey was struggling to break his bonds to get at Hopkins when the signal was given, and Casey and Cora fell to their deaths, Cora as quietly dignified as he had been throughout the proceedings, Casey futilely flailing away for a few more moments.

Afterward, it was known that a priest had given each man the last rites, and that Cora and Belle had been married. The volunteer firemen of Casey's Crescent Engine Company placed a monument over his grave at the mission, with the inscription: "The Lord have mercy on my persecutors." Belle, the harlot-wife-widow, preferred a plainer marker for her husband, who was also buried there.

Sherman and Johnson, although thoroughly disgusted at Coleman's betrayal and perhaps also at their own gullibility, hoped the matter would end here. As far as Sherman was concerned, the city was better off without both Casey and King. "Two birds are killed by one stone. Is this providence?" Such sarcasm did not blind him to the reality. "San Francisco is now governed by an irresponsible organization claiming to be armed with absolute power by the people. The government is powerless and at an end."

Then Sherman and Johnson realized that they had been misled on another score. What had the committee wanted? Only to kill a few prominent criminals, they thought, and then they would disband. But Coleman and the committee did not disband; rather they began to take over the whole governance of the city. They were not vigilantes; they were insurrectionists.

Sherman, for his part, began to plan for war, with the purposeful simplicity of mind that he would later show marching through Georgia. He wanted arms and ammunition from General Wool's arsenal in the north bay. He wanted naval support from Commodore Farragut at Mare Island. All he needed then was a sufficient number of volunteers; with them he would take possession of the thirty-two-pound gun battery at the marine hospital on Rincon Point, and he would then have no trouble dispersing the unlawfully armed force of the vigilantes, and arresting as many of their leaders as seemed appropriate. The previously cynical and detached Sherman was now showing another side of himself.

Others privy to his simple plan seemed a little frightened at what he was getting them into. General Wool, in particular, had come west to enjoy early retirement while still in uniform; he had not come to participate in a civil war. He finally agreed that he would provide arms if the committee acted in direct defiance of the state government. So the governor had Supreme Court Justice David Terry, someone the committee should trust as a Know-Nothing, present the committee with a writ of habeas corpus for one of the other prisoners they were now holding. Not surprisingly, the writ was defied. Johnson then issued a proclamation that the committee had committed an act of insurrection. Sherman now made no secret that his intentions were warlike, and some members of the committee were beginning to quail. Then General Wool did a little quailing of his own; he refused Sherman the promised armaments.

Johnson called a tense meeting of his councilors, including both Terry and Sherman, together with elements from the city who were trying to seek a compromise, such as Edward Baker. Sherman did not like a compromise, but given their weakness it was the only plausible course. Terry, however, had his blood up. Somehow his personal honor had been touched by the defiance of that writ. His solution to the problem was to "call the miners from the mountains who would sweep the damned pork merchants into the bay." As for Wool, Terry thought that he was a damned coward, something with which many others in the room enthusiastically agreed. Despite the enthusiasm all around him, Sherman was beginning to think that the whole enterprise was hopeless. While one of the other men, Joseph Crockett, was making what he thought a very realistic assessment of the situation, Sherman looked over at Terry: "All the time Crockett was speaking, Terry sat with his hat on, drawn over his eyes, and with his feet on the table." With the glowering Terry in that mood, the inexperienced Johnson was going to listen to nothing Crockett or Sherman had to say. Terry was dominating the meeting with scarcely saying a word.

Sherman pondered this coldly for a few minutes: "I found myself strangely placed: under a militia commission to quell a civil strife, the mass of people against me, arms refused by the only authority that could have given them, and the Governor under other influences than my own." He then took out pen and paper, and wrote out a brief letter of resignation on the spot, and handed it to the governor without a word—and, as he walked out, had occasion to glance at Terry again, who still had his feet on the table. From that moment on, Sherman went back to his accustomed role of acerbic observer.

The Committee of Vigilance then went about its real work, what apparently had been planned all along. They were going after Broderick and his Democratic machine. They were going to complete the work the Know-Nothings had started in San Francisco. In the 1855 city elections the Democratic Party had made a significant comeback against the Know-Nothings. Broderick and his men were just better organized and more determined than the reform-minded nativist politicians; and their wards of immigrants and laborers were just too loyal.

Now the Committee of Vigilance was going to end this once and for all, by removing from San Francisco as many leaders of the Democratic Party as they could. One after another of the boys was rounded up, and deported. "Dutch Charley" Duane, fearless Billy Mulligan, Martin Gallagher and Billy Carr (stalwarts of the solidly Irish First Ward), Bill Lewis, ugly Wooley Kearney, John Crow, Rube Meloney (of the big mouth and the wet leg)—all were deported. Yankee Sullivan would have been too; but a vigilante guard one night, knowing his fearful temperament, taunted him with hanging and left him alone. The former champion slit his wrists and saved the committee his passage.

Within a month of King's death, seventeen had been deported, all Irish, all Democrats, all trusted supporters of Broderick. The vigilantes were clearly working up to Broderick himself, and people were getting out of their way. Garrison, the recent mayoral candidate Broderick had supported, quickly decided he needed to look into his business interests in New York. Similarly, a prominent local judge of known Democratic sympathies felt weary, and decided that a sojourn in the Sandwich Islands would be just the thing. Sheriff Dave Scannel became a model of quiet and compliant probity.

The committee could not go after George Wilkes. He had recently had a falling-out with Broderick. Wilkes had fancied becoming a state Supreme Court justice, but Broderick did not think he would have a chance against the likes of Terry. In a huff Wilkes had returned to New York for a while; so he was out of reach. Ned McGowan, on the other hand, had sized up the situation early; the day that Casey and Cora were hung he went on the lam.

The committee now knew that McGowan had provided Casey with the gun that killed King, although the gun could not now be found. (Scannel probably "lost" it.) Clearly, the committee intended that he would be their next big execution, if they could only get their hands on him. But the Irish

Walrus proved remarkably elusive. Broderick helped arrange to get him out of town. Soon reports of his whereabouts became a staple of the San Francisco newspapers; McGowan seemed to be popping up everywhere in California, three or four places at a time. He would only resurface months later, when the danger was past, forty pounds lighter and with a new sobriquet of his own devising, McGowan the Ubiquitous.

The committee was going after anyone associated with Broderick. Even Tom McGuire was arrested for deportation, although he had nothing to do with politics except that he had provided Broderick and his friends with rooms. The sentence of deportation was passed on him, then postponed for two weeks, and then somehow forgotten in the crush of business.

The time had come to move on Broderick himself. The order was issued on July 19, 1856. But here a division emerged within the committee, for with this move there could be no denying that the committee was primarily concerned not with crime but with politics, party politics that was being settled by means other than elections.

From the beginning of the movement one newspaper, the San Francisco *Herald* (unrelated to Casey's Sunday paper), had denounced the committee in uncompromising terms. Its editor, John Nugent, himself a native of Ireland, had been a strong supporter of the 1851 vigilantes. This committee of 1856 was not, he insisted from the start, primarily interested in crime; it was a "mercantile junta." He added, mocking their symbol, "It cannot be said of this committee of vigilance eye, as of Banquo's, that there is no *speculation* in it." So Nugent had flailed away at the committee, as the *Herald* shrunk dramatically in size and circulation. (The day after Nugent first openly opposed the committee almost all advertisements in the paper were canceled, at the insistence of the committee and over the objections of Coleman.) Now others, in light of the recent deportations, were reluctantly coming to the same conclusion, among them Gerritt Ryckman.

Ryckman had been arguably the most important vigilante in 1851, at least after Brannan and Coleman. He was their most successful interrogator of suspected felons, apparently sympathetic to the accused while the investigation was under way but absolutely unyielding when guilt had been established. His idea of mercy was to provide clergy to the condemned. Coleman had been respected, the irascible Brannan feared—Ryckman had been both feared and respected. His saving grace—without which he might have become a California Robespierre—was that he had no love of power, was completely indifferent to it in fact.

Ryckman had early joined the movement this time as well, but had kept his distance when he learned of plans that were too political in his judgment. When Broderick heard that he was to be arrested, he shrewdly appealed to Ryckman as someone from the other side who on principle would oppose the blurring of criminal prosecution and party politics. Knowing Broderick as he did, Ryckman must have been stunned as Broderick emphasized his own weakness.

Broderick had to admit that he had been working behind the scenes against the committee. He had placed his hope in Sherman, but that was gone. The committee did not need to fear him anymore in San Francisco, for his machine had been smashed. All the boys were gone, or going, or in hiding. All he had left was his role in statewide government; if he was man-handled by the committee, his career would be over. But, if they tried to move against him, there would also be trouble.

To read Ryckman's account of his meeting with Broderick is painful. For the first time in his life Broderick seemed to be pleading. He was willing to admit defeat, to cut his losses, at the expense of his friends. If only he were left with a chance, just a chance still to become a U.S. senator. He was almost pathetic.

At least he had judged Ryckman correctly. The proposed arrest of Broderick confirmed his own worst suspicions concerning the true objectives of the 1856 committee. Ryckman confronted the executive committee in a fury: "I told you you were going to make a political engine out of it. If you don't countermand that order for the arrest of Broderick, I will tap the bell and order an opposition and arrest every damn one of you." And the committee knew well that Gerritt Ryckman did not make idle threats.

A compromise was reached. Broderick was not arrested. He came into the committee voluntarily, and cooperatively answered their questions. Then, when he was permitted to go, he left the city entirely. He went to the mining regions to campaign for Democratic candidates for the state legislature. He needed new supporters, and thought he might pick them up there.

By this time the committee had long since overreached itself. McGowan would later write, "The real motives of the Committee were beginning to be scanned, the people were coming back to 'second thoughts', the state was saved." There were radicals on the committee who were willing to entertain secession of California from the Union, but such drastic actions could only be taken at the risk of losing support, even within San Francisco. The revolutionaries among the vigilantes, Sherman thought, never did represent a majority, except perhaps in the executive committee. As for the majority, he wrote back to Saint Louis, "My own opinion is that the committee is tired of its position, but finds it difficult to withdraw from the complications in which they are involved."

Sherman's successor as head of the militia did not agree; he had written to Governor Johnson that events had left no doubt in his mind "that the insurgents aim at nothing less than an entire overthrow of the State government and secession from the Federal Union." Such secession would be unavoidable when the committee realized "that there is no safety for their leaders but in revolution and a separate government on the Pacific."

Certain members of the committee were undoubtedly pointing toward secession. (Coleman would later insist emphatically that he had never been one of them.) However, they had not yet reached a point of no return. They still could hedge their bets, moving toward secession without causing an irreparable breach with the state and federal governments. However, the situation had become so serious that an irreparable breach could occur without their having finally decided upon it. And it almost did.

The committee had come very close to such a breach shortly before Broderick was interrogated and just before Rube Meloney was deported. Meloney, trying to help the state government support the opponents of the committee, was involved in a scheme to smuggle arms into San Francisco. He had been caught by a vigilante patrol, released, and then ordered arrested again. The group sent to get him was led by Sterling Hopkins.

Meloney happened to be with David Terry when they came, an unlikely couple who had nothing in common except their hatred of these vigilantes. The result of the encounter was that Hopkins ended up with a bowie knife four inches into his shoulder near the neck, and that the committee had a state Supreme Court justice in its jail. As a regretful vigilante put it, "We started out to hunt coyotes, but we've got a grizzly bear on our hands, and we don't know what to do with him." If Hopkins died (which amazingly he would not), Terry was certain to be lynched. And some wanted to hang him whether Hopkins recovered or not, much as they had wanted to execute Casey even before King took a turn for the worse.

With this distinguished Southerner at risk, Gwin himself was forced to do something. Having up to now been as elusive as McGowan was proving to be, he made a halfhearted attempt to negotiate the release of Terry, and he got a glimpse of what the extremists on the committee were thinking. One of them dismissed Gwin's arguments for conciliation in strong terms: "We have proved ourselves superiors of the City and County government, and of the State government. And if the Federal government dares . . ." Presumably he was going to rant about fifty-seven thousand men ready for any action on a day's notice at the word of Citizen No. 1, but a naval officer Gwin had brought with him jumped to his feet and shouted, "Stop, sir!" And then treated all there to a handsome five-minute speech of earnest patriotism. All of which must have convinced Gwin that this was no place for him.

Outside of San Francisco, there was a rising cry against the vigilantes as a "sour flour and soft pork aristocracy," or a "mere political machine," or "the stranglers of Sacramento and Front streets," or a "hodge podge of potato vendors, small beer politicians and flour speculators," or a mob led by "Boston men and that ilk." (The last comment was from an uncompromising member of the Chivalry.) The taking of Terry seemed to undermine what support the vigilantes had outside of San Francisco. With Hopkins improving, they allowed themselves to be berated by Ryckman, then amicably interviewed Broderick and allowed him to leave the city.

Finally, when Hopkins was out of danger, the committee could release Terry. (For this reason one of the committee radicals would later write that Hopkins's failure to die was "the most unfortunate thing that ever happened" to the movement.) Coleman wanted the release done with great ceremony, but others feared that they could not control the situation—and Terry might well be lynched on the spot. Once again, Coleman was overruled. So they snuck him out of San Francisco at night, to the great displeasure of Hopkins's friends, who still wanted blood. Terry later received an elegant silver pitcher that was inscribed:

> Hon. D.S. Terry
> from the ladies of San Francisco
> who admire his courage, his honor, his patriotism and
> take the highest pride in his heroic resistance to tyranny.
> August 26, 1856

It was unclear whether the subscribers were ladies this son of the Chivalry would acknowledge as such. If Ned McGowan had not been temporarily unavailable for pranks, one would have suspected his hand in this, with the whole trophy being thought up late one night in a brothel.

The committee of 1856 did conduct another dual hanging, mostly just to show it still could. This hanging, unlike the first one, did not go well. One victim, who looked almost like a boy on the platform, became hysterical, and treated the crowd to an obscene diatribe against the committee. The other, a mature man of impressive bearing, was perfectly composed and dignified, and gave an eloquent oration arguing quite persuasively his innocence and the unjustness of this punishment.

With support waning, Coleman decided to disband the committee formally, unlike the committee of 1851, which had dribbled into nonexistence. There would be a holiday, and a great parade and show of force. Then the headquarters of the committee would be opened to the public, and women and children would be permitted to fondle handcuffs and nooses that had been actually used. Of this whole pageant so characteristic of Coleman, Sherman wrote with complete disgust, in particular at the power that the *Bulletin* (now edited by King's shady brother) still aspired to exercise over San Francisco:

> The Vigilance Committee have at last finished their task. We are now a highly reformed people. Today all their firms are parading the streets on a grand jubilee, celebrating their victories, and rejoicing at the regeneration of society. I have not been down the street to see who have closed their stores in

> obedience to the *Bulletin*'s orders, but we have not, and I do
> not think any of the bankers have. . . . I hear a good deal of
> under expression that it is all folly, this presentation of swords
> and banners to companies of armed men who at most have
> conquered their own fellow citizens and made the authorities
> of their own selection a by-word and laughing stock.

In the end Sherman's cynicism misled him. He could not bring himself
to realize that the committee had been a complete success, at least judged on
its own terms. It had executed the two men it had first wanted. It had
destroyed Broderick's political machine. It had deported most of the leading
Irish political activists of the city. Those merchants who had been on the
verge of bankruptcy had been given a respite of a few months from the
creditors. The commission merchants, moreover, had watched while their
overstuffed warehouses had now become depleted, thereby driving prices
back up. (Eastern suppliers had been understandably reluctant to risk sending
new goods to a city in turmoil.) So the committee had indirectly revived
business almost as effectively as a major fire would have.

Moreover, the committee had never quite succumbed to its occasional
visions of grandeur. So, despite the occasional bluster of Citizen No. 1, there
never had been a real test of strength with the federal government. Nor had
any irreparable breach occurred between the state and the city, although it
had been a close thing. So the vigilantes could return to their businesses
without fear of criminal prosecution. And yet, as Sherman could be excused
for not seeing, they were not going to return to business as usual.

Until now, the businessmen of San Francisco had largely remained aloof
from city politics. They had avoided public service as steadfastly as they had
avoided jury duty. Perhaps as a group they had been like the miners who
wished to make a killing and then return home. Nobody was making quick
killings now, either in the diggings or in San Francisco shops. Now, after
1854–55, the commercial boom was clearly over in San Francisco. What
growth there would be would be slow. Those who were not content with
modest profits would end up as James King of William had, in penury.

Even as the celebrations Sherman so deplored were ending, plans were
already well advanced for the businessmen of the 1856 Committee of Vigilance to continue their rule over San Francisco. The city officials had refused
to step aside, as the committee wanted them to. But that made no difference.
The committee would simply be transformed into a political party that would
be run by a central committee as the vigilantes had. There would be no
conventions, no primaries, only a slate dominated by businessmen, Protestant
businessmen of American birth. The People's Party, as it was called, would
rule San Francisco for more than a decade, thanks in part to its shrewd use
of alliances with regular political parties.

The committee of 1856 had learned well from the successes and failures of 1851. They had learned that the problem was not crime but politics. They had learned they wanted not justice but power. They had learned the value of secrecy and theatrical violence. They knew they needed a leader like Coleman, not Brannan. They knew, finally, that the ultimate enemy was not foreign conspirators but American democrats. And, despite what men like Sherman said, they had succeeded. Most of them would be right, when they looked back upon this summer as old men and said these few months were the most extraordinary in their lives. Their continued adulation for William Tell Coleman was understandable in light of that.

The Democratic Party was left to pick up the pieces. The committee had come into being at the worst possible moment for the Democrats. The Democrats had already weakened themselves by internal divisions to such an extent they had lost the state government. So they were in no position to act when the vigilantes organized. Broderick, who in this instance had been taken completely unawares, could no more effectively intervene for his people than Gwin could for Terry. One would not be surprised to learn that during much of this crisis he had also been immobilized by a deep depression.

The Democrats no longer had San Francisco to fight over. They had lost the largest city in California for the foreseeable future. Broderick virtually had conceded as much when he headed to the diggings to drum up new support. The Chivalry and the Shovelry had lost similarly in what was being called "the businessman's revolution."

Still, Johnson and the Know-Nothing officials had demonstrated themselves to be completely incompetent in this crisis; and the new party itself was deeply divided over the committee. That discomfort to the Know-Nothings was the only good thing to come out of this catastrophe for the Democrats, and showed where they had to start to rebuild. So, as the summer of 1856 was ending, the question for Broderick and Gwin was the same. Could the Democratic Party regain control of state government? The Know-Nothings might be swept out of office as suddenly as they had been swept in. However, that would require an extraordinary thing. David Broderick and William Gwin must cooperate. They could begin with the election of 1856.

7

William Gwin thought that the election of 1856 was his chance to get back into the United States Senate where he belonged. He certainly did not belong among the people of San Francisco as they had revealed themselves during the past wonderful summer. Perhaps this would be his last chance. Others among the Chivalry were beginning to eye higher office for themselves.

Notable among these was Milton Latham, the fair-haired boy of California politics who had been getting almost everything he wanted, without apparent effort—and was still head of the Customs House. Gwin had thought naturally that through the pliable Latham he would pretty much control the appointments at the Customs House. And he did, for a while—until, to be precise, he had failed in his initial attempt to get reelected to his seat. Then Milton Latham began to think of himself.

In the last two years the importance of the positions in the Customs House for the California Chivalry had increased significantly. The Know-Nothings now controlled the state government and through it all the patronage that Broderick and Bigler had so assiduously exploited. Of course, Gwin was no longer in the Senate; and Weller, the remaining senator, was ineffective in patronage matters. Weller, although his politics resembled Gwin's, did in other respects resemble his friend Solomon Heydenfeldt. In particular, he prided himself on his honor, and therefore did not like to dirty his hands with grubby political detail.

Latham now saw his opportunity to move past Gwin to the pinnacle of Democratic leadership. And Latham was not one to pass up opportunities, however winningly innocent he might seem to casual observers. So Latham, to the considerable annoyance of Gwin, had begun to spread these positions at the Customs House across the whole of the Democratic Party, including Broderickites, thereby making himself a most popular figure. He even at one point gave a position to the disreputable brother of King of William, thereby making the *Bulletin* an admirer. (King of William had written, "As Collector of this port, as far as our information goes, Mr. Latham has discharged his duties faithfully." Given his normal tone, this was approaching panegyric.)

Gwin, like everyone else, could see where all this was leading—to another run by Latham for governor, or (more likely) a serious run for the Senate.

One could not fault Latham's implicit reasoning, whatever one might say about his loyalty. He had calculated that the easiest way to the Senate was to become a candidate equally acceptable to the Chivalry and Shovelry—and, anyway, Latham always thought he should be liked by everyone. Although Gwin had no patronage at his own disposal, he had to make peace with the Shovelry. To become senator again, Gwin had only to forge a personal alliance with Broderick. However distasteful, it seemed feasible.

When the legislature met after the election of 1856, there would be two Senate seats open, Gwin's with a four-year term still remaining, Weller's with a full six. Gwin would be happy to support Broderick for the full six, if he in turn would be given the remaining years on his old seat. Latham and Weller would be left out in the cold. It seemed so simple, if one approached the matter rationally. But Gwin also knew that things were never simple when dealing with Broderick.

As early as April 1856, Gwin had felt out Broderick about an alliance that could take them both into the Senate. He had not talked to him directly, of course. Instead, he had sent a trusted intermediary for a secret meeting. (Perhaps it was James O'Meara, who is the source for this episode.) An understanding was quickly reached. They would cease to attack one another, and direct their followers to do likewise—and try also to control the newspapers, although that would not be so easy. Vituperation sold papers. Then, when the legislature met in January 1857, they would see to it by whatever means necessary that each received a Senate seat. In the intervening months, they would confide this secret arrangement to their supporters only as seemed appropriate. In outline the results from the two-hour meeting were everything Gwin could have wished. Nonetheless, the details, as they were recounted to Gwin (and repeated years later by a trusted aide), were disturbing.

Broderick's behavior had been frightening, not because he seemed unwilling to deal but because of the seething rage that the mere mention of the Senate seat seemed to occasion in him. Now that the prize was being placed by Gwin within his grasp, now that his old rival was suing for peace, Broderick only expressed his dissatisfaction.

Broderick rose from his chair in the small, dark backroom where the interview took place, and began to rant on and on, in tedious detail, about his determination one day to sit in the Senate. Finally he said, with what the listener must have taken as calculated hyperbole (he was a Gwin man, after all), "I tell you, sir, by God, that for one hour's seat in the Senate of the United States, I would roast before a slow fire in the plaza."

Now perhaps the Gwin man thought that with these histrionics over they could get down to the final details of the deal. But, no, Broderick began to review in obsessive detail his earlier efforts to achieve this end. Apparently he remembered every slight or betrayal, real or imagined. But why would

Broderick think the listener would be interested in this at all? As David Broderick progressed through this litany (one that he had obviously often repeated to himself), his voice began to rise and assume a tone that was not quite human: "Talk of friends! I have a few who are. But I know the others, damn them! For I have paid for them, and know the quality of their friendship. In the session of 1854 they cost me one hundred and seventy-five thousand dollars. They have nearly beggared me."

Rumor did have it that Broderick was nearly broke because of his continuous campaigning. He did own numerous lots in San Francisco, but many were tied up in mortgages or undeveloped. The truth was that Broderick seemed to lack a visible means of support, although he lived like a monk and so needed little for himself.

Broderick by this point had begun to speak of one man who had the gall to call himself Broderick's friend, but who required a bribe of $1,200 for his vote, and then had the gall later to demand in addition a gold watch, and when that was provided, then said he needed a gold chain to go with his watch. "I told Billy Graham to buy the dog a slide and ribbon, and if he was not satisfied with that he might go to hell."

Gwin's man could only have been perplexed by all this. What did Broderick expect to gain by providing such incriminating details to Gwin? Surely he must know this all would be repeated to Gwin. But still Broderick went on and on, in detail that now became embarrassing—and more than Gwin could possibly ever find a use for—about the others who called themselves his friends and were not. George Wilkes, his oldest friend from New York, had betrayed him to try to get a seat for himself on the state Supreme Court. Had gone behind his back to make a deal of his own with Bigler. Well, Broderick had taken care of that appointment, and so shamed Wilkes that the bastard pimp now had returned to New York rather than have to look Dave Broderick in the face anymore.

This litany had no calculated purpose; Broderick seemed to be losing his reason, right in front of his enemy's friend. As Broderick obsessively ticked off payoff after payoff and betrayal after betrayal, the increasingly fidgety Gwin man began to try to think of who if anyone was left. Suddenly it must have dawned on him. This man, so formidable, so beloved by his followers, does not think he has a single friend left. That is what his drive for the Senate has revealed to him. He has no true friends. And for the first time the Gwin man could look at Broderick with compassion.

Then Broderick, with the unconscious insight of the truly mad, immediately sensed this pitying condescension and with a wild smile shouted: "Ah, yes, I know these friends! I am going to that Senate. I'll go if I have to march over a thousand corpses, and every corpse a friend!" The interview was over.

Now, as the election of 1856 approached, Gwin was trying to fulfill his end of the bargain. He had confided the details of the arrangement only to his supporters who were not implacable in their personal feelings toward

Broderick. The others he would bring into line when they were needed. Of course, they might not be needed at all, since the California Democrats seemed to be vulnerable to a complete rout. Gwin's and Broderick's election to the U.S. Senate depended upon the Democrats regaining control of the California legislature in the general election of 1856.

On the surface the situation did not look promising. The Know-Nothings, of course, controlled state government, or at least occupied its chief offices. Neely Johnson and his administration would not be up for reelection until November 1857. The vigilantes had apparently broken Broderick's machine in San Francisco, or had at least removed many of his most loyal operatives. And their law and order campaign seemed to fit well with the broader nativist objectives of the Party of the Dark Lantern. There seemed little hope for the Democrats to pick up much ground in San Francisco.

The overall prospects in the state were, nonetheless, more promising. The leading Know-Nothings, notably David Terry and Neely Johnson, had been humiliated by the vigilantes—and were happy to ally with the state Democrats to try to humiliate them in turn. In the new legislative session Democrats and many Know-Nothings used every opportunity to repudiate Coleman and the all-seeing eye of vigilance. This intention became clear when the Assembly and Senate each chose their respective chaplain. The Assembly chose the Reverend William Scott, a Chivalry Episcopalian who had been the only Protestant minister in San Francisco to use his pulpit to denounce the vigilantes as un-Christian and un-American. Even more pointedly, the Senate selected as its chaplain Father Gallagher, the same priest whom King of William had denounced.

Governor Neely Johnson himself used the beginning of the new legislative session as the occasion to deliver an attack on the vigilantes. He explained, somewhat weakly, his decision to trust the early vigilante assurances that they would act within the law. "So loyal were the sentiments expressed and so positive the declarations made of their designed obedience to law and legitimate authority that I could not either disbelieve or doubt them." Soon, he reported, he had been disabused of his trust. Then the vigilantes had "assumed the character of a permanent organization, which designed not only to usurp the control of the legal authority in San Francisco; but . . . aimed also to extend its power to the subversion of State authority; and, if Federal intervention should ensue, the establishment of a government entirely independent of the Union." Johnson detailed how he had appealed to President Pierce for federal forces, but had been refused and thereby rendered "powerless to check the usurpation." (The one moment of partisan party politics in his address.) All he wished to do was "to arrest the treason and suppress the rebellion" and yet he could not. In conclusion, he wished to assure his listeners, "I know no *higher law* than the Constitution of my country; and as a rule of action alike incessant and inflexible, the observance of the duties it enjoins, will ever be paramount in my regard as a public officer and private citizen."

This speech was a handsome declaration as far as it went. The governor, before a joint session of the legislature, had publicly accused vigilantes of no less a crime than treason. He had, moreover, had his address published in the *Senate Journal* with numerous appendices filled with documents that supported his interpretation of the events. Nonetheless, this attack did on reflection only reveal what a weak governor Johnson had proven to be. This was clear when an important question was asked that Neely Johnson had avoided.

Now that regular government was operating once again throughout California, why were the vigilantes, or at least their leaders like Coleman, not being arrested? When this question was asked, Johnson's dramatic charges of treason and usurpation, as well as his grand evocation of the Constitution as the highest law, sound in retrospect like so much cowardly weaseling. In his speech Johnson had been careful to charge the vigilantes only with federal offenses—and then the Democratic president's refusal to suppress the rebellion left the state officials off the hook. Yet, if what Johnson said of the vigilantes was true, these same vigilantes were also guilty of other crimes, not least of which was simple murder. Much as he did during the crisis itself, Neely Johnson was more comfortable proclaiming than acting. Johnson was going to fulminate and then sit on his hands.

Moreover, the fact that the likes of Johnson and Terry were steadfastly opposed to Coleman and the vigilantes did not mean that all in their party were. At the statewide convention in the summer of 1856 Southerners in the party had tried to introduce a resolution that was clearly intended as a repudiation of the committee, only to be hooted down by some nativists of Northern origins, many presumably representing San Francisco.

This was encouraging for the Democrats. From its beginnings there had been tensions between the Northern and Southern wings of the American Party, as the Know-Nothings now called themselves. If there had not been such tensions right here in California, "Hangman" Foote would now be sitting in the U.S. Senate. Democrats could only hope that these tensions would become fissures. If the American Party broke apart, the Democrats could control the next election by a mere plurality. And breaking was what the Know-Nothings nationally seemed to be doing.

The American Party had shrewdly fielded a prominent ticket for national office in 1856, with former president Millard Fillmore at its head. Fillmore was just the man to waffle on the issues that threatened party unity. Nonetheless, there were omens from the start that his campaign was doomed. (For instance, Fillmore was notified of his surprise nomination while on a European tour; unfortunately, it did not escape the notice of the American press that the new standard-bearer of nativism in the United States had received this news shortly after he had arranged to have an audience with the pope.)

Fillmore's only practical hope for election was to carry enough Southern states along with California to throw the selection into the House of Representatives, where he would stand a fair chance.

As a result of this strategy, it was not popery but slavery that threatened to destroy the American Party as a national force. Many Northern nativists had long since connected popery and slavery as the twin evils that threatened the American republic. As one state party platform put it succinctly, "Whereas, Roman Catholicism and slavery being alike founded and supported on the basis of ignorance and tyranny; and being, therefore, natural allies in every warfare against liberty and enlightenment, be it Resolved, That there can exist no real hostility to Roman Catholicism which does not embrace slavery, its natural co-worker in opposition to freedom and republican institutions."

So to many Northerners abolitionism and nativism seemed two sides of the same coin. How could one be opposed to slavery spiritual and not be opposed to slavery physical? No one, for instance, gave more intemperate sermons against Catholicism than the Reverend Henry Ward Beecher; his sister, Harriet Beecher Stowe, while sharing his views on religion, had also written the immensely successful abolitionist novel *Uncle Tom's Cabin*. In short, many sincere Know-Nothings found it difficult to support a party that would fight to keep the pope out of America while allowing Uncle Tom to be sold down the river.

The leadership of the California Know-Nothings in 1856 tried to avoid the issue of abolitionism as best they could. At the state convention they called themselves a "reform party." They exhorted their members "to lend their energies in the aid of great and essential reform movements of the day." When pressed to be specific as to what particular movements these were, they responded that all true Americans should be "co-laborers with us in the glorious cause of union and regeneration." But what about concrete issues like the extension of slavery into the West? The leadership wanted to claim that they knew nothing about the party's position on such divisive issues— but would, if elected, do the right thing, whatever that was.

Nonetheless, even members of their own party were not satisfied with this less than artful dodging. So in the summer convention of the Know-Nothings members of the Chivalry frowned while being treated to abolitionist oratory by some Northern delegates. In return, these abolitionists got treated to official circumlocutions and parliamentary sleight of hand. So, in turn, they stormed out of the convention, threatening to establish their own party.

This was not an idle threat, for there already was a national party ready to embrace them. So it was that in 1856 the state senator who had blocked Foote's election to the U.S. Senate changed parties and became a Republican—and others accompanied him.

In retrospect, Gwin could see that he himself had in a sense been present at the founding of the Republican Party, had in fact played his own unwitting role in its becoming a national party. It had occurred when he was senator, in his last Congress, that of 1854.

In 1854 Gwin, just as he had during the Compromise of 1850, had placed himself thoroughly in the camp of Stephen Douglas, the camp of practical politics for the national good. The Democracy, as Democrats sometimes called themselves, was the one truly national party, the party that could transcend sectional bickering. Douglas understood that the price of this was, as he had put it pointedly in an earlier speech, "entire silence on the slavery question." Gwin was convinced that Douglas was also the man to negotiate the compromises to ensure this silence.

This meant that the Compromise of 1850 had to be periodically brought up to date. Clearly, at least clearly to Gwin, for this silence to be preserved further concessions had to be given to the South in light of the expansion of settlements into the territories. The so-called Free-Soilers within the Democratic Party wanted no extension of slavery into any of the territories. But for there to be peace there had to be the possibility of extending slavery. Douglas had worked out, with consultation with Southern senators and Southern sympathizers like Gwin, what looked in 1854 to be a brilliant compromise, a compromise that had had Gwin's enthusiastic support.

For Douglas as for Gwin, slavery was simply an economic issue. In some places it was profitable; in others not. A mode of social organization that was profitable in Mississippi might not be in New York because of differences in climate, soil, and topography. The moral dimension, which obsessed abolitionists, was simply beside the point. As Douglas put it with purposeful blandness, "The civilized world have always held that when any race of men have shown themselves so degraded by ignorance, superstition, cruelty, and barbarism as to be utterly incapable of governing themselves, they must, in the nature of things, be governed by others, by such laws as are deemed applicable."

The concrete issue that in 1854 had threatened the Compromise of 1850 had been the territory of Kansas, which lay west of Missouri. The Southerners were insistent that Missourians, if they so chose, should be able to colonize Kansas with their slaves. Free-Soil Democrats were equally insistent that such a colonization would violate the Missouri Compromise of 1820, which stipulated that no slavery be permitted above 36°30'.

To this Free-Soil contention Douglas had a brilliant if unexpected refutation that he formulated in a bill covering both the Kansas and Nebraska territories. The Missouri Compromise had already been set aside by the Compromise of 1850. The latter compromise had stipulated that territories like California could decide for themselves whether to be slave or free; henceforth slavery was an appropriate matter to be decided in their state constitutions when they applied for admission as states.

This move was typical Douglas. As a debating tactic, it was brilliant, putting his opponents off-balance and on the defensive. However, plausible as it initially sounded, this argument in the end would convince only those who already believed that Kansas should be open to slavery. If the Compromise of 1850 really negated the earlier compromise over Missouri, was it not peculiar that no one, including Senator Douglas himself, had mentioned this important point at the time—not once, during the months and months of debate in 1850?

Gwin naturally had stood by his friend Douglas throughout the debate over Kansas. But the Democratic Party had been badly split by it. The Free-Soilers had been apoplectic; they denounced this "gross violation of a sacred pledge," this "criminal betrayal of precious rights," this "atrocious plot to . . . convert it [Kansas] into a dreary region of despotism, inhabited by masters and slaves." To such arguments Douglas would reply with disdain. His opponents were merely posturing: "I do not believe there is a man in Congress who thinks it [Kansas] could permanently be a slave-holding country."

Here was a true statesman, the kind of man who as president could overcome sectional differences (while also finding for Gwin a place in his cabinet). Gwin, of course, knew Douglas well. "The Little Giant" was, most people agreed, more of a pugilist than an orator. Short, rotund, with a large forehead, dark hair, circled eyes, and a frequent scowl on his lips, he looked like a bulldog—and he fought like one too. This was the paradox of the man; he fought like a bulldog on behalf of compromise and quiet. His "compromises" had afterward more the feeling of victories in which whoever had stood in his way had been completely routed. Although he worked to similar ends as the Great Pacificator, Douglas was no Clay.

Once in a debate, Douglas would use anything that came to mind to win. Moreover, he seemed dominated at such times of intense struggle by a strange possessiveness, as if winning was less important than being the one who had won. Weller learned of this trait when during this debate over Kansas he had risen to offer a little help on the Senate floor to his champion. To Gwin's immense amusement, Douglas, like a pint-sized Achilles, had snapped at the junior senator from California, "Sit down, don't mix in, this is my fight." This possessiveness, the simple vanity that all depended upon him alone, made Douglas a whirlwind of energy. Friends, like Gwin, simply stood with him, and worked quietly on his behalf, gratefully allowing him to hold the whole center stage. Then, when he and they succeeded, they could also watch with smiling approval as Douglas crowed like a bantam rooster, as he did this time when his bill on Kansas and Nebraska passed: "I passed the Kansas-Nebraska Act myself. I had the authority and power of a dictator throughout the whole controversy in both houses. The speeches were nothing. It was the marshalling and directing of men and guarding from attacks with a ceaseless vigilance preventing surprise."

The bill had won in the Senate two to one, and would pass the House as comfortably. Yet, despite Douglas's crowing, Gwin had realized reluctantly that the slavery question was not going to pass into silence—and that a number of important Northern Democrats had been driven by the Kansas question into seriously considering bolting the party. Douglas had become as great a villain to them as Webster had been in 1850. He had sold his birthright for a mess of pottage—and in this case the pottage was possible Southern support for an eventual bid for the presidency. Or so they grumbled.

Gwin had hoped that the Kansans would in time resolve the issue as quietly as Californians had, even if that meant the new state would be free, as seemed likely since most immigrants to Kansas came from free states. But there had been a recurring theme among the opposition in the Senate that troubled him, especially because it had been enunciated by some men he respected.

Gwin knew better than to pay attention to the pedantic self-righteousness of Charles Sumner; the Democrats would be better off without such moralistic prigs as the senator from Massachusetts. On the other hand, Salmon Chase, the senator from Ohio, although given to grandiloquent speeches, was a more reasonable politician; that he would break party discipline on the Kansas question was worrisome for the future of the Democrats as a truly national party, for he with Douglas represented the growing power of the Northwest. Yet the senator who most troubled Gwin was a Whig from New York whom he genuinely liked, William Seward.

Seward had become a frequent guest at Gwin's house, and both he and Mrs. Gwin enjoyed his company. They purposefully had him with their more radical Southern friends like Jefferson Davis, and they all got on well at a personal level. Seward was a little man like Douglas, although sparse in build. And unlike Douglas, whose energy made him seem to grow in stature before your very eyes, Seward remained small in appearance when speaking, his oversized eyebrows comically distracting from his sternly composed expression.

Seward was usually almost offhand in his delivery of speeches, sometimes even twirling his spectacles distractedly. His was not the voice of a great orator, any more than Douglas's was. Yet his voice at times had an odd timbre, especially when he was aroused. If Douglas was ever the pugilist, Seward was at times the oracle. Like Shakespeare's Glendower, Seward had then the voice to call spirits from the vasty deep. Statements could on occasion come from his lips that sounded as if read in a trance from the scrolls of fate. So Seward's three-hour oration against the Douglas bill came to a disturbingly plain conclusion, a conclusion more like a prophecy than a peroration: "The slavery agitation you depreciate so much is an eternal struggle between conservatism and progress, between truth and error, between right and wrong." How could an experienced politician say such a thing and mean it? Worse—regard it as self-evident?

After the fight was over and Douglas had won, Chase drew the corollary from Seward's vatic assertion: "They celebrate a present victory, but echoes they awake shall never rest until slavery itself shall die." Coming from Summer, such might have been dismissed as self-righteous bluster. However, coming from serious men like Chase and Seward it had been disturbing to Gwin, all the more because it employed a kind of reasoning he could never comprehend. If they wanted to talk about progress, why not focus on tractable matters like improved mail or the transcontinental railroad?

The antislavery agitators, moreover, bore an odd resemblance to Broderick and his cronies. Defeats like this one, rather than opening them to compromise, only seemed to make them more determined. On this particular subject they refused reasoned calculation, but rather seemed to derive strength and conviction from outright defeat. But, of course, Chase and Seward were not truly like Broderick. Gwin knew that. They were gentlemen, senators, statesmen, the kind of men one welcomed into one's home, introduced with pride to one's family.

Since Gwin had left the Senate, he had watched from afar, horrified and helpless, as Douglas's Kansas compromise that had looked so promising, so reasonable, so clever had unraveled, thereby ruining Pierce's presidency as well as Douglas's chance to be his immediate successor. Kansas was now enduring civil war between proslavery and free-soil factions. The source of the violence was not only Northern antislavery agitators. As Edward Everett had put it sarcastically in his Fourth of July oration of 1855, "It has lately been maintained, by the sharp logic of the revolver and the bowie knife, that the people of Missouri are the people of Kansas!"

Some prominent Southerners had reasoned themselves into seeing Kansas as the last chance to achieve the sectional equality that Calhoun had insisted was necessary for the just continuance of the Union. This was the view, for instance, of David Atchison, the Missouri senator who had engineered the 1850 defeat of Tom Benton over the slavery question: "If Kansas is abolitionized, Missouri ceases to be a slave State, New Mexico becomes a free State, California remains a free State; but if we secure Kansas as a slave State, Missouri is secure; New Mexico and Southern California, if not all of it, becomes a slave State; in a word, the prosperity or ruin of the whole South depends on the Kansas struggle."

In this struggle there were atrocities on both sides—most notably, one massacre of slave owners by a fire-breathing abolitionist named John Brown who applied the Pauline maxim "Without the shedding of blood there is no remission of sins" more broadly than had the apostle to the gentiles. All the while Atchison was exhorting the border ruffians from his own state to take Kansas "if necessary with the bayonet and with blood." But, as the situation continually worsened, President Pierce, listening to his old comrade-in-arms Jefferson Davis, had tried to ignore the unignorable. Soon "bleeding Kansas" had two territorial governments (with Charles Robinson, late of the Sacramento squatters, as the head of the Free-Soil one), was in a virtual state of civil war, and had groups both in the North and South intent upon sending more arms and settlers. "Free state or proslavery?" had—it was reported—become the common salutation between strangers in Kansas, the answer to which was too commonly followed soon after by the report of a pistol. All the while Pierce dithered. "Pierce entered the presidency with little opposition," the quip went, "and he will leave with none." Pierce, for his part, may have had occasion to remember what a dear old friend, Nathaniel Hawthorne, had said to him upon his election: "Frank, I pity you."

Bleeding Kansas had supplied the lifeblood for the new Republican Party. Douglas's compromise had produced a "fusion party" of Northern Whigs and Free-Soil Democrats to oppose it. In the House about thirty representatives opposed to Douglas's bill had caucussed on May 9, 1854, and had decided to call themselves the Republican Party, a name that had been bandied about by other fusion groups. Douglas, Gwin, and other moderate Democrats had at first discounted this new party as a flash in the pan. A one-issue, sectional party could scarcely challenge a great national party.

But then the most dire Republican predictions concerning Kansas proved correct. Now many in the North were listening to the Republican call. All existing parties—Democratic, American, Whig—were too corrupted by their Southern wings. What was needed was a new party uncompromised by the past, or rather by the South.

Politicians who had spent their careers reluctantly on the fence were turning to the new party in considerable numbers. John Greenleaf Whittier, the poet laureate of abolitionism, had begun to rhapsodize about the coming 1856 election in apocalyptic terms. This would be the year "When Good and Evil, as for final strife, / Close vast and dim on Armageddon's plain." Of course, even given the inevitable victory destined for the forces of good, the Republicans still needed a standard-bearer to lead them through the grubbiness of an election.

Seward, having joined the new party along with most other abolitionist Whigs, was the natural choice for the Republicans—and yet he hesitated, perhaps because he regarded the likelihood of election as slight. So did Chase, who also had gone over to the new party. By the time each had decided he wanted the nomination, a celebrity candidate was showing surprising strength, for reasons summarized by one of his prominent supporters: "It will never do to go into the contest and be called upon to defend the acts and speeches of old stagers. We must have a position that will enable us to be the charging party. Frémont is the man for the operation."

Frémont had the advantage of being well known while lacking any detailed political record. Seward and Chase had said plainly that the restriction of slavery in the territories was but a first step down the path leading to complete abolition, an initial dose of medicine in a course of treatment that was to result in a complete cure. Frémont, with no record, could restrict his statements to the more limited objectives of the Republican platform, simply no extension of slavery into the territories. He could also claim that his brief career as a California senator—his only governmental experience—had been ended by a slave power conspiracy. He, or rather his handlers like Horace Greeley, could tailor his positions to the sentiments of the delegates to the first Republican convention.

So Frémont sketched in the vaguest terms his views on Kansas through a public letter to his California acquaintance Charles Robinson, now the leader of Free-Soil Kansans. But mostly he relied on his glamour to find him the path to the nomination. Soon Republicans were shouting, "Frémont and Jessie"—and campaign biographies were extolling this love match as well as John's manly exertions on the frontier, his many "hair-breadth 'scapes" (as one of them put it). The Republican convention in the summer of 1856 decided that, compared to such a swashbuckler, Seward and Chase were indeed little more than old stagers.

For the California Democrats Frémont was just the man for the operation to put them back in control of the state legislature. His reputation in California, especially in the mining districts, had never been lower—and no one could gull most Californians with his self-serving accounts of his completely inconsequential term as senator. Moreover, the vituperation from the Chivalry against the emerging new party was frequent and extreme. For instance, when Republicans held their first convention in the state in August 1856, it was denounced as a "convention of nigger worshippers." The Chivalry would have enough sense, it was hoped, to vote for the candidate most likely to keep Frémont and the Republicans out of the White House.

Moreover, while the Republican and American parties had fielded regional candidates, the Democrats had settled upon someone who for Gwin was an ideal national figure untainted by the Kansas debacle—former secretary of state James Buchanan, "the Sage of Wheatland" to his friends and "Ten-cent Jimmy" to his detractors, and simply "Old Buck" to much of the electorate. Having been safely out of the country as the ambassador to the Court of St. James during the Kansas crisis, he had been able to maintain a sagelike silence, although insiders like Gwin knew perfectly well that Buchanan's views were indistinguishable from those of Douglas.

Gwin could sympathize with the disappointment of his friend Douglas, but Douglas was a young man and there was still time for him. On the other hand, Buchanan, now in his late sixties, was at the end of a long and distinguished career of public service. A term of Buchanan, and then the American Democracy, with its Kansas distractions finally behind it, could turn to its true leader, the Little Giant.

Buchanan, as a pragmatic Democratic from Pennsylvania, did seem to embrace both wings of the Democratic Party. For instance, he was the only close friend of Gwin who had once written a letter of introduction for jolly Ned McGowan. He was apparently someone for whom both Broderick and Gwin could campaign enthusiastically, although Gwin knew from private talks that Buchanan was far more sympathetic to the South than many Northerners thought. Old Buck was just the candidate to allow Broderick and Gwin to carry out their earlier agreement while they positioned themselves for the subsequent elections to the U.S. Senate.

At the California state Democratic convention in the early fall of 1856 something quite odd happened, at least to those not in the inner circle of either Broderick or Gwin. Broderick had allowed the Chivalry to run the convention without any effective opposition. This was perplexing to many observers. Although it was not true (as one newspaper claimed) that "he had it in his power, as usual, to dictate the nominations," Broderick could have put up a good fight against Gwin and the Chivalry. Rather he allowed the Chivalry to have its own way. The reporter from the Sacramento *Daily Times*, in particular, was stunned: "Why was he not there as usual, and with his great parliamentary tactics, scattering in dismay and wonderment his ancient foes?"

So Broderick, uncharacteristically the personification of placidity, simply watched while the Chivalry garnered all the most prominent nominations, to Congress, to clerk of the Supreme Court, to the electoral college (should Buchanan win the state). Broderick sat through this with scarcely a peep. It looked as if his spirit had been broken along with his San Francisco machine. He did have votes in the convention but chose time and again not to call upon them. Finally, the newspapers began to speculate that a deal of some kind had been worked out between Broderick and Gwin.

Broderick would allow Gwin the various nominations to Congress and other high offices. In exchange Gwin would not interfere with Broderick as he quietly worked the county conventions to influence nominations to the state Senate and Assembly. Gwin would be allowed to play the grand old man of the Democratic Party, but Broderick would slowly collect the votes in the legislature that could assure his election as senator, votes he could also deliver to Gwin to return him to his old seat. By the end of September Broderick was writing confidentially to a friend in southern California, "Three fourths of the nominations for Senate and Assembly, thus far, are my friends."

Broderick's subsequent campaigning on behalf of the Democratic ticket was based upon a careful calculation. He knew that many of his remaining supporters in cities such as San Francisco and Sacramento were going to vote Republican because for them slavery eclipsed all other issues. He shared their commitment to free labor, but not the conviction that Republicans like Frémont were improving the situation by incendiary proclamations. Nonetheless, he conceded these votes to the Republicans, and left it to Gwin and the Chivalry to deliver the Southern Democrats from the temptation of Know-Nothing nativism. Broderick sought the swing vote for the election out in mining districts, where he presented himself as a workingman's politician.

The mines by now were starting to play out; larger and larger operations were required to get the remaining gold. Moreover, fraudulent land dealings and other financial speculations had created deep resentment among the ordinary people scratching out a living in the foothills of the Sierras. Of those resented none was more notorious than the owner of the vast Mariposa land grant, John C. Frémont. So out in the diggings he was the perfect candidate to run against. When election day arrived, Broderick was full of fight and confidence. Gwin himself was full of confidence, for Buchanan's election and for an end to the fighting between himself and Broderick.

Nationally the presidential election of 1856 was a solid victory for the Democrats, but far less impressive than it might at first have looked. Buchanan, thanks largely to a collapse of Fillmore's national campaign, had won through a solid showing in the South combined with a few narrow victories in the North. Buchanan, for instance, carried his native state of Pennsylvania with a bare majority of only one thousand votes. Frémont had needed to carry only Pennsylvania and one other state—Illinois, New Jersey, or Indiana—to have himself won outright. The election had been, despite appearances, a close contest.

It could have been close in California too, and for the simple reason that Edward Baker like his friend Lincoln had become a Republican. Baker on the stump was formidable, or would have been, had anyone but Frémont been the nominee. As it was, Buchanan carried the state easily, Frémont coming in a weak third. The vote was split in the cities and coastal counties, but inland the Democrats won by such overwhelming margins that Buchanan's overall victory was a landslide. Broderick's calculation had proven exactly correct.

The election results showed, moreover, that during the campaign Broderick had frequently been preaching to the converted. In districts where Frémont was well known, for instance, the Pathfinder scarcely got a single vote. Of course, this did not mean that Broderick's effort had been pointless, for he had in the process strengthened his own support in the region of the state where he had been the weakest, a useful side benefit given the damage done to him by the vigilantes in San Francisco.

At the beginning of the campaign one newspaper had written that the two wings of the Democratic Party could not possibly unite effectively, for they were as "inharmonious as fire and water." In practice, however, it had been the non-Democrats who were broken into inharmonious factions, over the issue of slavery. The Know-Nothing party, apart from the reasonable showing of Fillmore in California, had been virtually destroyed as a force in state politics. The amateur state legislators who had been swept into office in the last election were swept out in this one. Neely Johnson would finish out his term as the lamest of lame ducks.

The reform party of the vigilantes, once so full of bluster, had fizzled outside of San Francisco, thanks apparently to residual resentment of their excesses. There remained only the Republicans, who could not expect to win many elections as long as the fire of David Broderick could remain in harmony, or at least in tense alliance, with the water of Dr. Gwin. This in turn depended upon the agreement of last April being fulfilled in good faith by both men; however, Broderick, as he followed the election returns of 1856, had started to think he could do better.

What made him so confident was not the number of his supporters in the legislature. Despite his earlier hopes, he now knew that he would not control a majority of the Democrats there. One Chivalry supporter put his finger on the explanation when he said, "I notice that every man who had quit the Democrats for the Republican Blacks has been a Broderick wire-puller." The truth was that the rise of the Republicans had hurt Broderick's strength within the Democratic Party statewide as much as the vigilantes had hurt him in San Francisco. If one simply counted votes, then the Chivalry clearly dominated the legislature—or as another Chivalry man put it shortly after the election, "We have the materials to achieve a complete and brilliant triumph in this campaign if we use them properly."

What made Broderick confident was the simple fact that the Chivalry could not use its materials "properly" because it had three determined candidates for only two U.S. Senate seats. Weller and Gwin both felt that they should be returned to the Senate. Latham thought, however, that his own time had come —and he already had turned the two new Democratic congressmen from Gwin to himself. These ungrateful desertions Gwin found, almost to his surprise, mortifying personally. Why had they not at least waited to make sure that this change of allegiance was advantageous? It was as if they were personally ashamed of the man to whom they owed their present offices.

Gwin had to put aside his personal pique to consider the potential consequences. If Gwin was thought to be weak, how could he deal with Broderick as an equal? And it was only as an equal that he could expect to get justice from that man. Gwin had to exert his full energy just to hold his remaining supporters together.

With Latham having now demonstrated that he was going to be a formidable candidate, the Chivalry was at an impasse. Neither Gwin nor Latham nor Weller could be expected to give an inch to one another. Nor could they reasonably expect to gain support from the thirty or more legislators who were steadfastly loyal to Broderick. For a smooth opportunist like Milton Latham this loyalty was a fact he could acknowledge without any pretense of understanding; he wrote to a correspondent late in November, "You know he has the peculiarity of tying to him his supporters in the most wonderful degree."

If one of the Chivalry candidates did not withdraw, then the only possibility for any to be elected was the support of Broderick. And the price of that would obviously be his own election as senator to the other seat. Latham had already smelt out who was most likely to have already made such a deal. He wrote confidentially to a friend, "What I have feared is a fusion between Gwin and Broderick friends which would shut me out of the contest." Having fully committed himself to this candidacy and then not having had his accustomed effortless success, Milton Latham had begun to whine more than was seemly for a grown-up.

Broderick's present oddly dominant position, however surprising in light of his recent setbacks, was scarcely a secret to anyone who followed California politics. When Broderick himself arrived in Sacramento in late November just after the election, he was treated by Democrats as a conquering hero. Everyone was eager to praise him, including—one cynical newspaperman wrote—"some of the prominent Democrats who have been his bitter enemies, and in fact, persecutors." This was a delicious experience, which Broderick savored, and indeed intended to prolong.

In these circumstances Gwin knew better than to expect Broderick to live up to their April understanding, now that they were plainly no longer equals. In a letter he wrote on Christmas Day 1856, he summed up the situation plainly: "I do not think Broderick can be defeated, and if elected who so important to our section of the party to be his colleague as myself?" Broderick, for his part, was already predicting to friends his election on the first ballot.

As the legislature arrived in Sacramento in early January, the outlook for the Chivalry was as bleak as the weather. Broderick was holding forth, letting it be known that he expected both senators to be from his wing of the party. He was even floating the name of Joseph McCorkle as his personal choice for the second seat.

This was a mischievous choice, and not because of McCorkle's open Free-Soil sentiments. In Latham's early years in California, when he was getting everything he wanted, Latham had decided he wanted the woman McCorkle was wooing, and he got her too. She became Latham's wife, and Latham became a permanent object of McCorkle's hatred. Latham was now already rattled enough without having McCorkle glaring at him, a rival intent on settling old scores. One misstep, and Latham was likely to find himself challenged to a duel by a man who liked the sound of the phrase "the widow Latham." McCorkle's candidacy, on the other hand, was small comfort to Gwin, for McCorkle was the very congressman with whom Gwin had fought his duel, full of wrath and sausages.

So Broderick was having his fun, but behind the scenes he was seeking a deal. Despite his boasting he knew perfectly well that he did not have the votes to get himself elected. (As for McCorkle, he was a lost cause, but could take his satisfaction by making the whining Latham feel like, and at times start to look a little like, a stalked deer.)

Gwin had been shrewd when he had proposed back in April that Broderick take the six-year seat. Broderick now was convinced that this was the least he should get, the seat with a full term. The problem was that this seat would normally be voted upon second. What guarantee did he have that Gwin, for instance, once he was elected, would not renege on his promise?

Here he thought he had a piece of good fortune. Senator Weller was still in Washington. He had placed the management of his reelection in the hands of Solomon Heydenfeldt, with whom Broderick had maintained the most friendly relations ever since they were California state senators on the opposite sides of almost every issue. Heydenfeldt was a man as principled as Gwin and Latham were pliable. He would rather die than have his honor besmirched.

So Broderick met with Heydenfeldt for a lengthy discussion. They had strangely always liked each other, perhaps because they were so completely different, products of different universes who still managed to communicate with each other, in part (one suspects) out of a consistently bemused curiosity. As was usual between these two opposite men— one tiny and punctilious, the other hulking and coarse—the meeting was full of cordiality and disagreements.

Broderick told Heydenfeldt he repented that his rivalry with Gwin had almost destroyed the Democratic Party in California. He had consequently decided, for the good of the party, that he should not run against Gwin and thereby stir up old animosities. So he had reluctantly concluded that he must run against Weller, whom he nonetheless deeply respected. So, for the good of the party, he had a proposal. Heydenfeldt would nominate Weller for Gwin's seat rather than his own. If he did, Broderick could assure Heydenfeldt of sufficient votes to elect Weller, if in turn Heydenfeldt would assure Broderick of sufficient votes —the few votes he still needed—for the six-year seat.

Heydenfeldt listened to Broderick's elaborate scheme, as he frequently did, with pleasure and without assent. There was a kind of integrity about Broderick, but unlike anything Heydenfeldt himself could imagine acting upon. How much of Broderick's explanations of his decision to run for Weller's seat Heydenfeldt actually believed is hard to say. Probably almost none of it. But is it really lying when the liar does not intend to deceive you? Nonetheless, the deal that Broderick was offering was clear enough, and to it Heydenfeldt could respond clearly. No.

Heydenfeldt explained. If he agreed to this, he would be violating Senator Weller's trust, for he was certain that Weller would regard this arrangement as itself dishonorable. Even if he thought Weller might agree, he, Solomon Heydenfeldt, could not be a party to it. Moreover, Weller's supporters were all themselves honorable men, and he could not treat them as so many pawns to be moved about at his own caprice. (At this comment Heydenfeldt must have paused slightly to let Broderick appreciate its well-turned irony, since Heydenfeldt was indirectly but purposely describing exactly what made Broderick so formidable in his electioneering: his men welcomed being used by him like pawns.)

Broderick and Heydenfeldt, both full of good cheer, likely then went back over every possibility together carefully, Broderick trying one variation after another, Heydenfeldt patiently explaining why each was irreconcilable with his conscience, Broderick emphasizing how desirable the end that could be achieved, Heydenfeldt shaking his head at the unseemly means. Throughout the discussion they both could see the broader irony of the situation. What made Broderick want to make a deal with Heydenfeldt in particular made Heydenfeldt in particular unable to accept it. So they parted, as usual, in friendship and still on opposite sides.

So the simplest, and most pleasing, solution had eluded Broderick. Now the campaigning and skullduggery could begin in earnest.

Each candidate, except the absent Weller, did his best to spy on the others, although with varying degrees of gusto. Broderick, the most inventive, sent snaggletoothed Billy Williamson under cover as a Negro hotel waiter to find out what he could; much fun was had each night as Billy washed off his negritude while telling how this fellow or that had stared at him as if trying to place his obsequious smile. All sides courted the uncommitted legislators such as Assemblyman Charles Orvis from El Dorado, who was promised by both Latham and Broderick to become collector of the port of San Francisco—but who then had his head turned when Gwin told him he looked more like Tom Benton (Orvis's hero) than any man he had ever met.

Broderick next sought to make a deal with the worried Latham, but not one that depended upon trusting him. Broderick wanted the long-term senator chosen first; this meant an initial vote on changing the order in which the Senate seats were filled. If Latham went along, then he could have . . . Broderick's goodwill.

The next morning at the Democratic caucus it was proposed "that in making the nominations for the United States Senators the following order of business shall be observed: 1st. The nomination of a Senator to fill the long term, to succeed Hon. John B. Weller; 2nd. The nomination of a Senator to fill the short term, to succeed the Hon. Wm. M. Gwin." At this point the supporters of Gwin and Weller must have smelled a rat. Then, as the vote was taken, they realized the rat's name was Milton Latham. His men voted uniformly for the measure, and it passed 42 to 35.

Quickly the caucus turned to the nominations for the long term. Only Weller and Broderick were put forward. Broderick won on the first ballot, with 42 votes. He was going to be a United States Senator, but the Broderick men had no time to celebrate yet because the caucus immediately set about filling the short term.

Heydenfeldt refused to allow Weller's name to be put back in nomination for the second seat. The sense on the floor was that this nomination was wide open, although the Latham men expected Broderick to throw his support their way, sooner or later. The early votes showed that this was going to be later, if at all. McCorkle, Gwin, and Latham were all nominated, along with four minor candidates who hoped to slip in if the caucus deadlocked. The first vote had Gwin with 26, Latham 21, McCorkle 15, and the minor candidates together 18. When the second ballot produced no significant movement, everyone realized that Broderick was going to permit no one to be nominated for the short seat at least until he had been formally elected in the California legislature. So the caucus adjourned.

On the next day, Friday, January 9, the two houses of the California legislature met in joint session. On the first ballot, with the Democrats following strict party discipline, David C. Broderick was elected to the United States Senate for a term to begin on March 4, 1857, and to end March 3, 1863. His commission as senator was signed by Governor J. Neely Johnson, and formally presented to him on Saturday, January 10.

A Gwin supporter, James O'Meara, described what happened next in broadly disgusted terms: "The joy of the Broderick men was excessive. They were jubilant, hilarious, demonstrative: towards some, exuberant in their patronizing amiability; towards others, exasperating in their offensive exultation." They were gleeful not just over Broderick's election but also over his power to select his colleague. They could tweak self-important supporters of Gwin, Latham, even Weller—and these chivalrous gentlemen would have to take it, lest a disdainful or belittling word might be taken wrongly by Senator-elect Broderick and ruin the chances of their own candidate. It was the most fun for the Broderick crowd in a long time, and marred only by the thought of their exiled brethren. How much more fun this would be with little Billy Mulligan and loudmouthed Rube Meloney.

Broderick did not participate in the celebration, but he watched it approvingly, even encouragingly. He was their champion, and the stonecutter's son had triumphed for them. His enemies were now suppliants at his feet, and he intended to make the most of this situation. He said to one of his exultant followers, "It is my turn now; and not one of them shall get his head to the front until I have pulled out his claws and put my brand on him."

Gwin at this point was shaken by the developments. He was not troubled by Broderick's failure to live up to the April agreement. Much had changed since April, and politics was politics. What troubled him, made him at times uncharacteristically close to despondency, was the behavior of his own followers. Once it became clear that some kind of understanding had been reached between Broderick and Latham, they began to look for excuses to desert him. He had not expected their support to be based on anything more than self-interest and expedience, but facing that now was somehow unsettling. What did it feel like to be Broderick, surrounded by men who at a word would fight to the death for you? How did he engender such loyalty when he would quite happily march over the corpses of all these men to reach the Senate?

Gwin's closest political advisers were now telling him that he should look for an honorable way to retire from the field rather than endure the humiliating defeat that seemed almost certain. On Friday morning, January 9, as Broderick was being elected to the Senate, Gwin announced his acquiescence. He was withdrawing, and would take the 2:00 P.M. boat back to San Francisco. As he was making preparations to leave, he had an unexpected visitor. David Douglass had been a close political friend of Gwin, although never a Democrat. He was one of those steadfast members of the Chivalry who had formed the backbone of the Know-Nothing party. He was now secretary of state in the Know-Nothing administration; as such, he would have to draw up that afternoon the commission to Broderick from Governor Johnson.

This was not a happy day for him, and he felt that the South needed the experienced Gwin in the Senate to balance Broderick. He knew that Latham's election was thought certain, and had inferred that Gwin might be thinking of withdrawing his own candidacy. All this Douglass said, and then he seems to have become cryptic. He had been hanging around various legislators, hearing this and that. Some allegations had come to his attention that, if true, would make Latham's selection unlikely, if not impossible. That was all Douglass could say, except that he certainly hoped Gwin would take heart and continue his candidacy a little longer.

This was all Gwin needed to hear. The reservation on the steamer was immediately canceled. What could Gwin do now to improve his chances? If there was some scandal about Latham that might come out, then Gwin needed to play for time. In particular, he needed to get through the caucus balloting that night without a bolt of delegates from him to the Latham bandwagon. Gwin and his people decided to approach Colonel A. J. Butler, the closest Broderick adviser with whom Gwin had maintained a friendship. They needed a particular favor from him that would help them keep their delegates from stampeding to Latham. Butler was to go into the popular saloon of the Orleans Hotel and confidently offer a wager of $2,000 that Gwin was going to win the short seat. (Gwin, of course, would provide the bankroll.) Soon word would be out that Butler, a confidante of Broderick, knew something no one else did—and nervous delegates might decide to wait a little longer before trying to pick the eventual winner.

Butler was delighted with this sly piece of mischief, and agreed to do it. But, on reflection, he decided he had better first check with the "old man," as he called Broderick. Shortly later he returned to say regretfully that the old man had countermanded the plan. So Gwin and his people approached the evening caucus wondering if everything was over for them. It was not.

Four ballots were taken that evening, with no substantial changes in the voting. There was a small movement toward Gwin, but Gwin's people could not tell whether this was a genuine trend or just Broderick trying to put pressure on Latham.

Broderick had in fact decided that after the Friday vote the time had come to declaw Milton Latham. He informed Latham that the price of his support was a statement in writing in which he renounced control of all federal patronage, conceding it to Broderick. Latham, understandably, balked—and tried to negotiate a less humiliating arrangement, one that left him with a little more maneuvering room. Then suddenly Latham's whole candidacy began to crumble.

The ubiquitous Ned McGowan, although still worried about a possible indictment as an accessory to the murder of King of William, had slipped into Sacramento, and was beginning to hold court— as only he could—to select audiences on his recent adventures. He also proclaimed that San Francisco still needed to be, as he delicately put it, "de-loused of lynchers." McGowan, of course, was happy to specify the biggest louses—and one happened to be named Milton Latham. McGowan charged that Latham while collector of customs had quietly cooperated with Coleman and the 1856 vigilantes. For this charge, McGowan had a letter of confirmation signed by a leading vigilante. McGowan claimed that even Coleman admitted Latham's role, although for that he had no letter. This allegation against Latham was likely what Douglass had heard rumored when he urged Gwin to stay in the race.

Then something even worse for Latham happened, who now seemed to be paying for his earlier inordinate luck. A state senator began to denounce Latham. He had had a written agreement with Latham that if Latham became senator he would be named collector of customs. Now someone, undoubtedly on Latham's orders, had stolen this written commitment. Later, it would turn out that the aspiring collector of customs had just misplaced the document, but this would be too late to rectify the damage that had been done to the innocent Latham, who understandably was starting to look like a man whose nerves were unraveling (while Joseph McCorkle may have begun to think that there was justice in the universe after all).

Broderick could infer from this contretemps a whole range of unpleasantries. Latham, despite what he said, was in fact quite happy to enter into written agreements on future patronage. Latham probably resisted deferring to Broderick because he had already committed himself to a series of appointments. Latham did not live up to his written commitments, anyway, and would even try to retrieve them by skullduggery. All this boiled down to one result: Latham was simply the wrong man with whom to try to make an arrangement over patronage.

When the caucus met the evening of January 10, another series of inconclusive votes was taken, with Gwin still leading Latham, and with McCorkle still having enough votes to swing the election either way. The next day was the Sabbath, but there was no rest for the politicians in Sacramento as they ran down rumors while planting their own, such as one from the Broderick people that former Governor Big John Bigler was going to emerge as a compromise candidate. (Big John had about as much chance as I, John McDougal.)

Gwin had seemed inexplicably cheerful during that day, and only desultorily interested in the various plans for the new week, the very plans that would ordinarily absorb him. His friends were surprised that evening when Gwin announced he was going to bed early and did not want to be disturbed the rest of the night. The "shadows" Latham had placed on Gwin's hotel headquarters to note any unusual activity were also surprised when they saw Gwin at the window of his room ready for bed. Then the light went out.

These shadows, if they had kept their watch diligently rather than dozing off, could have seen a couple of hours later, shortly after midnight, two men, darkly dressed, descending the back stairs of Gwin's hotel, and making their way through a back alley and then down the unlighted J Street (dark because there were no saloons there) toward the back of the Magnolia Hotel. It was Gwin and a bodyguard, perhaps James O'Meara, who had been so disapproving of the jubilation over Broderick's election (and is the chief source for this event). When they reached the darkened back of the hotel, one of them knocked lightly on a door so deep in the gloom a person might not notice it if he did not already know it was there. On the knock it was immediately unlocked and opened. In the doorway Gwin could barely make out Colonel A. J. Butler. Butler then guided Gwin and O'Meara down a hall, and pointed up a staircase, while whispering "Six." He himself remained at its base, on lookout.

They went up the stairs, and then Gwin tapped on the door of number six. After a short pause, it opened. The glare from the room temporarily blinded them, but a large figure was saying, "Good night, gentlemen. Walk in. Dr. Gwin, I am glad to see you. Be seated." Gwin shook hands with Broderick and did as he was told. The bodyguard knew he would soon be leaving them alone. But before he did he had a chance to glance around the room. It was a workingman's room—a bed, a pair of chairs, a table with a pitcher and basin, nothing else. He sat briefly on the bed while the two men exchanged empty pleasantries about things in which obviously neither had any interest. Then they both turned to him expectantly. He quickly got up, left the room, and closed the door behind him.

The caucus of the California Democratic Party reconvened on schedule the next night. Gwin had been calm during the day, going through his normal conferences with his various supporters as if nothing had changed—but they noted about him a continued cheerfulness that buoyed them. They realized something was up when he announced that he wished to go to the hall of the state Assembly, where the caucus was being held, in order to wait in an adjoining room, just on the chance that the election might be concluded this very night.

On the first vote Latham moved within one of Gwin. Was there a drift in Latham's direction? On the second, a minor candidate dropped out, which resulted in Gwin's gaining two votes, Latham one. Still, neither was anywhere close to a majority. One delegate consequently concluded that the caucus wasn't going anywhere tonight, and moved that it be adjourned. His motion was overwhelmingly defeated, to his wondering surprise. Then, on the third ballot, the thirteenth since the caucus had started to try to fill the seat, one voter after another began to shift, as if by a prearranged agreement. Gwin's total quickly went from 31 to 47, a comfortable majority. The next day the California legislature, meeting in joint session, voted to return William McKendree Gwin to the United States Senate.

The incensed Latham and his supporters were naturally convinced that Gwin had struck the same deal with Broderick which Latham had refused—and more incensed still because Latham would obviously have accepted the deal if he had known it was the final offer. They demanded to know what concessions Broderick had extracted from Gwin as the price of his support. But Gwin was not around to answer their inquiries, and Broderick himself was mum.

Gwin had quickly left Sacramento for San Francisco the afternoon of the election. Unlike Broderick, he was not one to gloat. But he could show the former saloon-keeper a thing or two about how the Washington elite celebrated joyous occasions. The next day he and his wife spent planning an elegant San Francisco victory party for the following day. It was to be the kind of grand but tasteful social event for which William and Mary Gwin were well known in Washington. This celebration, however, turned into a glum affair when that very morning a newspaper known to be controlled by Broderick published an open letter signed by William Gwin:

> To the People of California:
>
> I have thought it proper in view of the senatorial contest which has resulted in the election of Mr. David C. Broderick and myself to the Senate of the United States, to state to the people of California certain circumstances and facts which pose a part of the history of that arduous struggle.
>
> After a laborious service in the United States Senate, during a term of six years and at a juncture in the history of the State when the energy and fidelity of a representative could be most fruitful of results, I found myself at the expiration of the term, and after having, as I supposed, outlived the misrepresentations of my enemies, engaged in a struggle which has been again rewarded with the confidence of the Legislature. My election

was attended by circumstances which rarely occur in the course of such contests. A representative whose evil destiny it is to be the indirect dispenser of Federal patronage will strangely miscalculate if he expects to evade the malice of disappointed men. But the hostility, malignity, and abuse which have pursued my senatorial career, when at a distance from the maligners, and which have accompanied me during the strife just closed, are such, as I believe I may say, as a representative has never before endured to survive.

The opposition I have sustained comes from an unexpected quarter, and from those whose friendship I had believed, strengthened as it was by personal obligation, nothing could weaken or sever. Ardent, devoted, disinterested friends I had, whose fidelity remained unshaken from first to last, through storm and sunshine alike, and to these, one and all, my grateful acknowledgements are due.

But even the force of their attachment, faithful and zealous as it was, would have proved unavailing, if unaided, to meet and conquer the opposition which open hostility and secret treachery had arrayed against me. I had learned in the struggle that he who aids in conferring great official power upon individuals does not always secure friends, and that the force of deep personal obligation may even be converted into an incentive to hostility and hate. In a word, to the Federal patronage in the State do I attribute, in a great degree, the malice and hostile energy which, after years of public service and toward the closing period of life, have nearly cost me the endorsement to United States Senate. From patronage, then, and the curse it entails, I shall gladly in future turn, and my sole labor and ambition henceforth shall be to deserve well of the State, and to justify the choice of the Legislature in honoring me a second time as a representative of its interests.

I have hinted above at other aid than that received from those whom I had regarded as friends; I refer to the timely assistance accorded to me by Mr. Broderick and his friends. Although at one time a rival, and recognizing in him even a fierce but manly opponent, I do not hesitate to acknowledge in this public manner his forgetfulness of all grounds of dissension and hostility, in what he considered a step necessary to allay the strifes and discords which had distracted the party and the State. To him, and to the attachment of his friends to him, I conceive, in a great degree, my election is due; and I feel bound to him and them in common efforts to unite and heal, where the result heretofore has been to break down and destroy.

Wm. M. Gwin
Sacramento, January 13th, 1857

Other than his inability to disguise his bitterness at his friends who had deserted him (in contrast to Broderick's loyal friends), this remarkable letter is Gwin at his most persuasive and plausible. However, in some circumstances, no manner of persuasiveness and plausibility can hide the reality. Finishing reading this letter, everyone involved knew exactly what it meant. As one Gwin supporter put it baldly, "Gwin has sold his friends for the sake of being elected."

Not surprisingly, the newspapers chose to embellish the matter in their own ways (which were not Gwin's way). One ran a mock obituary: "Died— At Sacramento, on the 12th instant, of political bargaining affecting his honor, W. M. Gwin, the relict of David C. Broderick, aged about 60 years. His obsequies will take place from the Capitol, at Washington, in 1860. The body is carefully embalmed." A Broderick newspaper thought irony the wrong tone, preferring rather vindictive glee: "If Broderick's thrall, Gwin, sticks to his sale, and Broderick uses the power he has thus grasped, the only thing left in the hands of the Chivalry is the Stockton Insane Asylum. They will need it for their own use."

So Broderick had gotten more from Gwin than he had even tried from Latham. He had gotten both a disavowal of federal patronage and an expression of gratitude to Broderick for having been responsible for his reelection. He got this in writing, in a document which Broderick could make public whenever he wished. And so Broderick chose to make it public just when there were gathering for a champagne and caviar celebration those very aristocratic friends whom Gwin had sold for the sake of being elected.

Broderick must have thought he had not just declawed Gwin but defanged and gelded him as well—and then strung him up so that all could review at their leisure the maimed remains with the letters *DB* proudly branded on the rump.

The situation, however, was not quite so one-sided as Broderick and many others obviously thought. Gwin had expressed himself precisely when he wrote in the letter that he as a senator had only been an indirect dispenser of federal patronage. A Republican newspaperman, who was delighted at Broderick's election, made the same point when he reminded his readers that Broderick "will not have a single appointment to make except by sufferance." The whole arrangement depended upon the cooperation of President-elect James Buchanan.

Broderick was not worried. He had campaigned tirelessly for Buchanan. Moreover, he was going to be accompanied to Washington by John Bigler, whose brother as a senator from Pennsylvania was one of Buchanan's closest political associates. Back in San Francisco, Broderick celebrated in his own way: he went out to a quiet dinner with William Tecumseh Sherman.

Sherman had returned to California after a sojourn in New York. He had finally convinced his St. Louis partners that California was not a good place to do business. So he had come here a last time to liquidate their holdings, including the fine building of which he had been so proud. He was having mixed feelings, not because he thought the decision was a mistake but because it meant, he thought, an end to his ambition to distinguish himself from the common run of men. His business career had ended, as had his military, without a single noteworthy achievement. He was trying to take cold comfort at the prospect of living out his remaining life in a humdrum existence.

Dining with Broderick was a welcome break from these morose thoughts. He was thoroughly amused at the recent senatorial selections. He wrote back to St. Louis, "Notwithstanding the great moral reforms, the old State corrupt politicians, Gwin and Broderick, have been elected to the U.S. Senate."

As for the recent presidential election, Sherman, although voting for Buchanan, had not worried about a Frémont victory. "Our government ought to be strong enough to endure the Devil himself for president for four years." Anyway, Frémont himself had no real principles; so Sherman guessed that within six months of his election he would have broken with the radical abolitionists to try to increase his own chances for reelection.

Sherman did not know what was being reported to the East about the California senatorial election. But it was going to introduce a whole new kind of slavery into the highest governmental circles. The new senator from California, the uncouth David C. Broderick, it was said here, would be bringing the old senator, the genteel William M. Gwin, back to the Capitol in chains. The spectacle might just turn a few Southern senators into earnest abolitionists.

The two new senators from California traveled back east together, via Panama, arriving in New York on February 13, 1857. There Gwin had to endure a dockside welcome of Broderick that was fit for a conquering hero. All the guns of the harbor boomed, crowds rushed on board seeking the great man (perhaps also wanting a sidelong look at his senatorial captive), and a reception had already been organized in his honor with the leaders of the New York Democracy vying with one another for a place on the speakers' list to sing the praises of this successful son of the laboring poor.

The newspapers entered into the mood, devoting feature articles to his career. They were also interested in Gwin, although this interest was not kindly. Before the arrival of Broderick and Gwin, no one in New York apparently had heard about the deal between the two senators-elect. So Gwin, picking up a New York newspaper, could see the text of his extraordinary letter printed in full. Worse still was the interpretation placed on it. The chief Republican paper, the New York *Tribune,* had the most fun with what it termed "the glorification of Broderick and this singing small of Gwin": "A defeated faction never announced their humiliation with such circumstance and such eclat." Again: "The annals of political warfare will be searched in vain for a triumph as complete or a defeat so humiliating." Gwin was going back to Washington as a mere "appendage" to the mighty Broderick.

Gwin, needless to say, left New York as quickly as possible for Washington. Broderick, not surprisingly, lingered there. Broderick seemed genuinely surprised by all the attention, almost overwhelmed. This was all he could have ever wanted, more than he had ever wanted. Strangely, though, it seemed to make him uncomfortable. As much as being celebrated pleased him, he also did not like it. So he soon had retreated to a familiar circle of old cronies, a few of the very men the vigilantes had deported in 1856, like Billy Mulligan and Rube Meloney. Meloney was already loudly planning to sue William Coleman the next time the lion of the vigilantes showed up in New York for business. If Rube couldn't come to Coleman's city, then

Coleman shouldn't be able to show his face in Rube's, at least not without being slapped with a subpoena.

Broderick could not encourage the boys to come back. San Francisco was no longer his city, and he wouldn't be there much anyhow. He was now going to be concerned with national issues. He did not have to say, although surely they would have sensed it, that he was now above them, and their presence would be a liability to him. There must have been something sadly forced or artificial about Senator-elect David Broderick returning to his old haunts. For one thing he was too well dressed, although the fancy clothes did not quite look right on him.

Broderick had said, in that moment of uncontrollable rage, that he would march to the Senate over the corpses of his friends if need be. He had not done so. But he had gotten there at the cost of many friendships. Not friends discarded or betrayed, but old friends now timid around him, uncharacteristically restrained as if unwilling to offend his new dignity. No more street fights or saloon pranks.

One of the old group whom Broderick had most hoped to see was Mike Walsh. Walsh had succeeded in New York politics, as he was determined he would when he resisted the lure of California. He had first made it to the state Assembly. And then in 1854 Walsh had been elected to the U.S. Congress for a term. There he had treated his fellow representatives to his familiar themes, the Northern radical at times sounding strangely like a Southern apologist: "The only difference between the negro slave of the South, and the white wages slave of the North is that the one has a master without asking for him, and the other has to beg for the privilege of becoming a slave. . . . The one is the slave of an individual; the other is the slave of an inexorable class." Hearing from Mike himself what Washington was really like would have been an education—a last lesson—for this former member of the Spartan Band who had now surpassed him. However, while Broderick was on his way back to New York, Walsh had been killed. He had been celebrating Saint Patrick's Day in his usual uninhibited manner, and was last seen lurching home at about 2:00 A.M. The next morning his body was found on Eighth Avenue. He had been beaten to death, apparently for his gold watch and diamond ring, which were missing. The condition of his body showed that he'd gone down fighting.

The news must have cast its own pall over Broderick's triumphant return. Perhaps this was what made him seek reconciliation with George Wilkes. He had not expected ever to reconcile with him, for he was convinced that Wilkes had betrayed his trust. When he had spoken about the corpses of friends, he must have been thinking particularly of Wilkes. And Wilkes, most of all, he had missed at his triumphal election in Sacramento. Broderick was not someone who forgave, but he now forgave Wilkes. Wilkes of all his old cronies from New York could understand the world in which Broderick was going to move, and had the education to be a marginal part of it. With Wilkes alone he could share something of this new life.

So they became intimate friends once again, Broderick and his mentor to whom he felt he owed so much. Never again was there the slightest suggestion of a breach between them. And when Broderick died it was found he had left the bulk of his estate to the older man.

William Gwin, much as he had not wanted to watch the apotheosis of Broderick in New York, also had good reason to hurry to Washington. Since his term as senator was supposed to have begun in 1855, he could be sworn in immediately (unlike Broderick, who would have to wait until March). So Gwin returned to his true home, the nation's capital. He had no sooner taken his seat than he cast the deciding vote in favor of an appropriation for the laying of a transatlantic cable, just the kind of project he loved. It was a good omen.

The story of his election had, of course, long since reached Washington. But that California embarrassment seemed so unreal now that he was here, especially with his old friend James Buchanan in the White House. Broderick's true social world was the saloons of New York; Gwin's was the salons of Washington. And no one enjoyed a pleasant evening of good food and talk more than James Buchanan, especially when the old bachelor had a beautiful woman like Mary Gwin attending him.

Buchanan's social life was being organized by his accomplished young niece, Harriet Lane, who had already excelled in this role when he was ambassador to Great Britain. The White House was going to be quite a different place from what it had been under the pinched New Englanders, Franklin Pierce and his reclusive wife.

Moreover, Stephen Douglas, after years as a widower, had a new wife from a prominent Washington family. She was obviously taking him in hand, and the Little Giant, in the recent past quite slovenly, was now looking quite dapper. Adele Douglas, moreover, understood the role of parties and entertainments in government, and was determined that her husband as a likely future president would play his role. She, for instance, had them take a box next to Buchanan's at the Ford Theater. Washington for the next four years promised to be a most amusing place.

The Gwins themselves always had been generous entertainers. Now, having been away for so long, William Gwin seems to have realized how much he had missed it all, the give-and-take both on the Senate floor and in the drawing room. Now, Gwin was determined, they were going to entertain not just generously but splendidly. He encouraged his wife to outdo herself as a hostess. It would soon be all the buzz in Washington. No longer would they talk of Gwin's chains but of his lavish parties. The alleged slave entertained like a real king. The common estimate would be that the Gwins were spending at least $70,000 a year on their various affairs. Nowhere did James Buchanan, the Old Squire, like better to come.

Virginia Clay, the wife of the Alabama senator, looked back upon this period half a century later with more than a little amazement. "While a life-and-death struggle rages between the political parties and oratorical battles of ominous import were fought daily in Senate chamber and House, a very reckless gaiety was everywhere apparent in social circles." She, a self-styled "belle of the fifties," even as she participated in this life unrestrainedly, realized that "people are mad with rivalry and vanity." Yet, looking back upon all this vanity and rivalry, all this reckless gaiety, she thought it "lent a charm to life in the Government circles of that day which lifted the capital to the very apex of its social glory." A glory, she did not need to add, it had never achieved since.

Such glory, as Gwin's outlays would show, did not come cheaply. Fashions for the ladies changed rapidly. And only clothes and accessories of European origins were acceptable. (The diplomatic corps of Washington was an invaluable source of supply for aspiring hostesses, and was cultivated accordingly.) Now that Harriet Lane was in the White House, she could dictate style. The young, buxom Miss Lane enjoyed plunging necklines and lace berthas; so they were now all the rage. So were silk or kid gloves—embroidered on the back—that reached only halfway to the elbow; lovely shoulders and arms could then be left bare, or teasingly revealed through lace. In fact, during Buchanan's administration fashionable ladies of Washington were frequently showing so much skin that an unsophisticated Westerner could have been almost forgiven if he had mistaken them for soiled doves.

The men themselves entered into the spirit of all this. The rather somber swallowtailed evening dress of the period was but the background for spectacularly colored vests of richest satin and velvet, brocaded and embroidered. These were coordinated with an elegant silk cravat (although the president himself idiosyncratically insisted that his own always be white). The ensemble was then completed with an ample display of expensive jewels in cravat pins and studs, all the accoutrements that in San Francisco would have identified one as a professional gambler.

David Broderick finally arrived in Washington in March, just in time for the inauguration. He had grown up with stories of his father's role in the building of the Capitol. He may even have had some dim memories of the place. Now at the age of thirty-nine he was returning as the second-youngest member of the U.S. Senate. He certainly would have expected the capital to look finished by this time, but it did not. Washington was still a city of vast distances and largely unfulfilled hopes; the half-done buildings themselves were perfect architectural expressions of the divisions and indecision within the federal government itself about the future of the American republic. The half-done Washington Monument looked more like the ruined chimney of an abandoned factory than a fitting tribute to the Father of the

Country. The wings and dome of the Capitol itself were little further along; so, as a senator, Broderick would not even have his own office, but would be expected to do his work at his desk when the Senate was not in session.

But the capital city and boardinghouse accommodations in it were not the chief source of Broderick's disappointment. Nor was the unwelcome recognition that he was now living in the South. Of course, in Washington he could see firsthand what the California Chivalry revered. Many wealthy planters spent part of each year in Washington, with their family and servants. Amid the unfinished capital, there was a dazzling display of wealth in which many leading politicians like Gwin participated without restraint. This was on so much greater a scale than the silk stocking crowd in New York that it could be almost beguiling. But Broderick knew he never would be welcome in this Washington society, and did not want to be. Repulsed as he was by it, he had no expectations from it, and could not be disappointed there.

His life was politics, and to that all else was secondary. It was here, at his most vulnerable point, that he almost immediately sensed Washington had in store for him bitter, almost unbearable, disappointment. Broderick had naturally expected that he, as the new leader of the California Democracy, would be warmly received by his president. He was, after all, the tireless campaigner who had helped carry the state for Buchanan two to one. This expectation was the first of many to be rudely dashed.

Broderick seems to have had trouble even getting an appointment with the new president, who was filling his cabinet largely with Southerners and Southern sympathizers. So Broderick had to use Bigler to appeal to Buchanan through a Pennsylvania intermediary, a minor humiliation that must have stung. In a note James Forney reminded Buchanan that Broderick was now "the most important man from California," an unmistakable reference to Gwin's chains. Forney added almost pleadingly, "He is a man of the people and was your devoted friend in the last struggle. He feels most anxious to see you. But for my regard for you I would not ask your attention to this case."

Broderick finally got his audience with Buchanan. Buchanan was a pleasant-looking man, tall and portly (his well-known love of good food and drink was confirmed at a glance) with an easy-featured face topped by a shock of wavy white hair. Yet his face was hard to read despite its usual affability of expression. Perhaps it was his eyes, one hazel, the other blue. Or the fact that when listening to someone he always tilted his head to compensate for a weak ear. ("Which way does Buchanan tilt his head?" the joke went after his administration was well under way. "Always to the South.") Or the distraction of the unlit, half-chewed cigar that usually protruded from the side of his mouth. The effortless affability of Buchanan in fact hid real toughness that at times could become something worse. James Buchanan, when pressed, frequently became downright pigheaded.

In his brief meeting with the new president Broderick, never good at the small talk Buchanan cherished, would try invariably to make a few political points. The California delegation to the national Democratic convention had disregarded the wishes of Broderick's wing of the party when it delayed supporting Buchanan. That was the California Chivalry which thought Pierce would be better for the South. They were not loyal to Buchanan as Broderick had been.

What Broderick had to say, he could not know, weighed not at all against the good companionship Buchanan enjoyed at Gwin's table. Moreover, Buchanan knew that Gwin the pragmatic party regular would always be a loyal supporter of this Democratic president while some thought this brash New Yorker would soon be acting in concert with the Republicans. Perhaps someone had shown him the New York *Tribune* article which claimed delightedly that Broderick would have under his control "the entire dispensation of Federal pap in the gift of Old Buck for these regions." The *Tribune* was no friend of James Buchanan. So Buchanan was affable but evasive, while the young senator tried futilely to get some tangible sign of support or appreciation.

Finally, Broderick was done with being discreet and indirect, and brought up the subject of patronage—but only to be waved off. Buchanan told Broderick that any patronage recommendations should be submitted to his administration in writing. Buchanan acted as if he could not be bothered with what was a matter of political life and death for Broderick. Was this just presidential decorum or was he really getting brushed off?

Broderick knew that his position in California was not as strong as the recent election might have suggested. His power in San Francisco was largely gone, with the political descendants of the vigilantes now thoroughly in control. The Chivalry did control a majority of the Democrats in the legislature, and the Republicans were growing at his expense while Southern Know-Nothings were daily returning to the Democratic fold. The circumstances that had led to his election as senator were not likely to repeat themselves. Nonetheless, as senator he could rebuild his power in California, but only with President Buchanan's help. Broderick needed, in particular, Bigler appointed to the San Francisco customshouse in place of Latham. But the president had waved him off as if he were an importunate schoolboy.

Broderick must have left his interview with Buchanan stunned, perhaps too stunned to be angry, at least for the time being. Washington was so different from what he had expected that it disoriented him temporarily, a town of magnolias and slaves and Southern belles. His political instincts told him he was going to be betrayed by this president for whom he had worked so hard, but he could not be certain. And then late in March the California appointments began to be announced.

Broderick's chains on Gwin only worked if Washington acknowledged their existence. And Washington, it became increasingly clear, most certainly did not. If anyone should wear chains, it should be the stonecutter's son. Amid all the studied politeness, Broderick came to realize that he was being mocked, and tried to fight back.

Assuming now that Buchanan would appoint no one Broderick suggested, he in desperation staged a falling-out with Bigler, who with his brother was an old political ally of Buchanan. He then had Bigler suggest Broderick's candidates as if they represented a new anti-Broderick faction. But Broderick's most complicated maneuvering could be undone by only a few words from Gwin. Gwin wrote a friend, "I spent yesterday with the cabinet and the President. They will not forget us."

Even the appointments Broderick did get were harmful. Bigler, having been passed over for collector of customs (in favor of a loyal member of the Chivalry), was appointed ambassador to Chile, a position after which he had long hankered. Bigler was pleased, but Broderick could see the malice in this. It removed his most effective political ally from California altogether.

Broderick, as would not have surprised him at all, had become a subject of humor between Buchanan and Gwin during their frequent evenings together (which Gwin duly recounted to his friends). Buchanan, for instance, was said to have asked Gwin to resolve a puzzlement for him. Gwin recommended no one for federal positions, and yet how the devil did it happen that all his friends were getting appointments? "Why, Mr. President," the smiling Gwin reportedly replied, "my friends are just the best-qualified men for the jobs." They laughed, and Mary Gwin moved through the blue haze of cigar smoke to open another bottle of wine.

Broderick finally began to attack Buchanan privately. One newspaper reported that Broderick had said, "I will not cross the threshold of the White House while the present incumbent occupies it." Gwin in response would simply regret that the barkeep-senator found himself unable to behave as befitted his new station.

Gwin, being fair, would admit on occasion that Broderick was being provoked unmercifully. For instance, when Buchanan appointed a Gwin man to head the San Francisco customhouse, Gwin admitted smugly that the president had administered to Broderick a "fatal stab." Gwin lamented that Broderick simply did not take the wound like a gentleman: "His denunciations of the President are gross in the extreme." But what could you expect from someone from the slums of New York?

Broderick had not been in Washington a month, and he was already being declawed and defanged. And it was Gwin's brand on his rump, and all this Gwin had achieved apparently without having lifted a finger.

However, Broderick was not the only loyal Democratic senator who was being bitterly disappointed by Buchanan's federal appointments. Another was no less than the Little Giant himself. Stephen Douglas had had his own discussion with Buchanan at the beginning of Old Buck's term. Douglas was facing reelection in 1858, and expected a strong challenge from the Republicans. (He was particularly worried about the former congressman Abraham Lincoln, the cleverest campaigner the Illinois Republicans had.) Douglas needed Buchanan's help to shore up his own strength. Unlike Broderick, he had approached Buchanan aggressively; like Broderick, he was met with polite evasions. Douglas had been in Washington long enough to know what that meant. He had left the White House convinced that federal patronage in the Northwest had already been promised to his rivals in the Illinois Democracy. This incited Douglas to characteristic bluster as he girded his loins for come what might: "I shall fight all my enemies and neither ask nor give quarter."

The feisty Douglas, full of his own self-importance, was just the man to bring out the worst in James Buchanan. When the subject of Douglas's demands and threats was raised subsequently to Buchanan, he responded sarcastically, "I trust in Heaven I may be President myself and think I shall be."

Of course, Douglas's situation and Broderick's were in many respects far different. Whatever his particular problems with patronage and his personal tensions with Buchanan, Douglas was a respected leader of the national party, whereas Broderick was at most a promising newcomer. Moreover, Douglas was clearly in Buchanan's conservative wing of the party, while Broderick's loyalty had yet to be tested. And Douglas's own presidential ambitions were tied to Buchanan's successful resolution of the divisive Kansas issue.

Patronage, however embarrassing, was secondary to this. Here Buchanan shared with Douglas and Gwin a piece of wonderful news that must have confirmed their own earlier estimate of Buchanan's potential to become a successful president.

Pierce's governor of Kansas had been John Geary, the early mayor of San Francisco. Geary, having behaved heroically in a situation that had been rendered impossible by Pierce's dithering, now needed to be relieved. Buchanan had chosen as his successor Robert Walker. This was the same Walker whose successful campaign for senator from Mississippi Gwin had managed decades before, the same Walker who when appointed to Polk's cabinet had done everything he could to get Gwin named as his replacement. Here was a Southerner of impeccable credentials, and a shrewd and experienced moderate fully committed to the Union. The new governor was someone in whom the South could trust and with whom the North could deal. Moreover, Buchanan had Walker, before going to Kansas, pay a courtesy call on Douglas as chair of the Senate Committee on the Territories to show him his instructions from Buchanan. Walker was to call a constitutional convention, and then have the resulting constitution submitted to a vote of the people. In short, he would follow Douglas's policy of popular sovereignty.

This more than satisfied Douglas. The antislavery forces were growing in the Northwest, and in practice were his only threat for reelection. But with Walker there he could expect that Kansas would not give the Republicans the incendiary issue they needed. With Bleeding Kansas bleeding no more, the Little Giant had little to fear from the Republicans in 1858. And, federal patronage or no federal patronage, he could control the Illinois Democracy.

Robert Walker, before he left for his peacemaking mission to Kansas, had also tried at making peace between Broderick and Gwin. Broderick had already recognized that after only a month in office his own political future was at risk. Buchanan's decisions had backed him into a corner. He had made many promises in the course of his past election campaign, and had been able to keep almost none of them. Moreover, he was now being attacked back home for being disloyal to the president for whom he had campaigned so vigorously. And there was still the bad feeling in California over his deal with Gwin, a deal that now had proven to be entirely worthless. So Gwin was looking to Californians more like the honest victim who was, nonetheless, proving himself to be an able senator with the interests of California and his supporters at heart.

By early April Broderick had decided that his only way to shore up his position would be to return to California, and use the upcoming state elections as the basis for regaining initiative. Once again, he would have to offset federal patronage from the Chivalry with his control of state and local offices. He needed another friendly governor who could do for him what Ambassador Bigler had done for him a few years ago.

To pursue this strategy Broderick would have to set up an anti-Buchanan Democracy in California. If such a movement was successful, it might encourage similar defections in New England or the Northwest; this in turn could be disastrous to the party nationally. But Broderick was not thinking of the party nationally.

So, now that the patronage had all been distributed for the time being, the administration sent Walker to try to do a little fence-mending. However, now that the patronage had been distributed, the two California senators had little to talk about, or bargain over. So Walker called together Broderick and Gwin for the meeting, as if what separated the two leading Democrats from California were simply personal. It was personal, of course; but also much more.

Perhaps Walker expected that Broderick would start shouting at Gwin, or make cutting remarks. (He knew, of course, that the urbane Gwin was above such things.) Broderick showed Walker that he knew how to behave himself. There was nothing to be gained by causing a fuss here; the damage had already been done, and Broderick had already decided what he could do to try to repair it. Gwin had won in Washington, and Broderick now had to carry on the fight back in California. So in the presence of Walker, Gwin and Broderick exchanged forced pleasantries, and wished Walker well in his important new assignment (which Walker secretly hoped might lead to his own nomination for president).

Gwin, for his part, could hardly wait to write back to California to describe what had happened: "Since the appointments were made we have met once on business and he was very social. I have never heard of his saying a word against me or blaming me in any way, although he must have known where the blow came from." In another letter dealing with Broderick, Gwin could add smugly, "I don't think I shall hereafter be charged with bargaining of the patronage of the government to Mr. B."

It had all fallen apart for Broderick with breathtaking swiftness. Little more than a month after taking the oath of office, Senator Broderick was on his way back to fight against the man he had helped elect to the presidency. Gwin, quietly remaining in Washington to pursue his legislative work, made sure through a series of letters that his friends in California understood perfectly well what Broderick was going to try to do.

Broderick's was, Gwin wrote, "a bold game in which he loses everything if he fails." Gwin urged them to "stand by the administration." Broderick was now trying to divide the party, as he had once before, without any concern for the party, the state, or the nation. In contrast, there were the statesmanlike actions of James Buchanan. Gwin concluded, "The President, in making appointments for California, has been governed by the desire to secure the most faithful public officers, and in doing so has sought to consult the wishes of the people and of *our* party in all sections of the state."

Broderick may not have lost everything in his return to California, but he certainly did fail miserably. Once he sized up the situation in California, he must have been appalled. The Know-Nothings as a political party had now completely collapsed, thereby sending nativist followers into Gwin's wing of the Democratic Party. In contrast, the Republicans were flourishing, continuing to gather strength—it seemed—daily, and mostly from the staunchest supporters of Broderick. It was a measure of Broderick's desperation that he published his own "Letter to the People of California" in which he categorically denied much of what everyone knew to be true about his and Gwin's senatorial elections. For instance: "Between Mr. Gwin and myself there was no condition whatever in regard to the distribution of patronage."

He then tried to resort to intimidation, organizing rallies of his most aggressive followers; but the Chivalry would have none of it. They simply put on counterrallies, and in both San Francisco and Sacramento the result was open riots in which the police stood by until the rioters exhausted themselves.

His activities had been pointed toward the state party convention in July, but by the time that occurred his situation was so obviously futile he did not even bother to attend. Some of his followers did, and tried to oppose the Chivalry slate for state offices. Joseph McCorkle, for instance, represented the Broderickites for governor against former Senator Weller, the hope of the Chivalry. It was no contest. Weller won on the first ballot 254 to 61.

During the convention, Broderick's men had tried to use every tactic they could to distract the convention from the business at hand. They wanted to expel all those who had ever supported the Know-Nothings; they repeatedly tried to get a condemnation of the vigilantes of 1856. Time and again, they tried to stir things up; time and again, they were either voted down or outmaneuvered. In the end they were usually little more than a nuisance, and sometimes just comic relief.

Broderick and his people sat out the subsequent election, but that made no difference. The Democrats, or rather Chivalry Democrats, swept back into complete control of the state government. By then Broderick was already on his way back to Washington. His was a despair that cleared the mind.

David Broderick came back to Washington in late 1857 a changed man. The fulfillment of his senatorial ambition had resulted in ashes, all ashes. He had failed, and to his failure he could see no remedy. So Broderick came back to the capital a dangerous man, a man who felt he had nothing to lose, an ambitious man who had had the ambition seared out of him. He was going to be defeated one way or another in the next election—or perhaps he already was defeated.

He had apparently decided that he was going to go down to defeat boldly, even honorably. But how could a junior senator from California put up a fight that anyone would notice? He could flail away against Buchanan, Gwin, and the rest of them. But he was so weak. Anything resembling revenge seemed far beyond his reach. If he persisted, would he do anything but make himself look more foolish than he already did?

This seems to have been Broderick's state of mind as the Thirty-fifth Congress convened that December 1857. Then, to his amazement, he discovered that he had the perfect issue with which to belabor Buchanan and the Buchaneers (as his loyal supporters like Gwin jokingly referred to themselves). The issue was Kansas. More amazingly still, he had found the perfect ally to lead him into battle. Stephen Douglas.

While Broderick was failing in California, Robert Walker, through no fault of his own, had been failing in Kansas. He had held elections for a constitutional convention, but the Free-Soilers had boycotted it. The result was that the constitutional convention held in Lecompton was dominated by proslavery delegates. They naturally drew up a strongly proslavery constitution. For instance: "The right of property is before and higher than any constitutional sanction, and the right of the owner of a slave to such slave and its increase is the same and as inviolable as the right of the owner of any property whatever."

Of course, the framers of the Lecompton constitution knew that it had to be submitted to a general vote, and knew too that the Free-Soilers, being a clear majority in Kansas, would vote it down decisively. They tried to avoid complete defeat by a piece of cleverness. Citizens of Kansas were offered the choice of voting for the constitution with slavery or without slavery. The trick was that a vote for the latter meant only the substitution of a provision that slavery would no longer exist in Kansas "except that the right of property in slaves now in this Territory shall in no measure be interfered with." Moreover, this provision, according to the constitution, could not be amended until 1864. In short, the choice presented to the voters of Kansas was simply between unlimited slavery and limited slavery.

Walker was furious, and more furious still when he learned that Buchanan, after giving assurances to the contrary, had decided to support the Lecompton constitution. And Walker, when furious, was not a man to remain discreetly quiet: "I consider such a submission of the question a vile fraud, a bare counterfeit. I will not support it, but I will denounce it, no matter whether the Administration sustains it or not." (He wrote this by way of threat after he had learned privately that Buchanan had decided to reverse himself and was soon to announce his support of it.)

The Democrats of the Northwest were furious too, and also afraid. Buchanan's support of Lecompton handed the already strong Republicans just the issue they needed to sweep the state legislative elections, and subsequently take Douglas's Senate seat as well. The Republicans would say—and who could now argue with them?—that the Democrats had shown themselves once again to be so dominated by the South that they were incapable of treating the issue of slavery evenhandedly.

For Douglas this was a matter of both political principle and political survival. The Lecompton constitution violated his principle of popular sovereignty. And the Lecompton constitution meant that Douglas, if he continued to support the administration, would be finished in Illinois politics—"as dead as a herring," one of his loyal supporters wrote him. On top of all else, Douglas felt betrayed, since he had not even been consulted as chairman of the Senate Committee on the Territories. Douglas responded to all this with a belligerent arrogance that for once was fully justified: "By God, sir, I made Mr. James Buchanan! And by God, sir, I will unmake him!"

The gravity of the situation was recognized by all the leading Democratic politicians in Washington. The very day Douglas arrived in Washington for the beginning of the next session of the Thirty-fifth Congress, a meeting was hastily arranged between the Little Giant and the president whom he intended to unmake. To say that it did not go well would be the blandest of understatements. It started badly, and only got worse. Finally Buchanan was on his feet, towering over Douglas, while saying with rigid anger, "Mr. Douglas, I desire you to remember that no Democrat ever yet differed from an Administration of his own choice without being crushed." Pausing briefly, Buchanan then, his head tilted, reminded Douglas of the fate of two Democratic senators who had opposed Andy Jackson only to be crushed by him. This gave Douglas the opening for his decisive counterpunch: "Mr. President, I wish you to remember that General Jackson is dead." With that left hook having landed squarely on the chin, Douglas turned and stormed out of the Oval Office.

This breach between his two good friends, apparently irreparable, was painful for Gwin. From now on he tried to effect reconciliation, or the appearance of reconciliation, whenever that seemed even faintly possible. But it never worked. Buchanan had come truly to hate Douglas—"that perfidious man," he would soon begin to call him, refusing to pronounce his name. And there was no reasoning with the proud Douglas. When asked if he realized where his defiance of the president was leading, Douglas would snap, "Yes sir, I have taken a through ticket and checked all my baggage."

What was painful for Gwin was a godsend for Broderick. Douglas solicited his support in the fight against the administration. Broderick enthusiastically also took a through ticket and checked all his baggage. So now Broderick joined Stephen Douglas and Charles Stuart of Michigan in open defiance of the leader of their party and nation. Many thought that for a beginning senator to defy party discipline was suicide. One adviser thought he "had let his passion and bitterness run away with him, against the wishes and counsel of his best friends." What they did not realize was that Broderick already calculated his political career dead. Douglas gave him some little chance to revive it, and much chance for revenge.

The Senate of the Thirty-fifth Congress was overwhelmingly Democratic, although seven new Republicans had been returned to the Senate to raise their number to twenty. The Know-Nothings, or American Party, had only five senators, all from the South. The Democrats numbered thirty-seven, and twenty-five of these were from slave states.

Two of the new senators from the South were particularly prominent. Jefferson Davis had been returned from Mississippi, after having been Pierce's closest adviser in his cabinet. Davis had emerged unquestionably as the new Calhoun, a personification of the Deep South. His erect military posture (befitting a hero of the Mexican War) gave the impression of strength, until one realized how emaciated his frame. Six feet and ramrod straight but hardly 130 pounds. His high, almost aristocratic cheekbones were mocked by sunken cheeks, leaving his face with an unpleasantly pinched, ascetic look. And the left eye gazed with piercing power, but this impression was partly the result of a contrast with the right, which was permanently clouded and often inflamed. Davis seemed a bundle of contraries, like the South itself, strong but diseased, erect but frail—the contraries obvious to everyone but himself.

His much younger wife, after their first meeting, sensed this about him: "The fact is that he is the kind of person I should expect to rescue one from a mad dog at any risk, but to insist upon a stoical indifference to the fright afterward." One admirer said that he spoke with a heat that threw out no sparks or flashes. Another said that Davis might be a fire-eater but if so he ate his fire à la mode, with a fork and napkin. He was polite, but unyielding and ever vigilant. While in Pierce's cabinet, he had objected to the statue of the goddess of Liberty planned for the Capitol because it had a Phrygian cap that according to Davis's researches was the type most frequently worn in ancient Rome by freed slaves—the headdress of Liberty was changed. Davis's Calhounesque defenses of the peculiar institution were dominated by intricate, even crabbed reasonings from constitutional law, but reasonings clearly being made by a man passionately willing to fight and die for his syllogisms.

James Henry Hammond of South Carolina was of a different sort. Immensely wealthy, owning reputedly a thousand slaves who worked his ten thousand acres, Hammond looked like an aristocrat among aristocrats. His elegantly receding hairline, aquiline nose, gently doubled chin, uniformly aloof—even condescending—expression made him seem to the manor born, as did his expensively understated clothes. Gwin would know the true story, however, a story that would never be vouchsafed to the likes of Broderick.

Hammond had been an aspiring ne'er-do-well who gained his wealth by wedding a fifteen-year-old heiress (over her family's strenuous objections), and then had a most promising political career apparently cut short while governor because of sexual improprieties with four young nieces. His belated election to the Senate was a fluke, feuding South Carolina factions coming together behind him to thwart one another; but that did not stop Hammond from acting as if he were the true heir of Calhoun. He had published widely in defense of slavery as a social system morally superior to free labor. (Slavery, he had written, was "especially commanded by God through Moses and approved by Christ through his Apostles"—and those who objected to it were "ignorant of the essential principles of human association revealed by history.") He now relished the prospect of lecturing the Senate on the subject. Sensing in him a rival for sectional preeminence, Hammond had little patience with Jeff Davis—the "most irascible man I ever knew . . . as vain as a peacock, as ambitious as the Devil," he sniffed. The irascible part about Davis was right, if one believed in cold anger; but the peacock and the Devil, most senators would have thought, were more aptly laid at the feet of James Henry Hammond himself.

On December 8, Buchanan read his State of the Union address to a joint session of Congress in which, amid many other points, he contended that the Lecompton convention had been "in the main fair and just." Immediately afterward, a number of senators rose to respond. Loyal Democrats praised Buchanan's statesmanship. On behalf of the Republicans Seward dismissed his treatment of Kansas as "very lame and impotent," the weak policies that could quickly return Kansas to civil war. Douglas, for his part, did his best to praise the message, all except for the words on Kansas, with which he profoundly disagreed. Douglas's own words on Kansas, brief as they were, were a declaration of war on his president, a war that began the next day.

On December 9, Douglas went on the offensive, with a three-hour oration against the administration's policy in Kansas. The measures regarding Kansas would be submitted later. Now could begin a pure debate over administration policies, with Douglas taking on all comers, a situation he obviously relished.

It appeared to the gallery as if Douglas alone were opposing all the rest of the Senate. Seward had instructed the Republicans to stay out of it; however much they might deplore civil war in Kansas, they should be able to view bloody civil war within the Democratic Party with complete equanimity. Stuart and Broderick, on the other hand, knew Douglas well enough to realize that they were not to intrude on his fight until he gave them permission.

So one administration champion after another waded into battle against the Little Giant only to be repulsed. Gwin himself, during this time, stayed away from the Senate floor as much as possible. Instead, he tried to use his special committee on the transcontinental railroad—he was chair again—as a private seminar where Douglas, Seward, administration men like himself, and fire-eaters like Davis could seek common ground for the national good. He was amazed how the reasonable discussions he heard among these men in private would flair into partisan bickering on the floor. So he stayed away, lest he be drawn in and thereby compromise his usefulness—to California, to the Democratic Party, to the nation.

For much of December Douglas single-handedly held the Senate Democrats at bay, but with tempers fraying. Then, on December 23, the last day before the Christmas break, Douglas permitted Stuart and Broderick to speak. This would be Broderick's maiden speech before the Senate, and for that reason alone would have excited some interest.

Broderick spoke only briefly. He owned that he was "very much embarrassed" to have to criticize in his first speech as a Democratic senator a Democratic president, especially one whom he had so enthusiastically supported in the recent election. Nonetheless, embarrassed as he was, he would not hesitate: "I do not intend, because I am a member of the Democratic party, to permit the President of the United States, who has been elected by that party, to create civil war in Kansas." He held the president himself personally responsible for the misuse of his office: "It is the first time, I believe, in the history of this country that a President of the United States ever stepped down from the exalted position he held to attempt to coerce the people into a base submission to the will of an illegalized body." There may have been a few snickers at the inept coinage "illegalized"—but Broderick pressed on. However, he may have been reddened by the snickers, for his concluding words were probably harsher, less diplomatically expressed than he had intended.

He went on. As for the delegates to Lecompton who had perpetrated this fraud, he said, he thought that the liberty-loving Kansans had treated them with considerable forbearance. Had the Kansans rather seized them and "flogged them, or cut off their ears, and driven them out of the country, I would have applauded them for the act." Having said that, Broderick sat down, to a stunned silence. And the Senate then recessed to celebrate the birth of the Prince of Peace.

Buchanan formally received his copy of the Lecompton constitution at the end of January. In early February he sent it to Congress, with his recommendation for approval. If the Congress rejected this constitution, Buchanan said, he feared for the future of the Union itself. In the Senate it went to Douglas's Committee on the Territories where administration loyalists outvoted the alliance between Douglas and the Republicans. So on March 1 the Lecompton constitution was once again before the Senate.

But first there was an awkward moment for Gwin, and a sarcastic exchange between him and Broderick. Poor Gwin had come to the Senate session because the transcontinental railroad was the first item on the agenda. Senator Stuart, Douglas's ally from Michigan, was in the chair—and announced that Kansas was going to be discussed first. Gwin was immediately on his feet objecting to the change in the agenda. Let the Senate first vote on the railroad, and there will be plenty of time to discuss Kansas.

This remark seems to have been met by the Senate with jollity. Virtually everyone in the chamber knew of Gwin's single-minded concern with this project. And perhaps his colleagues had also noticed his repeated absences when Kansas was being heatedly argued. Now, it seemed, he was caught. And once the Lecompton constitution began to be discussed, there was no telling how long it would take.

Douglas immediately realized that Gwin's objection presented him with the occasion for a little mischief. He rose to his feet to agree with Gwin. All the major candidates in the last presidential election fully supported the transcontinental railroad. He thought that the Senate ought to act on this before addressing the divisive issue of Kansas.

Douglas had just given administration supporters a preview of his strategy. Douglas knew that he was going to lose in the Senate. He intended only to lose as slowly as possible. This was more than sheer orneriness. They could guess that while the debate continued anti-Lecompton newspapers were going to be hammering away against the administration policy in Kansas. By the time the issue came to the House there just might be enough opposition to stymie the administration.

Stuart as chair now smilingly had to inform the senior senator from California that a private arrangement had already been reached. Kansas was going to be discussed first. So Gwin, the purported insider, had then to admit publicly that he had not participated in the discussions of the Democratic leadership, the price he paid for trying to avoid Kansas. He apologized to Stuart, and mumbled that he would never have objected if he had known of this arrangement. He now probably hoped that the Senate would get to

Kansas immediately so that his faux pas could be forgotten without any more fuss. What had just happened was embarrassing enough.

Douglas, however, was not quite ready to let it go, although he undoubtedly had been party to the agreement about the agenda change. So he intoned another impassioned little paragraph more to amuse his colleagues—both friend and foe—at his feistiness than to have any effect. Stuart, for one, must have been having a hard time keeping the proper composure for a chair. Senators on the floor apparently were starting to regard this little contretemps as quite comical.

There was something healthy at a little good-natured fun before taking up the grave matter of Kansas when the future of the administration if not the Union itself was going to be at risk. Douglas had sat down, having enjoyed his performance as much as everyone else; and Gwin was probably smiling sheepishly and shrugging it off, when another senator demanded the floor. And his tone was not jocular. It was Broderick.

Gwin may not have heard the beginning of Broderick's brief extemporaneous remarks, but he heard the end: "I expected my colleague to state the importance of his bill to California. I did not expect that he would take his seat quietly after the laugh that I heard on this side of the chamber." Before Gwin could rise to respond, Seward, his eyebrows working mischievously, had jumped up in agreement with his distinguished colleagues from the other side of the aisle, Douglas and Broderick.

Now Gwin had arisen again, and now he was speaking in anger: "I am not so sensitive as my colleague is to any laugh that may occur in the Senate to a motion I make." The Senate as a whole was still mightily amused at what was transpiring, but Gwin was not paying attention to anyone but Broderick. He was starting to lecture him in the third person on what it meant to be a senator. "When he has been here as long as I have. . . ."

With laughter rolling about the chamber, Broderick was once again on his feet to express his gladness that his colleague is not so sensitive to laughter as he seemed. He then added, with sarcastic politeness, "It is very true that I have not occupied a seat in this body as long as my colleague; and perhaps when I have been here a few years, I shall not be so sensitive as I am at present. I am very thankful to my colleague for reminding me of that fact." So the Senate had one last laugh, and then turned to Kansas, which no one thought a laughing matter.

This time the Republicans did not remain aloof. On March 3, Seward rose to present the Republican view. There were two contradictory systems of labor in the United States, slave and free. As the country grows and expands, as communication improves and population increases, these are brought into collision. "Shall I tell you what this collision means?" Seward's voice was beginning to take on that timbre which made his friend Gwin so nervous. "It is an irrepressible conflict between opposing and enduring forces, and it means that the United States must and will, sooner or later, become either entirely a slave-holding nation, or entirely a free-labor nation."

Moderates like Gwin listened in vain for something in this speech that was negotiable. Toward its end Seward asserted, "I know, and you know, that a revolution has begun. I know, and all the world knows, that revolutions never go backwards." Seward then bragged over the growing strength of the abolitionists in Congress. Eventually these forces, led by the Republican party, would "confound and overthrow, by one decisive blow, the betrayers of the Constitution and Freedom forever."

What could Gwin say to a speech like this? If these words were taken seriously. . . . Well, it did not do to think of what would happen if these words were taken seriously.

The next day the elegant Senator Hammond answered Seward's metaphysics with realism—or so he would have framed the issue. Hammond was himself beginning to have visions of grandeur. He had become a Unionist of a rather idiosyncratic sort. He thought that in the American republic either the North had to rule the South or the South had to rule the North. (The Northwest of Douglas or the Far West of Gwin did not enter into his calculations.) He thought he could prove that the South, because of its superior social system, should rule the North. This made it absolutely imperative that the next president of the United States be from the Deep South. Indeed, Hammond thought that he knew just the man for the job, and his name was not Jefferson Davis. So Senator James H. Hammond rose in the Senate not to address the specifics of the Lecompton constitution and Kansas, but to talk sense to the nation.

The North had to recognize the international importance of the South, and its economic strength. The South, he declared, is already strong enough, without another foot of territory, to be independent and prosperous. Did Seward really expect there to be a conflict between North and South, a war of conquest?

The cotton supplied by the South is essential to the well-being of industrialized Europe, especially Britain. The European powers would not stand for a disruption of this supply. And that meant they would not stand for any conflict of the kind Seward predicted and welcomed. In such a revolution Europe would stand with the South. "No, you dare not make war on cotton. No power on earth dares make war on it. Cotton is King."

And what about slavery? Here the Northern partisans in their demagogic posturing are willfully ignoring indisputable and inevitable facts of social organization.

Hammond was speaking very slowly, painfully slowly. He said later that he had done this intentionally. He wanted to avoid all the showy histrionics that so dominated Senate debates. He was announcing evident truths that all should be able to see as such. He did not wish to distract his listeners by oratory. He wanted them only to attend to what he was saying, soberly, reflectively:

> In all social systems there must be a class to do the mean duties, to perform the drudgery of life. . . . Such a class you must have or you would not have that other class which leads progress, refinement and civilization. It constitutes the very mudsills of society and of political government; you might as well attempt to build a house in the air, as to build either the one or the other, except on the mudsills. Fortunately for the South, she found a race adapted to that purpose.

Seward had objected yesterday that the whole world had abolished slavery. To that Hammond had a simple response: "Aye, the name, but not the thing." And the thing was worse in the North than the South. The Southern slave owner, unlike the Northern employer, was obliged to his workers even during hard economic times. So a Southerner will see more beggars during one trip to New York City than he will in a lifetime in the South. (This point was particularly painful because the North had in 1857 suffered an economic collapse that had left tens of thousands out of work in New York City alone.) Moreover, the Southerner has enslaved members of a race who as a result are "elevated from the condition in which God first created them." So they are "happy, content, unaspiring, and utterly incapable, from intellectual weakness, ever to give us any trouble by their aspiration."

Hammond charged, "Yours are white, of your own race, you are brothers of one blood. They are equals in natural endowment of intellect and they feel galled by their degradation." Moreover, in the North they vote, and are in the majority. If they ever appreciate the power of the ballot box, these slaves are going to rise, have in fact already begun to rise up to seize the reins of government in their own degraded hands, and if successful will make our great republic the prey of demagogues.

Now Hammond could address his Northern colleagues as fellow members of the class that led progress, refinement, and civilization. They must think of the consequences of such a workingman's revolution: "Where would you be? Your society would be reconstructed, your government reconstructed, your property divided." Hammond sat down, even more pleased with himself than he usually was.

The response to the speech, at least in the South, was all Hammond could have hoped. Tens of thousands of copies were printed and distributed. Among the widespread praise there was a particularly gratifying comment from the Charleston *Courier* (which Hammond liked so much he had it put in his scrapbook). With "one bold stroke of Senatorial eloquence," it reported, Senator Hammond "leaps into the almost inaccessible niche occupied by Calhoun."

In Hammond's speech was distilled everything hateful to Broderick about Washington, but he could not himself respond immediately. Douglas, although he had to let Broderick and Stuart speak, wanted to make certain that he would not be upstaged, even to the limited degree he had been by Broderick's terse, biting remarks on December 23. He arranged for them once again to speak during the last day of the Senate debate, March 22; but after they spoke there would be a final evening session in which the Little Giant would hold forth alone. It made no difference, for Hammond had provided the stonecutter's son with the perfect pivot for his speech.

That day Stuart spoke without notable effect. And then Broderick rose to speak. Broderick began by making the conventional abolitionist dichotomy between slavery as old, decrepit, consumptive, and freedom as young, strong, vigorous. He particularized this by asserting—perhaps with appropriate glances at Gwin, for he was now attending the debates—that he came from a state "where labor is honorable," where "no station is so high and no position so great that its occupant is not proud to boast that he has labored with his own hands." There may have been a few guffaws from the Southern side at this, but he now turned to face Senator Hammond, who in the next few minutes sat impassive as if he were hearing not a word.

Broderick read from the text of Hammond's speech at length, to make sure everyone had it fresh in his mind. Then he began his attack:

> I, sir, am glad that the Senator has spoken thus. It may have the effect of arousing in the working men that spirit which has been lying dormant for centuries. It may also have the effect of arousing the two hundred thousand men, with pure white skins, in South Carolina, who are now degraded and despised by thirty thousand aristocratic slave holders.

This comment was telling, and produced a murmur across the floor and in the gallery. Before silence had settled, Broderick was already reading some of his cherished Romantic poetry, on power. The power that "Linked with success, assured and kept with skill, / That moulds another's weakness to its will, / Holds with their hands, but still to them unknown / Makes even their mightiest deeds appear his own."

The laborers of the North as well of those of the South, those that Hammond deprecates as the "white slaves" and the "mudsills" of society, must realize what they themselves have done for progress, refinement, and civilization. Progress, refinement, civilization are properly considered their achievements—and not the achievements of those who exploit, degrade and despise them.

> I suppose the senator from South Carolina did not intend to be personal in his remarks to any of his peers on the floor. If I had thought so, I would have noticed them at the time. I am, sir, with one exception, the youngest in years of the senators

upon this floor. It is not long since I served an apprenticeship of five years at one of the most laborious trades pursued by man, a trade that from its nature devotes its follower to thought, but debars him from conversation.

I would not have alluded to this if it were not for the remarks of the senator from South Carolina, and that thousands who know that I am the son of an artisan and have been a mechanic would feel disappointed in me if I did not reply to him. I am not proud of this. I am sorry it is true. I would that I could have enjoyed the pleasures of life in my boyhood days, but they were denied to me. I say this with pain. I have not the admiration for the men of that class from whence I sprang that might be expected; they submit too tamely to oppression, and are too prone to neglect their rights and duties as citizens. But, sir, the class of society to whose toil I was born, under our form of government, will control the destinies of this nation. If I were inclined to forget my connection with them, or to deny that I sprang from them, this chamber would not be the place in which I could do either. While I hold a seat here, I have but to look at the beautiful capitals adorning the pilasters that support the roof to be reminded of my father's talent and handiwork.

Then, almost by way of afterthought, he turned from his father, whose refined handiwork he respected, to another old man, James Buchanan, whose degraded handiwork he did not: "I hope, sir, that the historian, when writing the history of these times, will ascribe the attempt of the executive to force this constitution upon an unwilling people to the fading intellect, the petulant passion, and the trembling dotage of an old man on the verge of the grave!"

The Senate then adjourned until the evening. Then Douglas claimed the floor. He spoke that night for three hours to a packed gallery, and it was a sterling performance. Before it, Gwin made his only contribution to the debate over Kansas. He noted to the chair that the galleries seemed dangerously crowded, and begged that ladies be allowed on the floor of the Senate. Preening, Douglas thanked his colleague for his thoughtfulness. And then, once the ladies were settled, he launched into his magnificent oration, which was meant for the ages.

Yet no less a figure than Seward himself judged that in the whole debate "the courageous young senator" from California had in his one speech carried off the rhetorical laurels, a judgment that would have scarcely gratified the Little Giant, had he learned of it.

The vote in the Senate was a foregone conclusion. With only four Democratic senators voting against the administration, the Kansas measure passed 33 to 25. The fight in the Senate had, however, achieved what Douglas had hoped by allowing the anti-Lecompton forces in the House to organize themselves more effectively, once the representatives realized how strongly opinion was running against the administration in their districts. Despite immense pressure from the administration on Northern Democrats, the opponents in the House narrowly managed to replace the Kansas bill with one that would require elections on the constitutional question of free soil versus slavery. The Buchaneers consequently wished only to save face. They came up with a compromise bill that would allow Kansans to vote on the slavery provisions of the Lecompton constitution, but only indirectly.

This was now a situation in which Gwin felt that he could be effective. He apparently helped arrange a meeting between Douglas and Robert Walker. Walker, like Gwin always the practical politician, was himself satisfied with his de facto victory over the administration. When they met, Walker conveyed to Douglas his own willingness to support the compromise.

Douglas was agitated, and in a worrisome condition. The months of frenetic work—which of course he had to do all himself, refusing to delegate—had driven Douglas near to one of his physical collapses. He was in no condition to think coolly. As Walker patiently presented the arguments for accepting the new bill and for trying consequently to reassert party discipline, the Little Giant paced the room, sweating profusely. Finally he agreed, and the delighted Gwin informed the president. Douglas was also to telegraph his supporters to have them cease their attacks upon the president.

The next day—April 25, 1858, a Sunday—Douglas met with his congressional supporters in Broderick's modest room to inform them of his decision. One who was there, James Forney, recounted what happened next.

Broderick took the initiative: "Mr. Douglas, I understand you propose to abandon this fight." Douglas weakly appealed to political realism: "I see no hope of success. They will crush us and if they do there is no future for any of us, and I think we can agree upon terms that will virtually sustain ourselves." At this Broderick exploded. He sarcastically professed not to be able to understand Douglas—but he meant that it was Douglas himself who did not understand. Douglas did not understand that they were all doomed politically. They were all now clearly destined to be crushed eventually between the Republicans and the Southern Democrats. (As much as he admired some Republicans such as Edward Baker, Broderick apparently never did consider the Republican Party a possibility for himself; this is odd until one remembers the connection in his mind between nativism and abolitionism.)

Of course, such reasoning was incomprehensible to the Little Giant. So Broderick would give Douglas something more immediate to worry about, something he could understand, the prospect of a public humiliation. If Douglas supported the new administration bill, Broderick threatened, "I will denounce you." Broderick had by this point worked himself up into a complete rage, a side of him that perhaps Douglas and others in the room had never seen before. They listened stunned, as Broderick informed Douglas that he would be better off dead than to abandon the fight now: "You had better, sir, go into the street and blow your damn brains out. You came to me of your own accord and asked me to take this stand and I have followed you. I have committed myself against this infernal Lecompton constitution. If you desert me, God damn you, I will make you crawl under your chair in the Senate."

For one of the few times in his life, the Little Giant was cowed. The next week Douglas spoke against the administration compromise, which was passed handily. The whole debate had been an extremely painful one for Gwin, who had consistently tried to play the role of mediator to no avail. First he had spoken with the president on Douglas's behalf. Then he had served as intermediary between Walker and the president when Walker thought he had persuaded Douglas to accept a compromise. Gwin's highest appeal consistently was to party loyalty.

He had at one point managed to get the Chivalry-led California legislature to send to both Gwin and Broderick instructions that they were to vote with the president on the Lecompton constitution. But this only served to provide Broderick with the opportunity for histrionics. Gwin had read the instructions before the Senate with a certain amount of self-satisfaction. Broderick then rose to announce that he would ignore the instructions "here, now or in the future." He was certain that "four-fifths of the people of California repudiate the Lecompton fraud. I shall respect the wishes of the people."

From then on, when Gwin tried to speak on behalf of California, he was heckled by Republican senators. This was more than Gwin could tolerate. At one point he lost his composure completely. He responded to an attack of Senator Henry Wilson, Sumner's colleague from Massachusetts, by accusing him of "practicing demagoguism." Senator Wilson responded that he would rather be a demagogue than a thief. Senator Gwin called Senator Wilson "a liar, a cowardly, slanderous traducer of character" and offered him a horsewhipping for good measure. When the two senators then began to move toward each other to settle the matter without words, they had to be physically restrained, by Jefferson Davis and William Seward, each playing peacemaker on his side of the aisle.

Ironically, this same session witnessed Gwin's own greatest triumph, at least as a host. As the debate over Kansas became more and more bitter, Gwin and his wife apparently tried to bring everyone back to his senses by having a grand party. On April 9, Gwin and his wife had put on a fancy dress ball so elaborate that everyone immediately understood how they could spend more than $70,000 a year on entertainment, for this party alone was estimated to have cost $12,000.

It had been planned for months—and was so great a success that Mrs.

Clay, reminiscing in 1905 about Washington social life of the 1850s, devoted a whole chapter just to this party:

> Surely no hostess ever more happily realised her ambition! When the function was formally announced, all Washington was agog. For the ensuing weeks men as well as women were busy consulting costumers, ransacking the private collections of the capital, and conning precious volumes for coloured engravings in a zealous search for original and accurate costuming. Only the Senators who were to be present were exempt from the anticipatory excitement, for Senator Gwin, declaring that nothing was more dignified for members of this body than their usual garb, refused to appear in an assumed one, and so set the example for his colleagues.

The effort at costuming can be seen from Mrs. Clay's own household. The three young women of her family went, respectively, as "a gypsy fortune-teller, a Constantinople girl, and Titania." The costume of the Constantinople girl, in particular, was so accurate that when she appeared a group of Turkish onlookers—presumably from the embassy—broke into spontaneous applause. Mrs. Clay herself daringly came as a character from a recent popular novel, as Aunt Ruthy Partington, an old crone given to malapropisms. Mrs. Clay remembered proudly, "It was the one character assumed during the memorable evening, by one of my sex, in which age and personal attractions were sacrificed ruthlessly for its more accurate delineation." Mrs. Clay created even a greater sensation than Mrs. Emory, a noted beauty who came as a Quaker maiden.

Everyone who was anyone had been invited. (Broderick was not.) President Buchanan danced the first dance with Mrs. Gwin, and received the guests at her side. Mrs. Gwin's costume had been the subject of much speculation; she was dazzling as the "Queen of Louis Quatorze": "Skirt of white moire antique, trimmed with flounces of pointe aiguille; train of cherry satin, trimmed with a ruche of white satin; coiffure of the time of Louis XIV." The Gwins, apparently, were trying gently to remind Washington society that they were the class that led progress, refinement, and civilization—they were the ancien régime of America. They had to get ahold of themselves, lest there be a revolution and a terror.

Elaborate accounts of the evening were widely published, as well as a long poem in its honor. This was Washington the way the Gwins liked to envision it, as if aristocratic ostentation could smooth over all political differences. Stephen Douglas himself was there, with his ravishing young wife dressed up as Aurora, more beautiful than ever. In the midst of the cheerful glamor of this evening it could almost seem as if Gwin were right in his hopes for a Union preserved by moderation and compromise and guile. This was a glittering evening that would be remembered decades later as the last great party of a bygone era, remembered by those who survived the maelstrom to come. The few there that night who remained in Washington during the Civil War would note sadly when the Gwin ballroom used for this great party was taken over for a military court. This particular court, as one of its first cases, would try Mary Gwin's dear friend Rose Greenhow as a spy for the Confederacy.

9

David Broderick by 1859 seems to have known that he was a beaten man, and among confidants began to refer to his own political career as a thing of the past. In the Senate that sense of failure had made him even more reckless. Not content to attack just the Buchanan administration, he now began to use the floor of the Senate for personal attacks upon Gwin himself, attacks that Gwin dexterously brushed aside. Attacks that consequently became more savage.

Sensing how spent Broderick was, his friends urged him not to return to California for the election of 1859. This was only going to be for state offices, such as the governorship. His wing of the Democratic Party was certain to go down once again to embarrassing defeat, with or without Broderick. He should save his strength for the presidential election of 1860 when his ally Stephen Douglas might still be the nominee of the Democratic Party. Broderick should just get away from Washington and politics—take a tour of Europe, for instance, see for the first time the Old Sod. Broderick refused the advice.

He explained, "I am determined that my friends should succeed in the next state election in California, not on account of its being any political service to me in the future (for I am sick and disgusted with politics) but for the purpose of showing my enemies that I have not lost any of my energy and strength."

The revealing aspect of this statement is that it would be true as far as his personal strength and energy were concerned even if he lost decisively. Like a warrior going into his last battle, Broderick seemed more concerned about showing his mettle than winning. But the defiant confidence of this statement was intended for public consumption. Those close enough to Broderick saw the private man and they winced.

He was struggling with his old enemy depression; a few of his friends, to their horror, saw signs that he might in fact already have given up the struggle. He conceded as much to one of them, James Forney, the same Forney who had intervened unsuccessfully on Broderick's behalf with Buchanan at the beginning of his stay at Washington and who had witnessed Broderick's threatening of Douglas. Broderick met Forney one evening in Philadelphia as he traveled to New York to catch the steamer back to California.

From the first sight of him the friend could see that he was "much depressed." Broderick no longer believed that the breach in the Democratic Party nationally could be healed, and the Democratic Party was the only hope for the nation to hold itself together. The futility of it all was epitomized by the quixotic campaign he was returning to California to wage. Then Broderick began to speak personally, which unnerved the friend even more.

"I feel, my dear friend, that we shall never meet again. I go hence to die. I shall abate not a jot of my faith." Broderick was composing his own obituary, and clearly he expected his friend to remember what he was saying word for word. Now he was continuing with slow emphasis, "I shall be killed." The friend did not want to hear any more of this nonsense. Broderick was still young, scarcely forty—and he was brave—and he would live to gather even greater laurels for himself. Broderick smiled sadly, "No, no, it is best. I am doomed." He then bade him to be sure to write all this down, and left for New York. And the friend could not help sensing that the shadow of his fate was so heavily upon Broderick as to be actually palpable—but then he quickly tried to shake this melodramatic nonsense from his mind.

Upon returning to California Broderick did try to effect an alliance between his anti-Lecompton Democrats and the Republicans. The Republicans were full of praise for Broderick's performance as senator; one of their own could scarcely have been more adamantly opposed to Buchanan's slyly proslavery policies. Nonetheless, the Republicans also had their eyes on 1860; the collapse of Broderick's wing of the Democratic Party was, in the judgment of many, the key to the Republican's having a chance to sweep California in 1860. An alliance with the anti-Lecompton Democrats now, moreover, would make the Republicans into junior partners, scarcely an independent party at all. As one leader put it, Broderick's was an "invitation for us to commit suicide this year with the promise of glorious resurrection next." Republican leaders, therefore, were willing to lose on their own in 1859, if that meant forcing the choice on moderate Democrats in 1860 between the Republican Party and the Chivalry. So they praised Broderick, but refused an alliance. (As one prominent California Republican, Cornelius Cole, put it, Broderick "carried the war under the Democratic flag but fought with Republican weapons.") At this refusal Broderick could scarcely have been surprised.

Now Broderick's anti-Lecompton slate would lose the election of 1859 for certain. Two other factors made it unlikely that his group would make even a respectable showing. Broderick had expected strong support from those committed to Stephen Douglas for the next Democratic nomination for president, but in this he had misjudged practical politics. Douglas needed some support from the South, or at least some support from Southern sympathizers, such as those who would likely dominate the Californian delegation to the national convention. Hence his backers in California, far from being enthusiastic about Broderick's divisive electoral tactics, were interested in compromising with Gwin for the sake of party unity. So they stood aloof from Broderick's faction.

If that were not bad enough, there was simple political opportunism, which might dictate desertion and betrayal. Broderick was disgusted with politics and indifferent about the future, but not all those around him were. Many were in fact interested in their own personal prospects. These might not fancy reenacting the heroic defeat of Leonidas and his Spartans.

The increasing isolation of Broderick was embarrassingly demonstrated when the anti-Lecompton convention met at Sacramento in April 1859. The candidates who came in a close second for the congressional and the gubernatorial nominations immediately thereafter denounced Broderick's manipulation of the results and showed up at the Lecompton convention the next week. So did David Terry, who was seeking renomination to the state Supreme Court. He had actually tried first to get the support of the anti-Lecompton Democrats but could get nowhere because of his well-known ties to the Know-Nothings and the Chivalry.

Broderick, whatever demons were stalking him inwardly, did not act discouraged. The greater the odds against him, the greater the honor in doing battle. So Broderick focused the anti-Lecompton campaign on the great issue of slavery versus free labor, using Gwin's support of the Buchanan administration as well as the recent Dred Scott decision by the U.S. Supreme Court as examples of the wrong kind of leadership.

While he was beginning the campaign on these issues, the Lecompton Democrats themselves were meeting in Sacramento. The ragged, improvised character of Broderick's convention contrasted with the smoothly run, self-assured style of the regular Democratic Party. The defectors from Broderick were welcomed with open arms, even given featured time at the podium. The elections for nomination were fought in a gentlemanly manner. And the focus for the subsequent election campaign was set. The focus was to be not James Buchanan, not slavery or free labor, not Kansas or Dred Scott, not Gwin or the Chivalry, not even the Republicans. The focus that would assure an overwhelming victory was David C. Broderick himself.

The person who established most effectively this focus and set the tone was none other than David Terry. In his speech to the convention Terry described the California anti-Lecompton Democrats as "a miserable remnant of a faction flying under false colors." Far from being free men, they were "the personal chattels of a single individual, whom they are ashamed of. They belong, heart and soul, body and breeches, to David Broderick." And, Terry added, Broderick himself marched under the banner not of Stephen Douglas, a loyal Democrat, but of Frederick Douglass, the black abolitionist.

Terry's speech caused a sensation at the convention, but failed in its object to gain Terry his renomination. Given the reception of this speech, Broderick would ordinarily have felt called upon to comment on it formally. The speech was a betrayal all too familiar to him these days. Broderick had, after all, intervened on Terry's behalf with the vigilantes.

However, news of the speech came to Broderick unexpectedly at the International Hotel in San Francisco. At breakfast, on June 26, he was seated at a large table with a number of people including a lawyer friend of Terry, D. W. Perley. When he read Terry's speech in the morning newspaper, Broderick could not resist venting his anger, however inappropriate the time and place and company. (There were ladies present at this elegant breakfast.)

Tossing the paper toward him, he said to Perley, "I see your friend Terry has been abusing me at Sacramento." Perley decided to preserve decorum by playing dumb: "What is it, Mr. Broderick?" That blandness occasioned a verbal torrent: "The damned miserable wretch, after being kicked out of the convention, went down there and made a speech abusing me. I have defended him at times when all others deserted him. I paid and supported three newspapers to defend him during the Vigilance Committee days, and this is all the gratitude I get from the damned miserable wretch for the favors I have conferred on him." Broderick was hissing through clenched teeth by now, and the whole room must have realized that something extraordinary was happening, although his voice was not carrying. The ladies were staring wide-eyed, or trying to look away, while the men were straining to get every word, and the waiters were officiously fidgeting. Nothing could stop Broderick now; with the veins in his forehead bulging like small ropes (they always did when he was in a rage) and his clenched hands even more threatening than usual, he continued with scarcely a pause for breath, "I have hitherto spoken of him as an honest man—as the only honest man on the bench of a miserable, corrupt Supreme Court—but now I find I was mistaken. I take it all back. He is just as bad as the others."

Now everyone was looking at Perley, and he realized that something was expected of him. He tried the minimum: "Mr. Broderick, who is it you speak of as a 'wretch'?" The hiss came back, "Terry." Perley wished he were somewhere else. "I will inform the Judge of the language you have used concerning him." This polished politeness only riled Broderick more: "Do so; I wish you to do so: I am responsible for it." Now Perley, despite himself, began to feel, against his better judgment, his blood start to rise: "You would not dare to use this language to him." This was true in its way. If Broderick had said this to Terry, the judge would have been on him immediately with his cherished bowie knife. But then again, everyone knew that Broderick when angry—and he was surely angry now—spoke without considering the consequences. Broderick, further provoked by Perley's timid response, brought his full attention onto Perley, who was trying not to tremble. Broderick sneeringly threw Perley's words back at him: "Would not dare." The implied threat of Perley's words clashed with the effeminate rendition Broderick gave them. Broderick seemed to be saying, "I might not dare this or that with a man like Terry, but with a lily-livered gelding like you I can do whatever I please." And all this in front of the women, with the whole room watching.

Perley could take it no more: "No, sir. You would not dare to do it, and you know you would not dare to do it; and you shall not use it to me concerning him. I shall hold you personally responsible for the language of insult and menace you have used." This implied challenge seemed to amuse Broderick, and broke the tension. The incident was over, and everyone could go back to their breakfasts, although there was more clinking of china than talk in the aftermath, as if all had suddenly become obsessed with the plates in front of them.

Subsequently, Perley did issue a formal challenge to Broderick, who jokingly dismissed it because he said he had presently more important matters at hand than his personal honor. Upper-class shysters like Mr. Perley were not worth the killing. Or as he put it in his elegantly phrased response, "Your own sense of propriety should have taught you that the positions we relatively occupy are so different as to forbid my acceptance of your challenge." At times like these to be a U.S. senator was truly delicious, better than the elegant breakfasts at the International Hotel. And if the Chivalry interpreted this rejection as implying that Broderick would accept a challenge from Gwin, that would be just fine too. Broderick told his friends that now more than anything else he just wanted "to kill old man Gwin."

Broderick had begun the campaign by attempting to focus on the issues, but the attacks by Terry and others led him to respond in kind. Not wishing to be just on the defensive, he began making charges against Gwin as "dripping with corruption."

Gwin was in an odd position. The Lecompton Democrats had nominated for governor Milton Latham, who had still not forgiven Gwin for snatching the Senate seat away from him. In fact, they no longer spoke. Moreover, everyone admitted, even newspapers supporting the Lecompton ticket, that Latham was simply biding time until he could run for the Senate again. And, of course, Gwin would be the first to have to stand for reelection. So in supporting Latham actively Gwin would be bolstering an almost certain challenger to his reelection. Nonetheless, this was a question of party discipline. On that subject Gwin was inflexible. So he stumped the state on behalf of Latham and the Lecompton slate of Democratic candidates.

With Latham, Gwin, and Broderick as the three principal campaigners on the Democratic side, the subject of the joint senatorial election of 1857 was unavoidable, although amazingly the Democrats themselves were the ones doing most of the talking about it. In his speeches Latham himself provided his own self-serving rendition of the events.

He admitted that he had been offered the second senatorship by Broderick, on the condition of giving up federal patronage. His response had been virtue itself: "I told him I would not do an act of that kind to be Emperor of all of the Moguls." Much applause. Moreover, he did not just refuse the unseemly offer, but he also had had some free advice for Broderick. He warned Broderick that if he threw his support to Gwin "with the position he has in Washington, the social and political power he has there, he will completely overshadow you." Latham then could pause smugly surveying his audience, and report Broderick's response. Broderick had told Latham that he did not have the fear of Gwin people thought. Now the crowd rolled with laughter. Latham was not running against the other candidates for governor; he was running against Broderick and Gwin.

By temperament Gwin, now on his own independent electioneering tour of the state, would have preferred to have others like Terry do the rhetorical dirty work. He tried to keep a statesmanlike stance. He talked of how as a senator he had steadfastly avoided "controversy in debate in congress." Regarding Kansas, for instance, in supporting President Buchanan "I simply performed my duty." He tried to remind his audiences of the dangerous sectional hostilities threatening the well-being of the nation; during the last presidential election, for instance, "We appeared to be standing all the time upon the verge of civil war." The regular Democrats were the one truly national party, the hope of the Union. That was what voters had to realize.

Gwin had done his duty in that election of 1856 and in subsequently supporting the president. So he was doing his duty now. The anti–Lecompton Democrats would not be a factor, except as an annoyance. The Republicans were not yet strong enough to challenge seriously. And Gwin would do his duty in this election, even if that meant supporting the ungrateful Milton Latham.

But the newspapers kept reporting the wild attacks, the unfounded allegations, the sheer mudslinging of Broderick. In July a friend who happened to be in California wrote back to Jefferson Davis about the "bitter things" Broderick and Gwin were saying about each other—and also included copies of some speeches. He assured the concerned Davis, "In every way the Doctor will have the advantage, for his opponent cannot keep cool and gives way to violent impulses." Indeed, Gwin was doing so well on the stump, he reported, that his friends were openly talking about the next step for him, perhaps a run for the vice presidential nomination in 1864.

In fact, although he did have the clear advantage and Broderick was giving way to violent impulses, Gwin did not feel as much in control of this campaign as those letters to Davis suggested. The sniping of Latham he could tolerate. But Gwin found himself galled by the newspaper accounts of Broderick's speeches. Broderick should know as well as Gwin did that he was defeated in California, and of no account in Washington. And yet he would not stop. And Gwin, despite himself, was beginning to lose his calculating coolness. This was clear when in one speech he recounted Broderick's electioneering duplicities, and then asked in disgust, "What can you do with such an individual? If we club him, it will do no good; if we kill him, it will only make him a martyr." In another speech he began his vituperation with the regretful apology, "I am well aware that discussions of this description between United States Senators from the same State do not add to the dignity of the office."

For the two senators the point of the campaign now seemed less the upcoming election than a series of welcome occasions to attack one another. Significantly, at one campaign stop, with an audience ready to cheer him, Broderick upon his first mention of his rival heard a voice from the back shout that he should forget about old Gwin and get on with his speech. Occasionally he would, working his supporters into a fury against "Ten-cent Jimmy" and the Buchaneers, and then asking, "Can you support an administration that would bring slave labor into the West to compete with free labor?" (Of course, this was far from the way that Frederick Douglass would frame the issue, but more effective for garnering votes.)

Broderick, despite these successes, could no longer resist personal attacks on his two rivals. Did his audience know that in 1857 Gwin had privately described Latham as "one of the most ungrateful wretches in the State" and that Latham had judged Gwin "a corrupt old rascal"? Did hardworking Californians know, by the way, that Gwin had recently given a costume ball in Washington that cost him $12,000? At whose expense had the corrupt old rascal accumulated such a sum to be tossed away?

Even some earlier admirers of the two men began to be revolted at the spectacle. Frank Pixley, a Republican candidate for the Assembly, was typical of these. He wrote an open letter to a San Francisco newspaper admitting that he earlier had praised Broderick effusively: "I admired his undaunted courage, his indomitable resolution, his untiring energy." Pixley honestly thought that through much of his political career, even after he became senator, Broderick had been persecuted by his enemies. Nonetheless, his opinion of both Broderick and Gwin had changed in the last few months: "Messrs. Broderick and Gwin return from the Senate; themselves disclose the most astounding and infamous facts, telling but half the story of their shame. . . . I watch them as they disgrace themselves, as they disgrace the State; and I see that I have been the unconscious eulogist of a great political charlatan."

Broderick's charges were wild. He claimed, for instance, that a man who had witnessed the deal between himself and Gwin had subsequently been lured into a duel and "murdered." The fact that Gwin could rebut these particular charges in convincing detail made no difference. Broderick repeated them. Gwin had become so annoyed at them that he began to claim he could prove he had been elected without any assistance from Broderick at all; he had had enough votes on his own.

Broderick had always been a reluctant campaigner, but during this campaign he learned to play to the crowd. He would quietly talk of his early admiration for Gwin. He *had* respected him, until Gwin sold out his friends to get back to the Senate—but then he could feel only contempt for him. Now that he had witnessed how shamelessly Gwin was displaying himself in this campaign he could no longer feel even that. Gwin was not worthy of contempt, only of pity. Then Broderick mocked Gwin's complaints against the personal attacks: "If Dr. Gwin felt aggrieved at my conduct, he knew his remedy." Just so that all could understand what Broderick had just said, he repeated himself: "If I have insulted Dr. Gwin sufficient to induce him to go about the State and make a blackguard of himself, he should seek the remedy left to every gentleman who feels offense." The reporter for the *Alta California* certainly understood what Broderick was saying; his summary of the speech bore the headline BRODERICK INVITES GWIN TO CHALLENGE HIM.

The afterthought of an election went roughly the way it would have been predicted before the campaign began. Broderick's tireless campaigning and a last-minute, desperate partial alliance with the Republicans did make the election respectably close in some of the urban areas, but the rest of the state went overwhelmingly Democratic. Broderick's energy had succeeded only in drawing Gwin and the Chivalry into a street fight they won.

The Democratic Party now was entirely theirs, if there ever had been any doubt. One newspaper was scarcely exaggerating when it wrote, "The anti-Lecompton party so-called has been literally annihilated. There is, today, no such party in existence." If Broderick had not already been sick and disgusted with politics, this election campaign alone should have been sufficient.

Given the violent recriminations of the campaign of 1859, it was widely presumed that duels would be unavoidable in the aftermath. In particular, a duel between Broderick and Gwin seemed likely, so likely that the San Francisco newspapers openly discussed it. The San Francisco *Bulletin,* contrary as usual, reasoned against the expected duel occurring soon: "It would be late· in the day now, for either of the Senators, to avail themselves of the Code . . . after they have exhausted the torrents of mutual recrimination, and the time within which they could do harm has passed away with the motive which prompted it."

Even President Buchanan at the distance of Washington seems to have been worried about a possible duel between Broderick and his dear friend Gwin. Along with the news of his own administration's overwhelming victory in California, he was also told that Broderick was going to fight a duel but not with Dr. Gwin. Broderick, apparently on the very day before the *Bulletin* was expressing its contrarian optimism, had been challenged by David

Terry, whose honesty he had questioned at the breakfast table at the International Hotel.

Terry had planned to challenge Broderick since he first heard of his remarks. The man who had actually carried Perley's unsuccessful challenge to Broderick, Samuel Brooks, later had dinner with David Terry and his wife, Cornelia, at their home in Sacramento shortly after the episode and about a month before the election. The episode and its immediate aftermath were avoided during dinner conversation, but Terry's wife (who was also his cousin by marriage) did not seem her usually vivacious self. Then Terry excused himself to water his beloved garden. (During the grueling Sacramento summers delicate flowers could be killed if they were not watered every day—and the best time was the early evening.) As soon as Terry had left the room, "Neal" Terry burst into tears: "Oh, Mr. Brooks, Cousin David is determined to fight a duel with Broderick. Won't you do what you can to prevent it?" Brooks promised, but he also knew Terry. When he made up his mind about something, he was unyielding—and on this matter, when asked, he said simply to Brooks, "Never before has any politician or paper, in all that has been said about me, cast a reflection upon my integrity. No one shall do it."

Terry had planned to issue Broderick a challenge immediately after the election if an adequate apology or retraction had not been made by then. His friends, by arguing with him, had at least been able to have him first give Broderick the opportunity to do so. Rather than issue the peremptory challenge he had intended, Terry, following this advice, began by formally announcing to Broderick his displeasure at Broderick's remarks. He did this in a note of September 8.

> Sir:
>
> Some two months since, at the public table of the International Hotel in San Francisco, you saw fit to indulge in certain remarks concerning me, which were offensive in their nature.
>
> Before I had heard of the circumstance, your note of 20th of June, addressed to Mr. D. W. Perley, in which you declared that you would not respond to any call of a personal character during the political canvass just concluded, had been published. I have, therefore, not been permitted to take any notice of those remarks until the expiration of the limit fixed by yourself.
>
> I now take the earliest opportunity to require of you a retraction of those remarks.
>
> This note will be handed to you by my friend, Calhoun Benham, esq., who is acquainted with its contents, and will receive your reply.
>
> D. S. Terry

Broderick received the note at the Union Hotel on Kearny Street at 9:30 in the morning on September 8. Benham and Terry himself must have expected an immediate response, for the alternatives to Broderick were straightforward. He could retract his words (or insist they had been misrepresented or misconstrued—in this case unlikely), or he could stand behind them, and thereby occasion a formal challenge to a duel. Broderick said he had many other matters he had to deal with, and also friends to consult. A little annoyed, Benham requested a response by four o'clock the next afternoon. Broderick answered that he did not see any occasion to hurry. Now a little more annoyed, and perhaps with a bit of an edge in his voice, Benham assured him that there was no disposition on his or Terry's part to hurry the senator in the least. But there were others involved beyond the principals. He then suggested eight o'clock in the evening. To that Broderick said, rather absently, that this note had come as a complete surprise, which Benham likely took to mean that he had expected a challenge from Gwin, not Terry. The next morning Benham dashed off a quick note to Terry recounting the interview and explaining the delay. That evening Broderick gave him a written response:

Sir:

Your note of September 8th reached me through the hands of Mr. Calhoun Benham. The remarks used by me in the conversation referred to may be the subject of future misrepresentation; for obvious reasons, I have to desire you to state what were the remarks that you designate in your note as offensive, and of which you require of me retraction.

I remain, etc.
D. C. Broderick

Terry was perplexed by this further attempt at delay, and sat down that very day to specify the portion of Broderick's tirade which he found offensive. He specified just the remark that Terry was no longer considered by Broderick an honest man: "What I require is, the retraction of any words which were used calculated to reflect on my character as an officer and a gentleman."

On consideration, he thought Broderick was having him specify the words so that he could then retract precisely, or find some other way to remedy the situation short of a duel. He sent a note back to Neal in Sacramento to inform her of the good news: "I have reason to believe that my affair will be properly settled without the resort to the 'last argument.' " Cornelia herself then quickly sat down to pass the word along to Brooks. She hoped that "the Judge will come up on the boat tonight." That hope was the real reason she was writing to Brooks. In her state of agitation she wanted to write to someone, and a letter to Terry himself would likely pass him on the way home.

What Broderick had gained for himself was a day's delay during which he could consult his friends at his leisure. They were divided, but the most vocal were in favor of accepting the duel. The San Francisco *Bulletin,* on the other hand, having gotten wind of the challenge, was publicly calling upon Broderick to resolve the matter by "apologizing for his reflections upon the Judge, or placing his objections upon higher moral grounds than he has hitherto assumed." Such comments by a newspaper that had steadfastly during the campaign attacked Broderick for corruption only played into the hands of those advocating a duel with Terry. As one of them said to a Broderick man against the duel, "It is no use. You are too late. The fight has got to come, and this is the best time for it. Broderick never had a better chance, and he isn't going to get hurt. He can hit the size of a ten-cent piece at his distance every time. These Chivs have got to learn that there is one man they can't back down."

Broderick and his men believed that he could not avoid a duel against someone as a result of the acrimony and vilification of the last campaign. It was inevitable. They would have preferred to fight against Old Man Gwin. But more important was that Broderick be challenged rather than maneuvered into having to issue the challenge himself. If challenged, he would have choice of weapons—and he had become a crack shot with pistols, much better than Terry, especially in getting off an accurate shot rapidly.

But there was also much to be said against the duel. Broderick was exhausted, both physically and emotionally, by the ordeal of the campaign. He now looked much older than his years; in what should be his physical prime, he often, especially during times of relaxation, had the stooped look of an old man. Some worried that his recent exertions had permanently damaged his constitution. Certainly he now seemed susceptible to every passing illness, always seemed to be troubled by some cough or another. He could not be less prepared for the emotional ordeal of a duel. Moreover, he had never been psychologically suited for dueling, no matter how good a shot he had become. Broderick had the temperament of a prizefighter. His nerves steadied only after having given and taken a few good blows. He was even like that in his speeches, normally beginning weakly, like a rank amateur, and only gradually gaining his footing. There was no opportunity for such give-and-take in a duel, where everything came down to a single moment, where nerves—not simple physical courage—was what counted.

To Terry's second note, that of September 9, Broderick replied that very evening, acknowledging the questioning of Terry's honesty, repeating what he said "so far as my recollection serves me" and refusing to take back his words. He did tone down these words though, omitting both "damned" and "wretch." But other than that Broderick was defiant: "You are the best judge as to whether this language affords good grounds for offense." Of course, this left Terry no choice. Late on the night of September 9 Terry penned his formal challenge:

Sir:

Some months ago you used language concerning me, offensive in nature. I waited the lapse of a period of time fixed by yourself before I asked for reparation therefore at your hands. You replied, asking specifications of the language used which I regarded as offensive. In another letter I gave you specification and reiterated my demand for a retraction. To this last letter you reply, acknowledging the use of the offensive language imputed to you, and not making the retraction required. This course on your part leaves me no other alternative but to demand the satisfaction usual among gentlemen, which I accordingly do. Mr. Benham will make the necessary arrangements.

Your obedient servant,

D. S. Terry

This note was rushed to Broderick, who sat down immediately to dash off his reply:

Sir:

Your note of the above date has been received at one o'clock A.M., September 10th. In response to the same, I will refer you to my friend, Hon. J. C. McKibben, who will make the necessary arrangements demanded in your letter.

I remain, etc.,

D. C. Broderick

At this point the additional seconds were chosen. David Colton was chosen by Broderick, but Terry's choice must have caused some bitter remarks by Broderick. Colonel Jack Hayes, although like Terry a former Texas Ranger, had been elected as county clerk of San Francisco largely as a result of Broderick's support.

A meeting between the two pairs of seconds was then arranged. At it Broderick's seconds, because he was the challenged party, presented the articles for the duel. They were as detailed as the prescriptions for a religious rite:

1st. Principals to be attended by two seconds and a surgeon each; also by a person to load the weapons. This article not to exclude the drivers of the vehicles. If other parties obtrude, the time and place may be changed at the instance of either party.

2nd. Place of meeting, on the farm adjoining the Lake House ranch. The road to the farm-house leaves the old Lake House road, where you strike the first fence of the Lake House property, about a mile before you reach the Lake House. There you take a road to the left, which brings you to the farm-house, on the upper end of the lake (Laguna Merced), occupied by William Higgins. This is the general neighborhood; the precise spot to be determined when the parties meet.

3rd. Weapons, duelling pistols.

4th. Distance, ten paces; parties facing each other; pistols to be held with muzzles vertically downwards.

5th. Word to be given as follows to wit: the inquiry shall first be made "Gentleman, are you ready?" Upon each party replying "Ready," the word "Fire" shall be given, to be followed by the words "One, two." Neither party to raise his pistol before the word "Fire," nor to discharge it after the word "two." The intervals between the words "Fire, one, two," to be exemplified by the party winning the word as near as may be.

6th. The weapons to be loaded on the ground in the presence of a second of each party.

7th. Choices of position and the giving of the word to be determined by chance —throwing up a coin, as usual.

8th. Choice of the two weapons to be determined by chance, as in article 7th.

9th. Choice of the respective weapons of parties to be determined on the ground, by throwing up a coin, as usual; that is to say, each party bringing their pistols, and the pair to be used to be determined by chance, as in article 7th.

Time, Monday, 12 September, 1859, at 5½ o'clock A.M.

The seconds for Terry objected to the location, as if suspecting that this would somehow give Broderick an unwarranted advantage. But they more strongly objected against article five, which specified that the firing had to be finished before the count of two. This was unusual, if not entirely unprecedented. The common count was three. The reason Broderick's seconds had slipped this item in was obvious enough to everyone. Broderick was reputed a consummate shot at quick-draw firing. Both men would have to shoot with hardly any time for aiming. As Broderick put it to a friend who urged him to avoid the duel, "Don't you fear, John; I can shoot twice to Terry's once; beat him shooting every time."

Terry's seconds did everything they could to get Broderick's seconds to acquiesce to the customary count. But they were adamant. In the end the matter had to be left to Terry, and he decided that as challenger he was in no position to insist. So the articles, as originally submitted, were accepted.

Of course, if President Buchanan a continent away knew about the upcoming duel, then so did everyone in San Francisco. The local newspapers wrote about it as if it were a long-anticipated sporting event. The consensus was that Broderick had the advantage.

Here is the assessment of the San Francisco *Morning Call,* under the headline A DEAD SHOT: "It is generally understood that Judge Terry is a first-rate shot, but it is doubtful whether he is as unerring with the pistol as Senator Broderick. This gentleman, recently, in practicing in a gallery, fired two hundred shots at the usual distance, and plumped the mark every time. As he is also a man of firmer nerve than his opponent, we may look this morning for unpleasant news."

In fact, the unpleasant news was to be deferred for a day. Dueling was illegal (thanks to the provision Gwin had supported in the state constitution), and so the authorities had to cover themselves in a duel as widely publicized as this one. On the morning of September 12, when all the participants had gathered, a sheriff appeared to arrest the principals. Actually the sheriff had to wait to arrest the Terry party. They had ridden out from San Francisco along the coast, and had lost their bearings. They waited for three hours for Broderick and his men to show up before they realized they must be at the wrong place. It was so cold and damp there they had taken the blankets off their horses to wrap themselves with. Then they sent out a scout to find the others, which he did quickly. So they belatedly arrived at the site, only then to be arrested.

Ironically, Broderick had then to present himself before Judge Coon, who had been elected to his office by the support of the Committee of Vigilance. Presumably, everyone in the court knew that this was a charade, but the accused duly submitted themselves to the judge's authority, and he duly released everyone concerned on his own recognizance. As the *Bulletin* reported matter-of-factly, "It is supposed they will fight within a day or two." This time the *Bulletin* was right.

The seconds had quickly agreed that the duel should occur the next day, at the same time and the same place. Terry's surgeon, however, decided that he had had enough of this business, and left that afternoon on the Stockton boat.

Terry was not his usual confident self. Benham said lamely, "Judge, I hope you will be successful." Terry winced back, "I don't know. Broderick fires quick." Then, recovering himself a bit, "If he doesn't kill me, I shall hurt him."

Broderick spent the night with his close friend Edward Baker, the former partner of Lincoln who had defended Cora and was now a leading Republican. Broderick could not settle down that night. Probably it was his illness, a cold of some sort; but there were those in retrospect who sensed a foreboding in all his behavior in the last few days. What did he have left to live for? His political career seemed at an end. His party had deserted him. And the future of the country was in the hands of Southern slave owners and black Republicans; whether the likes of Stephen Douglas and William Gwin realized it or not, there was no longer any defensible middle ground.

The next morning the duelists came together at the same place. A cold morning made even more raw by a wind off the lake. Both men had on heavy overcoats and soft felt hats. Terry had his hat jauntily back on his head, whereas Broderick had his pulled down almost to his eyes. Terry seemed completely composed, as did Broderick. But those who knew the senator well could detect in him the rigidity of movement and lack of facial expression they usually took to mean that he was inwardly seething with rage.

A crowd of about eighty had gathered to watch the duel. Most had come by horse, but a few had walked. The horses were nibbling the grass, itself quite wet from the low-hanging fog that the sun might not be able to break this chilly day. There were seagulls in the air, some noisily swooping down, as if curious at this unusual human intrusion into this ordinarily deserted spot.

The human solemnity of the scene was broken only by the man, a German, whom Broderick had brought as his surgeon, Dr. Loehr. He bustled about, trying to be important—and with him he carried a sack of rattling instruments. From the sack protruded a long saw. As Broderick paced back and forth while waiting for the arrangements to be completed, the rattling surgeon tried to keep up with him, making conversation in broken English. It was funny in a grisly way—but no one laughed. Terry's newly chosen surgeon, Dr. William Hammond, was in contrast almost nonchalant. He shook Terry's hand—and then walked a suitable distance away, took off his overcoat, folded it, placed it on the grass, and sat on it, to be as comfortable as possible while he waited to see if he would be needed.

Broderick won the coin toss for position, and predictably chose to stand with his back to the sun, which was now finally visible over the low hills to the east. Terry would have to shoot half-blinded by glare, and yet he still did not pull down his hat. Terry won the toss for the pistols, and of course he chose his own, French dueling pistols that had been used for this purpose only once before. Their barrels were about a foot long, and the stocks oddly shaped. These pistols were then examined by the seconds, and loaded, Broderick's by a gunsmith in attendance and Terry's by a friend.

The duelists now tossed off their overcoats. From a distance they looked almost like twins, in their full black suits, with buttoned-up frock coats and collarless shirts. Both Broderick and Terry passed to their seconds the contents of their pockets, Broderick in particular handing over his watch. Now each man was examined by a second of the other to make certain that he had retained no object in his pockets that might deflect a bullet, an ominous process to anyone who remembered how Broderick's only other duel had turned out.

The two men were now called to their positions. Terry easily assumed his—erect, sideways to his opponent, eyes directly upon him, feet in line.

He put his pistol first behind him, out of view of Broderick, and then slowly brought it forward, with muzzle down, until it pointed just to the side of his front foot. From the relaxed position of his arm, it would have been hard to infer that he was holding anything at all.

If the two had looked to be twins before, they no longer did. There was something unnatural in the rigidity of Broderick's stance. Then Terry's chief second realized that he was not holding his pistol directly down—as specified by the articles—but at an odd, awkward angle out from his body. He immediately objected about this to Broderick's chief second, McKibben, who reluctantly agreed. Embarrassingly, he now had to go onto the field of honor to explain to Broderick that he had to hold his arm straight. Broderick nodded, but then to McKibben's horror Broderick seemed unable to straighten his shooting arm. He was so tense he could not straighten his arm. Finally, Broderick with disgust used his left arm to push down his right. When McKibben got back to his position, he realized that Broderick while straightening his arm had inadvertently partially squared himself to Terry. In his nervousness Broderick was presenting to Terry almost twice the target that he should. McKibben at this point must have had to suppress a growing sense that the duel had been a mistake, had to be stopped.

But it was too late. The other second of Broderick now began the call in a steady voice. "Gentlemen, are you ready?" "Ready"—Terry's answer had been immediate, although his voice was so tense as to be scarcely recognizable. Now all eyes turned to Broderick. Why was he delaying? His right arm was rebelling again, his hand fidgeted as he tried to get a relaxed grip on his pistol. After a few seconds that seemed like an hour (during which some thought he was mumbling something to himself about his seconds), he nodded, gestured with his left hand, and said, "Ready," all at once. Colton had informed the duelists that he would try to time his cadence to be as much as possible like the tolling of the hour in a cathedral clock. So he now tolled. "Fire." "One." "Two."

Broderick fired first, just as Colton said, "One." He had raised his arm quickly in a straight line toward Terry, but the pistol discharged prematurely and the bullet made a furrow in the grass, a minuscule cannonball heading directly toward Terry but dying in the grass only nine feet from Broderick, over whose face a look of simple surprise quickly passed. Terry barely made his shot before the final toll of "Two." But did clearly, all agreed later. A puff of what seemed dust came from high on the right side of Broderick's coat, from the lapel as if some invisible valet had begun to brush him off after a hard ride in the country. It seemed like nothing, although a tear could be seen where the ball had struck.

Terry in disappointment (it had felt like a good shot) exclaimed excitedly that he had hit him too wide, only winged him. He started to walk off, and happened to be heading directly toward his old friend Brooks, to whom Neal had confided his intention to fight this duel, Brooks who had been so adamantly against it that Terry had consequently decided not to have him as a second. But Brooks now was yelling at him: "Remain in your position; it may not be over." Terry looked at him blankly for a moment, and then quickly returned to his position, and waited there with folded arms.

But, in the meantime, Broderick had extended both his arms far out, as if he were trying to catch his balance. The pistol was still in his right hand. He looked ridiculous; so rigid, he seemed to be hanging in the air. Then his body shuddered, the right arm grotesquely; and the pistol dropped. Now not a shudder, but a full convulsion struck him. He turned to the left, more a marionette than a man, his head drooping—a marionette being played with by a gigantic child. Then his left knee gave way, then his right. He was praying now, or so one would think if one did not see the rigid left arm holding him up, or the look on his face that made his seconds cringe as they rushed up. He said apologetically to the first who arrived that he had tried to rise but "the blood blinded me." Nobody could see any blood, except a tiny amount about the mouth.

Suddenly someone in the crowd shouted, "This is murder." And there was a brief scuffle. During all this time Terry had remained in his place, arms still folded, the pistol still in his right hand. Seeing that Broderick had fallen, Brooks asked, "Are you satisfied?" This was not meant as an accusation, but Terry bristled, "For the present." Then Brooks was upset: "Why for the present?" "Because Broderick's defamation still remains. He must retract it." "Where did you hit him?" Terry tapped his right lapel. Brooks, now almost pleading, "Then you have injured him badly." Terry, matter-of-factly, "No. I do not think so. Anyhow, I did not want to kill him, but to wound him."

While this exchange was going on, Broderick's seconds were trying to determine how badly hurt he was. Unfortunately, Broderick's surgeon proved to be as big a fool as he had looked in the preliminaries. He was completely nonplussed, and in packing his bag of grisly contraptions he had apparently neglected to include the appropriate bandages. Terry's surgeon, Dr. Hammond, was called in. He examined the wound, and judged it not to be dangerous. There was no significant blood from the mouth, not more than a tablespoon worth. The ball had apparently not hit the lungs, only flesh. He bandaged Broderick, and gave him some brandy from his flask, probably Broderick's first drink in more than a decade.

Terry, who had resigned his position on the Supreme Court to take part in this duel, returned to Oakland still convinced that he had not seriously wounded his opponent. He said to one of his companions during this trip that if he had had time to deliberate when Broderick misfired he too would have thrown away his shot. But he was so tense with reports of Broderick's marksmanship, and so rushed by the need to get a shot in before the count of two, that he fired without thinking. He had apparently read the story in the *Morning Call*, and it had thoroughly frightened him as the Broderick men who edited that paper had probably intended it to.

Broderick's men carried him to a wagon; during the trip to a nearby house they exchanged worried looks when Broderick complained of an unbearably painful weight on his chest. But they repeated to him Dr. Hammond's judgment that the wound was not serious. Nonetheless, despite the lack of blood from his mouth, Terry's bullet had hit a lung. It was soon obvious that his case was hopeless. David Broderick, after lingering for three days, died at 9:20 on the morning of September 16.

Gwin and the rest of the Chivalry had followed the challenge and duel closely. The death of Broderick on the field of honor, killed by a Southern gentleman, for many of them was a fitting conclusion to the campaign of 1859, a cause for considerable satisfaction. Gwin, however, knew better.

Gwin had in the heat of the campaign come to hate Broderick as Broderick hated him. Nonetheless, when the election results came in, Gwin could regain his characteristic composure. This victory over Broderick, together with his gelding of Broderick in the Senate, was all that he could wish. He saw things as always in social terms; that was why he could hardly understand how Broderick could break party discipline to condemn a Democratic president. Broderick was no more fit to be a senator than he was to be a guest at one of Gwin's fancy dress balls. The man simply did not understand, did not know that he did not understand.

And that made everything all right now, now that Broderick had been reduced to complete inconsequence by the election of 1859. Without significant support in his own state, Broderick's career could not even have been helped by Stephen Douglas in the White House. And Douglas's desertion of Broderick in this election showed that the Little Giant understood this. His path to the presidency went through the South. What chance he had, did require shedding allies like Broderick in order to court men like Gwin. Anyway, Douglas probably still smarted over Broderick's domineering of him at the end of the struggle over Kansas, just the kind of thing the Little Giant could never forget or forgive. So, now, with the election of 1859, Broderick was truly and finally finished. But then came the challenge by Terry.

The only thing that could save Broderick, make him a formidable nemesis again, transform him into a phantom that had to be fought but could not . . . Gwin had already had a premonition of this during the campaign, much as Broderick himself seemed to know at times that this campaign would be his last. The only thing that could save Broderick now as a force in California politics, and perhaps make him an unconquerable force at that, was his own death.

Gwin could be forgiven if when he heard of the actual details of the duel he thought for a moment that Broderick had squared himself to Terry and then fired his pistol into the ground purposefully, knowing that this was now the only way to revenge himself on Gwin. While Gwin's friends were congratulating themselves on the honorable killing of a once formidable adversary, Gwin himself was full of foreboding. And Gwin did not have to wait long for this foreboding to be confirmed.

The newspapers, immediately and predictably, began denouncing the institution of dueling, and condemned those friends of the principals who had advocated it. So the *Bulletin* wrote, "Both principals seemed to have been surrounded by a set of bloody Hotspurs, who were disposed to urge on the meeting to a fatal issue, rather than allow on either side the minutest waiving of senseless punctilio." As for Terry, the *Bulletin* thought that he "should be marked as another Cain." Of course, about its own earlier interest in the duel, the *Bulletin* was silent.

There was a good deal of spontaneous grief for Broderick throughout the state that so recently had voted overwhelmingly against him. A diarist in Marysville, a small town north of Sacramento, recorded that when news of Broderick's death reached there "our men hung their heads and paced the streets in sullen silence." So Broderick men did also in San Francisco, where the flags on all public and many private buildings were being flown at half mast. But sullen silence soon gave way to loud demands for explanation and even revenge. Rumors began to swirl about, alleging a conspiracy.

Broderick, it was reliably reported, had been given a pistol with a hair trigger; Terry's seconds had whispered on the field to him that the fix was in; Broderick himself realized this as he stood at his dueling place fumbling with his weapon, and he had been heard to mutter that his seconds were "children." These rumors became so widespread that Broderick's seconds finally felt the need to publish a formal denial in a local newspaper.

These seconds insisted that they had performed their offices well. If there had been any advantage in the arrangements, Broderick had it. They had no indication that the pistols were at all different; they had brought their own gunsmith just to make certain. "Had we believed there was any unfairness, there could have been no meeting." This insistent public denial of any wrongdoing, of course, only served to confirm in the minds of many that there had been some.

By this time an autopsy had been performed. The bullet had entered high on Broderick's right chest where the puff of dust had been observed; it had traversed his body through the upper part of his left lung. The spent bullet had been found under his left arm.

Broderick's remains were now laid in state, in a rear room on the first floor of the Union Hotel on Kearny Street. A steady stream of mourners filed past the open metal casket, which itself rested on a row of stools. The only color in the room was from the flags that had been hung on the wall. Otherwise, the room was draped in black, as was the coffin. The drapes from the coffin fell in long, elegant folds upon the floor all around it, except at the far end where the drapes had been neatly tucked around his feet, covering them, so that you could not see whether he had on shoes. A strangely suggestive detail. Broderick in state, perhaps daintily barefoot, or with his crude hobnailed boots hidden beneath the elegant cover.

Broderick himself was dressed in a black suit. Everyone said he looked natural, if a little thinner. But there was something not quite right about his aspect. The rough stone cutter's hands were folded neatly on his chest. It was obviously Broderick, but he did not look like himself. He looked small—and placid.

Compared to this gloom, the inquest was almost comic relief. The gunsmith the Broderick people brought with them to the duel, a man named Lagoarde, testified about the pistols. He provided a lengthy critique of the pistols. They were poorly made in a number of ways, entirely unsuitable. He insisted, in particular, that he had told Broderick's seconds the guns were too light and would discharge with the slightest jar, a contention the seconds denied vehemently. As for Lagoarde's critique, it was well known that he thought no gun made well except those made by himself. It finally dawned on the court that what at first seemed important testimony was really just an expression of professional hubris. Lagoarde was using the inquest to promote himself as the best gunsmith in San Francisco.

The intelligently reasoned findings of the inquest made no difference, nor did the self-serving silliness of Lagoarde. Rumor was now a living thing, a minor goddess spreading her mischief and malice, with the San Francisco newspapers acting as her enthusiastic acolytes. The pistols had surely been tampered with, or at least Broderick's had been. They must have been marked subtly so that Terry would know which one to take. One of Terry's seconds had whispered to him just before the duel not to worry; Broderick had the trick pistol, so Terry could take the full time to aim. Now, somehow, the exact words of the second could be quoted. Moreover, Broderick's second running up to the wounded man now heard him say not that his vision was clouded by blood but the well-turned aphorism, "I die because I was opposed to a corrupt administration and the extension of slavery." (Others had him saying that as his last words.) If this were not all infuriating enough, eyewitnesses reported that after the duel, knowing full well that Broderick was dying, Terry and his Chiv friends went out and had a celebratory breakfast. There was, moreover, a well-advanced plot to use the code of honor to kill every politician who publicly opposed the transformation of California into a slave state.

Cornelius Cole, a leading California Republican, wrote back a despondent letter to Seward to inform him of Broderick's death. After quoting Broderick's aphorism on his own death (as his dying words), Cole then added, "His death was decreed by his enemies months ago and was not unexpected. Our sky is now gloomy, but some rays of hope penetrate the dark clouds. Mr. Broderick could hardly be spared in the Senate; California is in need of such men there." Sincere as was Cole's grief, he must have realized that the death of Broderick was going to drive thousands of wavering California Democrats into the Republican fold.

The funeral for Broderick, on Sunday, September 18, 1859, was the greatest yet held in San Francisco, far greater than that of King of William. Portsmouth Square, the site of so much of the tumult of the 1850s in which Broderick had played so great a role, was hung with wreaths, crepe, and other funeral trappings. The square was more than crowded; not just the square but every window and roof in the vicinity seemed filled with eager spectators. The total was generously estimated at thirty thousand.

At precisely 1:30 a path was cleared from the Union Hotel to the flagstaff on the square where a speaker's podium had been erected. Then an honor guard of seven horsemen was seen, behind them a crowd of pallbearers, dozens of them, all grim faced, and in the midst of them a huge cluster of flowers beneath which could be barely made out something black and metallic, the casket.

When the casket was finally resting on the bier in front of the podium, Edward Baker stepped up, and delivered a lengthy funeral oration. He began, "A Senator lies dead in our midst. He is wrapped in a bloody shroud; and we to whom his toils and cares were given are about to bear him to the place appointed to all the living."

Much of the following speech, naturally, eulogized Broderick as an exemplar of all the virtues. Baker conceded that Broderick's efforts to get elected senator were at times shady. (He used a softer term.) But this was Broderick's thirst for fame, "that last infirmity of noble minds."

Baker, as a seasoned orator, knew that the easiest way to praise Broderick was to contrast him with his opponents. For instance: "Consider his public acts—weigh his private character—and before the grave encloses him forever, judge between him and his enemies!" It was but a short step from this to making him a martyr for his political principles, indeed the victim of a plot. As Baker put it, "His death was a political necessity poorly veiled beneath the guise of a private quarrel."

Baker did return in his peroration to eulogize the fallen senator: "Who can speak for masses of men with a passionate love for the classes from whence he sprung? Who can defy the blandishments of power, the insolence of office, the corruption of administrations? What hopes are buried with him in the grave?"

Nonetheless, it was the suggestion of a conspiracy that gave the volatile audience a focus for its grief: "I am here to say, that whatever in the code of honor or out of it demands or allows a deadly combat where there is not in all things entire and certain equality, is a prostitution of the name, is an evasion of the substance, and is a shield, emblazoned with the name of Chivalry, to cover the malignity of murder." (Weaving in the word "Chivalry," as if incidentally, was a particularly nice touch.)

The oration itself, at the time generally regarded as the greatest ever delivered in California, was finished a little before 2:30. The casket then was lifted from the bier and carried to the hearse waiting on Kearny Street. Now the bells of City Hall, muffled in mourning, were heard leadenly tolling as the procession formed behind the hearse. The bells of City Hall then were being answered by echoes coming from all sides; the firehouses were honoring one of their own, the best of their own. The procession now began, with the hearse drawn by four stately black horses. The thirty-five official pallbearers surrounded it, and they were followed by 132 official mourners.

The *Alta California,* so often Broderick's opponent, had anticipated the mood of the day when it printed in large letters, within a black border: "The lion hunt is over. The jackals that long hung howling upon his tread are at rest after their feast of blood, while in the cold majesty of death sleeps the great victim of their murderous deed."

The procession slowly wound its way through the city so that all could see—from the Plaza to Clay, then down Montgomery to Market, off Market along Battery, and then up California—a gradual, serpentine procession but ultimately making its way toward the west where the sun was declining. Everyone in the city, it seemed, was somewhere in the procession. The firemen, more than a thousand of them, were particularly prominent marching together, four abreast, Broderick's own company distinguished by their black badges. They were followed by at least a hundred horse-drawn carriages and wagons. Now the casket had reached Vallejo and turned up Powell.

The procession stretched for almost a mile, as it wound up and down the hills toward the cemetery that overlooked the whole city to its east, and the ocean to its west, and the Golden Gate to the north. The procession took two and a half hours to reach the windswept cemetery of Lone Mountain. There, a priest said a few words, as if to justify his own presence since Broderick had never been known to darken the inside of a church willingly. The senator could not be buried in sacred ground, he explained regretfully, because he had died in a duel. However, the priest could assure those within hearing that Broderick had near the end confessed and received the last rites. Father Harrington then turned and loudly addressed Broderick himself: "Peace to thy ashes, joy to thy spirit, truest and most unselfish of friends, and most moral of public men."

Most moral of public men. When Gwin read those words and the excerpts of Baker's eulogy (the whole of it was soon published in the thousands as a popular pamphlet), he must have felt a sickness at heart that resembled grief. Not grief for Broderick but grief for himself.

Gwin was in an impossible position. To deny the rumors would be to seem only to confirm them. He might have hoped that the careful work of the inquest might eventually calm opinion—but he knew better. When he had headed the inquiry into the Hounds a decade before (had it really been only a decade?), he knew legal niceties were irrelevant. So were careful distinctions. Even irrefutable evidence.

Terry had killed Broderick. Gwin could not fault him. He had had sufficient provocation, and had followed honorable procedures; he had behaved like a gentleman. With his sense of honor at stake, Terry could not consider the consequences. But Gwin would have to live with them. Terry had killed Broderick, and Gwin would henceforth be regarded as his true killer. His cowardly killer who would not face the man himself. Not much better than a bushwhacker.

It quickly became commonplace to refer to Broderick's death as an assassination. George Wilkes called it simply "murder" and explained that "no one but a bitter wretch and murderer" would fire at an opponent who had already accidentally discharged his weapon. Even one usually levelheaded politician wrote that he was certain Broderick was assassinated because he had opposed breaking up California into a southern and northern portion. "Broderick's denunciation of this scheme, I have no doubt brought on the conflict which led to his assassination. It was pretty well understood that he was to be assassinated anyway. If Terry failed, somebody else was to kill him." Against such reasoning Gwin was helpless.

Now he had to leave for the next session of Congress. Usually the departure of a senator for Washington would be the occasion for a great celebration; that would be particularly so for a senator who has just led his faction to an overwhelming victory. The departure of Gwin showed that he had almost overnight become a pariah in the state he had so ably represented.

There was a crowd to see Gwin off, all right, but no celebration. As he and a new Chivalry congressman stood on the deck of the steamer, they realized that their own supporters had prudently stayed home. In their place was a sullen group not unlike those who had gathered to support the vigilantes at their executions. The mood of the crowd was expressed in a single large sign: "The will of the People—may the murderers of David C. Broderick never return to California."

Gwin must have expected much of this, although even he must have been surprised by its swiftness and its severity. Perhaps he consoled himself that this too might pass. He had been reviled before, only to recover. He would go to Washington, again be a good senator, and prove his worth by delivering patronage, the kind of patronage that always would outrage the Brodericks of this world, outrage them because they could not share it. Eventually the people would see reason, or at least their self-interest. The *Alta California*, so long his support in San Francisco, might sneeringly advise him to look at the empty seat near him in the Senate chamber, and consult his conscience if he yet had any left. But, once he got back into his element, he would retrieve what could be retrieved. Perhaps someday he would look back upon this moment and laugh. No, not laugh. But things would look different in even a few years.

They would, but not in the ways he hoped.

Nonetheless, it could not have helped his mood when he learned that a similar celebration of Broderick's life and vilification of his enemies had occurred in New York City. John Dwinelle had delivered an oration that was admired almost as much as Baker's. And the procession through the streets of New York was, if anything, larger than that through San Francisco. Broderick now was a sacrifice to the Minotaur of human slavery. In his grave he was larger than life, and a convenient exemplum with which Northerners could demonstrate their sense of moral superiority over their Southern brethren. That he, Gwin, the most dexterous of men, should have allowed himself to be involved in all this, that he a gentleman should have allowed a stonecutter's son to induce him to descend to his own level, to fight with him in the gutter . . . this was all a measure of the man's demonic power. He tainted everything he touched, including Gwin's own life. And yet now it all was over.

William Gwin, like the United States of America, was well rid of this Lucifer who did not know his place, well rid of him. And yet the question must have flickered, back and forth, again and again, across his mind as he thought about the outpouring of support in New York as well as his last glimpse of San Francisco. A question that gradually eclipsed reasoned calculations. Would he ever be truly finished with Broderick?

10

Gwin must have returned to Washington at the end of 1859 with a certain apprehension. He could not be sure what the reaction there would be to Broderick's death. Republicans, even a friend like Seward, were likely to try to make political hay out of this. How was Stephen Douglas going to respond? Broderick, of course, would be publicly lamented in the Senate as the most important American since Alexander Hamilton to die in a duel. Would Gwin be held responsible?

When Gwin did arrive in Washington, he quickly realized his worries over the death of Broderick were needless. Washington was in a furor, but not over the death of the junior senator from California. John Brown's attempt to incite a slave insurrection at Harpers Ferry reduced every other issue to inconsequence. He had never seen Washington so bitterly divided. Senator Hammond was only half-joking when he said that now in both the House and Senate "the only persons who do not have a revolver and a knife are those who have two revolvers."

The social life which his wife so enjoyed and which he saw as a balm that could soothe political differences had effectively come to an end. Now factions only socialized with other factions. Grand parties for all the Washington elite, such as the Gwins' now legendary costume ball, were fraught with peril, if not simply impossible. Mary Gwin realized this one evening as her guests were about to be called to dinner. One lady had to accompany Senator Seward to the table, and Mary Gwin realized at the last moment that no lady present would accept his arm. So she accompanied him herself.

With civility almost impossible among the leaders themselves, the government itself was scarcely functioning. One visitor to Washington in 1859, a lawyer, summarized ably the common view when he wrote, "We seem to be drifting into destruction before our eyes in utter helplessness. The Administration is utterly depopularized; the President is embarrassed with insoluble questions; Congress is paralyzed by party spirit; and everybody seems to despair of any help from man, though many are looking vaguely for they know not what interposition of Providence."

In all this, depressing as it was, Gwin saw for himself a clear role. And it was a role at which he excelled. Not the uncomfortable one of the public fighter, as he had had to be in the last election. But rather as the artisan of compromise. He had played this role once before during a national crisis; few had as much to do with the Compromise of 1850 as he did, except of course Clay and Webster and Douglas. And he wished to make his contribution this time as well, but not as unobtrusively. Now perhaps he could help save the Union once again.

He decided that to serve best in this crisis he first had publicly to make clear his own position so that all reasonable parties could recognize him as an honest agent of compromise. Southerners were saying, on the floor of the Senate in response to John Brown's raid, that if a Republican were elected president they of the South, as the senator from Alabama Clement Clay put it, would "tear the Constitution to pieces and look to our guns for justice." Back home, they were, if possible, even more intemperate. Jefferson Davis had told the Mississippi legislature in November that rather than recognize a Republican president Mississippi's star would be torn from the flag "to be set even on the perilous ridge of battle as a sign round which Mississippi's best and bravest should gather to the harvest-home of death."

Northern senators, however, were not taking such outbursts seriously enough. In fact, many tended to dismiss Southern contentions as all bluff and bluster. For compromise to be possible, the North had to recognize that the South was serious about secession. So Senator Gwin, who previously had done his best to avoid sectional issues, now rose to address them directly. He gave a lengthy oration on the floor of the Senate concerning what he called the "extreme peril" the nation faced.

He declared himself emphatically in favor of the preservation of the Union. But he also pleaded with the representatives of the North not to turn the government in Washington into one merely acting in their sectional interest. He spoke as a senator from the only Northern state that had voted in favor of the national administration in the recent election. It had to be recognized that the Republican Party was a sectional party: "It has no existence in the Southern States, and never can have any existence there." If the Republicans won the next presidential election, then support for secession in the South would be overwhelming. This was no bluff. The South would secede. And it could well flourish as an independent nation.

Gwin pleaded with the Northerners to face facts. The South did have the population, the resources, the harbors and waterways, the economy to become a prosperous independent nation. In light of this, secession was an eminently practical alternative. If the federal government did not behave responsively to Southern fears—and John Brown's raid showed that these fears were not groundless—the South would leave, diminishing forever the United States as a nation.

There will be no internal revolution in the South as the abolitionists hope, no spontaneous slave insurrection. John Brown's raid also showed that the slaves of the South are content with their lot. They love their masters. If they are content, why does the North want to interfere?

Gwin at this point was starting to sound like Hammond. But his intention was not to defend morally the institution of slavery (as Hammond did), but to try to get Northerners to realize that the only revolution likely in the South would be one that would take them out of the Union. This led him to his most important point.

Sectional divisions, grievous as they were at present, could be overcome. Gwin could speak to this as a senator from California. So he described in detail how those sectional interests had been transcended in the 1850 compromise that had resulted in the admission of California into the Union. To preserve the Union, the voices of contention and advocacy had to be quieted, and a reasoning together had to be resumed. The example of 1850 showed how this could be done. It was still possible if all kept their heads and acted for the common good.

So, trying to strike a note of calm, he concluded his speech plainly, almost blandly: "We revere this Union, we honor it, we desire to preserve it. My only object in the remarks I have made was to present to the country the idea that there is danger, and to submit whether it is not best to pause before parties get so much excited that it will be impossible to prevent collision."

Clearly, for once, he had hoped to make a great speech, a speech worthy of the grand triumvirate whose rule of the Senate had ended in 1850. But Gwin's métier was the committee room, the drawing room, the cloakroom. He had done the best he could, but eloquence that could move the nation was not in him. Even while he was delivering it, he must have realized that it would have absolutely no effect upon his colleagues. To try to play the pacificator in this befouled climate was futility itself. So he had to be patient, and hope the situation would somehow change.

The furor over John Brown's raid had so distracted the Senate that the announcement of Broderick's death was made only in February. Each Senate faction had a spokesman lament his passing, most in fairly perfunctory terms. Seward, however, in delivering the Republican eulogy could not resist a few opportunistic swipes at Gwin and the Chivalry.

He talked of how worried the Senate had been when reports of gold rush California reached it: "As we looked upon these tumultuous assemblages, we asked, how shall even peace and life be secured among them? How and when shall the political chaos be reduced into the solid substance of a civil state?"

Seward, of course, knew the correct answer to that question. Gwin could be certain of that. California had become a more or less civil state through the efforts and shrewdness of William Gwin and men like him. Seward had learned at least this much about California at Gwin's dinner table. But it was obvious where Seward was heading, and it was not toward giving Gwin his due: "Even while we were asking these questions, we saw that State rise up before us in just proportion, firm and vigorous, strong and free, complete in the fullest material and moral sufficiency, and at the same time, loyal and faithful to the Federal Union. The hand that principally shaped it was that of David C. Broderick."

Gwin knew well enough not to take this personally or even seriously, but it was galling to have to listen to an old friend lying through his teeth at one's expense. Worse still were the reports Gwin was getting back from California concerning his major speech on the sectional crisis. All the newspapers were willfully misrepresenting what he had said. It was headlined in one newspaper "Gwin's Disunion Speech," as if saying that the South could secede was the same as saying that it should. Another newspaper judged it "manifest treason and sedition." Moreover, the Chivalry-dominated legislature, with timing so bad as to be buffoonery, had chosen this moment to vote in favor of legislation to divide the state into two, anticipating the division of the Union.

Still Gwin tried to do his duty in Washington. Milton Latham, five days into his term as governor, had gotten himself elected to fill Broderick's seat in the U.S. Senate, this despite Gwin's throwing his support to Weller. On March 5, he presented his credentials and took his seat. When he arrived in Washington, he did his best to avoid Gwin. But Gwin had President Buchanan intervene on his behalf.

Latham was making a courtesy call to the White House when Buchanan scolded him, "But you haven't called on Mrs. Gwin yet." The surprised Latham tried to fend this off, but Buchanan would have none of it: "Oh, I have heard her speak very highly of you. She hopes to see you one of her circle." Soon Latham was a member of the Gwin circle, and on a first-name basis with the likes of Hammond, Jeff Davis, and Vice President John Cabell Breckinridge (who had emerged as Buchanan's choice to follow him). So the Sacramento *Union* reported at the end of March, "A reconciliation was brought about between the Senators by Buchanan, at whose insistence Gwin made the advances necessary for a reconciliation, which were accepted by Latham, and the result cannot but prove beneficial to California, at least as far as legislation in Congress is concerned."

Perhaps Gwin thought this was the beginning of his rehabilitation in California politics. Latham at least now understood that Gwin was a different man in Washington from what he appeared in California, a man at ease in his true station and among his true peers. And Buchanan, for his part, knew that in the impending crisis Union Democrats had to stand together, whatever their past differences.

Gwin, as he had for a decade, tried again to get the transcontinental railroad legislation passed. This time he did have the votes, or thought he did until they dribbled away in sectional wrangling. Seward and Douglas were sympathetic, but the railroad was dead until after the presidential election of 1860. While acquiescing to this, Gwin still allowed his bitterness to show itself when the measure was finally tabled for this session. That he was outraged was clear even from the gallery. He now expected that he would never get the bill passed himself, for he did not expect to be returned to the Senate.

Among his friends Gwin had apparently begun to say that he would not even try to get reelected. He even confided as much to Latham—a sign of his new trust in him—who was quickly and firmly told to keep this to himself by Mrs. Gwin, perhaps a sign that she did not altogether regard Latham as someone to be trusted. She obviously still had hopes that he would seek another term, but he was more realistic. If a moderate Democrat was elected in 1860, he would seek either a place in the cabinet or a diplomatic post. Compared to the prospects in Washington for the 1860s, Chile might look like an attractive locale.

Gwin had placed his dwindling political hopes on Breckinridge getting the Democratic nomination over Douglas. He was actually dining with Breckinridge at the home of Senator Hammond when they heard the news that the Democratic convention—held in Charleston, South Carolina—had deadlocked between Breckinridge and Douglas, and had chosen a compromise candidate from the border states. In fact, only the first part was true.

The convention had deadlocked and adjourned without selecting a candidate. Now each faction was going to hold its own convention, and to nominate its own slate, Breckinridge heading one, Douglas the other. If that were not bad enough, the Republicans passed over Seward for a one-term former congressman, Abraham Lincoln, Baker's friend, whose chief distinction was that he had almost unseated Douglas in the last election. Moreover, the Know-Nothings had revived themselves sufficiently to put forward their own slate that had a reasonable chance to carry border states, and thereby to throw the election into the House, where their candidate might have a chance. When apprised of this strategy, Douglas responded with characteristic vigor: "By God, sir, the election shall never go into the House; before it shall go into the House, I will throw it to Lincoln." During their debates in the senatorial contest Douglas had come to regard Lincoln as much more than a clever backwoods orator.

Lincoln himself followed the strategy that had brought him the presidential nomination; in public he said and did absolutely nothing. It was also the same strategy that another relative unknown, William Henry Harrison, had followed to the White House two decades earlier. One of Harrison's handlers, Nicholas Biddle, left a description of his candidate's approach to campaigning that could have been applied as well to Lincoln in 1860: "Let him say not a single word about his principles, or his creed—let him say nothing—promise nothing. Let no Committee, no convention, no town meeting ever extract from him a single word, about what he thinks now, or what he will do hereafter. Let the use of pen and ink be wholly forbidden as if he were a mad poet in Bedlam.''

As it worked out, the only truly national candidate was Douglas, one national candidate against three regional candidates; but he was a truly national candidate who was likely to run second just about everywhere. Douglas, to his credit, realized late in the campaign that he had no chance and that Lincoln was going to be elected with an almost exclusively Northern vote. When in October the Republicans carried both Pennsylvania and Indiana (four states voted early), Douglas said to his secretary, "Mr. Lincoln is the next President. We must try to save the Union. I will go South." The presidency was out of his reach, but the Union itself depended upon him, all upon him.

Having returned to California for the election campaign, Gwin could follow in the newspapers the Little Giant's heroic campaign swing through the Deep South, defending the Union against all comers. And Gwin could imagine the toll it was taking on Douglas physically. Douglas was magnificent in defeat, but his greatest cause proved too much for him. Broken by his effort, Stephen Douglas would be dead a year after the election, at the age of forty-eight.

For Gwin there were discouraging developments on the West Coast as well. In the 1859 election, Edward Baker had run for the House of Representatives in California as a Republican. He had been swamped in the overwhelming Democratic victory engineered by Gwin and his allies. Now, due in part to his friendship with Lincoln, Baker's prospects for office had revived. He campaigned in Oregon for Lincoln as president and—amazingly—for himself as senator. More amazingly still, Oregon, another of the four states that held its election in October, went for Lincoln and Baker.

To make matters even worse, Senator-elect Baker then had time to travel to San Francisco to campaign for the California Republicans. The Silver Eagle of Republicanism, as he was now called, was his usual spellbinding self. Newspaper accounts would routinely intersperse the texts of his speeches with the audience responses (as if the text of a play). "Sensation" would give way to "tremendous applause and cheering," which then a few sentences later would be followed by "profound sensation."

This was all to be expected. As someone said of Baker, he could talk people, even intelligent people, "out of their five senses and six wits." What was not to be expected, or at least was inexcusable, was the shameless manner in which Baker exploited the memory of David Broderick.

Time and again, he would remind his audiences of how he had stood "by the bedside of my slaughtered friend Broderick, who fell in your cause and on your behalf." Nonsense, of course, but the plausible nonsense of demagoguery. Then Baker would feign that Broderick's death had caused in himself a crisis of faith: "And I cried, 'How long, oh, how long, shall the hopes of Freedom and her champion be crushed!' The tide has turned. I regret my little faith."

What Baker failed to mention, of course, was that Broderick, if he were alive, would have been doing everything in his power to get Douglas elected, not Lincoln. But popular eloquence is not to be restrained by paltry factuality. So Baker could appeal to the hundreds—no, the thousands of men "who loved him in his life and will be true to his memory always." As for himself, he was going to report to the Senate that Broderick's "ashes repose among a people who love him well; who are not and never will be forgetful of the manner of his life, nor the method of his death." Baker himself, of course, had apparently forgotten his slaughtered friend's funeral, where it had been clear to everyone that the corpse had not been cremated.

The tongue of Baker and the ashes of Broderick managed to carry a much-divided California for Lincoln by a mere 614 votes. During the campaign Gwin himself had been continually on the defensive. He was being attacked even for his alleged opposition to a transcontinental railroad. The reasoning behind such a charge was impeccable: California would have its ties to the Union strengthened by this railroad; Gwin was a secessionist; therefore, Gwin must be against the railroad. The fact that he could produce dozens of speeches he had given in favor of the railroad (to say nothing of the hundreds of hours he had spent in committee promoting the project) was irrelevant. Or rather showed how devious and dangerous a man he truly was.

Gwin began his trip back to Washington as soon as possible after the election, on November 10 aboard the steamship Sonora. This was a trying trip, for also aboard was Edward Baker. Baker, understandably, was full of himself. He had seen the future, and it was his. Gwin, in contrast, was full of foreboding. His own political career apparently was over. When the California legislature met in January, his name would not even be mentioned as a possible candidate for his own seat. Yet it was not his personal troubles, grievous as they were, that most depressed him.

He had sincerely predicted what would happen if a Republican was elected president. The Union was over. Baker, of course, did not take seriously the Southern threats to secession. In fact, the only thing he seemed to take seriously were openings for himself to give great orations. Baker would welcome crises that gave him the opportunity to strike a profound oratorical pose. In that love of the grand gesture, he bore a strange resemblance to Frémont. If he was typical of the men Lincoln would bring to the fore, God help the republic, or what would be left of it after these smug amateurs were done. During the voyage back to Washington, Gwin stayed as much as possible in his stateroom.

So he returned to Washington to await the end of his term and the inauguration of Lincoln. So he watched firsthand, and played his own small role in what came to be called the Great Secession Winter of 1860–61.

Response in the South to Lincoln's victory showed that Douglas's heroic effort had been wholly without effect. Ordinarily moderate Southern newspapers outdid themselves in the radicalism of their pronouncements. The Atlanta *Confederacy,* normally a voice of restraint, proclaimed in an editorial that the time for restraint was over: "Let the consequences be what they may—whether the Potomac is crimsoned in human gore, and Pennsylvania Avenue paved ten fathoms in depth of mangled bodies, or whether the last vestige of liberty is swept from the face of the American continent, the South will never submit to such humiliation and degradation as the inauguration of Abraham Lincoln." Alabama congressman David Clopton agreed: "The argument is exhausted, further remonstrating is dishonorable, hesitation is dangerous, delay is submission. 'To your tents, O Israel,' and let the God of battles decide the issue."

Yet during that winter there was an air of regret more than defiance about the leading Southern fire-eaters. And also moments of genuine poignancy, none more so than the resignation of five senators from seceding states on January 21. Jefferson Davis addressed the Senate chamber in statesmanlike terms, as befitting the man who within a month would be President of the Southern Confederacy: "I wish you well; and such, I am sure, is the feeling of the people I represent toward those whom you represent."

Gwin seems to have thought through very clearly what his own role should be in his last months as senator. He had hoped that his friend Buchanan would prove in this moment of crisis a leader worthy to be compared to Andrew Jackson. Unfortunately, Buchanan behaved instead as Broderick would have predicted, like a dithering old fool incapable of decision. Gwin would later write that the president and his general, Winfield Scott, acted like weathercocks, pointing one way in the morning and another at midday and another at dusk. Even the Southern leaders to whom he had so often deferred were blaming Buchanan in 1860; Jefferson Davis himself wrote, "His weakness has done as much as wickedness could achieve." Buchanan had aged ten years in the last one; those who had not seen him in a while were stunned when they did. The hearty Old Buck had started to look as frail as he sounded depressed.

Given Buchanan's weakness, Gwin reasoned that secession would be a *fait accompli* before Lincoln was sworn in. He did not see how the North, especially with Buchanan as its commander-in-chief, could prevent it. So there would be two republics soon. And what of California? He imagined that after this dissolution was effected California would go its own way as well, forming a great Pacific Republic, perhaps with the Rocky Mountains as its eastern boundary.

It was rumored, probably correctly, that Gwin had a role in the appointment of Albert Sidney Johnston as head of the federal forces on the West Coast. Johnston was known to be an ardent Southerner. In any test of strength between North and South Johnston could hold his troops aloof.

Baker, in particular, was arguing that Johnston should be removed as soon as possible. And someone was attributing to Gwin the assertion that California would unite itself to the South. This was serious enough that he felt compelled to deny it on the floor of the Senate.

"I have never made that statement upon any occasion. I hope, Mr President, that this Union will be imperishable; but if it is ever broken up, the eastern boundary of the Pacific Republic will be, in my opinion, the Sierra Madre and Rocky Mountains." Latham openly agreed with Gwin on this, not realizing that Gwin's candor was that of someone who realized his own political career was likely ending.

Gwin's hopes for the Union that winter were placed in Seward. Seward was going to be the inexperienced Lincoln's secretary of state, and was expected to be the dominant figure in his administration. Seward's confidential plan for preserving the Union was to let "the erring sisters leave in peace"— in the hope that the goodwill thereby preserved between the sections would gradually bring the states back together. Men in the South like Gwin would then have the opportunity to work for the reestablishment of the Union. Let secession happen peacefully and it might prove ephemeral.

To try to achieve this before Lincoln's inauguration, Seward needed a reliable liaison with the Southern leaders, someone they trusted as much as Seward did. There was perhaps only one person capable of this, William Gwin.

This was the role that Gwin played, with increasing pessimism, between late January and early March. The ambiguity of his situation was epitomized by two stories rumored at this time. The first was that a group of five hundred Texas raiders was going to swoop down on Lincoln at the inauguration to kill him before he could take the oath of office; their leader, it was said, had already slipped into Washington, and was being hidden in the house of Senator Gwin. The second, likely true, was that Seward, amid the elaborate precautions taken to prevent Lincoln's assassination before he took the oath of office, actually borrowed Gwin's well-known carriage to carry the president-elect safely from the train station (where he had arrived under an assumed name) to his lodgings. So, depending upon whom one believed, Gwin was central either to the plot to assassinate Lincoln or to the plan to protect him.

The Southerners, as Gwin put it later, "trusted Seward personally—but did not think he could control Lincoln and his cabinet." Gwin was becoming increasingly doubtful himself, even about trusting Seward personally. When other sources contradicted what the unusually chipper Seward was telling him, Gwin would challenge his Republican friend, only to be met with evasion—Seward insisted that what he had said was true, but that some grave matter had necessitated a little trimming of the sails. What this was Seward was not at liberty to say.

Gwin understood that Seward had to be careful, for the war hawk his party, led by Salmon Chase, were making their own efforts to take over the Lincoln administration. A false step by Seward, and Lincoln might pass him over for secretary of state. And Seward was being candid with Gwin when he admitted that he had no assurances from the president-elect that he was determined to settle matters with the secessionists peaceably.

President Jefferson Davis had to make his own judgment about the likelihood of war. He could, if he judged war probable, buy the cotton crop with Confederate bonds, and then sell it in Europe and use the cash to fortify the South against a possible invasion. Seward implored Gwin to write Davis to advise him to avoid anything that could be taken as a belligerent act, for such was exactly what Chase and the others wanted to justify their own belligerent stance.

Gwin did write the letter and showed it secretly to Seward at his desk in the Senate. Gwin, moreover, was still trying to act on the conviction that a state of war did not exist between North and South. So he sent his letter to Davis through the U.S. mails. That alone might convince Davis to take it seriously.

Despite such acts of faith, Gwin was by February 1860 clearly losing heart. He now thought that the only reasonable hope was to avoid open war. He wrote to Calhoun Benham (one of Terry's seconds in the Broderick duel) five days before the arrival of Lincoln in Washington, "The cotton States are gone forever. The border States will follow; it is only a question of time. If no collision takes place, reconstruction is barely possible. The chances are there will be two republics, North and South, with amicable relations. Time will probably turn it into three."

Ominously, however, Lincoln had proven initially less pliable than had been expected. He listened to all advice given, but without assent or demurral. A worried Seward arranged an interview between Gwin and Lincoln, shortly before the inauguration, so that he could praise Seward as the secretary of state who could work with the Southern leaders to preserve the Union. Gwin was obviously uncomfortable with this, as he was becoming increasingly uncomfortable with the things Seward was asking of him, things that if they did not work out Seward could disavow while leaving Gwin holding the bag.

The interview, however, appeared to go well. Lincoln treated Gwin courteously, and seemed interested in all he had to say, while saying very little substantive himself. Of course, what could one expect? Here was someone who had won first the nomination and then the presidency itself without having given a single speech or having made a single policy statement.

As cordial as the interview itself was, Lincoln had struck Gwin, as he did so many others, as a cipher, a complete enigma. Gwin had absolutely no idea what the president-elect was thinking, or if he was thinking at all. He had expected to take the measure of this provincial amateur rather quickly, and was surprised to find that he had made no progress. Perhaps he had t'

disquieting thought that maybe it was Lincoln taking his and Seward's measure. This thought, if it had crossed his mind, would have been pushed aside—until, that is, the next day. Then Gwin was stunned to learn that the president-elect had selected not only the dove Seward as secretary of state but also the hawk Chase for his cabinet. Lincoln—could it be?—was going to be his own man. Or was this just inept temporizing?*

Gwin now realized that he understood not at all what was going to happen in Lincoln's administration. He felt that his earlier letter to Davis had unwittingly misled his old Mississippi colleague. He had, in writing it, compromised himself. Rather than showing him to be a friend of the Confederacy, it could now be used as evidence that he was its enemy, or at the least a dupe of its enemies.

So the very day that the appointment of Chase was announced Gwin wrote a note to Davis. There he forthrightly told him what Davis did not need to be told—namely, that the appointment of Chase constituted a victory for the war party in the new administration. Still trying to remain loyal to both sides, he sent a copy of this note to Seward, to give him the opportunity to respond before it was actually sent. Seward sent the note back to Gwin with its crucial sentence changed to read: "Notwithstanding Mr. Chase's appointment, the policy of the administration would be for peace, and the amicable settlement of all questions between the sections."

This left Gwin in a quandary. Clearly he was being used. Seward expected him to declare Seward's hopes to be Gwin's facts. This was useful for Seward, but extremely precarious for Gwin. He had been put in exactly the kind of situation he had so dexterously avoided throughout his career—and there was no clear way to extricate himself.

Nonetheless, to refuse to send the note as Seward wanted it would be to break off with the new administration, to end whatever influence he might have at this time of extreme crisis for the American republic. So he sent the note as Seward wanted—but with what reluctance could only be imagined. By now he must have had the growing feeling that he was simply playing out a losing hand.

Gwin did not bother to attend Lincoln's inauguration. Edward Baker was going to introduce his old friend—and to sit through another self-serving exercise in oratorical pyrotechnics was almost more than Gwin could manage, although he would hope that Baker had at least enough sense of the occasion not to invoke the ghost of that fallen martyr to justice, David Broderick. But, knowing Baker, one could not be sure.

---

*William Tecumseh Sherman's brother John, a prominent Republican congressman from Ohio, had also arranged a presidential interview. Sherman had recently completed a brief stint as commandant of a military academy in Louisiana. He detailed to Lincoln the ominous military preparations well under way in the South. His report was met with a blithe response from Lincoln: "Oh well! I guess we'll manage to keep house." Sherman in disgust left Washington for Ohio, but not before denouncing Washington politicians: "You have got things in a helluva fix, and you may get them out as best you can."

He heard of the moving moments at the inauguration. Douglas, now prematurely aged, had attended, and at a certain point had held Lincoln's stovepipe hat on his lap. Another changing of the guard, like 1850. Douglas and he had thought that they and a few others would rule the country as Webster, Clay, and Calhoun had, for decades. Yet he and Douglas had just strutted their few moments on the national stage, transitional characters between two sets of major players.

Douglas was now obviously a spent force, a truly tragic figure. Seward was conniving just to keep his place in Lincoln's cabinet. Davis still had a potentially great role as the founding father of the Confederacy. And Gwin, if he had one at all, would find it in an independent Pacific Republic. Yet this last possibility was unlikely because of the memory of Broderick, damned Broderick whose wound every demagogue would keep fresh.

Lincoln's speech at the inauguration was handsome. Seward had tried to provide a peroration that would extend the olive branch to the South. Lincoln, in what was becoming an all too familiar pattern for Seward, took the passage and revised it to his own purposes:

> We are not enemies, but friends. We must not be enemies. Though passion may have strained, it must not break our bonds of affection. The mystic chords of memory, stretching from every battlefield, and patriot grave, to every living heart and hearthstone, all over this broad land, will yet swell the chorus of the Union, when again touched, as surely they will be, by the better angels of our nature.

Handsome, but a republic that depends upon mystic chords and better angels is doomed. If something unexpected did not occur, battlefields and patriot graves were going to be the order of the day.

Out of a sense of courtesy and obligation, he paid a visit to his dear friend James Buchanan. It was a hard visit. Buchanan knew that he was blamed, hated by everyone. Or so he felt. He told Gwin that his was the first visit he had had since the inauguration. Gwin could not tell him he was not to blame, for he like everyone else thought he was. But unlike almost everyone he did not harbor ill feelings toward Old Buck. This charming gentleman, with whom he had spent so many exquisite evenings and with whom he had cut so many dexterous deals, was now a "hopeless, broken hearted man." How unlike the triumphant retirement of Andrew Jackson! Yet Gwin was struck not just with pity but with fear. He was still trying to occupy Buchanan's middle ground; he was, unlike Buchanan, not quite destroyed. Politically ruined perhaps, but not quite destroyed like the old man before him.

Given his sense of impotence, Gwin could have been only faintly encouraged when commissioners from the Confederacy arrived to be available after the inauguration, including Martin Crawford, the former senator from Georgia. They were authorized to propose a twenty-day truce during which neither side would seek military advantage. During that time negotiations would be conducted in the attempt to find a peaceful resolution of differences The commissioners were instructed to add orally that if this proposal was rejected the Southerners were "prepared to accept war." This was, in short, a final offer.

Seward, as was depressingly predictable, expected Gwin to serve as the secret intermediary between him and the Confederate representatives. Seward now thought that even meeting with Gwin would compromise him; so the messages Gwin got from the Southerners he was to pass to someone else who in turn would give them to Seward. This arrangement was, of course, complete nonsense. Now Gwin was being treated as somehow tainted simply because he was willing to talk to the Confederates. The only chance for the success of the Confederate mission was an open meeting with the Republican administration, although the hawks would be violently opposed to this because it would grant the Confederate government some small recognition as legitimate. Seward was finally going to have to take a stand.

On March 11 Gwin met privately with Crawford and the others. Crawford, with his complete agreement, insisted upon at least an unofficial interview with Seward for the sake of a preliminary exploration of the Confederate offer. If Seward could not even meet with them on these modest terms, then the Confederate emissaries, who had come as an act of peace, could only return home—and a final breach between the two governments would have occurred.

Gwin had an appointment with Seward to convey this demand the next morning, March 12, at ten o'clock. When he arrived precisely on time, he was told at the doorstep by a servant that Seward was indisposed. During the night he had suffered an extreme attack of lumbago or sciatica or something. Dr. Gwin had his own diagnosis of Seward's discomfort. He immediately went to Crawford's room, told him of Seward's indisposition, and informed him that he was no longer willing to act as intermediary. That evening Gwin left Washington for New York.

Gwin was now concerned not with saving the Union, but simply with saving himself, himself and his family and their prospects. His situation from the start was immensely complex. The basic question was where to make his stand.

He could declare for the South and be a patriotic citizen of the Confederacy at the plantation he still owned in Mississippi near Vicksburg. Or he could try to remain in Washington for the duration, carefully hedging his bets. Or he could return to California, either to work for the Confederacy or to promote a Pacific Republic or just to sit out this debacle at a safe distance. He seems to have entertained all these options at one time or another during the next few years, but in the end settled on an entirely different one.

First, he went to the South to tour and assess opinion before milita-

hostilities broke out. Gwin apparently was troubled by what he saw, for he soon had returned to Washington and then quickly left for California. He played the sphinx in California, trying to observe everything but committing himself to nothing. The situation there was not encouraging.

The Chivalry was becoming more and more indiscreet in its support of the Confederacy, thereby creating a backlash in the elections of 1861 that gave control of the state government to the Republicans. In April, Albert Sidney Johnston resigned his commission as military commander of the Department of California; and as soon as his replacement arrived late that month, he headed South with two hundred troops. Only thirty made it with Johnston all the way to Richmond, where Johnston himself was appointed a major general of the Confederate army.

With Johnston's departure the hope for establishing a Pacific Republic dissolved, until at least the Confederacy had successfully established its independence from the Union (which Gwin still judged likely). Gwin could only congratulate himself that he had not committed prematurely to the Pacific Republic. (In the increasingly hysterical atmosphere even Milton Latham's relatively innocent remarks about the Pacific Republic were being interpreted as treasonous; they eventually would be used to drive him out of politics altogether.) Deciding there was nothing to do in California for the time being, Gwin returned east, to join his wife in New York.

Mary Gwin had left Washington because she found it intolerable now. She had written to a friend in South Carolina that "Washington offers a perfect realization of Goldsmith's Deserted Village." Mary's whole world had dissolved in front of her. One friend had written of her a little earlier, "Mrs. Gwin is packed up ready to leave. Poor thing! Her eyes are never without tears."

Her eldest children were cause enough for tears. Willie Gwin, their teenage son, had already enlisted in the Confederate army without the consent of his parents. And their oldest daughter was taking the whole crisis as a splendid lark; she had moved to Richmond to live the life of a Confederate belle, another familial rebel.

Mary Gwin had also to worry about her own safety. Her dear friend Rose Greenhow had suddenly been arrested as a Confederate spy, a charge of which she admitted happily she was guilty. All Southern ladies remaining in Washington were openly suspected of being members of the same petticoat ring of traitors. Their charm and flirting that had so beguiled Northern gentlemen before was now dismissed as—in the phrase of one Republican—"the incandescence of their treason."

Mary Gwin might have thought that moving to New York would stop such talk as it applied to her. However, one New York newspaper soon thereafter reported categorically not just that she was still under suspicion but that she herself, along with another "accomplished high life secessionist," had in fact already been arrested. And when she wrote to demand a retracti the newspaper glibly responded that yes, its item was premature; it should have reported that she had been arrested "not yet."

So Gwin had good reasons, beyond the disappointing situation in California, for hurrying east. He had no sooner rejoined his wife in New York than he himself was arrested. (Actually, during his passage across Panama there had almost been an international incident when federal authorities had tried to arrest him on Colombian soil.) He suspected that Seward thought he knew too much.

Within the government itself even the remnant of the old civility Gwin so valued had long since disappeared. After the defeat at Bull Run, now-Colonel Edward Baker had actually shown up on the floor of the Senate in his uniform in order to charge former Vice President Breckinridge (now senator from Kentucky) with treason to his face, simply for advocating a policy not much different from the one that Seward and Gwin had tried to pursue covertly:

> Will the senator yield to rebellion? Will he shrink from armed insurrection? Shall we send a flag of truce? What would he have? These speeches of his, sown broadcast over the land, what clear, distinct meaning have they? Are they not intended to dull our weapons? Are they not intended to destroy our zeal? Are they not intended to animate our enemies? Sir, are they not words of brilliant, polished treason—even in the very Capitol of the nation?

Breckinridge would soon flee to the Confederacy. Colonel Baker himself would be killed in a minor inconclusive action shortly after this encounter, a loss at which Lincoln is said to have wept but at which Gwin would not have shed a single tear.

When Gwin was finally released from custody due to the intervention of Lincoln (whom he personally thanked), his only concern was his family. As he said to one friend, he had been living on a volcano for six months now and "knew too much but to keep clear of gunpowder."

He sent his wife and younger daughter to Europe. He himself retired to his plantation. He firmly recalled his older daughter from charming Richmond, and used all his influence to get his son discharged from the army. He did not succeed with his son; so for a year he quietly waited on his plantation for Willie's enlistment to run out, as it would in early 1863. Virtually nothing is known of Gwin during that year of 1862. He would have reacquainted himself with the rhythms of plantation life, from which his ambition had so long taken him away. Perhaps it was a time for reflection. He seems to have brought with him his papers, which he had assiduously preserved throughout his career. He could have begun to think how to use his memoirs to teach another generation practical wisdom while in the process of settling old scores.

Events were not going to leave him alone, however. By the time of Willie's discharge, there was little left of Gwin's plantation. It happened to be on a route Ulysses S. Grant had chosen to attack Vicksburg. It was destroyed by fire, and with it all Gwin's papers. He and his daughter had successfully fled. Once Willie had been mustered out, the Union blockade had to be run before the whole family could finally be reunited. His ship, *R. E. Lee,* barely made it, almost being run down by the USS *Iroquois.*

Dr. Gwin, former senator from California, ended up in Paris with his family intact. There he could observe, in the glittering court of Napoleon III, the diplomatic maneuvering for and against European recognition of the Confederacy. Gwin's sympathies were with the South, but he was more concerned to find something for himself and his family.

Among the Confederates haunting Paris and the courts of Europe was Gwin's old rival, Thomas Butler King. King's aristocratic manner fitted in well there, but as usual he was overreaching himself. The governor of Georgia had appointed him the state's ambassador to Europe before Georgia itself entered the Confederacy. King's position had been rendered needless by Georgia's action; but that did not prevent him from railing against the Union in the name of commerce, as if he were still an ambassador. He declared that this was "a war of conquest and subjugation on the the absurd pretext of preserving the Union." He reminded his European friends that Southern cotton was "as necessary to the working of the spindles and looms of France and England as bread is to feed those who operate them. Has Mr. Lincoln a right to forbid the supply of either?"

Gwin could not but sympathize with his arguments while wondering what precisely this private citizen hoped to achieve. If he had learned that King was trying to get European powers to establish a regular steamship run to Savannah, he would have only shaken his head. Some people just get stuck in time; here was old T. Butler King trying to repeat his achievement of subsidizing the steamship run to California. One could almost predict what King would do next: return home to try to use his service to get a post in Jeff Davis's cabinet—and failing in that, have an unsuccessful run for the Confederate senate. Both of which King did, before his death in 1864.

Gwin himself was past all that. Gwin had become disgusted with politics for the time being. Despite the loss of his plantation, the Gwins still had sufficient means, thanks to his usual shrewdness with financial matters. Nonetheless, they did not have the money they had had in Washington. But Gwin had come to Paris with a plan to take care of all that—and perhaps to leave the door open a crack for a triumphal return to politics eventually.

Napoleon III, he knew, intended to reestablish the French empire in the New World by making Archduke Maximilian of Austria the emperor of Mexico, although Maximilian himself did not seem altogether enthusiastic about the idea. What Gwin could offer Napoleon was a secure northern border. This would be achieved by allowing Gwin to supervise the colonization of Sonora with Americans experienced in mining. Sonora could be transformed as California had been—and with many of the same people.

The Civil War was now going against the South. Members of the California Chivalry would not want to be part of a Union that had been preserved by an aggressive war against the Confederacy. They could use their skills to develop Sonora, which was reputed to have greater mineral riches than even California. All Gwin needed was perhaps a thousand French troops to protect the prospectors from the Indians.

Gwin first presented his plan to French ministers whom he had known as diplomats while he was a senator. Then he dexterously worked himself up the French governmental hierarchy until he finally was granted an audience with Napoleon himself. In the Tuileries Palace he once again outlined his plan, and then had a good discussion of it with the emperor. The emperor impressed him as ambitious, shrewd, without undue scruples—just the kind of man with whom Gwin could happily do business.

Gwin warned Napoleon that "if the northern boundary of Mexico is left in its present defenseless condition" the French were risking losing northern Mexico altogether, especially after a Union victory in the Civil War. What was to prevent Sherman and Grant with their hundreds of thousands of hardened troops turning south, as American armies had already in 1846. He could prevent this by settling the area with thousands of Southerners who could exploit the mines and become "loyal citizens of Mexico, loyal to its Emperor and bulwarks to his throne."

Napoleon was enthusiastic about the plan. What Gwin did not realize was that the future emperor of Mexico, Maximilian, when informed, was suspicious if not outright hostile. He observed that the American Southerners Gwin proposed as the settlers "have always been and always will be the sworn adversaries of Mexico whatever the form of its government." As for Gwin himself, he might be an ideal pioneer, but Maximilian added bitterly, "Yes, a pioneer for the South."

Napoleon's plan was for Mexico to cede temporarily to France most of northern Mexico in repayment for outstanding debts. France could then support Gwin's colonizing efforts, and profit from his mining operations. Mexico could be content with an effective buffer between itself and U.S. power, a buffer that would allow Maximilian to consolidate his power in southern Mexico. Maximilian, not surprisingly, was not eager to have a major cession of territory be one of his earliest acts as emperor. He might be a puppet of the French empire, but he certainly did not want to look like one.

In Napoleon's court few things were secret for long. It began to be rumored about Paris that Dr. Gwin was about to be named the Duke of Sonora. And this rumor made its way back to the United States. On June 1, 1864, at Southampton en route to Mexico, Gwin wrote a confidential letter to a member of his family still in Tennessee to reassure him about his new plans:

My dear brother:

I am this far on my way to Mexico. A generation has almost passed away since I left the South. I have relatives and friends left, whom I love and value highly, but I cannot shut my eyes to the fact that I am not counted as one of the South, although highly valued because I am with the South in this contest.

You know I am the "Wandering Jew" of the family, and this is one of my excursions. Much fatigue and labor will result from this enterprise, but I do not mind that. In fact, it is necessary to perfect health and usefulness to me. It is a great work which I propose to do, to populate an important part of the empire, now held by wild Indians for more than a hundred years. It is the richest mineral country in the world, and will attract tens of thousands of enterprising men.

I intend to reverse my action in California. I went there determined not to make money, but to devote all my energies to obtaining and maintaining political power. Now I go for money alone, and shall let power alone. I want no dukedoms, nor any honors the emperor can bestow on me. Nothing can be as high as what I have been, a senator in the greatest body of the greatest nation on earth.

I may not succeed, as I have the prejudices of the Mexicans to contend against, who fear we will take the country away from them; but I am backed by the Emperor of France, and carry with me such authority from him that it is impossible for these prejudices to defeat me. Moreover, the Emperor of Mexico favors my plan, and does not share these fears of his subjects.

Gwin closed by instructing how to contact him by mail, but also advised possible correspondents, "Any letter to me would likely be opened, as the Federals are troubled about my movements."

They were troubled all right. Gwin's reception at the court of Maximilian in Mexico City, in particular, did not go unobserved by worried Union loyalists. Both in Washington and California it was reported that Gwin was at the head of a filibustering Confederate conspiracy. The *Alta California* went further. Gwin's plan was "to unite California with the Mexican States on the Pacific to form a Pacific Republic." This "sensation," as the *Alta California* termed it, the paper subsequently decided had its good side: "Discontented and unappreciated descendants of the delapidated Chivalry, go in, go in!"

General Grant saw no such rosy side to this development and wrote to warn the commander of his Pacific forces of a possible invasion:

It is known that Dr. Gwin, former United States Senator from Cal., has gone to Mexico and taken service under the Maximilian government. The Dr. is a rebel of the most virulent order. His being formerly a resident of California, and now getting to that State in Mexico bordering on the State of his former residence, portends no good to us. May it not be his design to entice into Sonora the dissatisfied spirits of California, and if the opportunity occurs, organize them and invade the State? I write, without having discussed this question with any one, to put you on your guard against what I believe may prove a great danger. Watch this matter closely, and should you find these apprehensions well founded, prepare to meet them.

The Confederate government was also following this matter closely through its agents in Paris, hoping that the worst fears of the North would prove true. The Confederate ambassador to Napoleon's court, in particular, thought his scheme had a "fair chance of success" and if successful would have "consequences . . . most beneficial."

The irony was that as the power of Gwin was more and more magnified in the common opinion of gringos, he was becoming more and more frustrated with the decadent court of Maximilian, who could not settle upon any decisive action about Sonora or anything else except to hold grand but meaningless ceremonials. So about the time Grant was writing to his Pacific commander to warn him of this "rebel of the most virulent order," Gwin, after six months of frustration in Mexico, was traveling back to France to try to get sufficient support to overcome the Mexican impasse.

What he apparently did not realize was that Napoleon had been doing his best to induce Maximilian to support Gwin. Maximilian had chosen to ignore the advice, and Napoleon had been reduced to writing almost pleading letters to Maximilian: "It is feared in Mexico that Sonora may become an American province, but, believe me, if nothing is done, it will become one by force of circumstances." As for Gwin himself he was "the man best able to be of service in the Sonora area."

To this particular letter of exhortation, Maximilian delayed a full month before replying. Moreover, his reply then was in a tone that could best be described as ironical. He certainly intended, he assured Napoleon, to do something about Sonora ("this interesting portion" of his empire)—exactly when, he was not sure, but "in a not too distant future." As for that most able pioneer, "I shall then be charmed to see Mr. Gwin attract there many American colonists who appear to be merely awaiting a sign from him to come and group themselves around him to seek their fortune."

While Gwin was in France the second time engaged in needless lobbying, the Civil War ended. American newspapers were openly hostile to the anti-Union plots in Mexico. One newspaper ran a cartoon in which Uncle Sam, with a large basket in hand, looked delightedly at "Two Fine Mushrooms

Nearly Fit to Pull." The larger was labeled "Maximilian," the smaller "Dook Gwin."

"Dook" Gwin was in fact being toyed with by Napoleon and his court. He apparently had judged that the success of Gwin's plan depended upon getting the colony in place before the Civil War ended. Now the United States could not be presented with a fait accompli, but rather could turn its full military attention to what it could regard as the beginning of a hostile act. Gwin's proposed colony would be plucked before it had a chance to set roots.

This seems to have been the reasoning of Napoleon. But there was no reason to confide in Gwin. In fact, Napoleon does not seem to have resisted having a little fun at Gwin's expense. He actually had Gwin carry back to Maximilian a confidential letter announcing that the French government was no longer supporting Gwin's plan because it could prove "expensive and dangerous." Maximilian was, nonetheless, encouraged to "decide what he can get from his [Gwin's] efforts and intelligence."

A relieved Maxmilian wanted nothing from Gwin. He confided to a correspondent, "I fear him most of all because of his extreme finesse and the great ability which I see in him." Gwin seems to have had no inkling of his lost support. He may have been deluding himself by this point. His letters back home certainly brim with confidence. Yet that might just have been an effort to keep Mary from worrying. To others he was bitterly complaining about the very kind of social whirl of which his wife had once been an empress in Washington. Gwin wanted to get down to business, but the Mexican government seemed more interested in preparing for a lavish wedding reception for one of its leading officials.

But on June 28, 1865, two weeks after the relieved Maximilian had confessed privately his fear of Gwin, a small item in the government newspaper, *El Diario del Imperio,* settled the matter in Gwin's mind once and for all:

> The emperor has not pledged, much less already alienated, the department of Sonora. Mr. Gwin has not received from his Majesty any mission, nor any of the titles attributed to him. He is not attached to the government in any relation whatsoever. It appears even that he is entirely unknown to members of the administration. His sojourn in Mexico has no political significance whatever, the gates of the empire being open to the whole world.

So Gwin had been formally repudiated by the Mexican government. He had failed. He wrote to his wife to apprise her of this, including with his letter a copy of the article. There was no rancor in his words. He thought he understood perfectly why this promising plan had come to nothing.

The unexpectedly sudden collapse of the Confederacy under the hammering of Grant and Sherman, he understood now, had been "the only obstacle to my complete success here"—but it proved to be an insuperable one: "Fear of the power of the United States seems to be the prevailing sentiment all over the world." The United States was now ascendant, and Gwin himself could not expect to escape "its long arm": "Then why not submit at once? Abler generals and greater men than I am have been defeated by them, and compelled to lay down their arms. Then why should we not do the same?"

He had done the best he could for his family, much as in the secessionist crisis he had done the best he could for his country, much as in the preceding decade he had done the best he could for his adopted state. With California he had succeeded, but with the later two enterprises he had failed abjectly. Failed but not through any fault of his own, or so his always easy conscience told him.

Gwin traveled to New Orleans, that site of one of his first triumphs, when everything had seemed possible for him. He presented himself to General Philip Sheridan, now in charge. He requested permission to travel to New York in order to reunite with his family, who were returning from Europe. Sheridan quickly agreed, but was countermanded when he routinely informed Washington. Lincoln was dead, and Andrew Johnson was apparently determined that prominent secessionists like Gwin should get what they deserved. Apologetically, Sheridan placed Gwin under arrest, and sent him to a fort on the Mississippi for a indefinite imprisonment. It was a fitting conclusion to five years of complete futility.

The carriages, through the swirling fog, begin arriving at the hotel early in the evening, depositing numerous elderly gentlemen, some with their wives, most without. As these men all make their way first into the hotel and then toward the grand ballroom, it is obvious that there is scheduled some large celebration this night at the Grand Hotel, itself still the finest in San Francisco (but not for long, for the Palace Hotel is now going up almost next door).

Lavish parties are not uncommon in the city these days. The nine years since the end of the Civil War have been good to it. No, more than good. A massive silver strike—the Comstock Lode of Nevada—has poured vast wealth into San Francisco. Conspicuous consumption and sumptuous celebration are the order of the day. Yet the city is not being overwhelmed by Nevada silver as it was earlier by California gold. Vast, unexpected wealth San Francisco has learned to take in its stride—or so the city fathers like to think.

But these men who arrive this evening, as they go into the ballroom that has been set up for a banquet, do not all look as if they are members of the wealthy class. Some do, but others are obviously uncomfortable in their formal attire and are trying not to gawk at the elegant fixtures.

There is much conviviality and laughter among the men as they have their drinks, although a small minority holds itself at a distance from the main group, with a few individuals moving easily between the two. The humor is broad, about thinning hair and expanding waists. Apparently this is a reunion of sorts. And despite the opulence of the surroundings, a few remarks are quite crude, although clearly some of the guests are uneasy at the crudities. Whatever the tensions, the general mood is celebratory.

Now conversation aplenty can be overheard. For instance, about the old Niantic Hotel, which was just torn down and carted off piecemeal. Charlie Low has now built a three- or four-story brick building in its place; the fruit and produce markets are said to be going in on the ground floor. Real progress, and Charlie will make a pretty penny. But they all could remember—or claimed they could—the Niantic before it was a hotel, when it was still a ship riding anchor in the bay, deserted by its crew, its captain frantic. It had been pointed out to them, when they had entered the bay together, twenty-five years ago today. It had been pointed out to them from the launches as they came in from the *Panama*. Or had it? There is some dispute whether the *Niantic* had lost its crew later. But everyone agrees that a little after that much of its rigging and the like had burnt. Here there would be another disagreement about whether this happened in the great fire of '50, the year after they arrived, or the one in '51. Most thought, upon reflection, '51. Certainly not later. Then someone—who was it? not the frantic captain, by this time—had gotten the bright idea to drag the hulk ashore, what was left of it, use it as the foundation of a hotel, the Niantic Hotel, with its prow sticking out into the street, and the name still right there for all to see. Someone remembered that Roby had been the first manager, and then the old men were silent for a while, remembering too that Roby had committed suicide a year or two ago. But then they were cheerful again. Laughing at all those easterners who thought that this Niantic Hotel was a clever piece of architectural whimsy, not just an expression of good old California laziness. And now the old Niantic, hotel and ship, was finally gone; sad in a way.

This was a story they obviously all knew, but enjoyed retelling bits and pieces of to one another. Then everybody had a good laugh at the stories of buried treasure under the doorstep of the Niantic. A thief had buried his booty there, and showed up after having done his time at San Quentin to get his wages of sin. But, or so the story went, a clerk had already found it, and soon had bought the hotel where he had long worked—but had vamoosed to parts unknown long before the thief returned to the scene. Even so, people in charge of its recent demolition had carefully sifted through the foundations of the hotel, digging for that treasure. And—remember?—finding only an old case of champagne, as effervescent as it was when put in the bottle a quarter of a century ago. Unlike us, one of the old gentlemen undoubtedly added. Then hearty laughter all around.

Someone being called Mr. Ambassador might be overheard talking about his old friend Bayard Taylor. He himself had seen a bit of the world, but had been no traveler compared to Taylor, who had arrived on the next trip on the *Panama* after theirs. Hadn't stayed long enough to set down roots though. He had a sweetheart back home; so he left but did come back just a few years ago, to write another book on California, this one on how it had changed since 1850, an interesting book but not nearly as good as the first one. Taylor now had been just about everywhere though. Africa, India, Arabia. He was actually with Commodore Perry when he opened up Japan. Now he is supposed to be writing about his travels to Egypt and Iceland. It seems like yesterday that he wandered Monterey after the convention, and got his first taste of abalone.

So the conversations meandered from one subject to another, being whimsical and wistful by turns. The men did talk of current events, of course. They were full of opinions about the recent Indian war in the north of the state against Captain Jack and his Modocs. Tecumseh Sherman, now head of the army with Grant as president, had directed the harsh punitive raids against them. Most people didn't know that he had once been a San Francisco banker, but all the men here did—and some thought his experience here had given him his hearty distaste for politics and politicians. Speaking of politics, what about the recent city elections? The Democrats actually had elected a mayor—and a native Irishman at that. First Democratic mayor since . . . well, since 1856. And so talk of the present would lead inevitably to talk of olden days, or at least of acquaintances from those times.

There was Davy Scannel. What a career he had had. Started as one of the Hounds, but somehow avoided being tried with them. Then became sheriff until the trouble of '56. Then resigned and devoted himself to the fire department, especially to Broderick Company No. 1 (the original Empire Company No. 1). Never married. Now revered as the grand old man of the San Francisco Fire Department. Oh, how different the dignified Davy Scannel was now from the days when he marched to fife and drum through Chiletown.

Then there was poor Billy Mulligan. Perhaps some of the group had not heard. He had come back to San Francisco, but in bad shape. The liquor had finally gotten to him. He was trembling all over and seeing things—thought everyone was out to get him. Barricaded himself in a hotel room, and killed two people before he was shot dead himself. One he killed was a bystander, the other a friend trying to help.

Ned McGowan was still around, the ubiquitous McGowan with his high white beaver, Old Ned still reveling in his reputation for vice. Oddly, it was said that he and William Tell Coleman, the lion of the vigilantes himself, had become friends—Coleman who had never reached the heights he seemed destined for, and now contented himself with beautifying the little country town of San Rafael, in which he had his summer home. Portly and balding, Coleman was no longer the second-handsomest man in San Francisco, but his eyes, though heavily circled, still burned. And Sam Brannan had finally gone broke, thank God. He had tried to develop a spa called Calistoga. The story went that he had meant to name it Saratoga, but when he got up during the opening to announce its name he was so befuddled with drink that he toasted "Calistoga, Sarafornia." The story was undoubtedly made up, but too good not to retell at Brannan's expense. Now Calistoga was belly up, and Brannan with it.

The men tried to sound sympathetic at his plight, but were unconvincing. (Although they did not mention it, some of them had taken to crossing the street to avoid him, lest he ask for a handout.) Their sympathy was sincere, however, when they talked of Emperor Norton. Joshua Norton had been one of the wealthy ruined in the hard times of the early fifties. Unlike King of William, he went benignly mad. Now he paraded San Francisco in a plumed hat and a fancy coat that boasted golden epaulettes; touching the hilt of the large ceremonial sword that dangled by his side, he would declare to all willing to listen that he was rightly the "Emperor of the United States and Protector of Mexico." He paid for everything with banknotes that he issued himself and San Franciscans accepted them out of kindness and pity. He insensibly reminded old San Franciscans how close they all had come, amid the toil and trouble of early San Francisco, to the edge of their own endurance, the edge over which poor Joshua Norton had tumbled.

So the conversations easily meandered from one subject to another, from past to present and back to past again. But an eavesdropper—a waiter, say, taking orders and serving the drinks—would gradually realize that all the conversations tended to turn on a certain June morning many years ago. Finally, perhaps, his curiosity would get the better of him, and he would ask one of these old gentlemen precisely what they had come to celebrate this June 4, 1874. And he would be told that it was the twenty-fifth anniversary of the first entry of the steamship *Panama* into San Francisco Bay. The men here were all her pioneer passengers. These '49ers were all on her deck that cold morning, full of hope and apprehension, as full as they were of memories and conversation now.

This might have satisfied our waiter—but, then again, he might have had one more question he could not resist asking. There was one man at this reunion who was clearly first among equals. He was older than most of the men at this banquet, looking threescore and ten, but clearly, too, still full of vigor. Much of the early activity of the evening had revolved around him, and now as the eleven-course banquet was about to be served he was moving toward the place of honor at the head table. Our curious waiter might have asked if that tall gentleman with the impressive white hair had been the captain of the *Panama*. His informant would smile and say no, that was Dr. William McKendree Gwin. And if the waiter looked blank at this, he would be met, for the first time, with a little impatience—and be informed that Dr. Gwin had almost single-handedly written the California state constitution and had been one of her first senators. He was also the man who first envisioned the transcontinental railroad, and many other improvements that made California what it was today.

The years since 1865 had been as satisfying for Gwin as the Civil War years had been frustrating. As he sat in prison in 1865 letting his beard grow as a tacit protest, it soon became clear that Seward was behind his arrest. Apparently Seward worried that a disclosure of his own efforts through Gwin to allow the Southern states to secede peacefully would undermine his position in the administration of President Johnson, who was determined to treat the South sternly after Lincoln's assassination. Gwin's friends appealed on his behalf, but were stymied by Seward. All Seward would say to Johnson and the rest of the cabinet, all of whom favored Gwin's immediate release, was a gnomic, "I have reasons, which I cannot explain, for Dr. Gwin's continued imprisonment, and cannot consent to his liberation." Eyebrows working up and down, voice portentous, meaning elusive—Seward at his oracular best. Eventually Johnson got tired of refusing appeals without being able to give a reason. He ordered Gwin's release without telling Seward. Against Seward, Gwin felt permanently bitter, especially since Seward pretended that he had nothing to do with the incarceration. Other than that, Gwin refused to dwell on the past.

Gwin eventually had made his way back to California. There was nothing left for him in the South now. He undoubtedly had heard how Senator Hammond, as Tecumseh Sherman marched to the sea a few miles from his plantation, had taken to his bed, announcing that it was time for him to die— which he did shortly after. Hammond was right when he said he was witnessing the end of his world. One had to turn away from it and look only forward—for to set eyes backward was to end up like Lot's wife and the elegant Senator Hammond.

Gwin was not going to be destroyed with the South, nor endure watching the humiliation of its reconstruction. He gathered his family about him in San Francisco, determined to live quietly and comfortably. He turned his shrewdness to business, and made a modest fortune investing in mines. He did occasionally enjoy watching political battles from a ringside seat, such as when he went to a Democratic national convention as a delegate. But he tried to play no role, even that of a gray eminence. He enjoyed his obscure life amid people largely ignorant of his former prominence, and now in his old age had come to prefer it. His ambition was all spent. Or so it seemed until plans began to be made for this reunion.

Here was a chance, if only for an evening, to relive his former glory. So when the desserts had finally been taken away, Gwin rose, as president of this anniversary celebration, to begin the formal program by giving an address that he hoped would set the right tone. No, which he knew would set just the right tone.

Twenty-five years had passed, twenty-five years in their lives, twenty-five years in the life of California. He reviewed for them the passenger list from that voyage, and what these passengers had become. There were two governors, three senators, two congressmen, two state Supreme Court justices, seven generals and an admiral, and two ambassadors, one of them to China, a son of the newest civilization sent to the oldest. They were by any measure as distinguished a cargo as any ship had ever belched up upon these shores.

And these shores, how they had changed! Twenty-five years ago the permanent population of San Francisco had been less than a thousand; now it was more than two hundred times that. The ground beneath them this moment was then a shapeless mound in a sandy desert, and now it was covered by one of the finest hotels on the continent. And across the street is being built at this very moment what is intended to be a hotel equal to any on the globe. Lots that sold for $16 in 1849 now sell for $300,000. Then we were worried if the gold would last; now California still dominates the world in its production. Then we were repelled by the barrenness of California, but now it leads the country in the production of wine and wool—and produces more grain than any country in the world, 40 to 50 million bushels a year, not counting hay.

We here gathered are now all in the evenings of our lives. Few if any of us will survive to see the golden anniversary of this arrival. On an occasion such as this it is fitting for us to reflect upon what we have achieved collectively with our lives. Few are so fortunate as daily to see this achievement all around them. But we do, and should be content. Such rewarded usefulness is the most for which a man can hope from this life.

Gwin remembered that during the debates over the admission of California as a state one of his most eloquent opponents had argued that it was too large. To Gwin's chagrin the opponent argued that in twenty-five years California would have the resources of a nation. Fortunately, nobody believed him. His vision of the future was too grand, and so his arguments were ignored.

Yet he was right, impossible as he was to believe at the time. Everything that has happened to California since those times is on the order of the miraculous. Unbeknownst to us, this was what we were beginning that cold morning a quarter of a century ago. We were beginning the creation of the equivalent of what in any other age would have been a nation, a nation that we can all see now has a limitless future. And we were its founding fathers.

Gwin's celebration of their collective achievements met with sustained applause. Then one speaker after another echoed its praise. Not all were as cheerful as Gwin, however. Some spoke more with a sense of surprise, not just at what California had become, but also that they were still here to see it. One said, "We went forth for a brief season of energy and effort in the hope of a speedy return with the golden results of our labor." He added that now he would not behave like the patriarch Jacob, who bade his children to take his bones out of Egypt with them back to Canaan. California was now his Egypt and his Canaan.

In that nicely turned phrase one could not help but hear a twinge of regret. Others were more explicit. Again and again, speakers alluded to the difficult, uncertain lives that they had, as a group, lived. For them California had been more Egypt than Canaan. For them as individuals it had not proven a promised land. The contrast with that day was for a number painful, for then "all were young, buoyant with hope and bright anticipation in the future." An evening like this could at least console them that it all had not been for nothing. Or as one succinctly put the sentiments of a number, "Our lives have been singularly checkered, but time has at last given our aims and purposes stability."

Certainly the president himself had lived a singularly checkered life, and in his speech he had exhorted them to realize how stable their aims and purposes had become at last. At last, finally, the glimmer would emphasize in their words—but at a time when they as pioneers got little credit for the suffering and disappointment contained in that bland word "checkered."

A few had tried to make Gwin realize that they had not forgotten what he individually had achieved, and what he personally had suffered. One ended his remarks by reminding the group that their president had been "one of the framers of our State Constitution, one of our Senators in Congress, whose senatorial career is familiar not only to you but to the whole country. . . . However some of us may differ with him in political views, we must all concede that he had ever been an earnest, able and untiring advocate for the interests of California."

The minutes of the after-dinner proceedings noted emphatically that this remark met with "loud and continued applause." Gwin's friend, the secretary, was being perhaps a little too emphatic. Gwin had in his opening remarks tried to avoid stirring up old embers of controversy. When he mentioned those who had subsequently gained military distinction in the Civil War, he dexterously referred to one not as a general but rather more circumspectly as someone killed early in the war while wearing the stars of a Confederate general. Gwin even made a brief nod toward the absent Jessie Frémont, wife of California's most prominent black Republican.

Although absent, Jessie was still capable of speaking for herself. She had sent, to be read at the dinner, a telegraph message from the East Coast, where she lived in seclusion with her husband, himself now a nonentity in the nation she had expected him to lead. Jessie summarized her perspective on the arrival of the *Panama* into San Francisco Bay in a bitter exclamation: "How maimed have been the lives compared to the bright hopes." For Jessie, in character to the last, the achievements of California were as nothing compared to the disappointments of John Frémont. The men at the banquet could only be grateful that she had been unable to attend, for she certainly would have done her best to put a damper on the festivities.

On the other hand, some at the dinner had apparently begun to think that William Gwin himself was having too good a time. They had come to celebrate this important anniversary, not to honor him. For the sake of this evening, they were willing to let bygones be bygones. During drinks they just had tried to avoid the group clustered around Gwin, which had not been hard. But now the extravagant praise for Gwin, the lengthy applause to it, and his obvious if dignified pleasure in it were galling to them. And two were, as a result, goaded into words that they may not have planned to say, and may have subsequently regretted, particularly if they had stared at Gwin when they firmly uttered them.

The next speaker, right after the sustained applause for Gwin, did give an amusing, lighthearted speech—but he could not resist closing his remarks by reminding the assembled that the great advances of California had been made as part of the Union. The use of the word "Union" was pointed. And everyone there, even the waiter if we imagine him still bustling about the tables, would have understood what was being pointed at.

Gwin's praise for California as virtually an independent nation could itself be taken as implicitly secessionist, a nostalgic evocation of a Pacific Republic that he thought would follow from a victory of the Confederacy. The emphasis upon the Union was an implicit rebuke. Of course, if pressed, Gwin would insist that he was not alluding to secession; then this emphasis upon the Union itself could be taken as a manner of expression. No offense need be taken.

The same could not be said for remarks made toward the end of the evening. Then S. W. Holliday rose to speak. Of the many passengers on the *Panama* who had subsequently distinguished themselves he had not been one. Consequently, of those called upon to speak this evening he had been near the bottom of the list, just before a reading of telegrams of congratulations from various functionaries.

At first Holliday, whom Gwin probably could barely remember, spoke conventionally of his own first impressions upon entering San Francisco. He had been one of those who had thought that the gold rush was already over, that the golden bubble had burst. Then he spoke, again conventionally, of all the material progress they had seen. Then his little speech took an awkward turn.

But this material progress, he insisted, was meaningless without moral improvement, and even material improvement should be measured only as it helped the common man. Gwin at this moment must have looked away, or just closed his eyes as if suddenly feeling very weary. Holliday continued, "The summit of glory in by-gone ages was to conquer and enslave." But now, he declared, we must seek our glory not just in truth, fair-dealing and integrity among elites. Our glory is to extend "justice and freedom to all mankind, everything wearing the shape of humanity."

Broderick, Broderick, would he never be done with Broderick?

SOURCES*

Preface

The classic statement of California exceptionalism is Carey McWilliams, *California: The Great Exception* (New York, 1949). David Potter's revisionist survey is *The Impending Crisis* (New York, 1976). Czeslaw Milosz's preoccupation with the recovery of the past is a central theme in Leonard Nathan's and my *The Poet's Work* (Harvard, 1991). Of Govan's work the best is *Nicholas Biddle* (Chicago, 1959).

General

Many contemporaries were fascinated by the Broderick–Gwin rivalry—but no one more than James O'Meara, a newspaperman and staunch Gwin supporter, who witnessed many of the events narrated in this book, at least those that occurred in California. Long after them, he published his small book *Broderick and Gwin* (San Francisco, 1881), apparently based on notes and interviews he had done at the time. O'Meara is not interested in analysis or the national scene. But he has preserved much detail that might have been lost. This book would have been, if not impossible, at least much diminished without his.

The book would have been much more difficult without the scrapbooks of Benjamin Hayes. Hayes seems to have been his own one-man clipping service. He duly clipped newspaper stories, classified them, and then put them in his appropriate scrapbook. Months of scouring California newspapers can be done in mere hours thanks to the dozens of scrapbooks of Hayes, which are held by the Bancroft Library of the University of California at Berkeley.

Broderick and Gwin have been the subject of one scholarly biography each: David Williams, *David C. Broderick: A Political Portrait* (San Marino, 1969); Hallie Mae McPherson, "William McKendree Gwin, Expansionist" (unpub. diss., Univ. of Calif. at Berkeley, 1931), both quite useful. They have also been each the subject of a popular biography: Jeremiah Lynch, *A Senator of the Fifties* (San Francisco, 1910), for Broderick; and Lately Thomas, *Between Two Empires*, for Gwin (Boston, 1969), both quite unreliable. Gwin also left rather unsatisfying memoirs, which were published in a number of installments in the CHSQ* of

*Abbreviations: CHSQ, *California Historical Society Quarterly*; OM, *Overland Monthly*; PHR, *Pacific Historical Review*; SCQ, *Southern California Quarterly*

1940; nonetheless, these are the only source for some important episodes, such as Gwin's early conversations with Calhoun. What survives of Gwin's correspondence and papers is at the Bancroft Library of the University of California at Berkeley.

California politics from the conquest to 1860 has received two classic interpretations: Josiah Royce, *California: A Study of American Character* (Boston, 1886); and Joseph Ellison, *A Self-Governing Dominion: California 1849–60* (Berkeley, 1950). Also consistently useful are: Hubert Howe Bancroft, *History of California* (San Francisco, 1888); Theodore Hittell, *History of California* (San Francisco, 1885–97); and W. H. Ellison, *California and the Nation 1850–1869* (Berkeley, 1927). The best guide to early California culture is Kevin Starr, *Americans and the California Dream* (New York, 1973). My own understanding of early California development has been sketched out in my *Broken Shore: A Perspective on History* (Salt Lake City, 1981).

The classic narrative of national politics in this period is James Ford Rhodes, *History of the United States, 1850–77* (New York, 1892–1907). A more recent account is Allan Nevins, *Ordeal of the Union* (New York, 1947), for 1847–57, and his *The Emergence of Lincoln* (New York, 1950), for 1857–61. Also notable is Michael Holt, *The Political Crisis of the 1850s* (New York, 1976), which should be supplemented by his recent collection of essays, *Political Parties and American Political Development* (Baton Rouge, 1992). Of recent books on regional culture, the two most germane to the contrasting backgrounds of Broderick and Gwin are: Sean Wilentz, *Chants Democratic: New York City & the Rise of the American Working Class 1788–1850* (Oxford, 1984); and Bertram Wyatt-Brown, *Southern Honor: Ethics and Behavior in the Old South* (Oxford, 1982). Those familiar with Richard Hofstadter, *The Paranoid Style in American Politics* (New York, 1966), will also see its influence throughout this narrative.

Chapters 1–2

The recollections of the entry of the *Panama* into San Francisco Bay are recorded in the anonymous pamphlet *Reunion of the Pioneer Panama Passengers* (San Francisco, 1874), which is also the chief source for my account of the reunion in Chapter 10. Jessie Benton Frémont's version of her journey is contained in her *A Year of Travel* (New York, 1878). Joseph Hooker's sojourn in California is the subject of Milton Shutes, " 'Fighting Joe' Hooker," CHSQ 16 (1937): 304–20. The first chapter of David Wyatt's *The Fall into Eden* (Cambridge, 1986) is a provocative interpretation of early responses to the California landscape, including Dana's.

Aspects of travel to California by ship have been exhaustively treated in a number of books: notably, John Haskell Kemble, *The Panama Route* (Berkeley, 1943); and Oscar Lewis, *Sea Routes to the Gold Fields* (New York, 1949).

Of the many evocations of early San Francisco, notable are Frank Soulé et al., *The Annals of San Francisco* (San Francisco, 1855); and the charming *Men and Memories* (San Francisco, 1873), by T. A. Barry and B. A. Patten. Also worth consulting is John H. Brown, *Early Days of San Francisco* (San Francisco, 1933).

A good recent survey of the apparently limitless material on the gold rush itself is Donald Dale Jackson, *Gold Dust* (New York, 1980). The classic firsthand accounts are: Bayard Taylor, *El Dorado* (New York, 1850); and Frank Marryat, *Mountains and Molehills* (London, 1855). A notable recent addition to this vast literature is J. S. Holliday, *The World Rushed In: The California Gold Rush Experience* (New York, 1981). An indispensable older work is John Caughey, *Gold Is the Cornerstone* (Berkeley, 1948).

The early governmental problems in California are well surveyed in Theodore Grivas, *Military Governments in California 1846–50* (Glendale, 1963), whereas they are placed in the context of the conquest in the last chapters of Neal Harlow, *California Conquered* (Berkeley, 1982). Thomas Butler King has been the subject of a competent biography: Edward M. Steel, *T. Butler King of Georgia* (Athens, Georgia; 1964). King's report on California, by the way, is contained as an appendix to Taylor's *El Dorado*. On his failed tour as well as other episodes from early California politics, see Charles Baker (ed.), *The Memoirs of Elisha Oscar Crosby* (San Marino, 1945).

The best treatments of the Hounds and their rampage are: Jay Monaghan, *Chile, Peru and the California Gold Rush of 1849* (Berkeley, 1973); and Edwin Beilharz and Carlos Lopez, *We Were 49ers!: Chilean Accounts of the California Gold Rush* (Pasadena, 1976). The August 2, 1849, issue of the *Alta California* has an extensive account of the trial. For Bancroft's patently biased views on this and subsequent vigilante episodes, see his two-volume work *Popular Tribunals* (San Francisco, 1887). Donald Biggs, *Conquer and Colonize: Stevenson's Regiment and California* (San Rafael, 1977), is the standard work on the subject. See also the memoir by a friend and admirer of Stevenson: Daniel Knower, *Adventures of a Forty-niner* (San Francisco, 1894).

Gwin's activities as a politician in Mississippi figure significantly in the standard early history written by a close associate of his, J. F. H. Claiborne, *Mississippi as a Province, Territory and State* (Jackson, 1880); but this has been superseded by Edwin Miles, *Jacksonian Democracy in Mississippi* (Chapel Hill, 1960). As for Gwin's views on race, Gerald Stanley has shown that, despite his attempts after the Civil War to claim otherwise, they were about what one would expect of a Southerner of his generation and station; see his "Senator William Gwin: Moderate or Racist," CHSQ 50 (1971): 243–55.

The social context of Broderick's own early experience is well analyzed in Richard Stott, *Workers in the Metropolis* (Ithaca, 1990); for Michael Walsh, see Robert Ernst, "The One and Only Mike Walsh," *New York Historical Society Quarterly* 26 (1952): 43–65. Broderick's coinage scheme is given technical treatment by Edgar Adams in his "Private Gold Coinage: Various Californian Private Mints, 1849–55," *American Journal of Numismatics* XLV (1911): 173–91.

Chapter 3

In addition to works already cited, important for the constitutional convention are: J. Ross Browne, *Report of the Debates in the Convention of California on the*

Formation of the State Constitution (Washington, D.C., 1850); Cardinal Goodwin, *The Establishment of State Government in California, 1846–50* (New York, 1914); Woodrow Hansen, *The Search for Authority* (Oakland, 1960); and the more specialized thesis by Mary Oyster, *Gwin in the Constitutional Convention of 1849* (unpub. diss., Univ. of Calif. at Berkeley, 1938).

The best source for the social life of Monterey is perhaps Walter Colton's entertaining *Three Years in California* (New York, 1850). Personal perspectives on the convention are offered in: Taylor's *El Dorado;* E. Gould Buffum, *Six Months in the Gold Mines* (Los Angeles, 1959); James Jones, *Two Letters* (Carmel, 1928); Francis Lippit, "The Boundary Question," *Century* 11 (1890): 794–5; and William Tecumseh Sherman, *Memoirs* (New York, 1892), which also has much to say about subsequent events in California during the 1850s.

Larkin has been the subject of a full-length biography: Harlan Hague and David Langum, *Thomas O. Larkin* (Norman, 1990). On Semple, see Zoe Radcliffe, "Robert Baylor Semple, Pioneer," CHSQ 6 (1927): 130–58; on Halleck, Milton Shutes, "Henry Wagner Halleck, Lincoln's Chief of Staff," CHSQ 16 (1937): 195–208.

As for Frémont, the destruction of his reputation that was begun by Royce's *California* in the late nineteenth century has been ably continued—if not completed—by Bernard De Voto, *The Year of Decision, 1846* (Boston, 1943), arguably the single best piece of historical writing on America near midcentury. Of course, Frémont still unfortunately does not lack defenders—notable among them is Allan Nevins, *Frémont, Pathmarker of the West* (New York, 1939). A recent attempt at a psychoanalytic approach—in this case appropriate—is Andrew Rolle, *John Charles Frémont: Character as Destiny* (Norman, 1991). Jessie has gotten her own full-length biography in Pamela Herr, *Jessie Benton Frémont* (New York, 1987).

The best separate account of the Compromise of 1850 is probably Holman Hamilton, *Prologue to Conflict* (Lexington, 1964); Hamilton has also written the most detailed account of Taylor's brief presidency, *Zachary Taylor: Soldier in the White House* (Indianapolis, 1951). The compromise is ably presented as the last stage of three distinguished careers in the final chapters of Merrill Peterson, *The Great Triumvirate: Webster, Clay and Calhoun* (Oxford, 1987). A convenient collection of sources and interpretations is Edwin Rozwenc (ed.), *The Compromise of 1850* (Boston, 1957). Of course, the debates over this compromise and other legislative issues of the 1850s can be followed in detail in the official record, *The Congressional Globe.*

Chapter 4

The basic source for the California legislative debates is the offical record, the *Journal,* supplemented by various newspapers. Leonard Pitt, "The Beginning of Nativism in California," PHR 30 (1961): 23–38 is an excellent introduction to this subject. Also worth consulting are: Pitt's *The Decline of the Californios* (Berkeley, 1971); Robert Heizer and Alan Almquist, *The Other Californians* (Berkeley, 1971); Rudolph Lapp, *Blacks in the Gold Rush* (New Haven, 1977); and Richard

Peterson, "Anti-Mexican Nativism in California, 1848–53," SCQ 62 (1980): 309–27, as well as his *Manifest Destiny in the Mines* (San Francisco, 1975).

The classic treatment of the Sacramento squatters riot is Josiah Royce, "Squatter Riot of '50," OM 6 (1885): 225–46. This should be supplemented by Frank Blackmar, *The Life of Charles Robinson* (Topeka, 1902), chap. 2; and C. E. Montgomery, "The Lost Journals of a Pioneer," OM 7 (1886): 173–81, which treat the event from the squatters' and speculators' perspectives, respectively. The repeated flooding of Sacramento is the subject of Marvin Brienes, "Sacramento Defies the Rivers," CHSQ 58 (1979): 2–19. On the land title question generally, see the two articles by Paul Gates: "The Adjudication of Mexican Land Claims in California," *Huntington Library Quarterly* 21 (1958): 213–36, and "The California Land Act of 1851," CHSQ 50 (1971): 395–430; they correct common misapprehensions that are often repeated.

Mary Floyd Williams did the basic scholarly work on the vigilantes of 1851 by first editing their papers in the *Publications of the Academy of Pacific Coast History* 4 (1919) and then providing a detailed narrative history, *History of the San Francisco Committee of Vigilance of 1851* (Berkeley, 1921). A more readable account is George Stewart, *Committee of Vigilance: Revolution in San Francisco, 1851* (Boston, 1964); whereas Kevin Mullen, *Let Justice Be Done* (Reno, 1989), is an important revisionist history that refuses to take the vigilantes at their word. (Mullen's account has much influenced my own.)

Jay Monaghan has told the story of the Gold Rush from the perspective of Down Under in his *Australians and the Gold Rush* (Berkeley, 1966); this should be supplemented by Sherman Richards and George Blackburn, "The Sydney Ducks: A Demographic Analysis," PHR 42 (1973): 20–31. The fullest account of Broderick's challenge to the rally is A. J. Moulder, "Broderick's Moral Courage," *Argonaut* 3, no. 24 (1878): 9–12. (Although I have chosen to take this account at its word, it should be pointed out that certain details are not corroborated by other sources.)

A more general perspective on vigilantism is offered by: Richard Maxwell Brown, *Strain of Violence* (Oxford, 1975); and Eugene Hollon, *Frontier Violence* (Oxford, 1974).

On the economic life of San Francisco, see Peter Decker, *Fortunes and Failures* (Cambridge, Mass.; 1978); and Roger Lotchin, *San Francisco, 1846–56* (Oxford, 1974); as well as the memoir by Daniel Coit, *Digging for Gold Without a Shovel* (Denver, 1967). Gunther Barth, *Instant Cities* (New York, 1975), is an excellent comparative study. For information on the early mayors of San Francisco, see William Heintz, *San Francisco Mayors, 1850–80* (Woodside, 1975).

Chapters 5–6

On the railroad question the standard monograph is Robert Russell, *Improvement of Communication with the Pacific Coast* (Cedar Rapids, 1948). On the social life in Washington a number of memoirs are helpful: Mrs. Clement Clay, *A Belle of the Fifties* (New York, 1904); Marcy Ames, *Ten Years in Washington* (Cincinnati,

1874); Marion Gouverneur, *As I Remember* (New York, 1911); and Mrs. Roger Pryor, *Reminiscences of Peace and War* (New York, 1904).

On the city of Washington itself I have found consistently useful: Constance Green, *Washington: A History of the Capital* (Princeton, 1962); and John Reps, *Washington on View* (Chapel Hill, 1991).

Detailed accounts of two early governors of California are: William Franklin, "The Political Career of Peter Hardeman Burnett" (diss., Stanford; 1954); and Lionel Fredman, "The Bigler Regime" (diss., Stanford; 1959). Particularly interesting also is F. F. Low, *Some Reflections* (Sacramento, 1959).

The standard survey of nativism is Ray Billington, *The Protestant Crusade* (New York, 1938); but this needs to be supplemented by the more analytic study by Tyler Anbinder, *Nativism and Slavery* (Oxford, 1992). Nativism in California and New York, respectively, are ably surveyed in: Peyton Hurt, "The Rise and Fall of the 'Know Nothings' in California," CHSQ 9 (1930): 16–49, 99–128; and L. D. Scisco, *Political Nativism in New York State* (New York, 1901). Foote's brief California foray is the subject of John Carter, "Henry Foote in California Politics, 1854–7," *Journal of Southern History* 9 (1943): 224–37.

Amid the large literature on the 1856 Committee of Vigilance, one interpretive work stands out above the others by presenting the committee as a culmination of trends that began with the Gold Rush itself: Robert Senkewicz, *Vigilantes in Gold Rush San Francisco* (Stanford, 1985). (Senkewicz is influenced by Maxwell's *Strain of Violence,* and convincingly refutes criticisms of him by Decker and Lotchin. I have found this account invaluable.) Stanton Coblenz, *Villains and Vigilantes* (New York, 1936), is notable for its hagiographic treatment of James King of William; John Myers, *San Francisco's Reign of Terror* (Garden City, 1966), for its love affair with Ned McGowan.

The three most important eyewitness accounts—Coleman's, James O'Meara's (the same O'Meara who wrote *Broderick and Gwin*), and Sherman's, all published in the late nineteenth century—have been usefully collected in Doyce Nunis, *The San Francisco Vigilance Committee of 1856* (Los Angeles, 1971), which also provides a fine bibliographical guide, especially to manuscript sources. Other significant reflections are: Henry Gray, *Judges and Criminals* (San Francisco, 1858); and Samuel Webb, "A Sketch of . . . San Francisco Vigilance Committee of 1856," *Essex Institute Historical Collection* 84, no. 2 (1948). Gerritt Ryckman's unpublished memoir "Vigilance Committees" is held by the Bancroft Library of the University of California at Berkeley. Sherman's fascinating correspondence of the 1850s—which is an indispensable supplement to his *Memoirs*—is the primary source for Dwight Clarke, *William Tecumseh Sherman: Gold Rush Banker* (San Francisco, 1969); while James Scherer sees everything about the committee rosily through Coleman's eyes in *The Lion of the Vigilantes* (Indianapolis, 1939). McGowan's own version has been been conveniently reissued as *McGowan vs. the Vigilantes* (Oakland, 1946).

Also worth consulting as sources are: Richard Dillon (ed.), "Rejoice Ye Harlots," CHSQ 37 (1958): 137–69; and Flocken Horburt, "The Law and Order

View," CHSQ 14 (1935): 350–74, and CHSQ 15 (1936): 70–87, 143–62, 247–65. On King's newspaper, see John Denton Carter, "Before the Telegraph," PHR 11 (1942): 301–17. R. A. Burchell, *The San Francisco Irish, 1848–1880* (Berkeley, 1980), provides a competent overview of its subject; while John McGloin, *California's First Archbishop* (New York, 1966), provides reliable information about the early history of the Roman Catholic Church in American California. For more detail on the cemetery, see Ann Hart, *Lone Mountain* (San Francisco, 1937).

Chapter 7

James O'Meara's *Broderick and Gwin* remains the crucial source for the contest that led to the election of both men to the U.S. Senate. A more recent account that adds little is William Thompson, "M. S. Latham and the Senatorial Contest of 1857," CHSQ 32 (1953): 145–54.

On the rise of the Republican Party nationally, I have found particularly helpful: Eric Froner, *Free Soil, Free Labor* (New York, 1970); William Gienapp, *The Origins of the Republican Party, 1852–6* (New York, 1987); and Gienapp, "Nativism and the Creation of the Republican Majority," *Journal of American History* 72 (1985): 529–59. A good insight into its rise in California is offered by Catherine Phillips (ed.), *Cornelius Cole* (San Francisco, 1929), 82 97. Also important is Ray Albin, "Edward D. Baker and California's First Republican Campaign," CHSQ 60 (1981): 280–89.

For the general politics of the nation, the best single work is Kenneth Stamp, *America in 1857* (Oxford, 1990), which presents a convincing alternative to Nevins's portrait of Buchanan; also on Buchanan and his presidency, see Philip Klein, *President James Buchanan* (University Park, 1962); Elbert Smith, *The Presidency of James Buchanan* (Lawrence, 1975); and Roy Nichols, *The Disruption of American Democracy* (New York, 1948). Particularly good memoirs for this period are: J. W. Forney, *Anecdotes of Public Men* (New York, 1873); L. A. Gobright, *Recollections of Men and Things* (Philadelphia, 1869); and Ben Poore, *Perley's Reminiscences* (Philadelphia, 1886).

Chapters 8–9

On Broderick's antagonist, see Drew Faust, *James Henry Hammond and the Old South* (Baton Rouge, 1982). For a presentation of these events and others from Douglas's point of view, see George Milton, *The Eve of Conflict* (New York, 1934); and from Seward's, Glyndon Van Deusen, *William Henry Seward* (Oxford, 1967). Also worth consulting is Edgar E. Robinson (ed.), "The Day Journal of Milton Latham," CHSQ 11 (1932): 3–28. On Gwin's fancy party, see John Haviland, *A Metrical Description . . . 9th April, 1858* (Washington, 1858), as well as the work of Mrs. Clement Clay already cited.

The letters on the campaign of 1859 to Jefferson Davis are printed in Dunbar Rowland, *Jefferson Davis Constitutionalist* (Jackson, 1923), vol. 4, pp. 91–92.

On the duel itself, see: A. Russell Buchanan, *David Terry of California* (San

Marino, 1956), a competent general biography; and especially Carroll Douglas Hall, *The Terry-Broderick Duel* (San Francisco, 1939). A good example of the early hagiography is George Wilkes's 1859 biographical eulogy, which has been conveniently reprinted with useful annotations in CHSQ 38 (1959): 197.

Chapter 10

Of the many works that attempt to treat the events leading to secession, particularly good are: Henry Adams, "The Secession Winter of 1860–1861," Massachusetts Historical Society *Proceedings* 43 (1910): 660–87; Buchanan's own version, *Mr Buchanan's Administration on the Eve of the Rebellion* (New York, 1866); the unjustly neglected Horatio King, *Turning on the Light* (Philadelphia, 1895), part 1; Kenneth Stamp, *And The War Came* (Baton Rouge, 1950); and the early chapters of the engaging *Reveille in Washington* (New York, 1941) by Margaret Leech. Also worth consulting are the senatorial responses to John Brown, including Gwin's, which are contained in Clement Clay, *Invasion of Harpers Ferry* (Washington, 1849). On California during the secession crisis, especially Baker's role, see the unfortunately tendentious Elijah Kennedy, *The Contest for California in 1861* (Boston, 1912). On the ungrounded fears about Johnston, see Benjamin Gilbert, "The Mythical Johnston Conspiracy," CHSQ 28 (1949): 165–73.

Evan Coleman, Gwin's son-in-law, has written for the *Overland Monthly* a series of articles on Gwin's career in the late 1850s and early 1860s: "Dr. Gwin and Judge Black on Buchanan," January 1892; "Gwin and Seward," November 1891; and "Senator Gwin's Plan for Colonization" May and August 1891.

Hamilton Cochran, *Blockade Runners of the Confederacy* (Indianapolis, 1958), provides a perspective on Gwin's voyage to Europe. Of the various treatments of Confederate activity in Europe, germane to Gwin is Beckles Wilson, *John Slidell and the Confederates in Paris* (New York, 1932). Of the many treatments of the Second Empire and its New World adventure, I have found particularly useful Alfred and Kathryn Hanna, *Napoleon III and Mexico* (Chapel Hill, 1971), especially chapter 16, "The 'Duke' from Mississippi," the most balanced treatment of Gwin's efforts in France and Mexico. A good general account of the Confederates in Mexico is Andrew Rolle, *The Lost Cause* (Norman, 1965). Various specialized articles also contribute to understanding what Gwin was involved in: Simon Ellison, "An Anglo-American Plan . . ." *Southwestern Social Science Quarterly* 16 (1935): 42–52; Hallie McPherson, "The Plan of William McKendree Gwin . . . ," PHR 2 (1933), 193–214; and W. H. Watford, "Confederate Western Ambitions," *Southwestern Historical Quarterly* 44 (1940): 161–87.

On the Niantic, see George Tays, *The Niantic Hotel* (Berkeley, 1936). My narrative, by the way, reflects the common contemporary view that it had been completely demolished. Recent archaeological work has shown that it was only buried in the foundation of the new building.

INDEX